THE PSYCHOLOGY OF LEARNING AND MOTIVATION

Advances in Research and Theory

VOLUME 49

THE PSYCHOLOGY OF LEARNING AND MOTIVATION

Advances in Research and Theory

EDITED BY BRIAN H. ROSS

BECKMAN INSTITUTE AND
DEPARTMENT OF PSYCHOLOGY
UNIVERSITY OF ILLINOIS AT URBANA-CHAMPAIGN
URBANA, ILLINOIS

Volume 49

ELSEVIER

AMSTERDAM • BOSTON • HEIDELBERG • LONDON
NEW YORK • OXFORD • PARIS • SAN DIEGO
SAN FRANCISCO • SINGAPORE • SYDNEY • TOKYO
Academic Press is an imprint of Elsevier

Academic Press is an imprint of Elsevier
84 Theobald's Road, London WC1X 8RR, UK
Radarweg 29, PO Box 211, 1000 AE Amsterdam, The Netherlands
Linacre House, Jordan Hill, Oxford OX2 8DP, UK
30 Corporate Drive, Suite 400, Burlington, MA 01803, USA
525 B Street, Suite 1900, San Diego, CA 92101-4495, USA

First edition 2008

ISBN: 978-0-12-374316-9
ISSN: 0079-7421

For information on all Academic Press publications
visit our web site at books.elsevier.com

Printed and bound in USA
08 09 10 11 12 10 9 8 7 6 5 4 3 2 1

CONTENTS

WHAT GOES WITH WHAT? DEVELOPMENT OF PERCEPTUAL GROUPING IN INFANCY

Paul C. Quinn, Ramesh S. Bhatt, and Angela Hayden

CO-CONSTRUCTING CONCEPTUAL DOMAINS THROUGH FAMILY CONVERSATIONS AND ACTIVITIES

Maureen Callanan and Araceli Valle

THE CONCRETE SUBSTRATES OF ABSTRACT RULE USE

Bradley C. Love, Marc Tomlinson, and Todd M. Gureckis

AMBIGUITY, ACCESSIBILITY, AND A DIVISION OF LABOR FOR COMMUNICATIVE SUCCESS

Victor S. Ferreira

LEXICAL EXPERTISE AND READING SKILL

Sally Andrews

CONTRIBUTORS

Numbers in parentheses indicate the pages on which the authors' contributions begin.

Sally Andrews (247), School of Psychology, University of Sydney, Sydney 2006, Australia

Ramesh S. Bhatt (105), Department of Psychology, University of Kentucky, Lexington, Kentucky 40506

Maureen Callanan (147), Department of Psychology, University of California, Santa Cruz, California 95064

Zhijian Chen (49), Department of Psychological Sciences, University of Missouri, Columbia, Missouri 65211

Nelson Cowan (49), Department of Psychological Sciences, University of Missouri, Columbia, Missouri 65211

Simon Farrell (1), Department of Experimental Psychology, University of Bristol, Clifton Bristol BS8 1TN, United Kingdom

Victor S. Ferreira (209), Department of Psychology, University of California, La Jolla, California 92093

Amanda L. Gilchrist (49), Department of Psychological Sciences, University of Missouri, Columbia, Missouri 65211

Todd M. Gureckis (167), Department of Psychology, New York University, New York, New York 10003

Angela Hayden (105), Department of Psychology, University of Kentucky, Lexington, Kentucky 40506

Stephan Lewandowsky (1), School of Psychology, University of Western Australia, Crawley, Western Australia 6009, Australia

Bradley C. Love (167), Department of Psychology, The University of Texas, Austin, Texas 78712

Candice C. Morey (49), Department of Psychological Sciences, University of Missouri, Columbia, Missouri 65211

Paul C. Quinn (105), Department of Psychology, University of Delaware, Newark, Delaware 19716

J. Scott Saults (49), Department of Psychological Sciences, University of Missouri, Columbia, Missouri 65211

Araceli Valle (147), Department of Psychology and Education, Mount Holyoke College, South Hadley, Massachusetts 01075

Marc Tomlinson (167), Department of Psychology, The University of Texas, Austin, Texas 78712

SHORT-TERM MEMORY: NEW DATA AND A MODEL

Stephan Lewandowsky and Simon Farrell

Abstract

We review the extensive benchmark data on short-term memory for order, and discuss the prominent computational theories accounting for serial order memory. On the basis of recent diagnostic results, we identify four explanatory constructs that we suggest must be instantiated in a model to provide an adequate account of those data. We present one such model, called C-SOB, and show that it handles existing benchmark data as well as recent diagnostic results. We conclude by exploring some of the model's novel predictions.

I. Short-Term Memory: A Wealth of Data and Theories

A. The Engine of Cognition

What could be simpler than reading a few items, such as the digits in a phone number, and recalling them in the right order a short while later? Simple as this short-term serial recall task may appear, it has been shown to contribute to language abilities such as vocabulary acquisition (Baddeley, Gathercole, & Papagno, 1998) and utterance production (e.g., Adams & Gathercole, 1996).

THE PSYCHOLOGY OF LEARNING
AND MOTIVATION VOL. 49
DOI: 10.1016/S0079-7421(08)00001-7

Short-term memory (STM) for serial order can also be a critical element in mental arithmetic (Fürst & Hitch, 2000) and, when a task combines short-term storage (e.g., retention of digits) with a processing component (e.g., mental arithmetic), the resultant "working memory span" measure is highly predictive of higher-level cognitive functioning including fluid intelligence and reasoning ability (e.g., Oberauer, Süß, Wilhelm, & Sander, 2007). Accordingly, STM is an acknowledged core component of cognition and there is some consensus that extending our understanding of STM will ultimately contribute to solving other puzzles of cognitive functioning. The importance of STM is also reflected in the wealth of existing data and the varieties of existing quantitative theories.

In this chapter, we first survey benchmark results in STM research and introduce some of the current computational theories that vie for their explanation. We then explore a new generation of results to identify and select the most appropriate explanatory constructs for a theory of STM. Following this, we present a computational model that instantiates those constructs, known as C-SOB, and we conclude by exploring some of the model's novel predictions.

B. Wealth of Data

We focus on situations in which people are presented short lists (usually no more than 5–7 items) for study and immediate (or nearly immediate) retrieval. Memory for the order among items—in addition to memory for their identity—is considered crucial, and thus most of the relevant data were generated using serial recall tests or other order-sensitive tasks such as serial reconstruction. In serial recall, people must report the list items in the order in which they were presented, either from the beginning of the list (forward recall) or from the end (backward recall). In a reconstruction task, by contrast, all list items are shown again at retrieval in a random sequence and the participant's task is to rearrange the items into their original presentation order.

With some 13,000 papers published on STM to date,[1] the rich database necessarily escapes concise summary; fortunately, however, there is some agreement on a set of findings that are considered benchmarks. Table I lists those benchmarks and additionally shows which of the currently available theories can handle the results at a quantitative level of description. We discuss the various theories later and, for now, invite the reader to focus on the rows, which report the core data on STM. In order to keep the quantity of information manageable, the table considers only those findings to which

[1] According to an online search of PsychLit.

TABLE I

SUMMARY OF CONTEMPORARY THEORIES OF SHORT-TERM MEMORY AND THE PHENOMENA THEY CAN ACCOUNT FOR AT A QUANTITATIVE LEVEL

Phenomenon	B&H 92	B&H 99	B&P 06	Oscar	PM	SEM	C-SOB	SIMPLE
List length	√	√	√	√	√	√	√	?
SPC								
Primacy	√	√	√	√	√	√	√	√
Recency		√	√	√	√	√	√	√
Errors								
Transposition proportion	√	√	?	?	√	√	√	?
Transposition gradient	×	√	√	√	√	√	√	√
Fill-in vs infill	?	?	√	?	√	?	×	×
Repetitions	×	√	√	×	?	√	√	×
Omissions	√	√	×	√	√	√	√	√
Intrusions	√	√	×	√	√	√	√	√
Protrusions	×	√	×	×	×	√	×	√
Phonological similarity								
Overall	√	√	√	√	√	√	√	√
Transpositions	√	√	√	√	√	√	√	√
Mixed lists (old)	×	√	√	×	√	√	×	?
Mixed lists (new)	×	×	√(?)	×	×	×	√	×
Reversal with delay	×	×	×	×	×	×	√	√
Grouping								
SPC	×	√	×	√	×	√	√	√
Interpositions	×	√	√	√	×	√	√	√
Modality effect	×	√	×	×	×	√	×	×
Word length								
Basic effect	√	√	×	×	√	×	×	√
AS abolish	×	√	×	×	√	×	×	×
Word frequency (pure lists)	×	×	×	×	√	×	√	×
Modality effect	×	√	×	×	√	√	×	×
Backward recall	×	×	×	√	√	×	×	×

Note: B&H 92 = Burgess and Hitch (1992); B&H 99 = Burgess and Hitch (1999); B&P 06 = Botvinick and Plaut (2006); OSCAR = Brown et al. (2000); PM = Primacy model, Page and Norris (1998); SEM = Start–end model, Henson (1998a); C-SOB = Farrell (2006), Lewandowsky and Farrell (2006), and the present article; SIMPLE = Brown et al. (2007) and Neath and Brown (2006).

more than one computational theory has been applied. On the basis of that criterion, we excluded the interaction between articulatory suppression and phonological similarity plus a number of interesting neuropsychological findings that have been explained by the model by Burgess and Hitch (1999). We also excluded the detailed account of the Hebb repetition effect—that is, the memorial benefit associated with surreptitious repetition of a list on every third study-test trial—provided by a later variant of the same model (Burgess & Hitch, 2006). The fact that no other model has been applied to those important areas of research attests to the power of the theory developed by Burgess and Hitch and must be borne in mind during the remaining discussion. We also excluded data gathered with probed recall, recognition, and judgments of recency, which only the OSCAR model (Brown, Preece, & Hulme, 2000) accommodates. Finally, we excluded latency data because only the SOB model (Farrell & Lewandowsky, 2002) provides response time predictions as a consequence of its architecture; however, we show later that response latencies may distinguish between rival explanatory constructs underlying theories of STM.

Even after exclusion of data that are unique to the domain of a single theory, the table shows that there is no shortage of phenomena that have been quantitatively explained. Before turning to a summary of the competing theories, we highlight a subset of benchmark results that are well replicated and have shaped the development of models of STM.

1. Serial Position Curve

The serial position curve for forward serial recall is the *sine qua non* of modeling in STM; all theories accommodate the extensive primacy (i.e., superior performance for early list items) and limited recency (i.e., advantage for terminal items). This pattern reverses with backward recall, in which case steep and extensive recency but little primacy is observed (e.g., Li & Lewandowsky, 1993). Symmetry of primacy and recency is achieved with a reconstruction task (e.g., Lewandowsky, Nimmo, & Brown, 2008; Nairne, 1992). Perhaps somewhat surprisingly, few models (if any) accommodate backward recall and reconstruction, and we therefore restrict consideration to the serial position curve for forward recall.

2. Error Patterns

The forward serial position curve is accompanied by a highly regular pattern of different types of errors. When a list item is recalled in an incorrect position, this is considered a transposition error (it is the only error possible with a reconstruction task). Most transpositions involve neighboring list positions, such that the third item might be recalled in the second or fourth output position (rather than in the first or seventh). This property of transpositions is known as the "locality constraint" (Henson, Norris, Page, & Baddeley, 1996), and it obeys the orderly property that increasing displacements of list items are increasingly unlikely.

A further analysis of transposition errors reveals several reliable subtleties in the data that are not apparent from consideration of pairwise transpositions alone. Suppose an anticipation error has been committed, for example, if the second list item is recalled first (i.e., "B" is recalled first from the list "ABCD"). This error can be followed by report of the first item (i.e., "BA ... "), an error known as a "fill-in," or it can be followed by report of the third item (i.e., "BC ... "), an error known as "infill," which preserves the relative ordering of the second and third items. Fill-in errors are known to be roughly twice as frequent as infill errors (e.g., Surprenant, Kelley, Farley, & Neath, 2005).

On occasion, people will mistakenly introduce an extra list item into their recall. These "intrusions" frequently involve items from the immediately preceding list (Drewnowski & Murdock, 1980), in which case they are also known as "protrusions" (Henson, 1998a, 1999) and are likely to occur at the same serial position as on the original list (Henson, 1999). The probability of intrusions appearing in people's recall is known to increase across output positions (e.g., Henson, 1998a). When people are permitted to "skip" items, the resulting omission errors also become more likely across output positions. (Only models that capture this pattern across output positions are identified in Table I as explaining intrusions and omissions.)

Finally, erroneous repetitions of an item—for example, reporting the first list item twice during recall—occur notably infrequently. Henson (1996) reported that erroneous repetitions constituted 2% of all responses, and Vousden and Brown (1998) cited a figure of 5%. Despite their infrequency, repetition errors have a distinct distribution, with most repetitions involving early list items that are reported a second time late in recall. In consequence, repetition errors are typically separated by three or four output positions (e.g., Henson, 1996, observed an average separation of ~3.5 output positions). The spacing of repetition errors can give rise to a subtle violation of the locality constraint for transpositions involving the last output position. Specifically, when a moderate number of repetition errors are present, the last output position may involve more reports of the first item than of the second or third if repetitions are not excluded from analysis (Henson et al., 1996).

3. *Phonological Similarity Effect*

The phonological similarity effect refers to the ubiquitous finding that lists composed of similar sounding items are less accurately recalled in the correct order than lists in which items do not sound alike (e.g., Baddeley, 1966, 1968; Conrad, 1964; Henson, et al., 1996; Wickelgren, 1965a,b). The effect is of considerable generality and occurs with consonants (Baddeley, 1968) as well as with words (Baddeley, 1966; Coltheart, 1993; Henry, 1991) and for the most part is due to an increase in transposition errors. With increased retention interval, the detrimental effects of phonological similarity are either reduced (e.g., Farrell, 2006) or reversed (e.g., Nairne & Kelley, 1999).

The phonological similarity effect also occurs when phonologically similar (e.g., B, P, T) and dissimilar (e.g., K, Q, R) items are mixed together on a single study list. Mixed lists are particularly diagnostic because performance on dissimilar items can differentiate between competing theories of memory. We consider mixed lists in detail in a later section.

4. *Grouping Effects*

When a list is explicitly grouped, for example, by inserting a temporal pause after every third item, recall performance improves considerably overall (Ryan, 1969) and there are within-group recency and primacy effects, thus creating a slightly scalloped appearance of the overall serial position curve (Hitch, Burgess, Towse, & Culpin, 1996). The size of the grouping effect does not appear to depend on the duration of the pause between groups (0.9 s vs 3.4 s; Ryan, 1969), and grouping effects may even emerge spontaneously without any objective cue to group (Henson, 1996; Madigan, 1980), indicating grouping to be a natural manner in which information is organized in STM.

Grouping of a list also affects the pattern of errors, primarily by reducing the frequency of transpositions overall. When transpositions do occur between groups, they tend to preserve within-group position, in which case they are referred to as "interpositions" (Henson, 1999).

5. *Effects of Word Length*

There is no doubt that lists of words that take longer to articulate (e.g., "hippopotamus," "retromingent," "plethysmograph") are recalled less accurately in correct order than lists composed of shorter words such as "bat" or "putt" (Baddeley, Thomson, & Buchanan, 1975), and this pervasive result has been taken to support the view that information in STM is subject to time-based decay (e.g., Mueller, Seymour, Kieras, & Meyer, 2003; though see Brown & Hulme, 1995). This conclusion has been subject to considerable controversy and alternative interpretations (e.g., Service, 1998). In particular, unless the number of syllables is kept constant between short and long words, the word-length effect likely reflects differences in complexity of the material rather than the net effects of the passage of time (Service, 1998). When the number of syllables is kept constant but words of differing pronounciation directions are compared (e.g., "platoon" vs "racket"), there is a small effect of word length but it appears to be confined to selected sets of stimuli (Lovatt, Avons, & Masterson, 2000).

Moreover, although the sheer volume of interest in the word-length effect mandates its inclusion in our list of benchmarks, it is important to bear in mind that word length is a mere surrogate manipulation for the real variable of interest—namely, the effects of time on memory; we therefore suggest that examinations of word length are best replaced by other, more direct manipulations of encoding or retrieval time (e.g., Lewandowsky, Duncan, & Brown, 2004). We take up the role of time in STM in a later section.

6. *Data and Theory*

Although our survey of benchmark results was necessarily brief and selective, it should nonetheless be apparent that the existing database poses an enormous theoretical challenge. Can we find a tractable and coherent explanation for the overall pattern of results, given that no single model handles all phenomena listed in Table I (although some handle the list of benchmarks just reviewed)? Is it worth pursuing the possibility of an overarching computational model or might it be preferable to strive for broad verbal explanations?

In our view, the precision and reliability of the data demands equally precise and exacting theorizing which can be achieved only by computational modeling (see Hintzman, 1991; Lewandowsky, 1993; Lewandowsky & Heit, 2006, for discussions of the benefits of computational modeling). Without such modeling, even seemingly clear-cut empirical dissociations defy unambiguous interpretation (Brown & Lamberts, 2003). We therefore restrict the remaining discussion to computational models. By implication, the influential working memory model of Baddeley and Hitch (e.g., 1974) is considered only in its explicit computational instantiations, that is, the primacy model (Page & Norris, 1998) and the models by Burgess and Hitch (e.g., 1999).

C. Varieties of Theories

A complete review of the available theories goes beyond the scope of this chapter; nonetheless, to place our own theoretical development into context, we find it helpful to at least provide a broad classification of models according to their architecture and underlying explanatory constructs. Table II provides this classification using 10 attributes that we find useful. (The last digits of the section numbers from here on refer to column numbers in the table to facilitate cross-referencing; the role of the shading of various cells in the table is discussed later.)

TABLE II

SUMMARY OF CONTEMPORARY THEORIES OF SHORT-TERM MEMORY AND THE EXPLANATORY CONSTRUCTS ON WHICH THEY RELY. SEE TEXT FOR EXPLANATION OF COLUMN NUMBERS AND SHADING

Model	1 Nature of Representations	2 Locus of Similarity Effects	3 Type of Associations	4 Role of Time at Encoding	5 Role of Time During Forgetting	6 Primacy Gradient	7 Response Selection Mechanism	8 Output Interference	9 Response Suppression	10 Energy-gated encoding
Burgess & Hitch (1999)	Localist (except context)	Separate confusion stage	Item↔Item and Item↔Context	Temporal context	Decay	No	Context + CQ	No	Yes	No
Primacy Model (Page & Norris, 1998)	Localist	Separate confusion stage	None	None	Decay	Yes	CQ	No	Yes	No
SEM (Henson, 1998a)	Localist	Separate confusion stage	Item↔Context (× 2 markers)	None	Decay (certain applica-tions), interference otherwise (?)	Yes (+ recency gradient)	Context + CQ	No	Yes	No

SIMPLE (Brown et al., 2007)	Localist	Primary stage	Item↔Temporal context	Temporal information crucial	Interference, but temporally based	No	Context + Luce	Possible	Possible	No
OSCAR (Brown et al., 2000)	Distributed	Primary stage	Item↔Temporal context	Temporal context	None (interference)	Yes	Context + CQ	Yes	Yes	No
C-SOB (Farrell, 2006; Lewandowsky & Farrell, 2008)	Distributed	Primary stage	Item↔Context	None	None (interference)	Yes	Context + Dynamic deblurring (or Luce)	Yes	Yes	Yes
Botvinick & Plaut (2006)	Distributed	Primary stage	Recurrent	None	None	No	Recurrent + CQ	No	Optional	No

1. *Nature of Representations*

Concerning representations, Page (2000) has provided arguments in favor of localist storage—that is, dedicating a unique place in memory to each item—whereas others (e.g., Hinton, McClelland, & Rumelhart, 1986) have provided arguments in favor of the opposite notion, namely, that each item is represented by multiple units of information and that the same units contribute to storage of all items. The latter approach implements distributed representations.

2. *Locus of Similarity Effects*

The locus of similarity effects, and, in particular, the need for a second output stage to explain phonological confusions, is likewise subject to debate (e.g., Page & Norris, 1998 vs Lewandowsky & Farrell, 2006) and we address this issue further below.

3. *Type of Associations*

After the fading from prominence of chaining models (e.g., Lewandowsky & Murdock, 1989), the nature and type of associations is now considerably less controversial, and Table II shows the (near) consensus toward what we call "item marking," namely, associations or "binding" between items and some independent representation of order such as time, temporal context, or ordinal list position. For example, in OSCAR (Brown et al., 2000), items are associated with a temporal "context" signal that autonomously evolves over time driven by a set of oscillators. The temporal distinctiveness mechanism in SIMPLE (Brown, Neath, & Chater, 2007) can be understood in a similar manner. An alternative class of markers involves ordinal position rather than time, as instantiated in the start–end model (SEM) (Henson, 1998a) and in the model we present below.

4. *Role of Time at Encoding*

It is important to underscore that item marking can equally involve time-based encoding—as in the oscillator-based OSCAR model or SIMPLE—or event-based encoding, as in SEM or the model we present below. In the former case, items are associated to a continuously changing signal whose temporal evolution is unaffected by encoding or retrieval events but depends on the passage of chronological time alone. In the latter case, items are associated to a signal that is unaffected by the passage of time per se but is assumed to evolve with retrieval and/or study events.

5. *Role of Time During Forgetting*

Within a given model, the role of time at encoding is not always mirrored by the role of time during retention; for example, the primacy model (Page & Norris, 1998) relies on temporal decay to explain forgetting whereas time plays no role during encoding. Conversely, even though OSCAR associates events to a temporal signal during encoding, forgetting is not driven by temporal decay.

6. *Primacy Gradient*

Another property that characterizes many, but not all, models is the presence of a primacy gradient. A primacy gradient embodies the assumption that the quality of information available for retrieval of an item decreases across serial positions. In some cases, this is achieved by one or two weighting parameters that reduce encoding strengths across successive items (e.g., Brown et al., 2000; Houghton & Hartley, 1996; Lewandowsky, 1999; Lewandowsky & Li, 1994; Lewandowsky & Murdock, 1989; Page & Norris, 1998). By contrast, in SOB (e.g., Farrell & Lewandowsky, 2002) the primacy gradient arises as the natural consequence of weighting the encoding strength of any new item in proportion to its novelty.

7. *Response Selection Mechanism*

Response selection mechanisms fall into two broad classes, depending on whether or not they involve item marking and, hence, cueing by context. In context-free competitive cueing models ("CQ" in Table II), items compete with each other for recall through mutual inhibition between items and self-excitation. In the most basic version of such models, this competition is based only on the intial strengths of the items (e.g., Page & Norris, 1998), whereas in other architectures the items' activations enter into several cycles of excitation and inhibition until they settle into a final pattern (e.g., Farrell & Lewandowsky, 2004). In contrast, models that rely on item marking typically postulate a CQ response selection mechanism that processes the activations elicited by the context cue (e.g., Burgess & Hitch, 1999), with items whose stored contexts most closely match the cueing context being more highly activated. Finally, in more abstract instantiations of the response selection mechanism, an item is selected not only in proportion to its own activation but also in proportion to its own activation compared to those of all other items, as described by Luce's choice rule (Luce, 1963).

8. *Output Interference*

There is considerable evidence that the act of recalling an item interferes with the accessibility of other items yet to be recalled (see Anderson & Neely, 1996, for a review). Accordingly, when input and output order are dissociated in serial recall, a contribution of output interference to primacy can be empirically identified (Cowan, Saults, Elliott, & Moreno, 2002; Oberauer, 2003). For example, Oberauer (2003) randomized the temporal and spatial input order of items by presenting them—separated in space and time—in a spatial array of boxes. Output order was dissociated from input order by randomly and successively cueing individual boxes for report of the presented item. Oberauer found that primacy was particularly pronounced when performance was plotted as a function of output position, aggregating across all input and spatial positions, suggesting that output interference contributes to the primacy effect. Given the evidence for output interference, it is perhaps surprising that this does not form a core assumption of any models of memory for serial order (though see Brown et al., 2000; Farrell & Lewandowsky, 2004).

9. Response Suppression

A nearly universal property of models is the presence of response suppression. Response suppression refers to the assumption that each recalled item is temporarily suppressed and unavailable for further report. In any pure competitive cueing model with a primacy gradient (e.g., Page & Norris, 1998), in which the strongest or most active item is chosen for report without cueing by context, suppression is essential for maintaining serial reproduction. Without suppression, only the first (and strongest) item would be produced at each successive retrieval attempt. Suppression naturally accounts for the relative infrequency of erroneous repetitions noted earlier. Response suppression is also implicated by the fact that people are reluctant to repeat themselves during recall, even when a list does contain repetitions (e.g., Henson, 1998b). Because this deficit for report of a repeated item persists even in conditions in which people can detect repetitions, if instructed to do so, with more than 85% accuracy (Henson, 1998b), response suppression is typically understood to be an obligatory and automatic process.

10. Energy-Gated Encoding

Finally, Table II identifies SOB as the only theory to incorporate a process known as energy-gated encoding. Energy-gated encoding instantiates the idea that the strength of encoding into memory is a function of the novelty of the incoming information: Novel or surprising events are encoded strongly, whereas familiar and unsurprising events that are similar to existing information in memory are encoded with reduced strength. Energy-gated encoding thus resembles the feedback signal instantiated in some other distributed memory models, such as the "closed-loop" version of the theory of distributed associative memory (TODAM) (e.g., Lewandowsky & Murdock, 1989; Murdock, 1982).

D. Model Selection

Where do we go from here? How might one choose a preferred model from the set shown in the first two tables? By what criteria might one best propose a new model? The most obvious possibility, quantitative model comparison, suffers from the constraint that some results can be handled equally by different models, as is obvious from Table I. A more specific illustration of this problem is provided in Fig. 1, which shows the predicted serial position

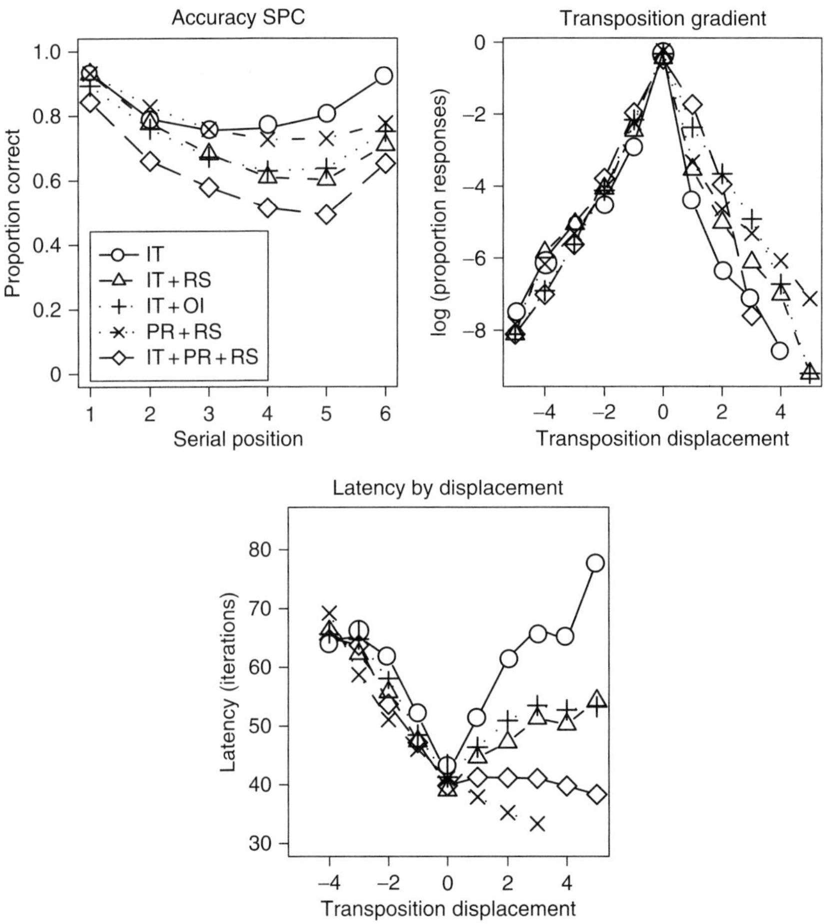

Fig. 1. Predicted accuracy serial position curves (top left panel), transposition gradients (top right panel), and latency–displacement functions (bottom panel) for a number of explanatory constructs implemented in a common architecture. IT = item marking; RS = response suppression; OI = output interference; PR = primacy gradient.

curves (top left panel) and transposition gradients (top right panel) of several models that are based on a variety of quite different explanatory constructs (whose identity is irrelevant for now but will be revealed later). Although there is some heterogeneity between predictions, they do not qualitatively diverge, which may make identification of the preferred model difficult.

We therefore pursue an alternative approach by seeking direct evidence for specific explanatory constructs. Although Tables I and II show that there are a variety of ways in which constructs can be combined to account for (largely) the same set of results, we now show that evidence has become available recently that favors some constructs over others.

II. Explanatory Constructs and New Data

We review four recent findings that can help identify the preferred explanatory constructs of STM, either by providing new constraints or by reevaluating earlier benchmark results in a new light. Specifically, (1) we present empirical support for energy-gated encoding and show that this evidence also favors a primacy gradient and speaks against the presence of a separate phonological confusion stage. (2) We then show that encoding and retention in memory are best understood without assuming that time plays a causal role; (3) we present evidence for the existence and role of response suppression; and (4) we underscore the importance of item marking (i.e., item-to-context associations). The constructs that are directly supported by evidence are shaded gray in Table II.

A. Energy-Gated Encoding

Although all viable models of short-term order memory accommodate the basic phonological similarity effect, their predictions differ for lists on which similar and dissimilar items are intermixed. A number of early studies (e.g., Baddeley, 1968; Bjork & Healy, 1974; Henson et al., 1996) showed that dissimilar items on mixed lists were recalled with the same accuracy as those on pure dissimilar lists. The immunity of dissimilar item recall to list composition compelled several theorists to propose that serial recall involves two independent stages of processing, with order errors occurring between positionally encoded tokens in a primary stage and similarity-based confusions occurring in a separate secondary stage that affects only similar items but lets dissimilar items pass unhindered (e.g., Burgess & Hitch, 1999; Henson, 1998a; Page & Norris, 1998).

However, the absence of a mixed-list advantage is arguably counterintuitive. Consider an extreme case of a single dissimilar item being embedded in a similar sounding list (e.g., the letter *X* in the list B D G *X* T P); on any notion of distinctiveness, the dissimilar item should be recalled more accurately from this list than when it is surrounded by other mutually dissimilar items. Several recent studies have reevaluated the mixed-list effect and have concluded that when guessing is controlled (unlike in the earlier experiments), dissimilar items on mixed lists are in fact recalled more accurately than their counterparts on pure lists (Farrell, 2006; Farrell & Lewandowsky, 2003; Lewandowsky & Farrell, 2008). One implication of these new, revised mixed-list effects is that all models that predict identical performance for dissimilar items regardless of list context—that is, those identified as handling the "old" mixed-list effect in Table I—are challenged by the empirical reevaluation of that phenomenon.

In support, a comparison of several theories by simulation by Lewandowsky and Farrell (2008) and Farrell (2006) showed that the mixed-list advantage for dissimilar items cannot be accommodated by two-stage models (the primacy model by Page & Norris, 1998, and the SEM by Henson, 1998a) and instead supports an alternative view based on a single memorial stage involving energy-gated encoding (i.e., SOB; Farrell & Lewandowsky, 2002; Lewandowsky & Farrell, 2008).

Energy-gated encoding refers to the weighting of the encoding strength of new list items on the basis of their novelty compared to already encoded information. We use the term "energy-gated" because within the SOB model, novelty of an item is measured by its "energy" with respect to the weight matrix of previously stored associations (Farrell & Lewandowsky, 2002). Items that differ from earlier memorized information are encoded more strongly than items that are similar to the contents of memory. In consequence, dissimilar items on mixed lists receive a memorial advantage because the mutual similarity of the list neighbors implies that they are encoded less strongly. On a pure dissimilar list, by contrast, list neighbors are all dissimilar to each other and hence encoded with greater strength, thus providing more competition to each other. To illustrate, consider the expected gradients of encoding strengths for two three-item lists: one consisting only of dissimilar items (referred to as "D" in abstract notation; hence, DDD) and one that has a dissimilar item sandwiched between two items that are similar to each other (SDS). The first item is stored with the same strength on both lists, as there are no previous items which could affect its novelty. The second item is also stored with the same strength in both cases, as it is (likely) equally novel with respect to the first item. However, the third item on the SDS list receives a smaller weight than its sibling on the DDD list because its similarity to the first item reduces its encoding strength by the energy-gated encoding scheme. It follows that the isolated dissimilar item on the list SDS will be recalled more accurately than its counterpart on the DDD list because the third item on the SDS list, having been encoded with less strength, will offer reduced competition during recall. Because the recent data (Farrell & Lewandowsky, 2003; Lewandowsky & Farrell, 2008) conform to this prediction, we identify energy-gated encoding as a preferrred explanatory principle in STM.[2]

Energy-gated encoding, in turn, naturally gives rise to other explanatory constructs, including the primacy gradient. Although the primacy gradient is often motivated by the need to predict a recall advantage for early list items (e.g., Brown et al., 2000; Lewandowsky, 1999; Lewandowsky & Murdock, 1989), there are independent reasons for its existence. For example, Brown et al. (2000) justified the primacy gradient by appealing to the "intuition that each successive item . . . is progressively less 'surprising' or attention demanding than the previous one" (p. 151), an intuition that Brown et al. considered to be consonant with the demands on an adaptively rational organism. This intuition is formalized by energy-gated encoding, which naturally yields a primacy gradient (Farrell & Lewandowsky, 2002).

B. No Role for Time

Do STM representations involve a temporal component? Are memories temporally organized? Do they inexorably decay over time? Or are our memories built and altered on the basis of events, irrespective of the time that lapses between events? Few issues have been debated as intensely as this fundamental question concerning the nature of our memories. Turning first to the role of time at encoding, we consider whether temporal distinctiveness is a useful principle to characterize performance in STM. According to temporal distinctiveness theories (e.g., Bjork & Whitten, 1974; Brown et al., 2007; Crowder, 1976; Glenberg & Swanson, 1986), the temporal separation of events at encoding is a crucial determinant of memory performance. All other things being equal, distinctiveness models predict that the memorability of an event increases with its temporal separation from neighboring events. In consequence, people are more likely to remember details about widely separated events (e.g., biennial holidays) than about events that are more closely spaced (e.g., frequent trips to conferences).

Contrary to this expectation, there have been numerous recent reports showing that temporal isolation does not facilitate serial retrieval from STM. Across a number of studies employing a variety of retrieval tasks (serial recall, probed order recall, and serial recognition) and presentation modality

[2] Page, Madge, Cumming, and Norris (2007) recently suggested that the mixed-list advantage observed by Farrell and Lewandowsky (2003) was due to their method of presenting all lists of the same type in a contiguous block, which followed the precedent of Henson et al. (1996). Page et al.'s (2007) explanation is unlikely given that the mixed-list advantage has also been observed when all trial types were randomly intermixed (Farrell, 2006; Lewandowsky & Farrell, 2008).

(auditory vs visual), it has been demonstrated that items closely preceded or followed in time by other items are no worse recalled than items that are temporally isolated (e.g., Lewandowsky, Brown, Wright, & Nimmo, 2006; Nimmo & Lewandowsky, 2005, 2006). There are, however, two known exceptions to this general conclusion: First, isolation can benefit memory if the presentation schedule is predictable and people can use it for strategic encoding of the list (Lewandowsky, Wright, & Brown, 2007). Second, isolation can benefit memory if output order is unconstrained; that is, when people are free to choose which item to report (by selecting a serial position for report in a reconstruction task), isolated items are recalled better than temporally crowded items (Lewandowsky et al., 2008).

We acknowledge those exceptions, and we acknowledge that they mandate a mechanism by which people can switch attention to time and use it to govern retrieval (even retroactively, after list presentation; see Farrell & McLaughlin, 2007; Lewandowsky et al., 2008). Nonetheless, we set aside those exceptions here because our declared focus is exclusively on forward serial retrieval. Within those constraints, we identify the *absence* of temporal representations as the preferable explanatory principle of STM. By implication, we reject the idea that temporal distinctiveness presents a viable explanation for short-term serial recall, although we acknowledge the power of the approach in other domains of memory such as free recall (see Brown et al., 2007; Brown, Morin, & Lewandowsky, 2006).

Turning to the role of time during retention, we have already noted the limitations of the word-length effect. Lewandowsky et al. (2004) introduced a paradigm in which retention time was experimentally manipulated while simultaneously blocking rehearsal (to avoid potential refreshing of memory traces) without introducing extensive interference. Participants orally recalled a list of letters while repeating an irrelevant word ("super") aloud in between retrievals, thus preventing articulatory rehearsal. Lewandowsky et al. found that recall performance was unaffected by the number of times people articulated the distractor in between memory retrievals, implying that time per se did not cause forgetting in serial recall. We conclude that processes other than the passage of time are responsible for forgetting in STM.

C. Response Suppression

Whereas output interference refers to a deleterious effect of retrieval on other items that have yet to be recalled, response suppression refers to a temporary inability to access an item just recalled. Notwithstanding the widespread appeal to response suppression, it has proven difficult to find direct evidence for its existence. Farrell and Lewandowsky (2007) tackled this issue by noting that many models rely (at least in part) on response suppression to explain recency (e.g., Brown et al., 2000; Farrell & Lewandowsky, 2002; Henson, 1998a; Lewandowsky & Murdock, 1989). When items must be reported in serial order, any competitive response selection mechanism predicts recency if the number of potential response candidates decreases across output position—a decrease that is achieved very naturally by response suppression. A causal link between response suppression and recency entails the prediction that the fewer list items are recalled (thus leaving more list items unsuppressed), the less recency will occur. Because a list item will remain unsuppressed if it is replaced by an intrusion (i.e., recall of an extra list item), the extent of recency should decline with the number of intrusions during recall. Importantly, this prediction can be tested while controlling absolute accuracy: if two items are transposed during recall (i.e., two items are recalled in the wrong position), accuracy—as measured by proportion correct recall—is identical to the case in which two intrusions are reported; however, in the former case two more list items are suppressed than in the latter.

Figure 2 shows the results of a conditional reanalysis of seven published and unpublished serial-recall experiments conducted by Farrell and Lewandowsky (2007). For all studies, only those lists were considered on which people committed exactly two errors during recall of all items barring the last one. Performance on the last item was then examined as a function of how many list items were suppressed during commission of the two errors,

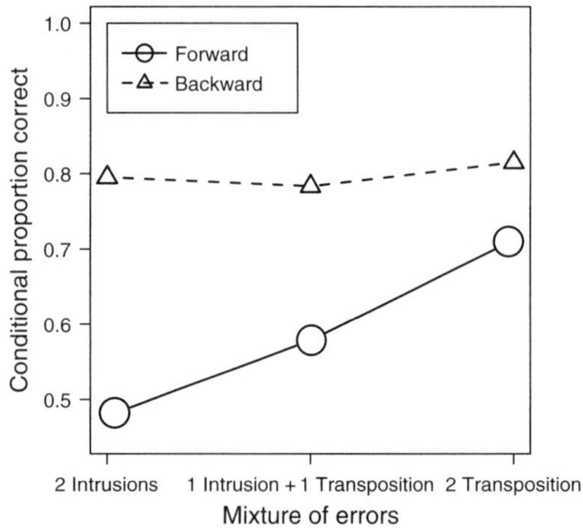

Fig. 2. Average performance across seven experiments for the terminal list item (forward) and for the first three list items (backward) conditionalized on the types of errors committed on the remaining list positions. See text for further explanation.

which ranged from 0 (two intrusions) to 2 (two transpositions). The results, shown by the line labeled "forward" in the figure, are quite straightforward: Performance on the last item increased with the number of list items that were reported previously, exactly as predicted by the suppression account of recency.

One potential problem with this analysis is that it might reflect a correlation between two measures of memorial information; even though accuracy is identical between the different mixtures of errors, one might argue that intrusions occur only when both item and positional information is lost whereas transpositions reflect loss of positional information in the presence of intact item information. On that view, two intrusions might be associated with lower terminal item performance than two transpositions not because of response suppression but because of overall poorer memory for those lists.

This problem can be addressed by reversing the directionality of conditionalization and considering performance on the early part of the list as a function of errors during the later part. The line labeled "backward" in Fig. 2 shows performance on the first three serial positions as a function of the mixture of error types observed during recall of the remaining list items (again keeping accuracy constant by considering only those lists on which exactly two errors were made). In contrast to the forward conditionalization, the mixture of late-list errors was not predictive of accuracy for early-list items. This result allays fears that the forward conditionalization merely revealed a correlation between two measures of memorial quality.

We therefore identify response suppression as a viable explanatory construct in STM. We additionally conclude that response suppression contributes to the occurrence of recency.

D. Item Marking

The first two panels in Fig. 1 demonstrated that the serial position curve and underlying transposition gradients can be explained by several rival constructs. Farrell and Lewandowsky (2004) showed that when response latency is considered in addition to response proportions, the various competing explanations can be empirically differentiated on the basis of their predicted "latency-displacement functions."

The bottom panel of Fig. 1 shows a family of predicted latency–displacement functions, which plot response latency as a function of the displacement of the recalled item. A displacement of zero refers to a correct response, a negative displacement refers to an anticipation (e.g., the third list item recalled first would be a displacement of −2), and a positive displacement constitutes a postponement (e.g., the first item recalled in the second position would be a +1 displacement). It is clear from the figure that different explanatory constructs can predict qualitatively different latency–displacement functions.

The predictions shown in the panel were obtained using a common architecture, based on localist representations within an iterative competitive activation network. The network permitted the instantiation of various explanatory constructs in a common framework and generated both the probability and the latency of all possible responses (see Farrell & Lewandowsky, 2004, for more detail). The panel shows predictions from four explanatory constructs; namely, a primacy gradient (labeled PR in the figure), response suppression (RS), output interference (OI; instantiated by increasing the amount of noise added to the network across output positions); and an item marker (IT; instantiated by activating items according to the match between the position currently being cued and each item's list position). The predictions differ considerably between the various combinations of constructs instantiated in the network: Whereas an item marker on its own produces completely symmetric and nonmonotonic latency–displacement functions (with the fastest responses reserved for correct retrievals), the presence of a primacy gradient in conjunction with response suppression qualitatively alters the shape of the function and renders it monotonically negative. Addition of an item marker to the combination of a primacy gradient and response suppression flattens the slope of the function for postponements, without, however, removing monotonicity.

Farrell and Lewandowsky (2004) reported three experiments involving timed keyboard recall of lists of letters or digits. Across all experiments, the observed latency–displacement functions were consistently monotonic (or nearly so) with a negative slope, and additionally exhibited a reduction in slope for postponements compared to anticipations. As seen in Fig. 1, these data are most compatible with a model that includes a primacy gradient, response suppression, and an item marker.[3] The data clearly compromise models that are based on an item marker alone.

E. Summary

We argue that the evidence just discussed has considerably narrowed down the preferred set of explanatory constructs summarized in Table II. With the exception of Columns 1 and 7, which are neutral with respect to the available evidence, only the shaded cells in Table II are compatible with the set of recent results on STM. We next present a computational model of serial recall in STM that is based on those constructs. The model incorporates a set of principles that

[3] Farrell and Lewandowsky (2004) did not consider this model and instead focused only on the model including a primacy gradient and response suppression.

we have been elaborating for several years. The formal instantiation we present here brings together a simpler serial recall model that handled basic phenomena in a dynamic connectionist network (Farrell & Lewandowsky, 2002), and a generalized extension that we have recently implemented to account for similarity effects (Farrell, 2006; Lewandowsky & Farrell, 2008).

III. C-SOB: A Model of Serial Recall in STM

Farrell and Lewandowsky (2002) presented a distributed model of serial ordering known as SOB, or "Serial-Order in a Box," a name that acknowledges the model's reliance on the Brain-State-in-a-Box algorithm (e.g., Anderson, Silverstein, Ritz, & Jones, 1977). Briefly, SOB assumes that items are represented by vectors of features that are encoded into memory by adding their auto-associations to a common weight matrix. That is, the core architecture of the model consists of the continuous superimposition of new information onto items already presented. A crucial property of SOB is that encoding strengths are a direct function of the novelty, or "energy," of incoming items, which naturally gives rise to a primacy gradient.

Retrieval from SOB involves nonlinear iterative dynamics. Memory is probed by presenting a cue vector to the weight matrix. In contrast to many other networks, the first response of the model is not taken to be its final answer: Instead, the output is fed back into the weight matrix across multiple iterations until a stables state, known as an "attractor," is reached. If the model correctly recalls an item, that final state will be identical to the target item, whereas in the case of an erroneous recall, the model will reach an attractor that differs from the target. This iterative dynamic deblurring mechanism very naturally gives rise to latency predictions because each response in SOB takes a measurable amount of time to emit.

Farrell and Lewandowsky (2002) showed that SOB could explain a number of benchmark phenomena, including the basic shape of the serial position curve; the pattern of errors during recall, including the balance between transpositions, omissions, intrusions, and erroneous repetitions; the effects of list length on the distribution of errors, the overall level of recall, and response latency; and the effects of natural language frequency on recall performance.

In addition to providing an account of some benchmarks, the initial SOB resolved two problems that had previously been ascribed to distributed representations (e.g., Page, 2000); namely, the presumed inability to disambiguate responses and selectively to suppress items. The first problem, disambiguation, refers to the fact that except in special circumstances, distributed models of memory do not reproduce an exact copy of a studied item but a "blurry" approximation. SOB solves this problem because its dynamic deblurring mechanism is guaranteed to converge onto an unambiguous and identifiable response. The second problem, concerning suppression, pertains to the difficulties that can be associated with the selective removal of specific information from neural networks. SOB solves this problem by the use of antilearning, which is instantiated by removing the auto-association of each recalled item from the weight matrix by "relearning" it with a negative learning rate (see Anderson, 1991, for an introduction to antilearning).

The core assumptions of the initial SOB model have remained unchanged to date and are embodied in the C-SOB model being presented here. There are two major differences between SOB and C-SOB: First, whereas all items in SOB were necessarily orthogonal, this constraint is relaxed in C-SOB and interitem similarity is free to vary. Second, whereas SOB initiated retrieval by a random cue, in C-SOB items are associated to an item marker that is used as a retrieval cue. In recent applications of C-SOB in which the selection stage was not considered crucial to the predictions of the model, the computationally demanding iterative deblurring mechanism was replaced by a simpler response selection method using Luce's choice rule. Here, we focus on the complete version of C-SOB that incorporates the fully specified dynamic deblurring stage.

A. Architecture and Specification

1. Network Architecture

The model consists of two layers of units, an input layer ($N = 16$) used to represent item markers and an output layer ($N = 150$) representing list items, where N refers to the number of units in each layer. The two layers are fully interconnected by a weight matrix **C** (weights unidirectionally projecting from the input layer to the output layer) and an additional weight matrix **W** representing full interconnectivity between units in the output layer. The weight matrix **C** stores associations between positional markers and items, whereas the weight matrix **W** stores auto-associations (i.e., associations of items to themselves) that drive the dynamic disambiguation. The matrix **W** and its dynamic disambiguation properties are isomorphic to the core architecture of the initial SOB model (Farrell & Lewandowsky, 2002).

2. Positional Markers

C-SOB incorporates a marker for each list position to which items are associated (cf. Henson, 1998a). The similarity between any two positional markers is an exponential function of their absolute separation in list positions; that is,

$$\cos(\mathbf{p}_i, \mathbf{p}_j) = t_c^{(|i-j|)} \tag{1}$$

where i and j are the positions of the ith and jth items, $\mathbf{p}_i$ and $\mathbf{p}_j$ are distributed vectors representing positional markers, and t_c is a constant that was set to .8 in the majority of simulations below. Markers were generated from a weighted combination of orthogonal Walsh vectors of dimensionality 16, with the weights set to satisfy the similarity constraint embodied in Eq. (1). Note that the positional markers are not affected by the passage of time but are identified by position alone.

3. *Preexperimental Learning*

C-SOB assumes that participants come to serial recall experiments armed with prior knowledge of the experimental vocabulary, which plays a fundamental role in disambiguating noisy traces. In the original version of SOB, pretraining was accomplished by storing auto-associations in the weight matrix using Hebbian learning. In C-SOB, knowledge about items is captured by auto-associations that are pretrained using Widrow–Hoff learning:

$$\Delta \mathbf{W}_i = \eta_P \mathbf{v}_i (\mathbf{v}_i - \mathbf{o}_i)^T \tag{2}$$

where $\mathbf{v}_i$ is the item being learned, $\mathbf{o}_i$ is the current output of the network obtained when cueing with $\mathbf{v}_i$ (i.e., $\mathbf{W}_{i-1}\mathbf{v}_i$), and η_P is the learning rate. Items are represented by binary vectors whose elements are set to +1 or –1. For each simulation below, training lasted for 200 cycles, with each cycle k involving training of all items with learning rate $\eta_P = .03/k$. (Reducing the learning rate across pretraining cycles was found to facilitate learning.) The use of Widrow–Hoff learning is required when lists contain similar items; if all items are assumed to be orthogonal, Hebbian learning may be employed instead (Farrell & Lewandowsky, 2002).

4. *Encoding of Study List*

List items are associated with successive positional markers using standard Hebbian learning (see, e.g., Anderson, 1995):

$$\Delta \mathbf{C}_i = \eta_e(i) \mathbf{v}_i \mathbf{p}_i^T \tag{3}$$

where $\mathbf{C}$ is the matrix of positional marker-item weights, $\mathbf{v}$ is the vector representing the ith presented item, and $\mathbf{p}$ is a positional marker for the ith serial position. The learning rate η_e for the ith association, $\eta_e(i)$, was determined anew for each item using the energy between the association to be learned and the information in the weight matrix up to that point:

$$\eta_e(i) = \begin{cases} 1, & i = 1 \\ -\phi_e/E_i, & i > 1 \end{cases} \tag{4}$$

where ϕ_e is a free parameter, and E_i, the energy of the ith association, is given by:

$$E_i = -\mathbf{v}_i^T \mathbf{C}_{i-1} \mathbf{p}_i. \tag{5}$$

5. Retrieval

Retrieval consists of stepping through the positions using the markers to cue for their associated items, and then using pretrained knowledge to deblur the retrieved ambiguous information. Retrieval at position i is cued by placing the positional marker $\mathbf{p}_i$ across the input layer, and computing the item unit activations:

$$\mathbf{v}_i^{'} = \mathbf{C}_i \mathbf{p}_i \tag{6}$$

The retrieved vector, $\mathbf{v}_i^{'}$, is a "noisy" version of $\mathbf{v}_i$, containing a blend of the target $\mathbf{v}_i$ and the other items on the list, according to the overlap between the positional markers for those other items and the marker for the target. This noisy output is then disambiguated using dynamic iterative deblurring as follows.

The pattern of activations $\mathbf{x}$ across units in the item layer is intialized to $\mathbf{v}_i^{'}$ and scaled to unit length to yield an intial state $\mathbf{x}(0)$. The activations in $\mathbf{x}$ are then iteratively updated according to:

$$\mathbf{x}(t+1) = \mathrm{G}[\gamma \mathbf{x}(t) + \alpha \mathbf{W} \mathbf{x}(t)] \tag{7}$$

The two terms inside the function G in Eq. (7) are the activation patterns from the previous iteration t (weighted by γ; included as an inertia term, Anderson, 1995), and the activations resulting from passing the previous state $\mathbf{x}(t)$ through the weight matrix $\mathbf{W}$. This crucial second term uses the knowledge in $\mathbf{W}$ to reconstruct items; effectively, each item that contributes to the "blend" $\mathbf{v}_i^{'}$ cues for itself using the stored auto-association in $\mathbf{W}$. Generally, the extent to which an item is successful in cueing for itself will depend on the extent of its storage in $\mathbf{W}$ and the weight of its contribution to the blend $\mathbf{v}_i'$. Because all items are pretrained with an equal weight, the only systematic contribution to the updating will result from the weighting of items in $\mathbf{v}_i'$.

To prevent this iterative updating process from continuing indefinitely, the function G in Eq. (7) "squashes" the updated activations to lie between –1 and +1. Updating terminates when all units are saturated (i.e., all units equal +1 or –1), thus ensuring that deblurring ends in a final state that corresponds to a vertex (i.e., corner) in a zero-centered hyperspace. (It is for this reason that the algorithm is referred to as "Brain-State-In-a-Box.")

Although all list items, by definition, are vertices, the reverse is not true, and the model can therefore generate extra list intrusions. To model omissions, we assume a temporal criterion for convergence; if $I_{\max}$ iterations have passed without achieving convergence, a "pass" response is emitted. As in SOB, because each iteration is assumed to take a fixed amount of time, the time to convergence can be treated as recall latency, thus allowing the model to predict latencies for each response.

Once an item is recalled, it is suppressed by adjusting the weights between the positional marker layer and the item layer according to

$$\Delta \mathbf{C}_j = \eta_s(j)\mathbf{v}_{o,j}\,\mathbf{p}_j^T \tag{8}$$

where j is the output position, and $\mathbf{v}_{o,j}$ is the recalled item; Eq. (8) is identical to the Hebbian learning used at encoding, except that the learning rate is negative, thus causing "anti-learning" of the weights and attenuation of item representations (e.g., Anderson, 1991). To ensure that the extent of response suppression approximately matches that of learning, the learning rate for suppression, η_s, is also determined from the energy of the recalled item with respect to the association matrix $\mathbf{C}$ and the positional marker $\mathbf{p}$

$$E_j = -\mathbf{v}_{o,j}^T\,\mathbf{C}_{j-1}\mathbf{p}_j \tag{9}$$

The weighting of response suppression is given by

$$\eta_s(j) = \frac{-E_j}{\phi_s E_1} \tag{10}$$

where ϕ_s is a model parameter and E_1 is the energy of the first recalled item (see Farrell & Lewandowsky, 2002); this term reduces to $-\phi_s^{-1}$ for the first output position.

Response suppression is followed by generalized output interference due to retrieval of the item. Following Brown et al. (2000), output interference is implemented by adding Gaussian noise to all weights in **C** with mean 0 and standard deviation σ_O.

B. Account of Benchmarks

To establish the basic viability of C-SOB, we now show that it accounts for the usual set of benchmark results. For continuity with recent applications (Farrell, 2006; Lewandowsky & Farrell, 2008), the items in all simulations were assumed to be moderately dissimilar letters, and were constructed using the known multidimensional phonological similarity structure of the stimuli (see Lewandowsky & Farrell, 2008).

All simulations used a constant set of parameter values that were not estimated from the data but were based on previous applications of the model. The encoding parameter ϕ_e was set to 720, and ϕ_s was set to .8 (i.e., in the center of the range of previously used values, namely, .45; Lewandowsky & Farrell, 2008, to 1.2; Farrell, 2006). The convergence parameters γ and α were set to .2 and 1.1, respectively, similar to the values used in Lewandowsky and Farrell (2000). The omission threshold χ was arbitrarily set to 100, and the amount of output interference σ_O was set to 1.

1. Serial Position Curves

Figure 3 shows the predicted serial position curves for serial recall across list lengths 3 through 7. The left panel shows the accuracy predictions and the right panel the associated predicted latencies. The model captured the

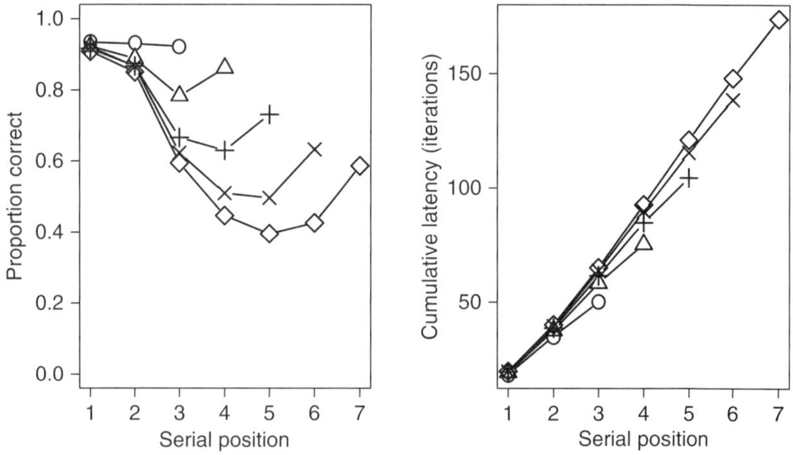

Fig. 3. Serial position curves for various list lengths predicted by C-SOB. The left panel shows predictions for accuracy and the right panel predictions for cumulative latency.

essential aspects of the accuracy data: It exhibited "fanning" from a common origin with increasing list length, it produced extensive primacy, and it showed limited recency.

Likewise, the model captured the known relationship between list length and cumulative response latencies (e.g., Dosher & Ma, 1998), particularly the fanning in the cumulative latencies, which reveals that making lists longer increases the time to recall individual items; a serial process in which items took a fixed amount of time to recall would predict the curves to be exactly overlaid.

2. *Transposition Gradients*

The transposition gradients underlying the preceding serial position curves are shown in Fig. 4 (averaged across all serial positions). The transposition gradients exhibit the usual "locality constraint"; that is, most errors involve items from neighboring list positions. Unlike the data, however, they show a slight asymmetry, with more anticipations than postponements at most displacement distances.

The predicted relative frequency of fill-in ("BA ... ") and infill ("BC ... ") errors was found to vary considerably with list length, with the ratio of fill-ins to infills decreasing from 53 to 10, 2, .8, and .5, respectively, for list lengths 3, 4, 5, 6, and 7. We know of no corresponding behavioral data that relate fill-ins to list length, with all available reports limited to list lengths 6–8 and citing a ratio of around 2 (Henson, 1996; Henson et al., 1996; Surprenant et al., 2005). It is clear, though, that C-SOB underpredicts the ratio of fill-ins to infills for the list lengths for which data are available.

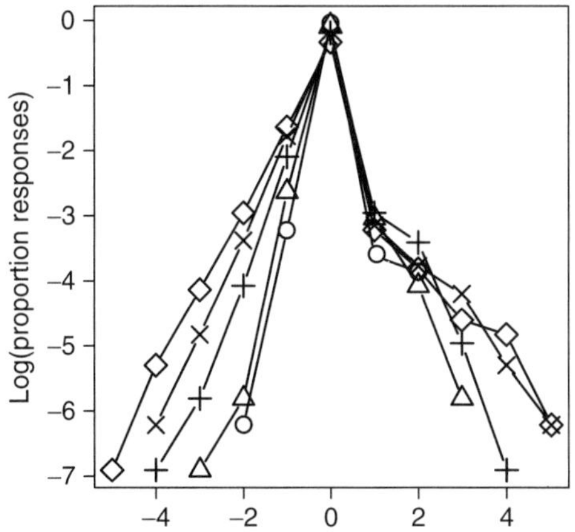

Fig. 4. Transposition gradients for various list lengths (averaged across serial positions) predicted by C-SOB.

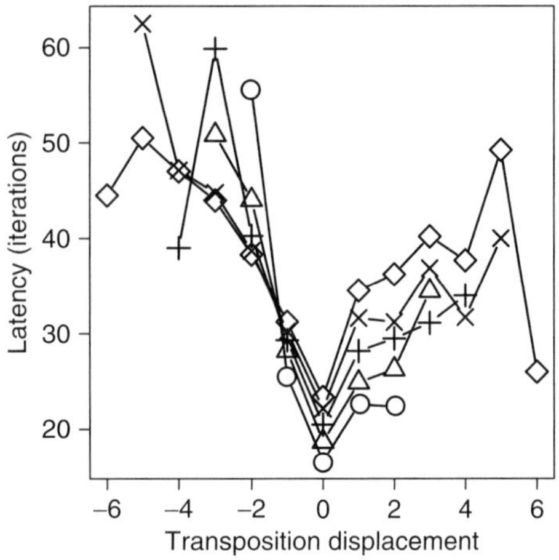

Fig. 5. Latency–displacement functions for various list lengths (averaged across serial positions) predicted by C-SOB.

3. Latency–Displacement Functions

Figure 5 shows the predicted latency–displacement functions for a number of different list lengths (averaged across serial positions in each case). The functions mirror the (roughly) monotonically negative trend in the data. The figure also confirms the modeling by Farrell and Lewandowsky (2004), which suggested that a primacy gradient in conjunction with response suppression is necessary to achieve negative monotonicity in the latency–displacement functions.

Moreover, the reduction in slope associated with postponements (i.e., positive displacements) mirrors the effects of introducing an item marker in addition to a primacy gradient and response suppression (see the bottom panel of the earlier Fig. 1), thus confirming that Farrell and Lewandowsky's analysis of a generic network architecture transfers to a completely specified instantiation.

4. Item and Repetition Errors

The predicted proportions of the various error types across output positions are shown in Fig. 6 for list lengths 5 (left panel) and 6 (right panel). In accord with the data, item errors (intrusions and omissions) increase across output positions whereas transpositions show an inverted U-shaped function, with a reduction in transpositions for the last one or two positions.

C-SOB also accounts for the proportion of repetition errors; for 6-item lists, 2.7% of all responses were repetitions, compared to values between 2% and 5% reported in the literature (Henson, 1996; Vousden & Brown, 1998). However,

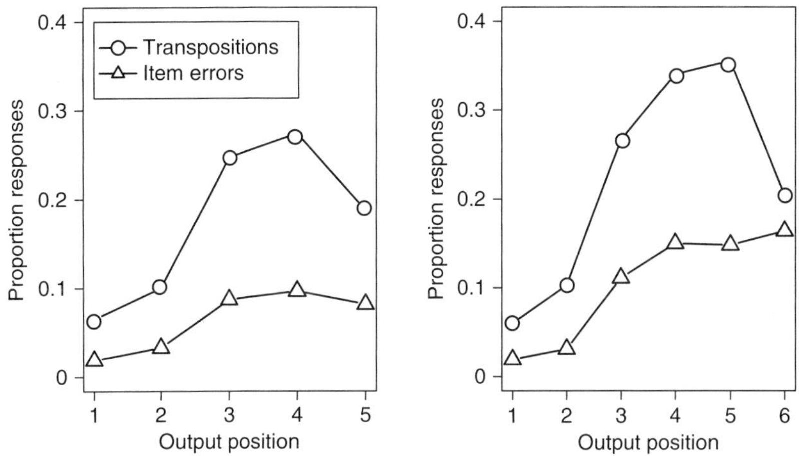

Fig. 6. Pattern of errors across output positions predicted by C-SOB for list lengths 5 (left panel) and 6 (right panel).

C-SOB fails to account for the separation of repetitions: Whereas in the data repetitions tend to be separated by three or four items (e.g., Henson, 1996), C-SOB predicted a considerable number of immediate repetitions. This result may reflect the fact that as recall proceeds, the current context marker will increasingly differ from the context that generated the first occurrence of a possible repetition, making remote repetitions unlikely.

5. *Similarity Effects*

Lewandowsky and Farrell (2008) provided a detailed analysis of SOB's ability to handle the effects of phonological similarity, and we briefly summarize their findings here. (Note that their model did not include dynamic deblurring but was identical to C-SOB in all other respects.)

Figure 7 is adapted from their paper and shows the predicted effects of similarity for pure lists (i.e., DDDDDD and SSSSSS) and various mixed lists, including two in which only a single dissimilar item was present in position 2 (SDSSSS) and 4 (SSSDSS), respectively. The figure clarifies that SOB predicts the detrimental effects of similarity and it also underscores the mixed-list advantage for dissimilar items—discussed earlier—that is a necessary consequence of energy-gated encoding.

6. *Effects of Grouping*

To model the effects of grouping, the item markers used in the preceding simulations were modified to a two-dimensional representation with the addition of a further 16 units which coded the position of the item within a

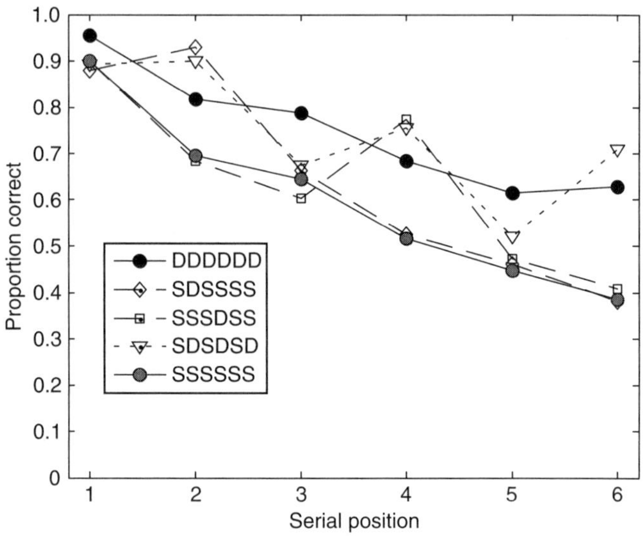

Fig. 7. Serial position curves for lists composed of similar (S) and dissimilar (D) items predicted by C-SOB.

group (as well as the position of the item in the list, carried over from previous demonstrations; cf. Brown et al., 2000; Burgess & Hitch, 1999). The same parameter t_c was used to determine contextual similarity for both dimensions of representation, and was set to .6. To account for the increased number of weights projecting from the context layer to the item layer, ϕ_e was set to the larger value of 1200.

The resulting predictions are shown in Fig. 8. The top-left panel shows that C-SOB predicts the scalloping of the serial position curves that is characteristic of grouped lists; the top-right panel shows the associated latency predictions; and the bottom panel shows the underlying transposition gradients. The grouped lists exhibit the classic peaks in the transposition gradients that reflect the increased likelihood of interpositions (i.e., transpositions of items from two groups in the same within-group positions).

7. *Summary*

Our simulations confirmed that C-SOB can handle the conventional set of benchmark results. As shown in Table I, this confirms that C-SOB ranks among competing alternatives in its ability to handle core results. Moreover, we showed that the model handles the particularly diagnostic mixed-list similarity effects. We next show that C-SOB makes novel predictions by turning to a further analysis of the effects of time on forgetting from STM.

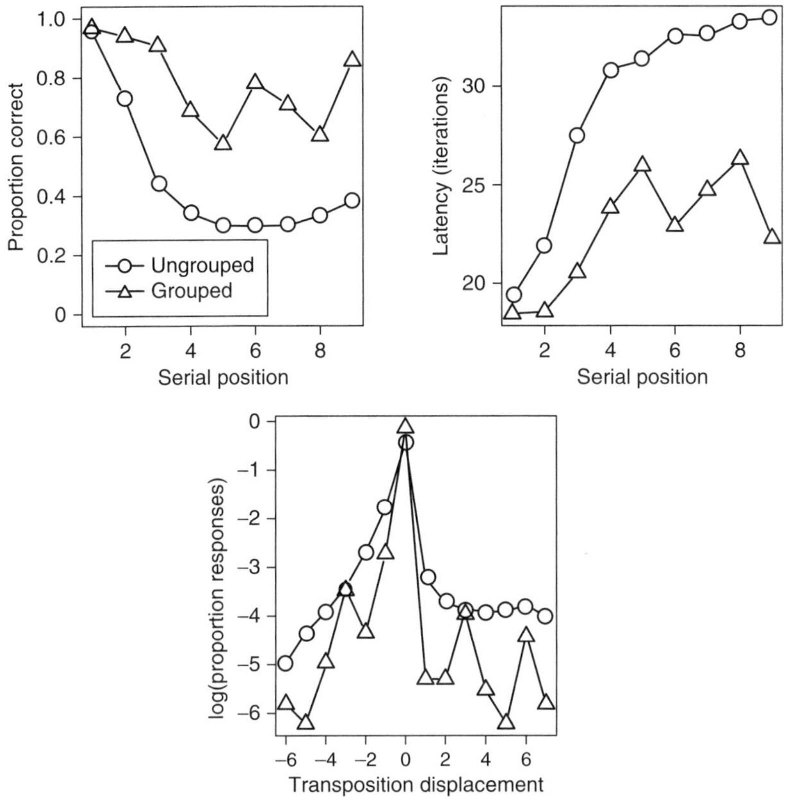

Fig. 8. Accuracy serial position curves (top-left panel), latency serial position curves (top-right panel), and transposition gradients (bottom panel) for grouped and ungrouped 9-item lists predicted by C-SOB.

IV. Experimental Predictions

A. Forgetting: Time Versus Interference

We noted earlier that the word-length effect, frequently cited in support of temporal decay, is fraught with problems of interpretation and replicability and we pointed to alternative means of examining the issue, as in the studies of Lewandowsky et al. (2004) in which increasing a distractor-filled delay at retrieval did not have a deleterious effect on performance. Oberauer and Lewandowsky (in press) extended the methodology of Lewandowsky et al. (2004) by comparing the effects of the irrelevant task to a quiet control condition and by adding an attention-demanding speeded choice task (with arbitrary stimulus–response mappings) on top of the articulatory suppression in between memory retrievals. Notwithstanding this added irrelevant load, manipulating the time in between retrievals—by varying the number of articulations and choices that had to be performed—had virtually no effect on memory performance.

The data from two of Oberauer and Lewandowsky's (in press) experiments are shown in the two panels of Fig. 9, together with the best-fitting predictions of C-SOB (Oberauer and Lewandowsky omitted the dynamic deblurring but their model was identical to C-SOB in all other respects). The figure makes two noteworthy points: First, as shown in the left panel, the addition of an irrelevant articulatory task depressed performance considerably compared to a quiet control (labeled B in the figure), but there was little indication that extending the duration of articulation (3R vs 1R) led to a further decrement in performance.[4] Second, as shown in the right panel, even if articulation is accompanied by an additional speeded choice task, the absolute duration of those two tasks (1 vs 4 AS + CRT) has no effect on memory performance. The figure also shows that C-SOB captures all those effects, namely, the dramatic decline of performance with introduction of an irrelevant task and the time invariance of performance across varying durations of the irrelevant activity (or activities).

The procedures of Oberauer and Lewandowsky (in press) and of Lewandowsky et al. (2004) are modeled by assuming that the distractor item (i.e., the irrelevant to-be-articulated word) is encoded into memory by being associated to a derivative of the current context marker. To model the differences in distractor duration between conditions, the distractor word was added either once or several times in between retrievals, mirroring the way in which people articulate once or multiple times. (For further details of these simulations, see Oberauer & Lewandowsky, in press) When combined with energy-gated encoding, these representational assumptions give rise to the best-fitting predictions in Fig. 9. Specifically, the first time a distractor is encountered, it receives a large encoding weight because C-SOB identifies it as novel. In consequence, the update to the weight matrix is quite distruptive of existing memories. If there are additional repetitions of the same distractor, those repetitions receive minimal encoding because they are identified as having little novelty. In consequence, there is little additional interference compared to the single distractor condition.

[4] The small divergence in the figure is not statistically significant and is also absent in a number of other experiments conducted in the first author's laboratory. If the effects of increasing the duration of articulation are expressed as the "loss of accuracy per second," in all experiments the 95% confidence intervals for those time-loss rates are narrow and generally straddle zero. The exact values are given later in this paper.

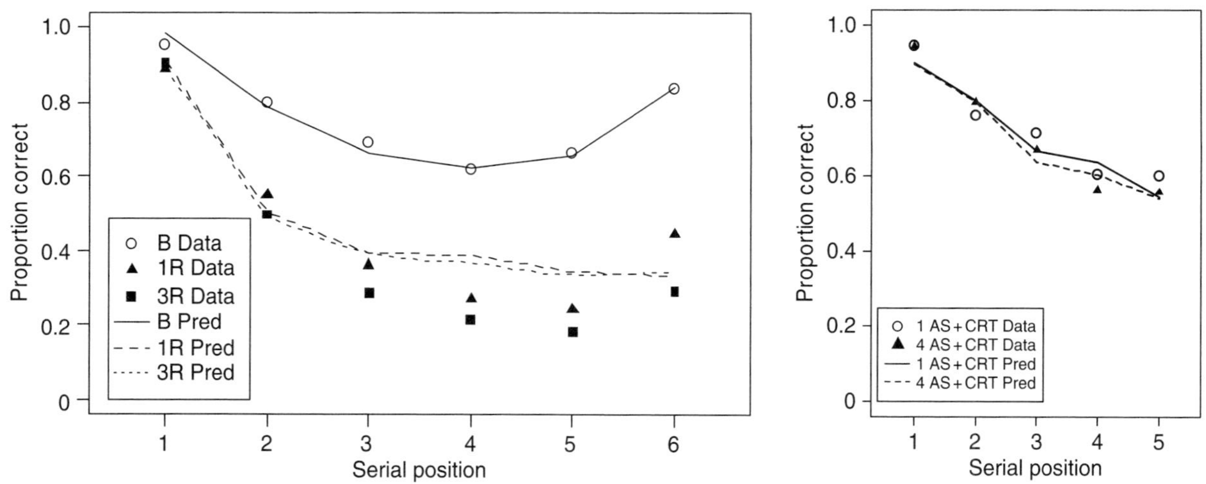

Fig. 9. Data (plotting symbols) and predictions from C-SOB (continuous lines) for two experiments by Oberauer and Lewandowsky (in press). The left panel shows an experiment that compared a quiet baseline (B) to two conditions involving one (1R) or three (3R) articulations of a suppressor before each retrieval. The right panel shows an experiment in which each retrieval was preceded by one (1 AS + CRT) or four (4 AS + CRT) interfering events, each of which involved articulation of a suppressor and a simultaneous speeded choice task.

B. Distractor Structure and Interference: An Experimental Test

The energy-gated encoding of distractors yields strong predictions involving the similarity structure of the to-be-articulated material. To illustrate, consider the extreme case in which every articulatory distractor consists of a different word; that is, people might say "table—horse—truck" after recall of the first item and "orange—zucchini—car" after the second item and so on. Within the energy-gated encoding framework, every distractor in this case is relatively novel and would be encoded quite strongly, hence maximizing the amount of interference and giving rise to considerable forgetting that increases in proportion to the number of articulations in between retrievals.

Figure 10 shows the complete set of predictions for all possible combinations of novelty within and between "bursts" of articulatory distractors. (A burst refers to the articulation sequence in between retrievals and thus refers to either 1 or 3 words being spoken aloud after recall of each list item.) The two lines shown in each panel represent one and three distractors, respectively, in between each retrieval. The top panels show predictions for "simple" bursts, that is, those involving repetition of the same word (as used by Oberauer & Lewandowsky, in press), whereas the bottom panels show predictions for "complex" bursts (consisting of three different words, not used in experiments to date). The left-hand panels show the predictions when bursts are steady across output positions, that is, when people have to repeat the same set of (one or three) items after each retrieval. The right-hand panels, by contrast, show predictions when the identity of bursts changes across output positions. All predictions were obtained using the best-fitting parameter estimates and representational assumptions used by Oberauer and Lewandowsky (in press).

In summary, the top-left panel corresponds to people saying the same word either once or three times in between all retrievals; the top-right panel represents people saying a word either once or three times after a retrieval, with the identity of that word changing across output positions. Finally, the bottom panels correspond to people articulating three different words at each output position, with the identity of those three words either repeating across output positions (left-hand panel) or changing after each retrieval (right-hand panel). In addition to predicting no fanning for simple bursts (cf. Oberauer & Lewandowsky, in press), C-SOB predicts only limited additional impairment when the distractor changes across serial positions (top left vs top right). However, changing the distractor within a burst introduces marked fanning (top vs bottom panels), with this fanning being most pronounced when the distractor bursts are repeated across output positions (bottom left vs bottom right).

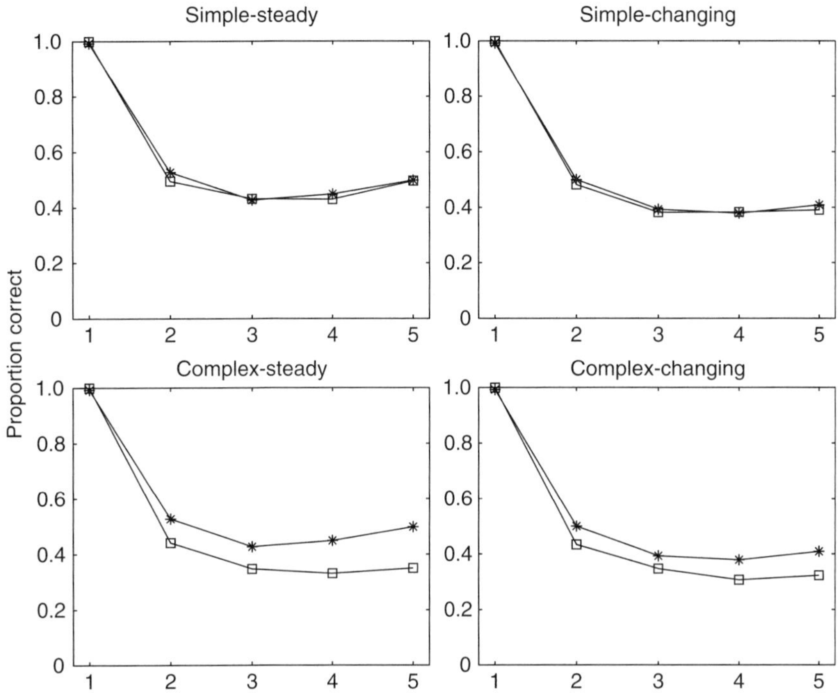

Fig. 10. Predictions from C-SOB for four different types of distractors during retrieval. The top row of panels refers to simple "bursts" of distractors, in which the same word is repeated once (lines with asterisks as plotting symbols) or three times (open squares) after each retrieval. The bottom row refers to complex bursts, in which each articulation involves a different word. The left column of panels refers to the case in which bursts of distractors remain unchanged across output positions, and the right column refers to the case in which the identity of words in a burst changes across output positions.

C-SOB's predictions are subject to fairly straightforward experimental tests. In a first, as yet unpublished experiment, conducted by Sonja Geiger and the first author, people were given a predictable and well-rehearsed sequence of distractors, namely, the months of the year. People studied lists of five letters for immediate forward serial recall. During recall, each oral report of a list item was followed by bursts of articulation of one or three names of months. The nature of the bursts (simple; "January-January-January" vs complex; "January-February-March") was manipulated between subjects, whereas the remaining two variables (number of distractors and whether or not the identity of distractors changed across output positions) were manipulated within subjects.

The results of this experiment are shown in Fig. 11 using the same layout of panels as for the C-SOB predictions. Comparison of this figure with the predictions in Fig. 10 confirms that the study in large part supported the predictions of the model. There was no fanning for the simple bursts, irrespective of whether or not they changed across output positions (mean difference between 1 and 3 distractors across serial positions 2 through 5 was a negligible .008, averaged across steady and changing bursts); there was fanning for complex bursts, and the extent of that fanning was greater for the steady condition (mean difference between 1 and 3 distractors across serial positions 2 through 5 was .1337) than for the changing condition (mean difference .0382). The one prediction that failed to be supported concerned

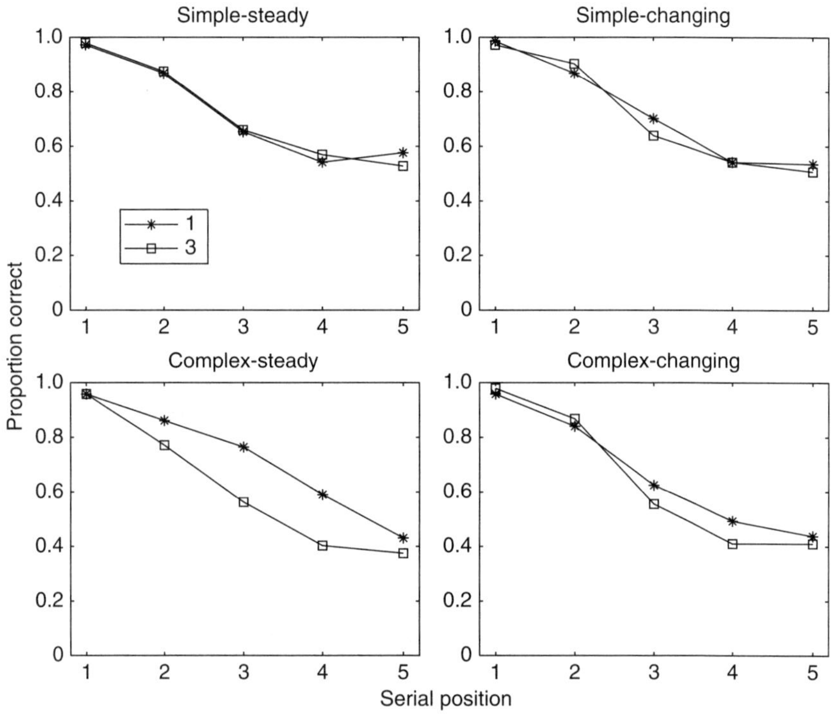

Fig. 11. Data from an unpublished experiment that compared four different types of distractors during retrieval. The top row of panels refers to simple "bursts" of distractors, in which the same word is repeated once (lines labeled 1) or three times (3) after each retrieval. The bottom row refers to complex bursts, in which each articulation involves a different word. The left column of panels refers to the case in which bursts of distractors remain unchanged across output positions, and the right column refers to the case in which the identity of words in a burst changes across output positions.

the differences between steady and changing simple bursts: Whereas SOB expected the latter to lead to slightly more interference than the former, the data showed no such effect.

To place these results into a wider theoretical context, it must be noted that a temporal view of forgetting would expect *all* types of articulation to engender the divergence between one and 3 distractors that in the experiment was limited to complex bursts. That is, because three repetitions of the word "January" take (roughly) as much additional time (compared to a single repetition) as does articulation of the sequence "January-February-March," a time-based model must expect equal forgetting in each case. The data clearly contradict this expectation.

We conclude that C-SOB's predictions differentiate it from theories that assign a role of time during forgetting (e.g., the primacy model, Page & Norris, 1998; SIMPLE, Brown et al., 2007), and that the successful test of those predictions (the results of the study just discussed were replicated and extended in two additional experiments conducted by Sonja Geiger and the first author) further supports one of the constructs on which C-SOB is built; namely, that the passage of time per se plays no causal role in STM. This encouraging outcome suggests that further exploration of C-SOB is warranted.

V. General Discussion

A. Limitations of C-SOB

Although we have shown that C-SOB can accommodate acknowledged benchmark effects in serial recall, and have demonstrated that the theory's predictions can be successfully tested, these successes were accompanied by two design decisions that, in turn, engendered two potential limitations: First, C-SOB explicitly rejects the notion that elapsed time plays a causal role in STM and, second, the theory as stated cannot be applied to multitrial effects. We discuss those limitations before placing C-SOB into a wider theoretical context.

1. The Role of Time in STM

By rejecting a causal role of time, C-SOB is an unequivocally event-based theory, and thus differs from several other current contenders, such as the primacy model (Page & Norris, 1998), SIMPLE (Brown et al., 2007), or the model by Burgess and Hitch (e.g., 1999, 2006). Is this strong theoretical commitment justified in light of the available data? Our response is twofold and considers the effects of time at encoding and during retention separately.

Concerning retention, we propose that there is now ample evidence to suggest that forgetting in STM is not caused by the passage of time per se. We presented some of the relevant studies earlier, and there is now clear evidence that if retrieval is delayed by distractor activity, recall performance is largely unaffected. At a quantitative level, this is best illustrated by considering the average "time-loss rate" across the experiments reported by Oberauer and Lewandowsky (in press). The time-loss rate captures the loss in accuracy for each second by which recall is delayed, and for the studies reported by Oberauer and Lewandowsky this value ranged from −.0012 (i.e., 1/10th of a percent loss per second) to −.011 (around 1% loss per second), with an average of −.005. In other words, no forgetting was observed despite delaying recall by as much as 12.5 s (for later list items). While it might be argued that the absence of forgetting reflected the operation of compensatory rehearsal that exactly canceled out the effects of decay or loss of temporal distinctiveness, we find it implausible to assume that rehearsal can take place when people simultaneously articulate distractors and perform a speeded choice task while also trying to recall a list.

Turning to the effects of time at encoding, the picture is somewhat more complex. We noted earlier that although there is considerable evidence that temporal isolation does not facilitate serial recall (e.g., Lewandowsky et al., 2006), there are two exceptions to this general finding that occur in known circumstances. Clearly, a comprehensive theory of memory must account for those exceptions as well as the general rule, and we acknowledge that C-SOB falls short in this regard. The first exception involves lists in which temporal isolation increases or decreases predictably across serial positions, as for example the list A.B...C...D....E, where each "." represents a unit of time (e.g., Neath & Crowder, 1996). Lewandowsky et al. (2007) showed that the benefit of temporal isolation that is observed under those conditions can be explained by assuming that people selectively focus attention at encoding on those items that they know will be widely separated. No existing theory of memory, C-SOB included, captures and describes strategies of this type. The second exception involves situations in which people are free to report items in any order, as in free recall (Brown et al., 2006) or in an unconstrained reconstruction task (Lewandowsky et al., 2008). The latter study is particularly relevant because it showed that isolation benefited performance even when output order was statistically controlled—that is, isolation affected performance directly, rather than indirectly by facilitating selection of isolated items for early report, thereby protecting them against the deleterious consequences of output interference. The study by Lewandowsky et al. thus constitutes strong evidence that even when controlling for strategic factors, temporal isolation can causally and directly determine STM performance provided report order is unconstrained (the study included a comparison condition in which reconstruction was enforced to be in forward order; in replication of numerous earlier studies, no isolation effects were observed in that condition).

Because C-SOB currently does not explain performance in tasks in which output order is unconstrained, we defer an account of these isolation effects, although we acknowledge that C-SOB might ultimately have to acknowledge a role of time during encoding. This might be most readily achieved by augmenting the context markers with a temporal component that evolves with elapsed time rather than being driven by study or retrieval events.

2. *Prior Knowledge and Multitrial Effects*

The present instantiation of C-SOB assumed that participants had access to preexisting knowledge about stimulus items, without, however, exploring the precise effects of that preexisting knowledge on short-term recall. This does not present an in-principle limitation of the theory: In earlier work, Lewandowsky and Farrell (2000) and Farrell and Lewandowsky (2002) accounted for the beneficial effects of word familiarity on short-term recall by giving more frequent items additional pretraining. Recent evidence suggests a more complicated relationship between word frequency and serial-recall performance. Hulme, Stuart, Brown, and Morin (2003) have shown that the high-frequency advantage disappears when high- and low-frequency words are mixed together on the same lists, suggesting that it is the associations that are formed between high-frequency items at encoding that drive the effect (see also Stuart & Hulme, 2000). It is unclear whether C-SOB would handle those effects.

Other evidence suggests that knowledge about sequential statistics also determines serial-recall performance (e.g., Baddeley, Conrad, & Hull, 1965; Botvinick & Bylsma, 2005; Thorn & Frankish, 2005). For example, Botvinick and Bylsma (2005) tested participants' immediate serial recall over many sessions with lists that contained sequential dependencies (e.g., *fie* might often be immediately followed by *kay* but less often by *tee*). Botvinick and Bylsma found that participants more accurately remembered sequences containing high-frequency transitions, and that they produced many regularization errors (i.e., erroneously replacing a low-frequency transition with a higher-frequency transition at recall). It is doubtful that C-SOB could handle those effects without further development.

Finally, learning can also be witnessed during experimental sessions in the form of the Hebb repetition effect, in which repeating sequences of items during an experiment cumulatively enhances recall for those lists relative to unrepeated control lists (e.g., Cumming, Page, & Norris, 2003; Hitch, Fastame, & Flude, 2005). In the light of claims that the fundamental role of verbal STM is to support the laying down of long-term phonological representations (Baddeley et al., 1998), phenomena such as the Hebb effect obviously represent valuable targets for models of serial recall. The revised model of Burgess and Hitch (2006) can provide a detailed account of the fairly intricate pattern of results surrounding the Hebb effect, and we therefore anticipate that any future development of C-SOB must involve its application to multitrial situations; not only to capture the Hebb effect but also more basic patterns such as the occurrence of protrusions (i.e., intrusions from the previous list which tend to preserve their original position). We expect that the inevitable retention of context–item associations across trials may lead to interesting interactions with similarity via the energy-gated encoding in C-SOB, perhaps giving rise to a possible mechanism for additional phenomena such as proactive interference.

B. C-SOB: Relationship to Other Theories

1. SOB and C-SOB

It is informative to compare C-SOB to its immediate antecedent, SOB (Farrell & Lewandowsky, 2002), both at an architectural level and in terms of its predictive power. There are two crucial differences between C-SOB and the original SOB: First, unlike SOB, C-SOB is not restricted to modeling memory for unrelated dissimilar items. Second, whereas SOB relied on a random endogenous cue to initiate retrieval, C-SOB includes a set of context markers. It turns out that those two changes necessarily go together. Within a distributed architecture, lists of similar items cannot be retrieved by a random cue alone because their attractors partially overlap, thus creating particularly strong basins of attraction that correspond to a blend of all similar items. Without context markers to cue retrieval, the model would retrieve only those strong blends which do not correspond to any of the list items.

The inclusion of context markers is also necessary for empirical reasons: First, recall that the analysis of latency–displacement functions points to the need for item markers. Second, item markers were required to enable the model to account for grouping effects. We explored numerous avenues to produce grouping effects without the use of context markers, all of which remained unsuccessful. The fact that the primacy model (Page & Norris, 1998), which includes no item markers, also cannot handle grouping effects supports the conclusion that grouping cannot be modeled without some type of external markers that are associated to the list items and that demarcate the various groups from each other.

These two architectural changes from the earlier SOB have yielded considerable payoff in terms of predictive scope: Not only does the model now handle similarity and grouping effects, but the presence of context markers additionally permitted modeling of distractor activity during retrieval (see the earlier discussion of the data by Oberauer and Lewandowsky, in press, and of the new experiment that explored the effects of varying the nature of distractors). The use of context markers does, however, entail a cost: As in many other models (e.g., SEM; Henson, 1998a), the structure of the markers across positions is assumed rather than explained by the model. That is, although it is entirely plausible to postulate that the contexts of adjacent items are more similar to each other than are the contexts of items separated by intervening events, the precise form of their similarity relationship is not derived from the model's architecture. Are there any candidate mechanisms on the horizon that might permit a more principled derivation of context markers? One model that contains a principled—albeit entirely time-based—mechanism for the evolution of context markers is OSCAR (Brown et al., 2000). OSCAR postulates that context is provided by a bank of independent oscillators that are operating at different frequencies and that, when considered together, uniquely identify any discrete moment in time. Accordingly, in situations in which list items are separated by constant temporal intervals, the similarity structure among the oscillator-based context vectors in OSCAR is nearly indistinguishable from that assumed for C-SOB.

2. C-SOB and Other Theories

C-SOB can be compared to alternative theories by once again considering Tables I and II. It is apparent that C-SOB matches or exceeds the predictive capabilities of most other contenders when the benchmark results in Table I are considered. However, to gather a more complete picture, we must consider two additional issues that were omitted from the table because, by our criteria, they fell outside the set of benchmarks: First, Burgess and Hitch (2006) presented an extension to their model that accommodated a wide range of data on the Hebb repetition effect. Second, the table does not include the results of the forgetting study presented ealier.

The first point reinforces our belief, stated at the outset, that the sequence of models by Burgess and Hitch (1999, 2006) present a powerful accomplishment and a formidable target for rival theories. That said, we must note that this accomplishment comes at the cost of a panoply of theoretical constructs: The architecture of the Burgess and Hitch model relies on item marking as well as competitive queueing; it contains two sets of weights with differing decay characteristics (slow vs fast); it contains two stages of retrieval, one of which involves feedback between two layers of phonemes; and its mechanism for response suppression is accompanied by decay of that inhibition. Although support can be adduced for each of those architectural features, their sum total can hardly be considered parsimonious. A desirable target for future theorizing must, therefore, be the attempt to match the theory's explanatory power within a more parsimonious rival framework.

The second point runs somewhat counter to the first one, because the results of the new forgetting study presented in this chapter are difficult to reconcile with a model in which forgetting is primarily due to time-based decay. In particular, neither the Burgess and Hitch models nor other time-based approaches (e.g., the primacy model of Page & Norris, 1998, or SIMPLE; Brown et al., 2007) can explain why performance in the absence of rehearsal is unaffected by the passage of time per se, and why a rather subtle change in the nature of the to-be-articulated distractors changes the outcome so profoundly. Similarly, unlike C-SOB, none of the existing models—with the possible exception of the model by Botvinick and Plaut (2006)—can accommodate the mixed-list advantage for phonologically dissimilar items reported by Farrell and Lewandowsky (2003), Farrell (2006), and Lewandowsky and Farrell (2008).

The comparison between C-SOB and other theories presented here is primarily qualitative; given that one strength of computational models is their ability to make quantitative predictions of the type presented throughout this chapter, a necessary next step in theoretical development in STM must involve quantitative comparison of models. By way of precedent, Lewandowsky and Farrell (2008; see also Farrell, 2006) showed that although some models could qualitatively account for the mixed-list advantage for dissimilar items, only C-SOB accurately captured the quantitative profile of the data. Similarly, Oberauer and Lewandowsky (in press) compared C-SOB to the primacy model and SIMPLE at a quantitative level in its ability to accommodate the effects of distractor activity during recall. We suggest that future work in STM should build on those precedents and should engage in quantitative comparisons of a number of models on the same data, rather than demonstrating that a single model can account for some data (see Navarro, Pitt, & Myung, 2004).

3. *Theoretical Conclusions*

What, then, is the current state of theoretical affairs in STM? Beginning with the specifics, we suggest that time-based forgetting is compromised as an explanatory construct. Instead, in the light of Oberauer and Lewandowsky's (in press) findings and the new data being collected in the laboratory of the present first author, we suggest that forgetting from STM is primarily due to interference, both in the cross talk between associations inherent in C-SOB's assumption of composite distributed representations, and in the novelty-sensitive encoding that reduces the quality of encoding of successive similar items.

Turning to the more general level, we conclude that there is strong evidence that implicates several architectural constructs in serial recall performance. Both response suppression and a primacy gradient are almost universally assumed in models of STM; when these assumptions are not incorporated into models, the ability of those models to account for the data is restricted (e.g., witness the lack of a primacy effect in the Burgess and Hitch model, which does not incorporate a primacy gradient). C-SOB arguably moves beyond other models in providing an endogenous account of the generation of the primacy gradient, and in specifying a learning mechanism responsible for response suppression. Another nearly ubiquitous assumption in Table II is that of item marking; given the empirical evidence in the form of latency–displacement functions and its apparent necessity to account for grouping and similarity effects in C-SOB, we suggest that the multidimensional contexts assumed by most models of serial recall are an essential representational device.

Finally, we point to some failings of current models, including C-SOB, as important areas for theoretical development. We suggest that theoretical development should focus on accounting for the rich set of constraints provided by the data on the Hebb repetition effect (Cumming et al., 2003; Hitch et al., 2005) and the role of long-term knowledge in short-term serial recall (Baddeley et al., 1965; Botvinick & Bylsma, 2005; Thorn & Frankish, 2005). We also suggest that models should ultimately account for working memory performance beyond short-term serial recall. Given the importance of processing and storage tasks in predicting higher-level cognitive functioning (Oberauer et al., 2007), we see this as a pathway for the current models to begin to contribute to a coherent and comprehensive theory of cognition.

VI. Concluding Remarks

We have presented and explored a theory of STM that we consider to be a welcome addition to the available theoretical contenders. We confirmed that the theory—with its assumptions of novelty-based encoding, response suppression, dynamic deblurring, and positional marking—accounts for conventional benchmark data, and showed that, unlike some of its rivals, the model additionally accommodates recent results that either forced a reevaluation of earlier data or provided new constraints on modeling. We also explored novel predictions of the theory that further differentiate it from rival models. We suggest that C-SOB—and, in particular, the energy-gated encoding that is central to its architecture—will provide a fruitful avenue for further exploration.

Acknowledgments

Preparation of this chapter was facilitated by various Discovery Grants from the Australian Research Council to the first author and by a Linkage International Grant from the Australian Research Council to both authors and Gordon Brown.

References

Adams, A., & Gathercole, S. E. (1996). Phonological working memory and spoken language development in young children. *Quarterly Journal of Experimental Psychology: Section A, 96*, 216–233.

Anderson, J. A. (1991). Why, having so many neurons, do we have so few thoughts? In W.E. Hockley and S. Lewandowsky (Eds.), *Relating theory and data: Essays on human memory in honor of Bennet B. Murdock* (pp. 477–507). Hillsdale, NJ: Erlbaum.

Anderson, J. A. (1995). *An introduction to neural networks.* Cambridge: MA: MIT Press.

Anderson, M. C., & Neely, J. H. (1996). Interference and inhibition in memory retrieval. In E. L. Bjork & R. A. Bjork (Eds.), *Handbook of perception and memory: Memory* (Vol. 10). San Diego: Academic Press.

Anderson, J. A., Silverstein, J. W., Ritz, S. A., & Jones, R. S. (1977). Distinctive features, categorical perception, and probability learning: Some applications of a neural model. *Psychological Review, 84*, 413–451.

Baddeley, A. D. (1966). Short-term memory for word sequences as a function of acoustic, semantic, and formal similarity. *Quarterly Journal of Experimental Psychology, 18*, 362–365.

Baddeley, A. D. (1968). How does acoustic similarity influence short-term memory. *Quarterly Journal of Experimental Psychology, 20A*, 249–263.

Baddeley, A. D., Conrad, R., & Hull, A. J. (1965). Predictability and immediate memory for consonant sequences. *Quarterly Journal of Experimental Psychology, 17*, 175–177.

Baddeley, A. D., Gathercole, S., & Papagno, C. (1998). The phonological loop as a language learning device. *Psychological Review, 105*, 158–173.

Baddeley, A. D., & Hitch, G. (1974). Working memory. In G. A. Bower (Ed.), *Recent advances in learning and motivation* (Vol. 8, pp. 647–667). New York: Academic Press.

Baddeley, A. D., Thomson, N., & Buchanan, M. (1975). Word length and the structure of short-term memory. *Journal of Verbal Learning and Verbal Behavior, 14*, 575–589.

Bjork, E. L., & Healy, A. F. (1974). Short-term order and item retention. *Journal of Verbal Learning and Verbal Behavior, 13*, 80–97.

Bjork, R. A., & Whitten, W. B. (1974). Recency-sensitive retrieval processes in long-term free recall. *Cognitive Psychology, 6*, 173–189.

Botvinick, M., & Bylsma, L. M. (2005). Regularization in short-term memory for serial order. *Journal of Experimental Psychology: Learning, Memory, and Cognition, 31*, 351–358.

Botvinick, M. M., & Plaut, D. C. (2006). Short-term memory for serial order: A recurrent neural network model. *Psychological Review, 113*, 201–233.

Brown, G. D. A., & Hulme, C. (1995). Modeling item length effects in memory span: No rehearsal needed. *Journal of Memory and Language, 34*, 594–621.

Brown, G. D. A., & Lamberts, K. (2003). Double dissociations, models and serial position curves. *Cortex, 39*, 148–152.

Brown, G. D. A., Morin, C., & Lewandowsky, S. (2006). Evidence for time-based models of free recall. *Psychonomic Bulletin & Review, 13*, 717–723.

Brown, G. D. A., Neath, I., & Chater, N. (2007). A temporal ratio model of memory. *Psychological Review, 114*, 539–576.
Brown, G. D. A., Preece, T., & Hulme, C. (2000). Oscillator-based memory for serial order. *Psychological Review, 107*, 127–181.
Burgess, N., & Hitch, G. (2006). A revised model of short-term memory and long-term learning of verbal sequences. *Journal of Memory and Language, 55*, 627–652.
Burgess, N., & Hitch, G. J. (1992). Toward a network model of the articulatory loop. *Journal of Memory and Language, 31*, 429–460.
Burgess, N., & Hitch, G. J. (1999). Memory for serial order: A network model of the phonological loop and its timing. *Psychological Review, 106*, 551–581.
Coltheart, V. (1993). Effects of phonological similarity and concurrent irrelevant articulation on short-term memory recall of repeated and novel word lists. *Memory & Cognition, 21*, 539–545.
Conrad, R. (1964). Acoustic confusions in immediate memory. *British Journal of Psychology, 55*, 75–84.
Cowan, N., Saults, J. S., Elliott, E. M., & Moreno, M. V. (2002). Deconfounding serial recall. *Journal of Memory and Language, 46*, 153–177.
Crowder, R. G. (1976). *Principles of learning and memory*. Hillsdale, NJ: Lawrence Erlbaum.
Cumming, N., Page, M., & Norris, D. (2003). Testing a positional model of the Hebb effect. *Memory, 11*, 43–63.
Dosher, B. A., & Ma, J.-J. (1998). Output loss or rehearsal loop? Output-time versus pronunciation-time limits in immediate recall for forgetting-matched materials. *Journal of Experimental Psychology: Learning, Memory and Cognition, 24*, 316–335.
Drewnowski, A., & Murdock, B. B. (1980). The role of auditory features in memory span for words. *Journal of Experimental Psychology: Human Learning and Memory, 6*, 319–332.
Farrell, S. (2006). Mixed-list phonological similarity effects in delayed serial recall. *Journal of Memory and Language, 55*, 587–600.
Farrell, S., & Lewandowsky, S. (2002). An endogenous distributed model of ordering in serial recall. *Psychonomic Bulletin & Review, 9*, 59–79.
Farrell, S., & Lewandowsky, S. (2003). Dissimilar items benefit from phonological similarity in serial recall. *Journal of Experimental Psychology: Learning, Memory, and Cognition, 29*, 838–849.
Farrell, S., & Lewandowsky, S. (2004). Modelling transposition latencies: Constraints for theories of serial order memory. *Journal of Memory and Language, 51*, 115–135.
Farrell, S., & Lewandowsky, S. (2007). *Response suppression contributes to recency in serial recall.* Unpublished manuscript: University of Western Australia.
Farrell, S., & McLaughlin, K. (2007). Short-term recognition memory for serial order and timing. *Memory & Cognition, 35*, 1724–1734.
Fürst, A. J., & Hitch, G. J. (2000). Separate roles for executive and phonological components of working memory in mental arithmetic. *Memory & Cognition, 28*, 774–782.
Glenberg, A. M., & Swanson, N. G. (1986). A temporal distinctiveness theory of recency and modality effects. *Journal of Experimental Psychology: Learning, Memory, and Cognition, 12*, 3–15.
Henry, L. A. (1991). The effects of word length and phonemic similarity in young children's short-term memory. *Quarterly Journal of Experimental Psychology, 43A*, 35–52.
Henson, R. N. A. (1996). *Short-term memory for serial order*. Unpublished doctoral dissertation, University of Cambridge, England.
Henson, R. N. A. (1998a). Short-term memory for serial order: The start-end model. *Cognitive Psychology, 36*, 73–137.

Henson, R. N. A. (1998b). Item repetition in short-term memory: Ranschburg repeated. *Journal of Experimental Psychology: Learning, Memory, and Cognition, 24*, 1162–1181.

Henson, R. N. A. (1999). Positional information in short-term memory: Relative or absolute?. *Memory & Cognition, 27*, 915–927.

Henson, R. N. A., Norris, D. G., Page, M. P. A., & Baddeley, A. D. (1996). Unchained memory: Error patterns rule out chaining models of immediate serial recall. *Quarterly Journal of Experimental Psychology, 49A*, 80–115.

Hinton, G. E., McClelland, J. L., & Rumelhart, D. E. (1986). Distributed representations. In D. E. Rumelhart and J. L. McClelland, the PDP Research Group (Eds.), *Parallel distributed processing: Explorations in the microstructure of cognition, Vol. 1: Foundations*. Cambridge, MA: MIT Press.

Hintzman, D. L. (1991). Why are formal models useful in psychology? In W. E. Hockley and S. Lewandowsky (Eds.), *Relating theory and data: Essays on human memory in honor of Bennet B. Murdock* (pp. 39–56). Hillsdale, NJ: Lawrence Erlbaum Associates.

Hitch, G. J., Burgess, N., Towse, J. N., & Culpin, V. (1996). Temporal grouping effects in immediate recall: A working memory analysis. *Quarterly Journal of Experimental Psychology, 49A*, 116–139.

Hitch, G. J., Fastame, M. C., & Flude, B. (2005). How is the serial order of a verbal sequence coded? Some comparisons between models. *Memory, 13*, 247–258.

Houghton, G., & Hartley, T. (1996). Parallel models of serial behaviour: Lashley revisited. Psyche *2*(25). Symposium on implicit learning and memory (http://psyche.cs.monash.edu.au).

Hulme, C., Stuart, G., Brown, G. D. A., & Morin, C. (2003). High- and low-frequency words are recalled equally well in alternating lists: Evidence for associative effects in serial recall. *Journal of Memory and Language, 49*, 500–518.

Lewandowsky, S. (1993). The rewards and hazards of computer simulations. *Psychological Science, 4*, 236–243.

Lewandowsky, S. (1999). Redintegration and response suppression in serial recall: A dynamic network model. *International Journal of Psychology, 34*, 434–446.

Lewandowsky, S., Brown, G. D. A., Wright, T., & Nimmo, L. M. (2006). Timeless memory: Evidence against temporal distinctiveness models of short-term memory for serial order. *Journal of Memory and Language, 54*, 20–38.

Lewandowsky, S., Duncan, M., & Brown, G. D. A. (2004). Time does not cause forgetting in short-term serial recall. *Psychonomic Bulletin & Review, 11*, 771–790.

Lewandowsky, S., & Farrell, S. (2000). A redintegration account of word-length, lexicality, and articulatory suppression effects in short-term serial memory. *Psychological Research, 63*, 163–173.

Lewandowsky, S., & Farrell, S. (2008). Phonological similarity in serial recall: Constraints on theories of memory. *Journal of Memory and Language, 58*, 429–448.

Lewandowsky, S., & Heit, E. (2006). Some targets for memory models. *Journal of Memory and Language, 55*, 441–446.

Lewandowsky, S., & Li, S.-C. (1994). Memory for serial order revisited. *Psychological Review, 101*, 539–543.

Lewandowsky, S., & Murdock, B. B., Jr. (1989). Memory for serial order. *Psychological Review, 96*, 25–57.

Lewandowsky, S.,Nimmo, L. M., & Brown, G. D. A. (2008). When temporal isolation benefits memory for serial order. *Journal of Memory and Language, 58*, 415–428.

Lewandowsky, S., Wright, T., & Brown, G. D. A. (2007). The interpretation of temporal isolation effects. In N. Osaka, R. Logie, and M. D'Esposito (Eds.), *Working memory-Behavioral and neural correlates* (pp. 137–152). Oxford University Press.

Li, S.-C., & Lewandowsky, S. (1993). Intralist distractors and recall direction: Constraints on models of memory for serial order. *Journal of Experimental Psychology: Learning, Memory, and Cognition, 19*, 895–908.
Lovatt, P., Avons, S. E., & Masterson, J. (2000). The word-length effect and disyllabic words. *Quarterly Journal of Experimental Psychology, 53A*, 1–22.
Luce, R. D. (1963). Detection and recognition. In R. D. Luce, R. R. Bush, and E. Galanter (Eds.), *Handbook of mathematical psychology* (pp. 103–189). New York: Wiley.
Madigan, S. (1980). The serial position curve in immediate serial recall. *Bulletin of the Psychonomic Society, 15*, 335–338.
Mueller, S. T., Seymour, T. L., Kieras, D. E., & Meyer, D. E. (2003). Theoretical implications of articulatory duration, phonological similarity, and phonological complexity in verbal working memory. *Journal of Experimental Psychology: Learning, Memory, and Cognition, 29*, 1353–1380.
Murdock, B. B., Jr. (1982). A theory for the storage and retrieval of item and associative information. *Psychological Review, 89*, 609–626.
Nairne, J. S. (1992). The loss of positional certainty in long-term memory. *Psychological Science, 3*, 199–202.
Nairne, J. S., & Kelley, M. R. (1999). Reversing the phonological similarity effect. *Memory & Cognition, 27*, 45–53.
Navarro, D. J., Pitt, M. A., & Myung, I. J. (2004). Assessing the distinguishability of models and the informativeness of data. *Cognitive Psychology, 49*, 47–84.
Neath, I., & Brown, G. D. A. (2006). SIMPLE: Further applications of a local distinctiveness model of memory. *The Psychology of Learning and Motivation, 46*, 201–243.
Neath, I., & Crowder, R. G. (1996). Distinctiveness and very short-term serial position effects. *Memory, 4*, 225–242.
Nimmo, L. M., & Lewandowsky, S. (2005). From brief gaps to very long pauses: Temporal isolation does not benefit serial recall. *Psychonomic Bulletin & Review, 12*, 999–1004.
Nimmo, L. M., & Lewandowsky, S. (2006). Distinctiveness revisited: Unpredictable temporal isolation does not benefit short-term serial recall of heard or seen events. *Memory & Cognition, 34*, 1368–1375.
Oberauer, K. (2003). Understanding serial position curves in short-term recognition and recall. *Journal of Memory and Language, 49*, 469–483.
Oberauer, K., & Lewandowsky, S. (in press). Forgetting in immediate serial recall: Decay, temporal distinctiveness, or interference? *Psychological Review.*
Oberauer, K., Süß, H.-M.,Wilhelm,O., & Sander, N. (2007). Individual differences in working memory capacity and reasoning ability. In A. R. A. Conway, C. Jarrold, M. J. Kane, A. Miyake, and J. N. Towse (Eds.), *Variation in working memory* (pp. 49–75). Oxford: Oxford University Press.
Page, M. P. A. (2000). A localist manifesto. *Behavioral and Brain Sciences, 23*, 443–467.
Page, M. P. A., Madge, A., Cumming, N., & Norris, D. G. (2007). Speech errors and the phonological similarity effect in short-term memory: Evidence suggesting a common locus. *Journal of Memory and Language, 56*, 49–64.
Page, M. P. A., & Norris, D. (1998). The primacy model: A new model of immediate serial recall. *Psychological Review, 105*, 761–781.
Ryan, J. (1969). Temporal grouping, rehearsal and short-term memory. *Quarterly Journal of Experimental Psychology, 21*, 148–155.
Service, E. (1998). The effect of word length on immediate serial recall depends on phonological complexity, not articulatory duration. *Quarterly Journal of Experimental Psychology, 51A*, 283–304.

Stuart, G., & Hulme, C. (2000). The effects of word co-occurrence on short-term memory: Associative links in long-term memory affect short-term memory performance. *Journal of Experimental Psychology: Learning, Memory, and Cognition, 26*, 796–802.

Surprenant, A. M., Kelley, M. R., Farley, L. A., & Neath, I. (2005). Fill-in and infill errors in order memory. *Memory, 13*, 267–273.

Thorn, A. S. C., & Frankish, C. R. (2005). Long-term knowledge effects on serial recall of nonwords are not exclusively lexical. *Journal of Experimental Psychology: Learning, Memory, and Cognition, 31*, 729–735.

Vousden, J. I., & Brown, G. D. A. (1998). To repeat or not to repeat: The time course of response suppression in sequential behaviour. In J. A. Bullinaria, D. W. Glasspool, and G. Houghton (Eds.), *Proceedings of the fourth neural computation and psychology workshop: Connectionist representations* (pp. 301–315). London: Springer Verlag.

Wickelgren, W. A. (1965a). Acoustic similarity and retroactive interference in short-term memory. *Journal of Verbal Learning and Verbal Behavior, 4*, 53–61.

Wickelgren, W. A. (1965b). Short-term memory for phonemically similar lists. *American Journal of Psychology, 78*, 567–574.

THEORY AND MEASUREMENT OF WORKING MEMORY CAPACITY LIMITS

Nelson Cowan, Candice C. Morey, Zhijian Chen, Amanda L. Gilchrist, and J. Scott Saults

Abstract

We review the evidence for various kinds of limit in the capability of working memory, the small amount of information that can be held in mind at once. To distinguish between types of limit in working memory, we invoke metaphors of space (capacity), time (decay and speed), and energy (control of attention). The review focuses primarily on recent evidence on a limit in how many chunks can be held in working memory, how this kind of limit can be measured, and how it can be distinguished from other types of limits. We explore the theoretical and practical importance of different working memory limits in research that is nomothetic (referring to general laws) and ideographic (referring to individual and group differences). The appropriate measure of working memory depends on one's holistic or analytic scientific interest.

THE PSYCHOLOGY OF LEARNING
AND MOTIVATION VOL. 49
DOI: 10.1016/S0079-7421(08)00002-9

I. Key Theoretical Issues

A. Introduction

Cognitive psychology casts a spotlight on both what people can do and what they cannot do. A person often can keep thinking about an important goal for some time, as when a driver knows he or she must watch for the second right turn. However, the driver can do so only by forfeiting other processing, such as complex conversation with a passenger. Watching a soccer game, a viewer can observe several players on the field at once but often will experience surprising (to the viewer) lapses in awareness of what is going on elsewhere on the field or in the stadium at that moment.

In describing the miracle of what humans can do, one inevitably is describing also the limits to what they can do. Although various animals including humans can visually scan an entire field or forest at once looking for predators or prey, humans excel at sequestering a small portion of the information to allow amazingly in-depth analysis of the selected portion. This is what the research literature shows. Miller (1956) wrote his famous article about humans typically being limited to remembering about seven items at once and, shortly afterward, Miller, Galanter, & Pribram (1960) wrote about how this limited memory may act as a "working memory" to keep in mind goals and other information that one needs to complete a task. In the present book series, Baddeley and Hitch (1974) wrote a seminal article on working memory suggesting that it must be composed of several parts that operate separately. Since then, research on the topic of working memory certainly has blossomed, both in the form of behavioral research on the topic and, especially recently, in the form of related neurobiological research. In our chapter, we focus on working memory capacity limits, with special attention on item limits like Miller (1956). To keep things simple we will not go into the various other terms that are used for similar concepts of a temporary memory, including short-term memory and immediate memory. These terms will be used interchangeably with working memory.

The topic of working memory limits is quite broad, considering that working memory is involved in almost every cognitive task and often sets boundaries for the performance of that task. For example, one cannot successfully complete arithmetic problems without some working memory of intermediate results and what types of calculation are still to be done. Probably for this kind of reason, researchers have approached the topic of working memory limits from a number of different theoretical vantage points. It is important to acknowledge these vantage points in order to avoid being stuck thinking that different investigators disagree on substantive points when, in many cases, they simply are interested in different issues.

Three issues that we introduce below refer to the type of working memory limits, the goal in studying these limits, and the level of analysis at which the limits are studied. We explain where our own recent research fits into this family of questions and what it is telling us.

The main emphasis of the present review is on the possibility of quantifying and characterizing limits in the number of chunks of information that individuals can retain in working memory at once, the theoretical and practical significance of this chunk capacity limit, and how it can be distinguished from other types of limits on working memory. We do not go into great detail regarding the specifics of different theoretical frameworks but we do have much in common with theorists who, in various ways, have emphasized a key role of attention in understanding the strengths and limits of both working memory storage and information processing (e.g., Awh & Jonides, 2001; Baddeley, 2000; Cowan, 1995, 1999, 2001; Davelaar, Goshen-Gottstein, Ashkenazi, Haarman, & Usher, 2005; Grossberg, 1978; Lovett, Reder, & Lebière, 1999; Unsworth & Engle, 2007).

B. Different Types of Working Memory Limits

After Salthouse (1985; also Kail & Salthouse, 1994), we point to an analogy between limits in working memory and limits in physical events, which occur within a certain time and space and involve a certain amount of energy. Working memory representations might be *limited in time*; they could fade quickly over time even in the absence of any sort of interference. Alternatively, working memory representations might last over time, but only until they are displaced by other representations that become active because of outside events or internal thoughts. The notion (Miller, 1956) that only a certain number of items can be held at once is like a space limit in which, say, only a certain number of eggs can fit in an egg carton. This is what we will term *chunk capacity limits*. The third possibility is that there is an energy limit, in which electrophysiological activity is in some not-quite-defined sense a type of energy. If the representation of each item required a certain amount of this neural energy per unit of time and other mental processes did as well, then any given representation would face competition from other representations in working memory or other mental processing that used the energy. This type of limit is often referred to as *resource limits*. This tripartite taxonomy is not meant as an assertion that no other factors can influence the fate of a representation in working memory. For one thing, multiple limits may apply (e.g., both space and energy). Moreover, there are additional factors. For example, the ability to use knowledge to form larger chunks of information eases the load on working memory (Miller, 1956). Thus, the letter sequence *irsciafbi* is much easier to remember in working memory if one notices that it is composed of three-letter acronyms for US government agencies, the Internal Revenue Service, the Central Intelligence Agency, and the Federal Bureau of Investigation. The present chapter is focused on identifying space or chunk capacity limits, and attempting to specify the relation between these types of limits and possible limits in time and energy.

C. Nomothetic and Ideographic Questions

Nomothetic questions relate to how a process normally or typically operates, whereas ideographic questions relate to how individuals (or groups) differ from this norm. Both of them are important and have played an important role in research on working memory. Perhaps most importantly, they should not be confused with one another.

Much of the early research on working memory was nomothetic in nature. Miller (1956) noted that the normal working memory limit was about seven items (give or take two) but he did not have much information on ideographic patterns. A large literature grew up following Baddeley and Hitch (1974) in which various manipulations were used to isolate components of working memory in the normal individual (Baddeley, 1986; Cowan, 2005; Gathercole & Baddeley, 1993; Logie & Gilhooly, 1998; Shah & Miyake, 2005). For instance, a phonological distracting task would interfere with verbal memory, but not spatial memory, whereas a spatial interfering task would do the reverse. A simple distracting task, such as repeating one letter would interfere with automatically held verbal memory, whereas only a more complex and engaging task, such as generating random numbers, would interfere with the central executive processes thought to be needed to control the flow of information from one memory store to another (Baddeley, 1996).

There also were ideographic approaches early on. The invention of the digit span task, in which the experimenter estimates how many digits the subject can repeat, was developed to help determine the maturational age equivalent of a particular child (e.g., Binet & Simon, 1916/1980; Bolton, 1892; Jacobs, 1887; Wechsler, 1944, 1991). That is, clearly the normal digit span increased with age in childhood and the question was the age norm that matched performance in a particular child. However, information carried over from nomothetic experimental methods can be of great help in solving ideographic questions. For example, the testing techniques developed by Alan Baddeley and colleagues have been used in many studies by Susan Gathercole and colleagues to study how different components of working memory change with age and how individual differences in each component are related to learning disabilities (for a review, see Baddeley, Gathercole, & Papagno, 1998).

It has also been tried in the other direction: ideographic differences have been used to try to help identify nomothetic principles. A good example is a study by Baddeley and Warrington (1970) on memory in amnesia. Informal study of amnesic individuals showed that they had great difficulty learning new information but still could interact rather normally (according to casual observation, at least) so that it seemed likely that they had preserved short-term memory. Baddeley and Warrington used an experimental method on amnesic individuals to verify that the typically nomothetic use of this same method provided separate measures of short- and long-term memory. In particular, it had been theorized that, in free recall, the most recent list items include a strong contribution of short-term memory, whereas earlier portions of the list are recalled based on long-term memory. Strongly supporting this division between short- and long-term memory and the measures of them in free recall, amnesic individuals were deficient in recall of earlier portions of the list but not in the last few list items. In more recent work, Engle and colleagues have shown that individuals with relatively low working memory span scores tend to be deficient in the control of attention compared to high-span individuals. They also have shown that high-span individuals with distraction perform similarly to low-span individuals without distraction (Kane & Engle, 2000; Rosen & Engle, 1997), and they have used that information to suggest that a key component of the normal operation of working memory is, in fact, the control of attention.

The use of ideographic differences to help identify nomothetic principles works fine to a point, but there are limits to its application. First, it is sometimes found that not all sources of individual differences converge on the same mechanisms. For example, Cowan et al. (1998) found that the effects of age on the timing of digit span recall were completely different from the effects of individual differences within an age group. If different sources of ideographic information yield different interpretations then one cannot tell which of them reveals the most important aspect of normal functioning. For example, according to one study on rapidly perceiving several items at once, or *subitizing*, there is no important individual difference in the number of items that can be held in working memory at once, in contrast to the pronounced individual differences in the control of attention (Tuholski, Engle, & Baylis, 2001). From this, one might reason that thinking of working memory as a capability of holding a certain number of items is the "wrong way" to think about working memory. However, other ideographic sources challenge this conclusion. In Section III.D, we describe a study by Basak and Verhaeghen (2003) that shows the subitizing range to change with adult aging, in contrast to the finding of Tuholski et al. (2001) in the examination of individual differences in young adults. Some studies have, indeed, used age differences in the holding capacity of working memory to explain developmental differences in cognition (Andrews & Halford, 2002; Pascual-Leone, 1970, 2005). In Section III.E, we will illustrate the importance of capacity with a procedure by Gold et al. (2006) that shows how space and energy constraints on working memory can be separated, strongly supporting space (i.e., chunk capacity) differences between normal and schizophrenic individuals; and we will examine a number of related examples.

A second limit to the research strategy of using ideographic information to discern nomothetic principles is that the latter can be theoretically important even without producing individual differences. To draw an analogy, most individuals do not differ in how many limbs they have (4), but the number of limbs is an important aspect of human physiology. The number of items retained in working memory at once is less visible than the number of limbs, but it similarly would be important even if it did not differ among individuals. Knowing that humans can retain 3 or 4 separate pieces of information at once, or can form 3 or 4 relations at once, allows many predictions about task performance that would not be possible otherwise (e.g., Halford, Baker, McCredden, & Bain, 2005; Halford, Cowan, & Andrews, 2007).

A key, capacity-limited part of working memory may comprise the contents of the focus of attention (Cowan, 2001). If so, it is not yet clear whether attention contents and attention control depend on separate mechanisms or a common mechanism. Here again, though, the ideographic information can be over-interpreted. Suppose it were found that there is a very high correlation between the control of attention and the holding capacity of working memory. Then it might be concluded that both of them stem from a single mechanism. For example, it might be that holding capacity depends on the ability to filter out extraneous, irrelevant items (Hasher & Zacks, 1988; Vogel, McCollough, & Machizawa, 2005). However, it would be going beyond the evidence to conclude from that that the control of attention and the holding capacity are not separate mechanisms, each with its own nomothetic importance. By analogy, the correlation of individuals' arm and leg length is rather high, but still one would not conclude that the arms and legs are indistinguishable. Arms and legs are independently important for overall active motor function, even if they strongly covary. As another example, having two eyes is important even though individuals do not vary in the number of eyes. Thus, one cannot use the ideographic uniformity of a component to rule out the nomothetic importance of that component. Thus, a particular measure of holding capacity would be nomothetically important even if it did not vary among individuals or age groups.

In our laboratory we have taken an approach that embraces both nomothetic and ideographic evidence, allowing cross-fertilization between the two while staying mindful that both approaches are meaningful in their own right. We will present our thoughts and our evidence on working memory limits that could be classified as space limits (i.e., chunk capacity limits), energy limits (i.e., the limits of total complexity and of attention control), and time limits (i.e., temporal decay of memory). These thoughts are tentative as the understanding of working memory limits is still evolving. Yet, we believe that considerable progress is being made by ourselves and others.

D. Holistic and Analytic Approaches

There are different attitudes toward research in psychology that one can term holistic and analytic. The holistic approach may be clearest to those interested in practical applications but they won't get far without including an analytic approach as well, in our opinion. Let us suppose that working memory is composed of multiple processes and components operating together, as Baddeley and Hitch (1974) assumed. (For now, it does not matter whether the components are just as Baddeley and Hitch thought.) Then a holistic approach is one in which we ask what is the combined effect of all components on working memory. In contrast, an analytic approach is one in which we ask what is the effect of each component. The components would have to be experimentally isolated to answer that question. If one adopts a holistic approach, it is not clear if good evidence could be found for time, space, or energy limits in working memory. That is because the components might operate differently and compensate for one another's weaknesses. If one sort of memory representation is lost as a function of time (i.e., decays), another working memory function might serve to counteract decay so that one cannot see it. A classic example is the use of covert verbal rehearsal to refresh representations that presumably would decay if they were not refreshed (Baddeley, 1986). If one sort of memory representation has a space limitation, another sort may have no such limitation so that the combined effect is to obscure the limit. If there is an energy limit, some strategies might have the effect of overcoming that limit too. So, as we will see, steps must be taken to examine each component in isolation. For example, assuming that one cannot rehearse memoranda while repeating a different word, it is possible to see whether memory is lost as a function of time during that repetition (Baddeley, 1986). (It turns out that the question of whether one can see decay in such a circumstance is still not satisfactorily resolved.) The issue of holistic and analytic approaches is a complex one to be revisited in Section IV.

II. Space (Chunk Capacity) Limits

A. A Brief History of the Capacity Concept

We refer the reader to Cowan (2005) for a more thorough exposition of the history of the capacity concept. Miller (1956) set the world on fire with his thorough demonstration that there are some real limits on how long a series of random items, such as words or digits, can be before people are unable to repeat the series (about 7 items). In the same paper, he demonstrated some similar limits on how many simple items, such as tones of different frequencies, can be included in an absolute identification test before people are unable to identify individual items (about 7 items), and how many items can be included in a set to be rapidly enumerated before it becomes necessary to count them one by one (about 7 items, he thought; actually it is closer to 4 items as in the subsequent literature reviewed by Cowan, 2005). Without making a strong theoretical claim, Miller provided evidence that inspired many researchers to imagine that there might be a very general mental resource with an easily quantifiable limit, and that the limit might be used to predict what materials are easily perceived, understood, or remembered, and what materials are so processed only with difficulty. Shortly afterward, when Broadbent (1958) published his famous book on information processing, it included a simple processing model in which information was dealt with in an effective manner only if it went through a limited-capacity system. It was natural to suppose that the limits such as those that Miller pointed out applied to the limited-capacity system that Broadbent proposed. A good metaphor for the limited-capacity processor therefore seemed to be a box that can hold only a certain, limited number of items of particular type because of its limited internal space (like an egg carton). That metaphor was advanced further by Atkinson and Shiffrin (1968), who reported in their book chapter some sophisticated empirical and modeling work related to storage capacity limits. Miller et al. (1960) discussed how this limited-capacity system for storing information temporarily was essential to keep in mind goals as one plans and carries out activities, and thus referred to it as working memory.

The storage limit per se was not the main contribution of Miller (1956). A more critical contribution was his noticing what type of measure one had to use to observe near-constant capacity. In the zeitgeist of that time, when general-purpose computers had recently been invented, it had been assumed that communicating devices impart information that is to be measured in terms of the number of choices that could have been made, called binary digits, or bits. Within a string of digits in which each one ranges from 0 to 9, there are 10 choices, which require between 3 and 4 binary decisions. (For example, one could often, though not always, guess a digit after only three yes-or-no questions. One could ask, is the digit less than 6? If so, is it less than 3? If not, is it less than 5? If so, it must be either 3 or 4. N binary decisions, reflecting N bits, allow perfect selection from 2^N choices, and there are ways to calculate the bit size of any number of choices, many of which require fractions.) By this metric, it should be much easier to recall digits, which come from a set of 10, than words, which come from a set of many thousands. Yet, Miller saw that people remember almost as many words as digits. For reasons like this, he proposed that the limit in capacity was to be measured not in bits, but in whatever units are psychologically meaningful, which he called chunks. He also explained how the process of chunk formation, or chunking, could be used to reduce the load on memory. A good example is the invention of the name ROY G. BIV to encode easily the seven colors of the rainbow: red, orange, yellow, green, blue, indigo, and violet.

From this point on, though, the situation became more complicated. A chapter by Baddeley and Hitch (1974) in this book series provided reasons why a single, general capacity-limited faculty would not suffice to account for the various evidences. Interference with verbal materials comes from other verbal materials and interference with nonverbal, spatial, or visual materials comes from other such materials, leading to the suggestion that there are separate verbal and visual/spatial types of active memory representations. Baddeley and Hitch allowed that there could be a central type of memory representation also, but Baddeley removed it from later versions of his model (e.g., Baddeley, 1986) and restored it only recently with the inclusion of the episodic buffer (Baddeley, 2000, 2001). Baddeley and Hitch also reframed the issue of temporary memory by emphasizing that it was essential in various types of higher-level cognition such as reasoning, and thus referred to the ensemble as working memory. In the model that evolved (e.g., Baddeley, 1986), working memory included low-level phonological and visual–spatial stores with a short time limit, managed by central executive processes.

Broadbent (1975) also recognized the contribution to working memory of processes other than a central, capacity-limited store, which, for example, could include the formation of multi-item chunks on line, other types of rapid memorization, and contributions of rehearsal. He therefore suggested that Miller's (1956) "magical number seven" was the result of an ensemble of processes, one of which is a central, capacity-limited store of not seven items, but three. One could observe it in certain restricted circumstances: when one looks at the number of items that can be repeated not half the time, but almost always without error, and when one looks at how many items are recalled from a category in long-term memory in a single, rapid burst. For example, a person trying to recall aloud as many countries as possible tends to recall them in small bursts such as Venezuela–Brazil–Columbia, United States–Canada–Mexico, and England–France.

Cowan (2001) elaborated upon Broadbent's (1975) approach by documenting many more situations in which it seemed unlikely that multi-item chunks could be formed and seemed likely that each presented item was a single chunk. In such situations, participants appear able to retain and recollect 3 to 5 items in immediate memory tests. Examples include many studies in which a random list of familiar words was presented acoustically, so that each word would be fully encoded into a single unit, and the participant was to carry out articulatory suppression (repetition of a single word over and over during the presentation of the list, in this case not loudly enough to prevent this encoding), so that verbal rehearsal could not be used to refresh the word representations or link words together to form higher-level chunks. In other examples, verbal lists were presented in an unattended channel within a selective attention task, or simple visual objects were presented all at once, both of which discourage rehearsal and chunking. A wide variety of procedures seemed to converge on an estimate of 3–5 familiar units that could be retained at the same time without further chunking.

What the approach of Broadbent (1975) and Cowan (2001) illustrates is an analytic view of working memory capacity limits, in contrast with the more holistic view of Miller (1956). They are not making the assertion that one can find this limit in every immediate memory task. Rather, the assertion is that if one analyzes tasks, one finds multiple mechanisms and one can isolate and thereby identify a mechanism that can hold just a few chunks at a time. Cowan (2001, 2005) suggested that the chunk-capacity-limited mechanism of working memory is the focus of attention. Oberauer (2002, 2005) took a similar view but suggested that there is a focus of attention that holds only 1 item and a fringe that holds the 3–5 items suggested by Cowan (2001). Cowan (2005) alternatively suggested that his evidence could be explained if there is a larger focus of attention that holds 3–5 chunks, but with some chunks at a higher priority than others. The resources of the focus of attention presumably must be divided among chunks, but cannot be divided among more than a handful of these chunks (with a range possibly spreading between 2 and 6 chunks in normal adults).

One special use of the focus of attention would be to form new chunks, which would require that the items to be associated or bound together be in the focus of attention at the same time. Thus, there would be a processing limit but any amount can, in principle, be remembered if enough time is taken to form higher-level chunks. An expert at forming chunks from a certain type of material can increase working memory substantially; several individuals have learned to increase their digit spans from the normal value of about 7 items to 80 or more (Ericsson, Chase, & Faloon, 1980). This acquired skill did not generalize to other materials such as letters. We assume that the fundamental capacities remain the same but that the size of chunks that mnemonists recall has increased enormously for the types of materials used in training (see also Ericsson, Delaney, Weaver, & Mahadevan, 2004).

In sum, holistically people typically can remember about 7 items but the value varies a great deal according to circumstances and training. Analytically, we believe that we can find evidence of a capacity limit of about 3 to 5 chunks, but probably with considerable individual variation (which we will discuss later). Other memory processes typically cloud the observation of a chunk capacity limit.

Instead of repeating in more detail the evidence from Cowan (2001) on the capacity limit as observed when the formation of multi-item chunks is prevented, below we search for various means of examining and controlling the chunking process and other processes that may cloud our observation of capacity limits. The basic hypothesis under investigation is that the same fundamental chunk capacity limit will hold in these more complex circumstances.

B. Further Evidence of Verbal Chunk Capacity Limits

Various attempts were made following Miller (1956) to determine how many chunks have been formed (e.g., Glanzer & Razel, 1974; Marmurek & Johnson, 1978; Slak, 1970; Tulving & Patkau, 1962). In what appears to be the first and perhaps the most relevant of these, Tulving and Patkau (1962) presented word lists following sequences with seven levels of approximation to English, for immediate free recall (i.e., with no constraint on the order in which the words should be recalled). The levels of approximation were formed by varying the number of words in a row that were syntactically and semantically reasonable according to participants who read them. For example, in one level, participants received two words that already had been judged to go together (e.g., *man thought*) and had to add a third word (e.g., *that*) whereas another participant was then to continue the process (e.g., *thought that* ___, which might be filled in with *way*, leading to the total sequence *man thought that way* ___, and so on). These associations could be used to lessen the load on working memory through the meaningful constraints of language. A medium-low level of approximation could be a sequence like, *Man thought that way we go home now or never think badly of him and us as.* Notice that although short subseries of words go together, the entire sentence is nonsensical and syntactically incorrect. The results from immediate recall of series with various levels of approximation to English were all scored according to a simple assumption of what forms a chunk. The assumption was that words within a chunk would be recalled in immediate sequence, whereas there would be no sequential succession for words recalled from different chunks. In the hypothetical example above, if the participant's recall protocol was *we go home never think badly thought that as* it would thus be scored as including four of what were called adopted chunks: *we go home*, *never think badly*, *thought that*, and *as.* It was found that, in every condition, participants recalled about 4–6 adopted chunks of information. The increasing levels of approximation to English simply resulted in larger chunks being recalled, not more chunks. This is what would be expected if there is a basic chunk limit but the size of chunks depends on the participant's knowledge of the materials.

The interpretation of Tulving and Patkau (1962) is similar to that of Ericsson et al. (1980, 2004) based on participants who learn to repeat long sequences of digits by forming large chunks, starting with multi-digit values they already knew as sports enthusiasts (e.g., 3:59, Roger Bannister's record when he broke the 4-min mile). In the latter case, it also was possible to learn to organize several chunks into higher-order chunks. Still, a basic capacity of just several chunks could be assumed.

Baddeley, Thomson, and Buchanan (1975) set off a firestorm that seemed to go against this finding that there is a fixed chunk capacity limit. They showed that, under some circumstances at least, a list of short (e.g., monosyllabic) words was recalled better than a list of the same number of longer (e.g., polysyllabic) words. They also found that an individual's recall was equal to the number of items that he or she could pronounce in about 2 s. This led to a theory that the limit in memory was not the number of chunks, but the amount of time for which the materials had to be remembered. The theory was that items were refreshed by rehearsal in a repeating loop (the *phonological loop* in the model of Baddeley, 1986). If a given item was not refreshed in about 2 s, it was lost from the working memory representation through temporal decay. These data were obtained using a procedure in which the task was serial recall (recall of the list items in order), the results were scored correct only for items recalled in the correct serial positions, and items were drawn from a small set used over and over throughout the experiment.

We will return to this word length effect of Baddeley and colleagues in the section on time limits. For now, what is notable is that the rehearsal strategy and scoring methods that yield this pattern of results is rather specific. If the materials are so long that using a repeating rehearsal method is impractical, or if free recall is used, participants seem less likely to apply a rehearsal strategy. Glanzer and Razel (1974) presented lists of 15 known proverbs for free recall. In that circumstance, one can see from a figure in their article, by adding the proportions across serial positions, that about 5.5 proverbs were recalled. Glanzer and Razel offered a smaller number of 2.2 by including only items recalled well because of their placement at the end of the list, assuming only those items to be part of a short-term store. Another way to look at the situation, however, is that most items have to be encoded in a form that allows them to be resistant to interference from subsequent items or from the process of recall. The last few items can be recalled immediately, in which case they are not susceptible to that interference and do not have to be encoded into working memory as thoroughly. (Recall might occur, e.g., from sensory memory.) If one replaces the scores in the recent positions with scores more like those throughout the rest of the list (with a recall probability of about .25 per item) then the total number of proverbs recalled (a summation of proportions correct across serial positions) would be about 4. By this alternative analysis, this number may approximate the number of chunks that can be well-encoded into working memory at the same time.

In our recent work (Chen & Cowan, 2005; Cowan, Chen, & Rouder, 2004), we have made several attempts to refine the methods used in the past to assess the capacity limit of working memory using verbal lists. We are no longer sure that our newer methods were successful, although they did yield important clues. Cowan et al. (2004) had participants recall on each trial, in order, the items in a list of 8 one-syllable, common words. Words in a list were always presented in pairs on the computer screen during a serial recall trial. Prior to this serial recall test, though, participants had studied the pairing of words to be used in most of the lists. Each word pairing was studied 0, 1, 2, or 4 times and these words were then used as the stimuli within lists in 0-pairing, 1-pairing, 2-pairing, and 4-pairing conditions, respectively. To equalize the number of prior presentations of the words themselves, along with the pre-exposure to pairs, the words also were presented as singletons 4, 3, 2, or 0 times in the 0-, through 4-pairing conditions, respectively, for a total of four presentations of each word (in the form of a singleton or a pair member or both) before the recall test. There were also lists in the recall phase of the experiment that were composed of nonstudied words.

This design yields predictions that appear to pit the phonological loop account against the capacity-limited account. A list of 8 singletons has as much speech material as a list of 4 learned pairs, but the latter has fewer chunks, with the number of chunks decreasing as the increasing number of pair exposures leads to a larger average size of chunks. In scoring the results, we allowed two types of chunks: (1) two-word chunks, comprising pairs of words that were presented together within a list and were recalled with the two words in immediate succession in the presented order, and (2) one-word chunks, comprising any other word recalled. A mathematical model took into account the possibility that two words could look like a single, two-word chunk in recall but actually could have been recalled as two separate one-word chunks; but that rarely happened according to the model. (The expected rate of that, based on such factors as the combination of first-word-only and second-word-only recall rates, was very low.)

The key results of this study can be observed in the top part of Table I. In contrast to the phonological loop hypothesis, the number of words recalled increased markedly with the number of word pairings. (Note that a result more consistent with a phonological loop hypothesis was obtained if the results were scored strictly according to serial position, as in Baddeley et al., 1975.) In keeping with a chunk capacity limit hypothesis, the total

TABLE I

WORDS RECALLED AND ONE ESTIMATE OF CHUNKS RECALLED IN FREE AND SERIAL RECALL

Experiment	Condition	Words per list	Words in free recall	Words in serial recall	1- and 2-item chunks in free recall	1- and 2-item chunks in serial recall
Cowan et al. (2004)	Nonstudied (=8n)	8	–	**4.64**	–	**2.83**
Cowan et al. (2004)	0-paired (=8s)	8	–	**4.88**	–	**3.33**
Cowan et al. (2004)	1-paired	8	–	**5.50**	–	**3.38**
Cowan et al. (2004)	2-paired	8	–	**5.69**	–	**3.48**
Cowan et al. (2004)	4-paired	8	–	**6.54**	–	**3.50**
Chen and Cowan (2005)	4n	4	3.45	3.75	1.88	1.97
Chen and Cowan (2005)	4s	4	3.73	3.88	2.03	2.09
Chen and Cowan (2005)	6n	6	4.36	4.34	2.67	2.72
Chen and Cowan (2005)	6s	6	4.52	4.00	2.79	2.56
Chen and Cowan (2005)	8n	8	4.76	**4.56**	3.12	**3.16**
Chen and Cowan (2005)	8s	8	4.76	**5.00**	3.18	**3.06**
Chen and Cowan (2005)	4p	8	6.67	**6.34**	4.15	**3.28**
Chen and Cowan (2005)	12n	12	4.70	3.88	3.03	2.47

(continued)

TABLE I *(continued)*

Experiment	Condition	Words per list	Words in free recall	Words in serial recall	1- and 2-item chunks in free recall	1- and 2-item chunks in serial recall
Chen and Cowan (2005)	12s	12	5.45	3.69	3.82	2.44
Chen and Cowan (2005)	6p	12	8.73	7.63	5.21	4.06

Note. The data are drawn from Cowan et al. (2004: Experiment 1) and Chen and Cowan (2005: Experiment 1, free recall and Experiment 2, serial recall). Cowan et al. (2004) conditions: where x is 0, 1, 2, or 4, "x-paired" refers to items paired x times and shown (4 − x) times as singletons. Chen and Cowan (2005) conditions: where x is 4, 6, 8, or 12, "xs" refers to x well-learned singletons; xn refers to x nonstudied singletons; xp refers to x well-learned pairs.

number of chunks recalled (1- plus 2-word chunks) was fairly constant at about three and a half chunks across pairing conditions, with slightly fewer chunks recalled in the nonstudied word condition.

Our subsequent work (Chen & Cowan, 2005) shows that there is a limit to this observation of a fixed limit in chunks recalled; it does not hold in just the same way across list lengths. However, it also suggests that we are making progress toward understanding the role of chunking and chunk capacity limits in immediate recall. Chen and Cowan used both free and serial recall, and used list lengths of 4, 6, 8, and 12 items. The main reason to manipulate list length was to examine the effects of list length with the number of chunks varied, and to examine the effects of the number of chunks with the list length varied. In the pretraining period, each word was presented only as a singleton or in a pair. The training continued until the participant was 100% correct in cued recall on the pairs (given the first member of the pair, correct recall of the second member) and 100% correct on the singletons (given the word, correct recall indicating that it had no paired associate). That way, all trained pairs could be assumed to be learned chunks. In 4s, 6s, 8s, and 12s conditions, the words had been studied as singletons whereas in 4n, 6n, 8n, and 12n conditions, the words were non-studied. The digit refers to the number of words (presumed one-word chunks) in the list. Critically, there also were 4p and 6p conditions consisting of 4 and 6 well-learned pairs (two-word chunks), respectively.

The metric of performance used by Chen and Cowan was proportion of words correctly recalled. Several comparisons were critical. If recall depended only on the length of the list, as the exclusive use of a phonological loop mechanism would imply, then recall should be identical for the 8s, 8n, and 4p conditions inasmuch as all of them include 8 words per list. In contrast, if recall depended on the exclusive use of a chunk-capacity-limited mechanism, then recall should be identical for the 4s and 4p conditions, inasmuch as both of them include 4 known, familiar chunks. Similarly, a length mechanism implies equality of the 12s, 12n, and 6p conditions whereas a chunk-capacity-limited mechanism implies equality of the 6s and 6p conditions.

Before introducing the results, it should be mentioned that there are different possible limitations of using free and serial recall to test capacity predictions. The traditional interpretation of these procedures is rather inconsistent. In serial recall, the traditional assumption has been that all recalled items are in working memory (e.g., Baddeley, 1986). Only short lists are typically used (e.g., 9 or fewer items) inasmuch as not many items can ever be recalled in the correct serial order. In free recall, the traditional assumption has been that only items at the end of the list are in short-term or working memory, whereas earlier list items have been memorized and occupy long-term memory (Davelaar et al., 2005; Glanzer & Cunitz, 1966). An alternative interpretation of long-term recall, however, is that some cue to recall of each list item must be saved in working memory, with the possible exception of the most recent list items. Often, the last item or items are recalled first, presumably in order to recall them without any input or output interference, so it is not clear if they have to be encoded into working memory in the same way as other items. If so, free recall might be judged a better measure of chunks held in working memory. In serial recall, participants might not be able to do their best because they are held responsible for the serial order of items whereas, as suggested above, the best strategy to recall all items that one knows may not be to recall them in the presented order, but to present the most recent items first.

In one important way, the results closely matched the chunk-capacity-limited prediction. As one can see in the upper, right-hand panel of Fig. 1, the proportion correct in the 6p condition was very close to the proportion correct for the 6s condition (and the 6n condition, for that matter), and much higher than the 12s or 12n conditions. This is very different from the phonological loop prediction and in concordance with the chunk-capacity-limit prediction. Comparing panels of the figure, one can see that the same applies to serial recall of these same lists, provided that the results are scored without regard for serial order. For other conditions, the results are not as clear and, if one examines the shorter, 4p condition for serial recall strictly scored, it matches the 8s condition as one would expect according to a phonological loop hypothesis (Fig. 1, bottom left). The conclusion appears to be that the phonological loop mechanism and a chunk-capacity-limited mechanism each have a separate role in recall and may often work together, in a balance that depends on the stimulus conditions and the data considered. When the materials fit within a period of about 2 s (as do 8-word lists, but not

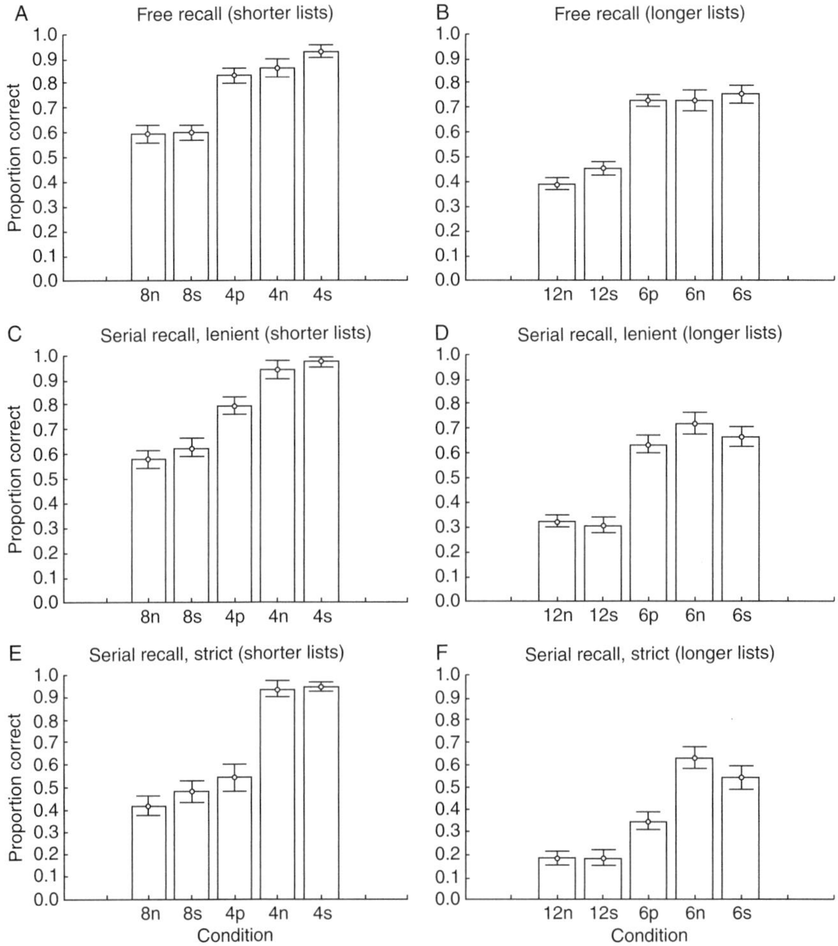

Fig. 1. From Chen and Cowan (2005, Fig. 1). Proportion correct in various conditions of two experiments. As listed in the figure, panels refer to free recall and to serial recall with strict or lenient scoring. Condition 8n = lists of 8 nonstudied words, 8s = lists of 8 words studied as singletons, 4p = lists of 8 words studied as 4 well-learned pairs, and so on. Error bars are standard errors. Capacity-limited performance is best exemplified in Panel B (free recall of longer lists); time-limited performance is best exemplified in Panel E (serial recall of shorter lists, strictly scored).

12-word lists) and when the serial order of responding is considered, it is the length of the list that counts. When the materials are longer and the scoring method ignores serial order, it is the number of learned pairs that counts. In-between conditions yield in-between results.

Given these findings, what are we to make of the results of Cowan et al. (2004), who examined the serial recall of 8-word lists and found a constant capacity in chunks? Those results were obtained with a scoring method that attempted to determine how many chunks were included in recall, regardless of the serial order of those chunks. However, there are limitations to both of the studies we have just reported. The study of Cowan et al. (2004) carefully examined chunks, but only for lists 8 words long. It is possible that the list length determines the amount of interference and therefore influences how many chunks can be reported. Chen and Cowan (2005) did vary list length, but the near-equivalence they found for the 6p, 6n, and 6s conditions was obtained with a straight proportion correct measure. We assumed that the equivalence in proportion correct meant that the same number of chunks was recalled in these conditions but that is not necessarily the case.

To provide a bridge between these two findings, we reanalyzed the results of Chen and Cowan (2005) in terms of chunks, counting singletons and intact pairs as 1- and 2-item chunks, respectively. As shown in Table I, the numbers of chunks recalled from 8-item lists in serial recall were fairly comparable for the data from Cowan et al. (2004) and from Chen and Cowan, as indicated by the bold entries. However, when the list length was changed or free recall was used, the equivalence was not as close (rightmost two columns of the table). Of course, the estimate of chunks recalled is necessarily limited by ceiling effects for 4-item lists, but the equivalence was not very close in 6-, 8-, and 12-item lists. That is true for free recall, for which the number of chunks recalled was an increasing function of list length. We also tried the scoring developed by Tulving and Patkau (1962), described above. Recall that, in this scoring method, any items recalled in a row were counted as a single adopted chunk. Again the number of chunks increased with list length. It showed the effect of learned pairing to be an increase in the number of chunks recalled as well as an increase in the average chunk size.

From this work, the question remains as to why we have not obtained a constant capacity estimate across list lengths. One possibility is that the process of verbal rehearsal is used to supplement the capacity-limited region of working memory, either by allowing memorization or by keeping some items in an active state in memory. In a still-unpublished follow-up study, we (Chen and Cowan) repeated the serial recall experiment of Chen and Cowan (2005, Experiment 2), but with the requirement that participants engage in articulatory suppression during the recall test. They were to repeat the word "the" at a rapid rate during the reception of the list. The results do show more equivalence across list lengths. Regardless of the list length, participants recalled about 3 words from lists of singletons and about 6 words from lists of learned pairs. This is consistent with the proposal of Broadbent (1975) that a basic capacity is about 3 items (or 3 chunks), and that one can observe this only in situations in which other mnemonic processes are curtailed.

C. Further Evidence of Visual–Spatial Chunk Capacity Limits

Most of the recent work on visual–spatial working memory has been conducted with arrays of objects to be retained in memory, inspired by Luck and Vogel (1997). In this task, a target array of simple objects is briefly presented on the screen (e.g., small squares varying in color). This brief presentation is followed by a probe stimulus (the same array, sometimes with a circle cue around one item; in later studies, a one-item probe). The question is whether there has been a change between the target array and the probe array, such as a change in color in one item. When one item is encircled in the probe array or a single-item probe is presented, the typical procedure is that only that item may have changed from the item in the same location within the target array. Adults can carry out this sort of task very well when there are four or fewer items in the array, and performance falls off as a function of the number of items in the array. Luck and Vogel found that performance levels were similar even when participants were responsible for four different features of bar objects (color, orientation, size, and presence or absence of a black segment in the center or "gap"). Thus, visual working memory seems to be limited in the number of objects that can be retained. This method of Luck and Vogel (1997) has an advantage over the earlier, classic method of Sperling (1960) that the items are nonverbal so that a purely visual–spatial store is probed. Often, articulatory suppression is used during the task to avoid verbal encoding of the items. However, there is little effect of articulatory suppression in this type of task (Morey & Cowan, 2004, 2005).

The ability to study capacity depends on a measure to convert the proportion correct to capacity. Obtaining such a measure may be easier for recognition procedures than it is for recall procedures because it is easier to take into account the role of guessing. (Therefore, it is unfortunate that recognition procedures have generally not been used to examine working memory capacity for verbal materials.) Pashler (1988) developed a method that logically seems to fit the method in which the probe is the whole array, in which any one item might have changed from the target array. The model assumes that for a target array with N objects, k objects are placed within working memory and can be compared with the probe array. Therefore, if an object has changed from the target array, the probability that the change will be noticed is k/N. If no change is detected, the participant guesses that it has changed with guessing rate g, which is taken as the proportion of incorrect responses on no-change trials. These assumptions lead to the formula, $k = N$ (hits − false alarms)/(1 − false alarms).

Cowan (2001; see also Cowan et al., 2005, appendix) modified this formula to be more suitable for procedures in which one item within the probe stimulus is cued or a single-item probe is presented. In these circumstances, it is assumed that the probability of knowing whether or not the probe has changed in comparison to the corresponding item in the target array is k/N, and the probability of guessing that it has changed is g. These assumptions differ from those of Pashler (1988) in that performance on no-change trials is not just based on guessing. These assumptions lead to the formula, $k = N$ (hits − false alarms). In many studies, though not all, it has been shown that the value of k increases with set size until reaching a rather constant, asymptotic level after about 4 items (e.g., Cowan et al., 2005). With such results, k can be taken to estimate the number of items in working memory and the asymptotic value can be taken to estimate the mean capacity across participants. The results typically show that between 3 and 4 items are held in working memory.

The assumption has been that each item presented in a brief visual array remains a single-item chunk. Although there is some evidence that chunking of visual items is indeed possible (Gobet et al., 2001; Jiang, Olson, & Chun, 2000), the pattern of results in which an asymptotic value of k is reached suggests that chunking is typically not an important factor with briefly presented, haphazard arrays of items.

Another issue is whether capacity is constant even for complex objects. Alvarez and Cavanagh (2004) found that the capacity estimate decreased as the complexity increased. The least complex was simple colored squares, with complexity increasing for line drawings, Chinese characters, irregular polygons, and the most complex set, cubes in different spatial orientations. However, Awh, Barton, and Vogel (2007) found that just as many items were held in working memory regardless of the complexity; it was just the perceptual resolution of the items in working memory that decreased with complexity. Thus, in a mixed target array that included some complex objects and some simpler objects, the ability to detect a change of a complex object to an exemplar of a different category (e.g., a change from a cube to a Chinese character) was no worse than the ability to detect a change from one color to another.

In a related neuroimaging study, Xu and Chun (2006) found slightly different brain areas to be involved in visual working memory, including an area that displayed activity in proportion to the number of objects in the display up to 4 (the inferior intraparietal sulcus), and other areas that displayed activity commensurate with Cowan's (2001) k measure, declining as the complexity of items in the array increased (the superior intraparietal sulcus and the lateral occipital complex). These studies show that the topic of working memory capacity is an exciting one in which the influences between behavioral and neurological sources of evidence may truly be bidirectional.

Additional work has gone into determining whether attention is needed to retain the binding between features within a visual item. One might expect so on the basis of the work on attention showing that it is much more difficult to search for a conjunction of features (e.g., a red square among red circles and blue squares) than it is to search for a single feature (e.g., a red square among blue squares only). However, a discrepant expectation could be formulated on the basis of the finding of Luck and Vogel (1997) that participants can retain just as many visual objects no matter whether the participants are responsible for one or four features of the objects. The findings seem to support the latter expectation. Studies using the Luck and Vogel procedure with simple objects have examined the effects of dual tasks on memory for features (e.g., whether the probe array contained a color that was not in the target array) and for feature binding (e.g., whether a particular color from the target array appeared at a particular location in that array). Although dual-task decrements have been observed, they have been shown to be of similar magnitude for feature memory and for feature binding memory (Allen, Baddeley, & Hitch, 2006; Cowan, Naveh-Benjamin, Kilb, & Saults, 2006). One possible resolution of all of the results is that attention is needed to enter objects into the attention-dependent part of working memory but that this process of entering objects into this part of working memory already includes the bindings between features within each item, so that no additional exertion is needed to retain the bindings. Location may play a special role in allowing features of an object to be bound (Treisman & Zhang, 2006). If features are bound as objects enter working memory, this concept assigns a high importance to the attention-related part of working memory (cf. Cowan, 1988, 1995, 2001; Cowan et al., 2005). That theme is to be reinforced in the next section.

D. Evidence of Cross-Modal Chunk Capacity Limits

One important question is why a visual and verbal working memory capacity limits exist. Given that the limits are similar in both modalities (and in other modalities: see Cowan, 2001), a key account states that the limits stem from the use of attention as a holding device regardless of the modality. This seems simpler than the alternative possibility that there are capacity limits that apply separately in the cases of verbal and visual information or, indeed, a separate capacity limit for each feature map (Wheeler & Treisman, 2002). A simpler alternative is that there are passively held, temporary representations that are not capacity limited, such as sensory memory representations in each sensory modality (for a review, see Cowan, 1995) or phonological and visuospatial buffer representations (Baddeley, 1986). A single, central capacity-limited mechanism such as the focus of attention would be able to retrieve information from a particular type of passively held representation if it still existed at the time of recall and if it proved to be relevant to the question asked about the memoranda. The central capacity limit would define how many items could be retrieved from any such representation into the central store.

If visual and verbal information both share a central storage area such as the focus of attention, then it should be possible to show that the need to retain stimuli in both modalities results in a decrease in performance in at least one modality, compared to a situation in which only retention in that one modality is required. Saults and Cowan (2007) were able to demonstrate this. The procedures that they used in five experiments are reproduced in Fig. 2. In Experiment 1, a visual array was presented at the same time as a simultaneous acoustic array of digits spoken from four different loudspeakers arranged around the participant at ear level, in four different voices to aid in perception (adult male, adult female, child male, and child female). The use of simultaneous sounds was intended to minimize participants' ability to rehearse the sounds. After a short retention interval, an array was presented in one modality or another and the task was to determine whether there was a change in a stimulus within that modality (i.e., in the digit identity of a sound or the color of a small square). In unimodal trial blocks, participants knew in advance which modality would be tested on each trial; that was not the case in bimodal trial blocks.

The question was to what extent performance in each modality was impaired in the bimodal condition. To the extent that both modalities depend on a common, central storage mechanism, the attempt to use this mechanism for both modalities at once should limit the availability of storage and compromise performance. In the limit, if only the central storage mechanism were used, then the capacity of the visual and auditory trials for bimodal trial blocks, added together, should not exceed the capacity of whichever unimodal condition has the highest capacity. (Given that the presentation of acoustic stimuli was somewhat difficult to perceive despite our best efforts, the measured capacity in that modality was lower than in the visual case.)

The results are shown in the left-hand panel of Fig. 3. Auditory capacities are stacked on top of visual ones in this figure. The modality-specific capacities were smaller in the bimodal condition than in the unimodal condition, suggesting that there was a central resource shared between the modalities. However, the fact that the sum of bimodal capacities is still higher than the visual unimodal capacity indicates that modality-specific sources of memory also contributed, in addition to a central store. The results were very similar in Experiment 2, in which the probe stimulus always included both modalities (as shown in the second panel of Fig. 3).

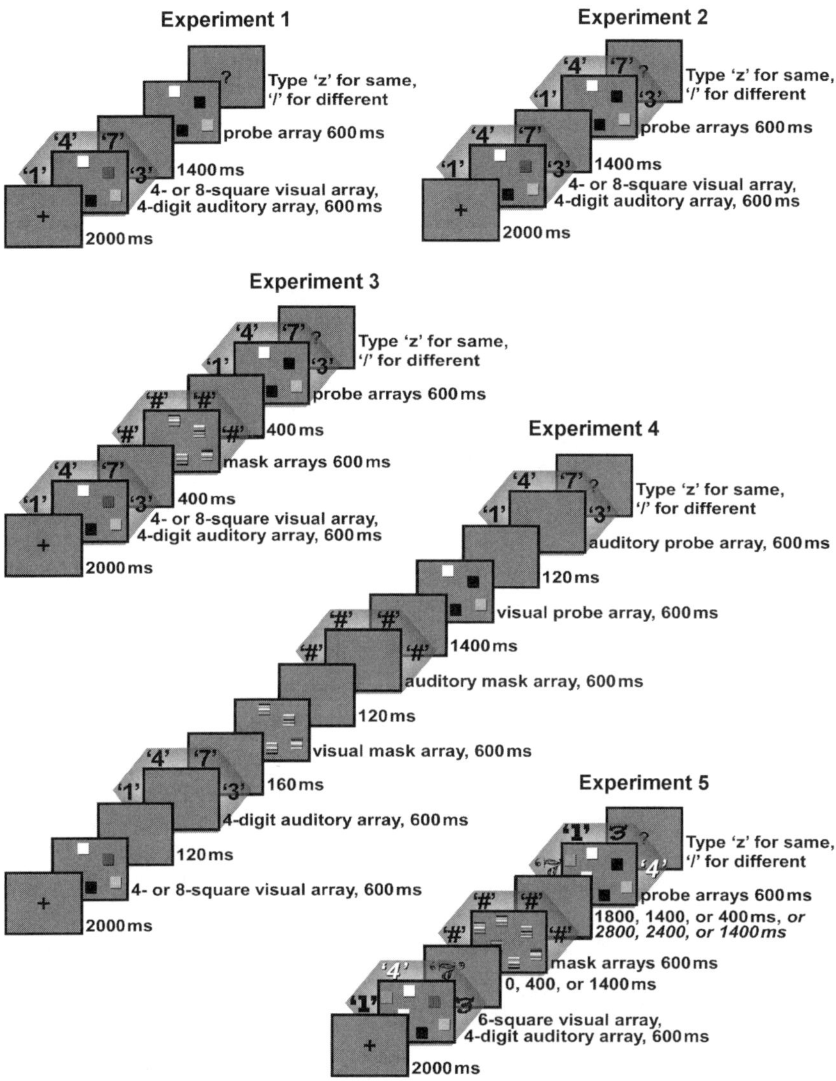

Fig. 2. From Saults and Cowan (2007, Fig. 1). Method in five experiments. Characters outside of the rectangles represent spoken stimuli, which differed in voice as represented by the different typefaces. For Experiment 4, only one of two orders of the memory sets is shown. Unimodal trial blocks were the same as bimodal trial blocks except that the participant knew which modality would be probed.

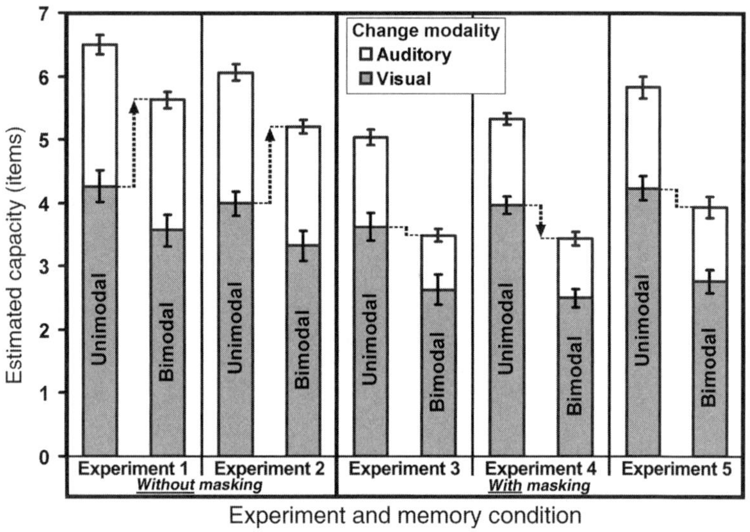

Fig. 3. Based on Saults and Cowan (2007). Results from five experiments. Provided that a postperceptual mask followed target stimuli (which occurred in Experiments 3–5), the sum of visual and auditory capacities in the bimodal condition did not exceed the visual unimodal capacity. Error bars are standard errors.

It occurred to us that we had not ruled out the possible contribution of modality-specific memory to performance. In previous studies in the visual modality, our assumption had been that the probe array would eliminate such contributions by overwriting the modality-specific representation of the target items before a decision could be made. However, that assumption had never been tested. Moreover, it might apply less to the auditory modality than to the visual modality. Perhaps participants can use the contents of capacity-limited memory and, if a discrepancy between it and the probe display is not found, they can refill the capacity-limited store with additional items from sensory memory and continue to make the comparison with the probe display. To address this possibility, in our subsequent experiments, we waited long enough after the target arrays for perception to be complete and then presented a bimodal mask on every trial, to wipe out any modality-specific memories that remained by that time.

As shown in Fig. 2, this procedure was used in Experiments 3 through 5. The mask included multicolored squares in the same locations as the squares in the visual target array and mixtures of all of the digits in each particular voice, presented through the same speakers as the target items had been presented. Experiment 3 resembled Experiment 2, but with the addition of the mask. Experiment 4 ruled out the contribution of resource limitations during stimulus encoding by presenting the target arrays in the two modalities in succession rather than simultaneously. Finally, Experiment 5 showed that the resource limitation was not simply the use of spatial codes for both modalities. In this last experiment, the spatial locations of spoken digits were rearranged between the target and probe arrays so that the participant had to rely on the association between digits and voices to respond. Moreover, different masking delays were tested to ensure that perception was complete by the time the mask was presented.

The results of three experiments using this postperceptual mask are shown in Fig. 3 (in the three right-most panels). In each such experiment, unlike Experiments 1 and 2, the sum of visual and auditory capacities in the bimodal condition did not exceed the unimodal visual (or the unimodal auditory) capacity. The close match between the unimodal visual and bimodal total capacities suggests to us that we have managed to isolate and estimate the contribution of a central capacity to working memory. On average it contributes between 3 and 4 items, in keeping with the theoretical estimates of Broadbent (1975) and Cowan (2001).

A closely related question is whether the cost of retaining two sets of materials presented in the same modality is any more costly than retaining two sets of materials presented in different modalities. In principle, the central store should not impose additional costs for materials all presented in one modality. However, the same cannot be said for the perceptual and conceptual processes needed to load materials into working memory. Cowan and Morey (2007) found a way to isolate a central maintenance component that is modality-free in this way, even though there are more modality-specific perceptual and/or conceptual processes. They included some trials with only one stimulus set and other trials with two stimulus sets. For the latter, as shown in Fig. 4, either set could be a verbal sequence or a visual array. (Articulatory suppression was used to prevent rehearsal.) After that, there was a cue with two boxes, one on top of the other, indicating that the first set should be retained (question mark in the top box), the second set should be retained (question mark in the bottom box), or both sets should be retained (question marks in both boxes). A 3-s retention interval followed and then a probe was presented for just one stimulus set, always one that the participant has been asked to retain. The results of this experiment are shown in Fig. 5. There was a cost of receiving two stimulus sets instead of just one, and that cost was larger when both sets were in the same modality. However, when two sets were presented, there was an additional cost of being asked to retain both sets rather than just one ("both cued"), and that additional cost was about the same no matter whether the two sets were in the same modality or not. Thus, after the items all had been loaded into working memory, the

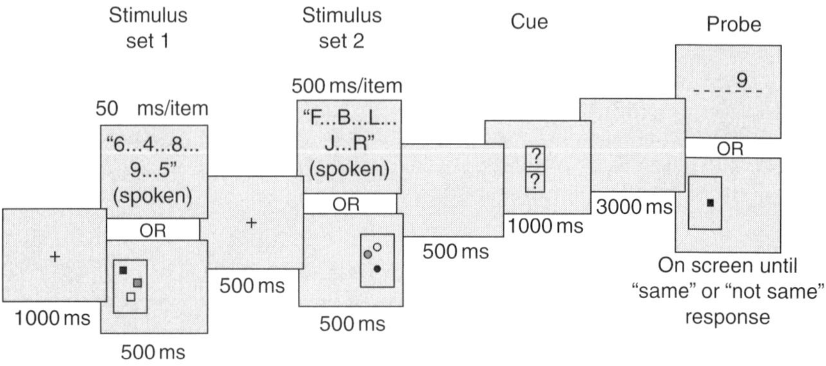

Fig. 4. From Cowan and Morey (2007, Fig. 1). Experimental procedure to isolate dual-task conflicts occurring during dual retention, as opposed to during encoding or responding. Shading of small squares or circles reflects variation in color. A spoken or visual first stimulus set is combined with a spoken or visual second set. If both sets are spoken they differ in voice and item category; if both are visual, they differ in the side of the screen and shape of objects. The postcue can indicate the need to retain the first set (top question mark), second set (bottom question mark), or both sets as shown here (two question marks, dual-retention trials). Only the processes after the cue differ between single and dual retention trials. There also were one-stimulus trials (not shown).

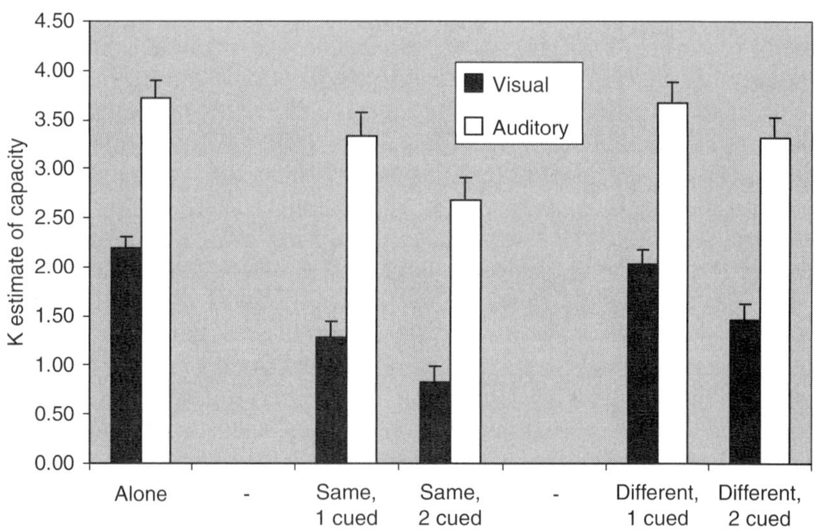

Fig. 5. Based on Cowan and Morey (2007). Visual and auditory capacities using the capacity estimation method of Cowan (2001) and Cowan et al. (2005). Error bars are standard errors. The experiment included articulatory suppression to prevent rehearsal of verbal lists. *Same* and *different* refer to whether the modalities of the two sets differ. Performance was higher when only one stimulus set was presented (*alone* condition) than when two same-modality sets were presented. However, the cost of dual retention (2 cued vs 1 cued) was about the same no matter whether the stimulus sets were in the same or different modalities.

continued retention of those items in working memory occurred in a central store that did not depend on modality.

III. Energy Limits, Time Limits, and Combinations of Limits

A. Multiple Limits

Although our own recent work has focused on space or chunk capacity limits, we do not wish to imply that these limits necessarily dominate working memory studies. Other major strands of research have produced findings more aptly described with the notion of energy or resource limits, and possibly with time limits. Bear in mind that much of the relevant evidence has focused on ideographic questions and will be deferred to the next section.

B. Energy Limits

Energy or resource limits refer here to processing limits that hold across many types of attention-demanding activities and must be shared between these activities. Often, it is a matter of judgment whether to classify a result as capacity limited or resource limited. The reasons are that (1) there appears to be a trade-off between capacity and resources used for other purposes, and (2) we often have insufficient evidence to determine which fundamental limit is restricting performance. Regarding the former (a trade-off between capacity and other resources), work in several laboratories confirms the use of attention at least in the case of visual working memory. Morey and Cowan (2004) used the procedure illustrated in Fig. 6, and found that an array-comparison task was impeded by the need to recite a random seven-digit load during the period between arrays, but was not affected by the need to recite a known seven-digit telephone number during that period. The effect of a seven-digit load was especially large when an error was made on the digit load. Moreover, the effect of the seven-digit load depended on that load being repeated aloud rather than silently rehearsed (Morey & Cowan, 2005). Stevanovski and Jolicoeur (2007) found that a simple tone identification task can impede array comparisons. These results suggest that attention must be shared between visual working memory and various sorts of retrieval. When little or no interference is found between a visual load and a verbal load (e.g., Cocchini, Logie, Della Sala, MacPherson, & Baddeley, 2002), that may be because it is possible to use a separate verbal rehearsal process to maintain the verbal information silently, and the rehearsal process is thought to require relatively little attention in young adults (Guttentag, 1984). To observe interference between tasks, one must not be able to rely upon an automatic, effortless process in either task.

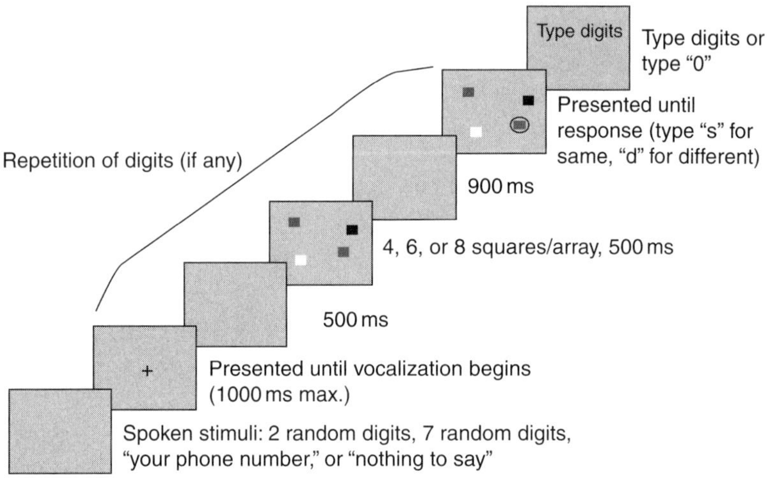

Fig. 6. From Morey and Cowan (2004, Fig. 1). Procedure to examine effects of a memory load, and of articulatory suppression, on array comparison performance. There was an effect of a random 7-digit memory load but not of a known 7-digit number (the equivalent suppression condition).

The converse trade-off effect may also be the case; there is an effect of a working memory load on nonmemorial tasks that rely on attention. Lavie, Hirst, de Fockert, and Viding (2004) introduced a theory that attention depends on the working memory load. They used an attention task in which the participant was to identify a target letter as x or z. It was accompanied by a distractor letter that was compatible (e.g., X with target x), incompatible (e.g., Z with target x), or neutral (e.g., L with target x). Meanwhile, one or six letters were held in memory for a search task. It was found that the incompatibility effect was larger with a high memory load. The interpretation was that a working memory load uses up resources that otherwise would be used to inhibit the irrelevant distractors.

More recent work has suggested that the effect is not consistent and that a working memory load can reduce, as well as increase, distractor interference (Kim, Kim, & Chun, 2005). As these authors pointed out, working memory is not unitary so it is possible to design situations in which the distractor has more in common with the working memory load (such as verbal processing) than the target does.

From this past research, it is clear that we need to know the results of a procedure in which the working memory task is limited to its attention-related components. It should then only increase distractor effects, as in Lavie et al. (2004), instead of sometimes decreasing distractor effects as in Kim et al. (2005). Even if that prediction is confirmed, it will not be clear how to interpret the attention-related working memory component(s). It may be, as we have suggested above, that attention can be used directly to hold some information in its focus. An alternative possibility more in line with the classic model of Baddeley (1986) is that central executive processes are needed to keep the items refreshed in more passive stores. In terms of Baddeley (2000), the question is whether attention-related storage occurs in an episodic buffer or occurs in more passive buffers with the assistance of central executive processes. So, more research is needed to understand the attention-related part of working memory.

A second reason why it is still a matter of judgment whether to classify a result as capacity limited or resource limited is that we have insufficient evidence on the nature of limits. Consider a classic procedure that has been used to examine resource limits, the procedure of Stroop (1935) in which color words are presented in different colors of ink and the task is to ignore the word and name the color of ink. Individuals are much slower and more error-prone in this task compared to a task in which the ink is presented in the form of noncolor words or nonwords. A capacity-based account of this finding is that, on some trials, the participant has dropped the goal from working memory and either erroneously makes the more natural, prepotent response of reading the word, or requires time to reload the goal into working memory before responding. A different, resource-based account is that the goal remains in working memory but nevertheless requires attention-related resources to overcome the difficulty of resisting the prepotent response, and to inhibit it while carrying through with the relevant response. Many results that are typically thought of as resource related thus can be alternatively described as capacity-related. To do so, however, one cannot simply think of capacity in equal chunks. If the only temporary memorandum of the Stroop task is the task goal, then this goal would have to count as more than one chunk in order to provide consistency with the literature above, indicating that several chunks can be held in working memory at once. Once one gets into the concept of a variable size of chunks in working memory, what is needed is a fluid resource that can be apportioned among the pieces of information as required. Attention would appear to be such a resource.

C. Time Limits

The field of working memory seriously shifted from an interest in capacity limits to an interest in time limits when Baddeley et al. (1975) published their work on the word length effect. Lists of short words were recalled better than lists of long words even when the short and long words were equated for the number of phonemes and syllables. Individuals recalled about as many verbal items as they could recite in about 2 s, so it was suggested that working memory is dependent on a decaying store that becomes useless within 2 s unless it is refreshed by a rehearsal process. The faster it can be refreshed, the more items can be held in storage at the same time and then recalled when the list ends.

Currently, however, there is no general agreement that the word length effect is obtained across different sets of materials when the short and long materials are equated for the number of phonemes and syllables (see Mueller, Seymour, Kieras, & Meyer, 2003; Neath, Bireta, & Surprenant, 2003) so there is no agreement that the word length effect supports the notion of time limits per se.

Some recent work using complex spans that include storage and processing components (operation span and reading span) have shown that time is an important variable for forgetting (e.g., Towse, Hitch, Hamilton, Peacock, & Hutton, 2005). Nevertheless, this is time filled with distracting items in order to prevent rehearsal. Given that these can cause interference, it is not clear that temporal decay is the cause of forgetting. Indeed, Saito and Miyake (2004) found that it is the number of distracting items rather than the time that is critical for performance.

Barrouillet, Bernardin, and Camos (2004) more specifically showed that it is the density of distracting events that is critical (i.e., the number of retrievals divided by the time in which those retrievals have to take place). They inserted numbers to be read aloud between items (letters) to be recalled. The faster these distracting numbers were presented, the poorer recall was. Their theoretical explanation involves a decaying memory that can be rehearsed during the breaks between distracting items. However, it is noteworthy that they do not find a large effect of time per se, as opposed to just the density of distracting events. If a certain density of distracting events is enough to prevent full rehearsal of the stimuli, there should be a memory leak that should be manifest as poorer performance with more time at a certain distraction density.

More recently, Lewandowsky, Duncan, and Brown (2004) carried out more direct tests of time limits. The amount of time between one item and the next in the recall period of a serial recall task was manipulated and, despite procedures designed to prevent rehearsal, no significant effect of time was obtained. The authors suggested that information is not lost as a function of time during the response, even when it is not rehearsed. A similar result was obtained by Cowan, Elliott, et al. (2006). Second-grade children were asked to recall items more quickly than usual and succeeded in recalling items as quickly as adults ordinarily do; yet their memory was not improved at all by this manipulation. We are currently conducting follow-up research to cross-pollinate the research procedures of Lewandowsky and colleagues versus Barrouillet et al. (2004).

Cowan and AuBuchon (2008) did find an effect of time in the absence of external interference by presenting irregularly timed lists; a long first half-list hurt performance, but only if the list timing had to be reproduced in the response. The assumption was that reproducing the timing prevents rehearsal and takes up attention during the response. In such circumstances, information can drop out of working memory during reproduction of a long first half-list. However, the detrimental effect of reproducing the timing of a long as opposed to a short first half-list occurred only in restricted circumstances (in the presence of a long second half) and its basis is not yet clear. Cowan and AuBuchon did not attribute it to a decay effect per se.

In sum, it seems fair to state that there is, practically speaking, an effect of time, though it may well result from the effects of interference spread across time (e.g., in the acid bath theory of Posner & Konick, 1966; see also Massaro, 1970) rather than from a pure process of decay even in the absence of interference. In the word length effect, each phoneme or syllable could interfere to some extent with memory for previous phonemes or syllables.

D. Combinations of Limits

If two or three different types of basic limitation on working memory exist, there is no reason why a particular procedure should tap only one of these limits. There are two ways in which different types of limits might be combined in working memory. The two limits can occur because they stem from a common mechanism, or the two limits can occur because different mechanisms affect performance separately. An example of two limits possibly stemming from the same mechanism and both affecting performance is the combination of space (chunk capacity) and energy (resource) limits. Both of these could be based on a common attention-related resource. A common attentional resource might have to be split between maintenance of items in working memory and central executive functions such as shifting attention, updating working memory, and inhibiting irrelevant items (e.g., Miyake, Friedman, Emerson, Witzki, & Howerter, 2000).

An example of two limits possibly stemming from different mechanisms and affecting performance together is the combination of space (chunk capacity) and time (decay) limits. Chen and Cowan (2005) found that the length of lists determined recall for short lists with serial scoring, but that the number of chunks governed recall for long lists without serial scoring. As shown in Fig. 1, the result was intermediate for other conditions. As we mentioned, in a follow-up study in which articulatory suppression was added, the chunk-based limit determined recall much more uniformly across list lengths. All of this suggests that there is a capacity-limited mechanism that governs performance except insofar as it is possible to engage in verbal rehearsal for the serial recall of short lists, and that the two mechanisms both can be used together for the same recall procedure (see also Mulligan & Lozito, 2007).

IV. Ideographic Evidence

A. Using Ideographic Evidence

We have already discussed (in Section I.C) the point that ideographic information is collected for several different and interlocking reasons. One is to find out about the classes of individuals being tested, but another is to shed light on nomothetic processes. The notion behind this approach is that if individuals differ in Trait X, then Trait X is nomothetically important too. An example of this line of reasoning is the idea that if individuals with high versus low working memory differ in their ability to control attention, then the control of attention is an important source of the human limitation in working memory. The paper by Kane, Bleckley, Conway, and Engle (2001) is a prime example. They used a *prosaccade* task requiring that the participant look at an appearing object, and an *antisaccade* task requiring that the participant look in the opposite direction. The antisaccade task, which is quite unnatural, is accomplished more successfully by high-span than by low-span individuals, who do not differ in the prosaccade task.

Despite the strength of such findings (for convergent evidence, see Conway, Cowan, & Bunting, 2001; Kane & Engle, 2003), several related points must be considered, as follows:

(1) Any Trait X distinguishing high- and low-span individuals may not be the only difference between the groups or individuals relevant to working memory. (Example: individuals may also differ in chunk capacity, which might be very important for the human limitations in working memory.)

(2) Trait X, though correlated with working memory capacity, may not be a key determinant of working memory. (Example: it could be chunk capacity rather than the control of attention that is critical for working memory capacity limits, if chunk capacity and the control of attention are highly correlated.)

(3) Trait X in a nonstandard population could impose a limit on working memory that is not critical for normal adults. (Example: vocabulary knowledge is not ordinarily a limiting factor for verbal working memory task performance in adults given the simplicity of vocabulary selected for the task, but it probably is a factor in the performance of young children on the same task.)

(4) Some other Trait Y may be a nomothetically important limit of working memory even if it does not yield individual differences. (Example: If it were found that chunk capacity did not differ at all among individuals, it

would still be possible that all individuals are limited to, say, 4 concurrently held objects in the central portion of working memory.)

As we will show, there are ways to begin to sort out these possibilities with experimental manipulations.

B. Individual Differences Among Young Adults

There are distinct individual differences on many cognitive traits and many of these are correlated with various working memory tasks. However, there has perhaps been too much of an attempt to seek evidence confirming particular accounts of the correlations and not enough seeking evidence of disconfirmation. For example, Baddeley et al. (1975) found a high correlation between the rate at which an individual could recite words and the number of words of the same type that the individual could recall. Their word length effect can be viewed as the result of an experimental manipulation affecting the rate at which a given individual could recite the words, and it did seem to confirm that rehearsal speed was important for serial verbal recall (cf. Schweickert, Guentert, & Hersberger, 1990). By equating short-word and long-word lists on the number of phonemes and syllables, there was an attempt to show that it was time per se that was important rather than a correlated difference between short and long words. (Recent research challenges the success of that control; see Neath et al., 2003.)

What was not established by Baddeley et al. (1975) and perhaps has not been established in subsequent research is the boundary conditions for the effect of individual rehearsal speed on working memory. There are many types of working memory that theoretically should not depend on rehearsal speed at all. We may not have such information at present. However, Conway, Cowan, Bunting, Therriault, and Minkoff (2002; see their Table 2) examined other kinds of simple processing speeds and the results indicate that these (in particular, for copying digits and letters, and for comparing pairs of patterns and letter strings) correlated with short-term memory in the presence of articulatory suppression much better than they correlated with short-term memory without suppression. This raises the possibility that the correspondence between individual speech rates and memory spans obtained by Baddeley et al. may have an unexpected path of causal relation.

The suggestion that the control of attention is causally related to working memory span (e.g., Kane et al., 2001) has been aided by research manipulating attention. This research shows that dividing attention during a memory retrieval task has a much larger detrimental effect on individuals with a high working memory span than it does on those with a low working memory span (Kane & Engle, 2000; Rosen & Engle, 1997). In fact, dividing attention removed most of the difference between the response patterns of high- and low-span individuals. That is exactly what would be predicted if the difference between high- and low-span individuals is that the high spans make more use of attention in the retrieval task, making them more vulnerable to divided attention.

Nevertheless, there are limits to what can be concluded from this kind of result alone. For example, it could be that dividing attention saps both space (chunk capacity) and energy (attention deployment) in working memory and then it would be unclear which is critical to task performance. By analogy, suppose that one person's home computer carried out calculations better than another's. Suppose, though, that a special program in the better computer, unavailable in the poorer computer, required an internet connection to do the best calculations. If one knocked out the internet connection in both houses and observed that the calculations were now equally mediocre in both computers located in the respective houses, one might incorrectly conclude that the difference between houses was in the ability to use the internet generally, when actually the difference is in the programs available in the two computers. In this analogy, attention is the internet and chunk capacity is the computer.

Cowan, Fristoe, Elliott, Brunner, and Saults (2006) carried out a study that included measures of both capacity (visual array comparisons) and attention. The measure of the latter was obtained in a situation in which spoken and printed stimuli were presented at the same time. The instruction preceding each trial was to attend to one of these modalities, and the measure of the use of attention was the extent to which memory for the to-be-attended modality exceeded memory for the to-be-ignored modality. These measures turned out to be correlated with one another ($r = .34$), but separate, among adults. They both correlated well with a composite IQ measure (visual array comparisons, $r = .52$; attention benefit, $r = .47$). However, the variance in IQ that they picked up was largely separate. Together they picked up 12% in shared variance in IQ, the arrays task uniquely picked up another 15%, and the attention benefit uniquely picked up another 10%, for a total of 37% of the IQ variance accounted for. In light of the importance that has been placed on accounting for variance in IQ (e.g., Engle, Tuholski, Laughlin, & Conway, 1999), this is an important indication that size as well as energy limits are worth discussing.

There has been research suggesting that the relation between working memory and intelligence (or, more narrowly specified, fluid intelligence) is increased by the presence of proactive interference from previous trials (e.g., Rosen & Engle, 1998). In both an operation span task and a probed recall task, Bunting (2006) included proactive interference, in the form of stimuli similar to the ones to be recalled appearing earlier in the list or appearing in recent lists. The correlation between memory scores and fluid intelligence (Ravens Progressive Matrices) was higher when proactive interference was present. In an fMRI study using a recognition procedure, Gray, Chabris, and Braver (2003) found that high-span individuals showed more activity than low-span individuals in the prefrontal cortex, but only on trials in which proactive interference was present in the form of a lure that was not in the current list but was in a recent list. These procedures clearly show the importance of proactive interference for individual differences in working memory but the exact theoretical interpretation of the finding remains unclear. It is not clear whether what is key is the ability to suppress memory for the items in previous trials (presumably a function of attention control), or the ability to remember whether an item was presented in the current trial (possibly a function of chunk capacity).

Similarly, the finding that low-span individuals have poorer control of attention in an antisaccade task (Kane et al., 2004) could be interpreted either as their inability to remember the unnatural task goal, or their inability to override the prepotent prosaccade response. In other studies, what is observed is the specificity with which relevant items are selected (Bleckley, Durso, Crutchfield, Engle, & Khanna, 2003) or the efficiency with which irrelevant items are excluded (Heitz & Engle, 2007). In each case, though, there remain several slightly different interpretations of the findings. It could be that the difficult goal was not maintained. This failure of maintenance could occur either because it was difficult to hold the goal while using working memory for other things during the task (a space limit), or because it takes considerable effort to maintain a goal (an energy limit). Another possibility is that the goal was still maintained in working memory but that the prepotent response (e.g., making a prosaccade) was so powerful that the goal could not control behavior. This would constitute a second type of energy limit.

A study by Delaney and Sahakyan (2007) seems to favor memory limits over energy limits. It investigated the finding that high-working-memory-span individuals do a better job of directed forgetting than do low-span individuals. One explanation is that the high spans are able to use more resources to suppress the material to be forgotten. An alternative explanation is that high spans have a richer use of context in the mnemonic encoding of stimuli and are therefore better able to separate the material to be forgotten from the material to be remembered. Evidence favoring the latter view was obtained in a word list memory study. If the participants were not told to forget the list but it was followed by a different task that greatly changed the context (45 s of imagining walking through their parents' house and describing the house and furniture to the experimenter), the change in context impaired memory of the word list more for individuals with higher operation spans and, in a replication, for individuals with higher counting spans.

Work by Saxe et al. (2007) provides conceptual support for this type of interpretation from a very different source of evidence. A type of X radiation was used in adult mice, and it had the effect of impeding neurogenesis in the hippocampus. This manipulation actually assisted memory for a radial arm maze in a particular situation, in which the memory load was low but the amount of proactive interference from previous trials was high. The notion is that, in some situations, rich contextual encoding can be an impediment to recall. The richness of contextual encoding in humans apparently is correlated with working memory, so better working memory can be viewed more as a mnemonic difference than as a resource difference. For a working memory task, this mnemonic difference may translate into a higher basic chunk capacity.

Vogel, McCollough, and Machizawa (2005) pitted space (capacity) and energy (attention control) constraints against one another in a version of the visual array comparison task designed to produce a lateralized, event-related potential signal indicating storage of items in working memory. There were arrays on the left and right sides of the screen and the task was to focus attention on one of these arrays. Within that task, there were 2 or 4 items. When there were 4, they all could be relevant or only 2 of the 4 were relevant (e.g., remember the orientations of 2 red bars and ignore 2 blue bars). If the irrelevant items were easily filtered out using attention, the 2 relevant, 2 irrelevant situation should yield a potential similar to the 2-item trials, whereas if the irrelevant items could not be filtered out and had to be held in working memory along with the relevant items, they should yield a larger potential similar to the case of 4 relevant items. It turned out that the irrelevant items were filtered out easily by high-span individuals but not by low-span individuals. However, questions remain about this result. It required selection of one half of the screen to do the task in every condition, and the split between high- and low-span individuals was based on this same task. Perhaps the results would be different if individuals were categorized on the basis of a different working-memory task that did not include an attentional filtering component in every condition. On the other hand, perhaps there really is a critical resource difference between high- and low-span individuals, in addition to a chunk capacity difference.

Overall, then, it seems that some aspect of individual differences related to attention is critically important in characterizing those who yield good versus poor performance on working memory tasks and on intelligence tests. (Intelligence and fluid intelligence are so highly correlated that it has been difficult to tell whether the contributions of working memory are specific to fluid intelligence, though see Hambrick & Engle, 2001.) The notion that a general attention component is involved is a convergent result, with generality across modalities or processing domains observed in the nomothetic evidence (e.g., Cowan & Morey, 2007; Saults & Cowan, 2007) and in a latent variable analysis showing that the relation between fluid intelligence and working memory is general across processing domains (Kane et al., 2004). It is less clear whether to interpret the individual differences as fundamentally space related, energy related, or both.

C. Childhood Development

We think it has been considered less convincing to use childhood developmental differences to discern nomothetic principles, as compared to individual differences among young adults. People generally realize that the nature of the processing limitations that young children have is, in some ways, very different from the nature of the limitations that young adults have. Nevertheless, we think there are some implications of developmental research for the nomothetic principles.

The observation that adults who rehearse more quickly recall more items in short-term memory tests was followed by the observation that, as children mature, they speak more quickly and remember more in these tasks (e.g., Hulme & Tordoff, 1989). It has not been possible to teach children to rehearse more quickly to determine whether they would recall more (Hulme & Muir, 1985). Anyway, such an attempt is confounded inasmuch as rehearsal requires more attention in younger children (Guttentag, 1984). However, it has been possible to get second-grade children to speed up verbal recall responses to a rate similar to what adults usually use, and this manipulation makes no difference for memory span (Cowan, Elliott, et al., 2006). Therefore, similar to the research with young adults, we believe that the correlation between speech rate and memory span across age groups may occur for reasons other than faster refreshing of a phonological memory trace before it can decay. We do not yet have a satisfactory account of that correlation.

Recent research has focused on the possibility of age differences in capacity in visual array comparison tasks modeled after Luck and Vogel (1997). An apparent discrepancy exists in the results. On one hand, Ross-Sheehy, Oakes, and Luck (2003) suggested that infants retained about 4 items by the time that they were 10 months old, similar to the presumed capacity in adults. This suggestion was based on a procedure in which arrays appeared on both sides of the display but changes in the arrays occurred only on one side. By 10 months, infants reliably looked more often toward the changing display when it included 4 objects, but not 6 objects. In contrast, Cowan and colleagues (Cowan et al., 2005; Cowan, Elliott, et al., 2006; Cowan, Fristoe, et al., 2006; Cowan, Naveh-Benjamin, et al., 2006) have used the standard procedure of Luck and Vogel and have found a marked increase in capacity from the early elementary school years to adulthood. How can both of these results be correct?

Assuming that the development of capacity from infancy to adulthood is monotonic (a very safe assumption, we believe), either the infant research provides an overestimate of capacity or the child research provides an underestimate. The infant research could provide an overestimate because of its necessarily atypical procedure. To detect the changing side of the display, it is not necessary that all changes be detected. It is possible to model performance in the infant procedure with a process in which capacity is relatively low (e.g., 2 items) and the proportion of changes noticed is enough to motivate sustained looking when there are 4 items in the array (in which case, half of the changes in successive arrays would be noticed when these arrays were examined), but not when there are 6 items (in which case, only a third of the items in successive arrays would be noticed when these arrays were examined). On the other hand, the child research could be an underestimate because children may not fill the available working memory as consistently as adults. We have found that the children do about as well as the adults when the set size is 2 items, so it is not simply that the children more often fail to pay attention to the stimuli. Nevertheless, it is possible that children load items into working memory more slowly and therefore fail to fill their capacity before the display ends. If so, children might do as well as adults if a much longer display time was used.

One useful research strategy is to find a way to nullify the differences between children and adults. If these differences can be nullified by eliminating certain processes in adults, then the processes that were eliminated may be the ones responsible for the developmental change. This strategy is analogous to the one that Rosen and Engle (1997) and Kane and Engle (2000) used to show that dividing attention can nullify high- versus low-span differences between young adults. Cowan, Naveh-Benjamin, et al. (2006) divided attention in an array comparison task with a tone identification task and found that dividing attention made the adults perform in a manner slightly better than third-grade children but worse than fifth-grade children. In another type of procedure, Cowan, Saults, and Morey (2006) examined memory for the associations between printed words and their locations on the screen. Several words (proper names) were presented one at a time, each disappearing from the screen shortly afterward, and then a probe word presented centrally had to be dragged to the location at which that word had appeared originally. There were several different trial types and a complex pattern of performance that was very age specific. However, the addition of articulatory suppression in adults resulted in a dramatically changed pattern of performance that closely resembled that of third-grade children (who did not receive suppression), as shown in Fig. 7. Without suppression, adults seemed to engage in a process in which the list of names and the path of spatial locations were rehearsed separately, favoring trials in which there was a one-to-one

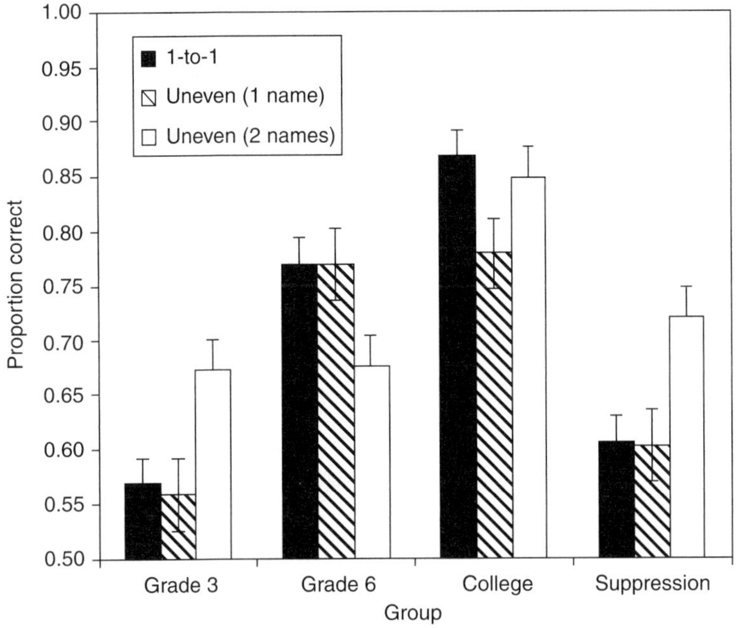

Fig. 7. From Cowan, Saults, et al. (2006, Fig. 3). Proportion correct recognition of the spatial location of a name from a target set. In the *one-to-one* condition, each name was presented at a unique location one at a time whereas, in the *uneven* condition, some locations received 2 names (not in immediate succession) on the same trial. There were 3–7 names in each target list. The two uneven conditions refer to trials in which the probed name was at a location by itself or with another name. Adults (college students) with articulatory suppression (right-hand cluster of bars) performed in a manner quite similar to third-grade children, which, as shown, was not the case for adults without suppression. Error bars are standard errors.

correspondence between the two. However, that pattern did not occur in children or in adults under articulatory suppression. Instead, they did best on trials with fewer locations used overall, even though some of those locations were used for two names on those trials. Taken together, these results suggest that strategic aspects of performance may well distinguish children from adults.

Nevertheless, there appear to be age differences in memory even when strategies are removed. Cowan, Nugent, Elliott, Ponomarev, and Saults (1999) investigated children's memory for spoken lists of digits that were presented while the children were busy playing a silent computer game that required thinking of rhymes. An occasional cue indicated that the computer game should be interrupted and the last list should be recalled. This procedure should minimize the ability to use strategies to encode the list items. In a

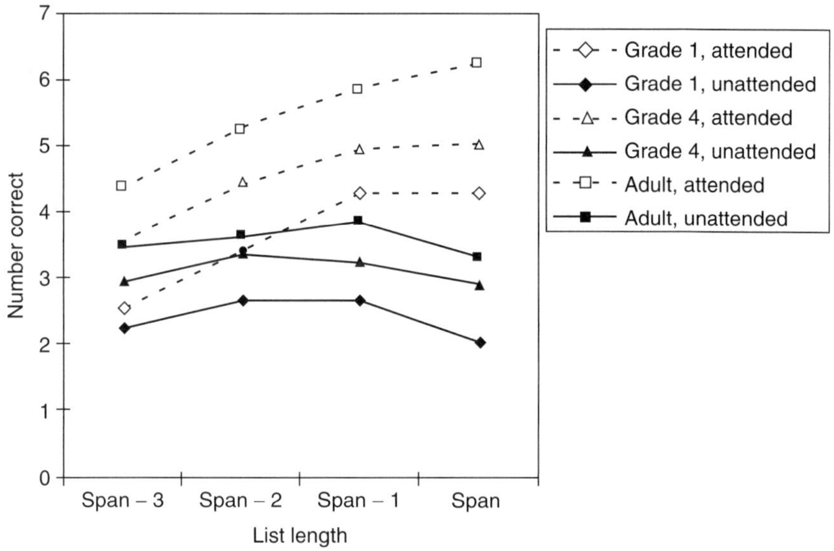

Fig. 8. From Cowan et al. (1999, Fig. 1). Number of items correct from unattended lists (solid lines) and attended lists (dashed lines) of spoken digits, in three age groups. Only lists unattended at the time of their presentation show roughly constant numbers correct across list lengths, presumably because of the absence of strategic encoding and the transfer of items to the focus of attention only after the retrieval cue.

control procedure, the lists were attended during their presentation. For unattended lists, presumably the focus of attention can be turned to the list only when the recall cue is presented. Figure 8 shows the results for attended and unattended lists. For unattended lists, the number of items recalled in the correct serial positions was constant across list lengths and increased with age. For attended lists, the number of items recalled was not constant across list lengths, and the age differences were slightly larger. However, most of the age difference in this procedure cannot easily be attributed to strategic differences during encoding. Cowan, Elliott, et al. (2005) replicated this result and obtained a similar result for a running memory span procedure, in which 12–20 digits were presented at a rapid, 4-per-second rate and ended at an unpredictable point, making rehearsal impossible. Both procedures showed similar age differences and correlated well with intelligence. For children too young to engage in strategic processing, but not for older children or adults, simple digit spans also correlated well with intelligence.

We do not yet have a reconciliation of results suggesting the great importance of strategic processing (Cowan, Saults, et al., 2006) and results showing marked capacity differences that cannot be attributed to strategic differences (e.g., Cowan, Elliott, et al., 2005). However, it can be seen in Fig. 7 that adults in the study of Cowan, Saults, and Morey with rehearsal suppressed still did recall slightly more items than young children recalled, so the contradiction may be more apparent than real.

There was an earlier era of research by neoPiagetians suggesting that children have fewer slots in working memory than adults (Case, 1972; Pascual-Leone, 1970, 2005; Weiss, 1995). Perhaps the clearest result supporting that idea is that of Burtis (1982). He presented matrices of letters to be recalled in their correct locations. The letters were presented in pairs within the matrix and the items within a pair were random or, in other conditions, contained redundancy in various ways (repetitions of the same letter; pairs presented in red to be distinct from the other pairs; pairs presented repeatedly throughout the experiment; pairs forming familiar acronyms, such as FM). The results were examined with the help of a simple model that incorporated results from both singletons and pairs. At every age for every set size, the results fell neatly on the line expected according to the capacity model with a capacity of 4 at 10 years of age, 5 at 12 years of age, and 6 at 14 years of age. The reason for the larger capacity estimates suggested by Burtis and other neoPiagetians compared to Broadbent (1975) and Cowan (2001) is an important unknown, but it might be attributed to the availability of rehearsal strategies in the procedure that Burtis used, or to other studies' use of procedures more challenging than Burtis' was, using up more capacity for processing.

In sum, there are some critically important questions remaining about the nature of the dramatic increase in working memory capabilities that are so evident between infancy and adulthood. We cannot yet be sure whether there are differences in space, energy, or both during childhood development but the evidence seems to favor both. Here we have emphasized space (capacity) differences, which are less commonly acknowledged in the literature than energy (resource) differences.

D. Adult Aging

In some ways, adult aging may be the converse of child development. For example, whereas the rate of verbal rehearsal and verbal short-term memory both increase during childhood as noted above, in adult aging the rate of rehearsal slows down and verbal short-term memory suffers accordingly (Kynette, Kemper, Norman, & Cheung, 1990).

In other ways, adult aging may not be the converse of child development, and the differences in mechanisms of processing make it difficult to make fair comparisons across age groups in capacity. In particular, older adults appear to have more difficulty than young adults associating or binding together the features within an object (Chalfonte & Johnson, 1996; Mitchell, Johnson,

Raye, Mather, & D'Esposito, 2000) or objects presented together (Naveh-Benjamin, 2000; Naveh-Benjamin, Hussain, Guez, & Bar-On, 2003). Given that one instance of binding is the formation of new chunks of information (e.g., Miller, 1956) we might expect that, in some situations, older adults will have to recall smaller chunks than young adults. To do so, they would have to recall fewer chunks even if the chunk capacity is the same in the two groups.

In several of our recent studies, we attempted to evaluate both the formation of associations and the capacity. Cowan, Naveh-Benjamin, et al. (2006) presented children (in third and fifth grade), young adults, and older adults with a visual array comparison task, similar to that used by Luck and Vogel (1997). For half of the trials in this task, the probe array did not differ from the target array (i.e., no-change trials). The probe array could differ from the target array in two possible ways for the other half of the trials (i.e., change trials). On some change trials, a colored square changed to a color that had not been seen in the original array; as a participant only had to keep track of the squares, these were considered item-change trials. On other change trials, a colored square changed to a color that was already present elsewhere in the first array. In this case, participants had to keep track of not only the colors present in the target array, but also the locations of each color. As correct detection involved successful binding of color and location features, these were termed binding trials. A cue encircled one item in the probe array, and only that item might have changed between arrays. Some key results are shown in Figs. 9 and 10. Figure 9 depicts results of an

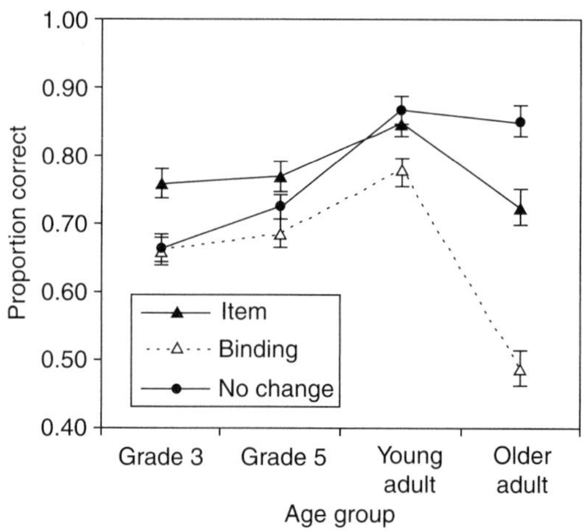

Fig. 9. From Cowan, Naveh-Benjamin, et al. (2006, Fig. 3). Proportion of trials correct for each age group (x-axis) in each condition (graph parameter) within Experiment 1a. Item and binding changes occurred in different trials within the same trial blocks. Error bars are standard errors.

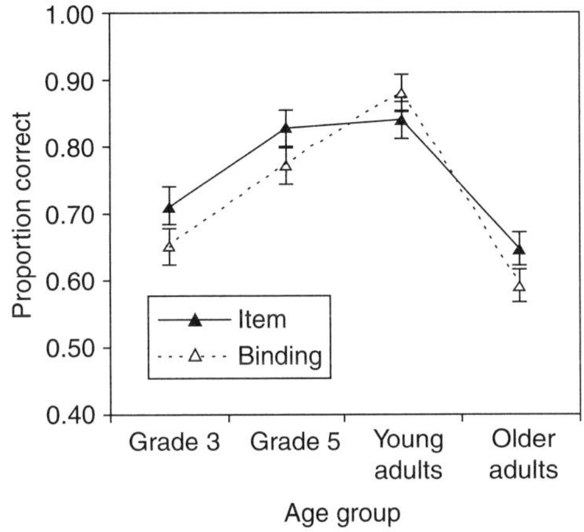

Fig. 10. From Cowan, Naveh-Benjamin, et al. (2006, Fig. 6). Proportion of trials correct for each age group (*x*-axis) in each type of trial block (graph parameter) within Experiment 2a. Item and binding changes occurred in different trial blocks, which allowed older adults to show no more binding deficit than children. Error bars are standard errors.

experiment in which item and binding changes were mixed together in the same trial block. One can see an inverted U-shaped developmental trend across the life span for item-change trials. Additionally, one can see that older adults did not do a good job of noticing the binding changes.

However, from those results it was not clear whether the older adults were incapable of noticing the binding changes or whether they simply did not attend to the correct information because the item changes were more salient. To address that question, Cowan, Naveh-Benjamin, et al. (2006, Experiment 2) developed a procedure in which item and binding changes appeared in separate trial blocks. The no-change control trials had to be adjusted accordingly. In the blocks with item changes, the cued item in no-change trials always was uniquely colored; in the blocks with binding changes, the cued item in no-change trials always had a color shared by another item in the array. Therefore, the participant could not guess whether the cued item had changed from the target array based on whether it was unique. The results are shown in Fig. 10. This study shows an inverted U-shape of developmental change in capacity, with little difference between children and older adults. A different pattern was found in an examination of bias; there was a monotonic trend to be less willing to indicate that a change had occurred. In terms of basic visual working-memory capacity, though, an inverted U-shape does appear to describe developmental change. Dividing attention with a tone identification task did produce lower capacity estimates in young adults, but did not reflect the other developmental trends that were unique to adult aging.

More work on aging has examined verbal working memory. Central to that work is the question of whether older adults' associative deficit will impede chunk formation, which should lead to smaller chunks than in young adults. It is critical to answer this question in order to address adequately the question of whether verbal working memory changes with adult aging. Allen and Coyne (1988) visually presented young adults and older adults with meaningless strings of letters. In this task, chunk size was externally manipulated by spacing between letters, with participants serially recalling between four and six letters when cued. For example, if six letters were to be recalled, the letter string was presented in the form "WRQB KX," influencing the formation of two chunks of different sizes. To examine how chunks were organized across age groups, error probabilities were computed for within-chunk and between-chunk boundaries; ideally, recall error should be lowest within a chunk, but higher between two chunks (Allen & Coyne, 1988). Although older adults recalled a fewer number of letter strings, there were no significant differences between age groups regarding the way that chunks were qualitatively organized (in terms of both number and size), suggesting that any deficits in memory were not due to organization in immediate memory. Similar studies confirmed these results, even when there was no spacing between letters to influence the number and size of chunks formed (Allen & Coyne, 1989; Allen & Crozier, 1992). Older adults are especially helped when stimuli in the environment support and influence recall, association, or grouping of items (Craik, 1983, 1986; Hay & Jacoby, 1999; Naveh-Benjamin, Craik, Guez, & Kreuger, 2005). Use of environmental support can greatly improve estimates in chunk size. In one study (Taub, 1974), older adults presented with letter strings that made words formed a greater number of chunks and had better recall than when the information was meaningless.

Naveh-Benjamin, Cowan, Kilb, and Chen (2007) examined chunking and capacity limits in working memory by presenting young adults and older adults with list of learned word pairs and lists of learned singletons (still presented in pairs within the list) to be recalled in serial order. This was the procedure of Cowan et al. (2004) in which, during a training phase, all words to be learned by participants received 4 different exposures, of which 0, 1, 2, or 4 exposures were as consistent pairs as opposed to singletons. There were also nonstudied control words. Several means were used to score the results so as to estimate chunks. In one simple method, a distinction was made between the number of pairs accessed and pair completion. Access referred to the number of pairs for which at least one item was recalled and pair completion referred to the proportion of accessed pairs for which both items were recalled. Figure 11 shows that there was a large, consistent difference in pair access favoring younger adults. Moreover, younger adults

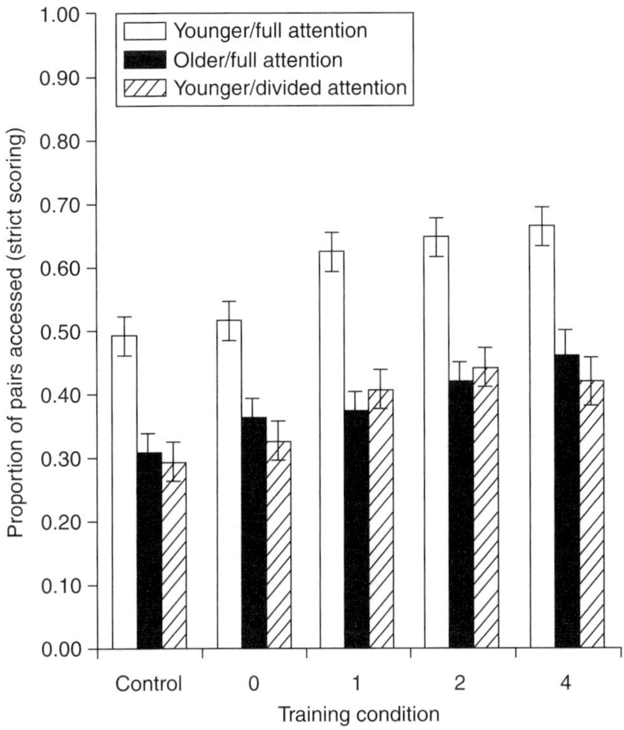

Fig. 11. From Naveh-Benjamin et al. (2007, Fig. 3). Proportion of presented pairs within a list to be recalled that were accessed in each pair-training condition. Access refers to at least one member of the pair being recalled. Older adults recalled fewer than young adults, but young adults under divided attention performed like older adults. Error bars are standard errors.

carrying out a divided attention task (tone identification) yielded pair access scores quite similar to older adults without divided attention. This result suggests that there is an adult aging decrement in capacity and that this decrement is attention related. A similar, clear result was obtained using various other estimates of chunk capacity. In contrast, there were only small and somewhat inconsistent group differences in the average sizes of chunks. It showed up in the 0- and 2-pairing conditions only. Across modalities and studies, then, adult aging sometimes results in a deficit in binding and association in working memory tasks but, regardless of those effects, consistently results in a deficit in some attention-dependent form of working memory capacity expressed in chunks.

There also has been considerable work emphasizing the reduction with adult aging in energy or attention control, as opposed to space or chunk capacity. Hasher and Zacks (1988) proposed that older adults have difficulty inhibiting irrelevant items, which allows them to take up valuable space in working memory. One type of evidence for this theory is comparable to the work on individual differences in proactive interference (e.g., Bunting, 2006; Conway & Engle, 1994). May, Hasher, and Kane (1999; also Lustig, May, & Hasher, 2001) used reading span and backward digit span tasks in two ways: with the usual, ascending order in which the list lengths get progressively longer across the session, and with a descending order in which the lists start at a relatively long length and get progressively shorter. The rationale is that ascending presentation allows considerable proactive interference to build up from one trial to the next by the time the difficult trials are presented. In the descending order, this was not the case. The deficit of older adults was eliminated with a descending presentation. One can, however, question the basis of this effect. Perhaps items in the first few trials are memorized and items only have to be held in a capacity-limited working memory store after a certain amount of proactive interference is present. Therefore, it is not clear whether the adult aging effect occurs because of space or energy differences. The same might be said of other results suggesting a resource limitation in child development or aging (e.g., Zelazo, Craik, & Booth, 2004). These could entail space limits, energy limits, or a combination of these limits.

A lot of work has documented that the speed of processing slows down in old age (Salthouse, 1996) and, as suggested above, this can have an effect on working memory performance. However, the literature still seems ambiguous about the fundamental causes of adult aging deficits in working memory. A speed deficit can increase the amount of energy needed to refresh representations in working memory, by making it necessary to remember more items at once rather than rotating among them rapidly. A faster decay rate requires a faster refreshing rate to rotate among items, making it more likely that items would be kept in an attention-based storage mechanism rather than successfully rotated. Energy limits and space limits may trade off, or insufficient space may have to be counteracted with an investment of energy. To some extent, these criticisms apply to all areas of the field; for example, Engle, Cantor, and Carullo (1992) found that an experimenter-paced version of the operation span task correlated with a cognitive measure (reading comprehension) whereas a subject-paced version did not. The capacity difference was critical only under speed pressure. Thus, the difficulty of separating causes of working memory limitations cannot be ignored.

Basak and Verhaeghen (2003) can be brought up as an example of how these difficult questions may be approached. They studied the range of subitizing, or apprehending small numbers of items without counting them. The classic literature shows that people can rapidly subitize about 4 items, after which a slower counting process is necessary (e.g., Mandler & Shebo, 1982). Recall that Tuholski et al. (2001) found no substantial relation between the range of subitizing and working memory in young adults. In contrast, Basak and Verhaeghen did find a difference between older and younger adults in the subitizing range; by their methods, younger adults were close to 3 items in that range, whereas older adults were close to 2 items. However, within the subitizing range, there was no difference in subitizing speed between younger and older adults. Rather than a general speed deficit (Salthouse, 1996), the results can be interpreted as showing that speed deficits in aging adults result from other deficits (in this case, engaging in slower counting processes for some lists that are more quickly subitized by younger adults).

E. Psychopathology

There is a vast literature on working memory deficits in diverse types of psychopathology, and it is beyond the scope of this chapter to review them. However, in this section we would like to point out that the recent literature has stressed the importance of energy (resource) limits in psychopathology, with emphasis on central executive processes and the frontal lobes (for reviews, see Engle, Sedek, von Hecker, & McIntosh, 2005). Here we issue a caution that this view may well be incomplete. An excellent case in point is provided by Gold et al. (2006). Their task was to compare two arrays of objects but some objects were irrelevant to the task (e.g., remember the orientations of red bars but ignore blue bars). Most of the time, the participants were tested on memory of one type of stimulus (e.g., the red bars) but, on occasional trials, they were tested on memory of the other type (e.g., the blue bars). In a separate test session, either type of bar could be relevant and each type was tested equally often. This test yielded evidence of how well attention was controlled: in particular, the steepness of the performance slope distinguishing between frequent, neutral, and infrequent conditions, with the highest performance for the frequent conditions and the infrequent feature attentionally filtered out. Better control results in attention more tightly focused on the frequent, most-relevant stimulus type and therefore better performance on it and a steeper slope when stimulus types are compared. The test also yielded evidence of how much visual working memory could hold: in particular, the sum of capacities observed in the frequent and infrequent conditions (e.g., red + blue bars in memory). Presumably, the number of items with the frequent feature plus the number with the infrequent feature make up the total contents of task-related working memory. As it happens, the total contents were less in schizophrenic patients than in normal control participants, but with little evidence of a change in attentional control (filtering). This finding is illustrated in Fig. 12.

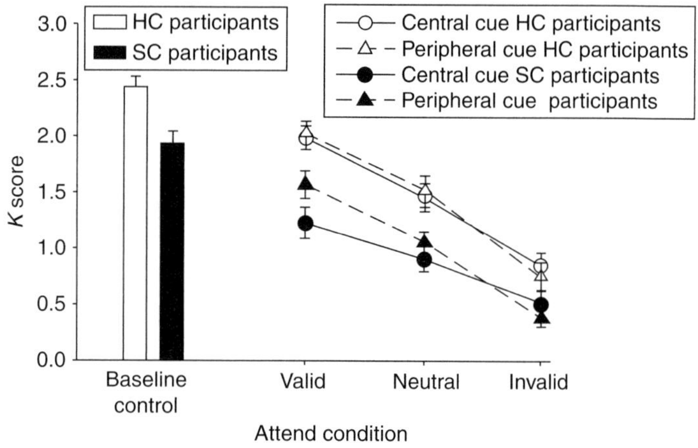

Fig. 12. From Gold et al. (2006, Fig. 2). HC = healthy control and SC = schizophrenic patient. The cue to look at colored squares on a particular side of the screen was valid on 60% of all trials, and a neutral cue was presented 20% of the time. The schizophrenic deficit showed up primarily in terms of capacity (lower intercept in patients) with only a small tendency for filtering out of invalid items to be affected (shallower slope in patients). Error bars are standard errors.

V. Addressing the Holistic-Versus-Analytic Distinction

We can surmise from the research on capacity that we have summarized that different levels of analysis lead to different measures for different purposes. If one is interested in what humans can accomplish, one finds that they can repeat up to seven or so verbal items (Miller, 1956); that the nature of the stimuli, such as how well it lends itself to verbal rehearsal, influences how well it can be recalled (Baddeley, 1986); and that people can learn to recall amazing amounts of information by grouping items together to form larger-level chunks (Miller, 1956) and data structures involving complex sets of associative relationships (Ericsson & Kintsch, 1995). However, that understanding is akin to knowing what an automobile does. If one wants to understand how an automobile works, or what makes one automobile more powerful or more efficient than another, one must adopt a more analytic framework in which one investigates how combustion engines work, how gear-shifting mechanisms work, and so on.

Research on capacity limits in chunks is of interest for at least two reasons. The first reason is that, as we have shown, there appears to be a simple limit of 3 to 4 chunks that, on average, occurs for adults across a large variety of test situations in which the contributions of rehearsal and other mnemonic strategies have been minimized. Knowing that limit can be of considerable use in predicting results in various new situations. The second reason is that, as we have further shown, the capacity limit appears to be a general limit that applies for items regardless of the modality in which they were presented, and for multimodal arrays of items; it is a limit vulnerable to distraction even from stimuli very different from the memoranda. This is of interest because it is what we would expect if what we are observing is the use of the focus of attention as a working-memory storage device. Given that this attention-related component of working memory is thought to be closely related to conscious awareness (e.g., Baars & Franklin, 2003; Cowan, 1995; Dehaene, Changeux, Naccache, Sackur, & Sergent, 2006), it may be that we are on the way to answering a fundamental philosophical question regarding how much information can be present in conscious awareness at once.

There are, however, multiple levels of analysis. After distinguishing between overall working memory ability and its division into components, an even finer level of analysis can be described. In specific, evidence of space (chunk capacity) limits can be further questioned as to their ultimate source. Attention-demanding, central executive processes presumably can be used to refresh items in memory (e.g., Cowan, 1992; Cowan et al., 1998; Hulme, Newton, Cowan, Stuart, & Brown, 1999; Raye, Johnson, Mitchell, Greene, & Johnson, 2007) and, at the macroscopic level, the process of doing so could look the same as using attention to hold the items concurrently. Therefore, at a microscopic level, we are still not sure what is going on and it is only at the intermediate level of analysis that we can draw conclusions about working memory capacity in chunks. At that intermediate level of analysis, the evidence is strong that (1) there is such a basic limit, (2) it is important in information processing and cognition, and (3) it appears to be important in understanding ideographic differences, including individual differences among young adults, life span developmental differences, and differences due to psychopathology.

VI. Conclusion

We have considered the concept of working memory according to separate potential contributions of space (i.e., chunk capacity), time (i.e., decay and speed factors), and energy (i.e., resources). The emphasis was in showing that the notion of chunk capacity is not intractable, can be separated from other factors, and plays an important role in both nomothetic and ideographic considerations of working memory according to an analytic perspective. Miller (1989) explained how he (Miller, 1956) was using only the magical number seven as a rhetorical device, and little more than a joke, to organize his presentation of several otherwise unrelated research areas. Although the approach in that classic paper may have set a skeptical trend in the field, we, after Broadbent (1975), believe that there are some important generalizations to be had regarding fixed capacity limits. The difficulty in reaching those generalizations is in identifying the chunks that individuals use and we have presented methods to examine what the chunks are. What appears to be a general capacity limit in working memory (Cowan & Morey, 2007; Saults & Cowan, 2007) is closely related to the contents of the conscious mind. It has the advantage of being easier to quantify than the resource limits that also appear to exist and to differ among individuals (e.g., Kane et al., 2004). The space and energy limits may occur for a common reason if, in fact, they share a focus of attention that can zoom out to apprehend a field of objects or zoom in to hold on to a goal in the face of a prepotent response going against that goal. With the devotion of enough time and resources, we will learn the truth about chunk capacity and its space metaphor.

References

Allen, P. A., & Coyne, A. C. (1988). Age differences in primary organization or processing variability? Part I: An examination of age and primary organization. *Experimental Aging Research, 14*, 143–149.

Allen, P. A., & Coyne, A. C. (1989). Are there age differences in chunking. *Journal of Gerontology, Psychological Sciences, 44*, P181–P183.

Allen, P. A., & Crozier, L. C. (1992). Age and ideal chunk size. *Journal of Gerontology Psychological Sciences, 47*, P47–P51.

Allen, R. J., Baddeley, A. D., & Hitch, G. J. (2006). Is the binding of visual features in working memory resource-demanding? *Journal of Experimental Psychology: General, 135*, 298–313.

Alvarez, G. A., & Cavanagh, P. (2004). The capacity of visual short-term memory is set both by visual information load and by number of objects. *Psychological Science, 15*, 106–111.

Andrews, G., & Halford, G. S. (2002). A cognitive complexity metric applied to cognitive development. *Cognitive Psychology, 45*, 153–219.

Atkinson, R. C., & Shiffrin, R. M. (1968). Human memory: A proposed system and its control processes. In K. W. Spence and J. T. Spence (Eds.), *The psychology of learning and motivation: Advances in research and theory* (Vol. 2, pp. 89–195). New York: Academic Press.

Awh, E., Barton, B., & Vogel, E. K. (2007). Visual working memory represents a fixed number of items regardless of complexity. *Psychological Science, 18*, 622–628.

Awh, E., & Jonides, J. (2001). Overlapping mechanisms of attention and spatial working memory. *Trends in Cognitive Sciences, 5*, 119–126.

Baars, B. J., & Franklin, S. (2003). How conscious experience and working memory interact. *Trends in Cognitive Sciences, 7*, 166–172.

Baddeley, A. (1996). Exploring the central executive. *Quarterly Journal of Experimental Psychology, 49A*, 5–28.

Baddeley, A. (2000). The episodic buffer: A new component of working memory? *Trends in cognitive sciences, 4*, 417–423.

Baddeley, A. (2001). The magic number and the episodic buffer. *Behavioral and Brain Sciences, 24*, 117–118.

Baddeley, A., Gathercole, S., & Papagno, C. (1998). The phonological loop as a language learning device. *Psychological Review, 105*, 158–173.

Baddeley, A. D. (1986). *Working memory*. Oxford, England: Clarendon Press.
Baddeley, A. D., & Hitch, G. (1974). Working memory. In G. H. Bower (Ed.), *The psychology of learning and motivation* (Vol. 8, pp. 47–89). New York: Academic Press.
Baddeley, A. D., Thomson, N., & Buchanan, M. (1975). Word length and the structure of short-term memory. *Journal of Verbal Learning and Verbal Behavior, 14*, 575–589.
Baddeley, A. D., & Warrington, E. K. (1970). Amnesia and the distinction between long- and short-term memory. *Journal of Verbal Learning and Verbal Behavior, 9*, 176–189.
Barrouillet, P., Bernardin, S., & Camos, V. (2004). Time constraints and resource sharing in adults' working memory spans. *Journal of Experimental Psychology: General, 133*, 83–100.
Basak, C., & Verhaeghen, P. (2003). Subitizing speed, subitizing range, counting speed, the Stroop effect, and aging: Capacity differences and speed equivalence. *Psychology & Aging, 18*, 240–249.
Binet, A., & Simon, T. (1916/1980). *The development of intelligence in children*. Nashville, TN: Williams Printing Company.
Bleckley, M. K., Durso, F. T., Crutchfield, J. M., Engle, R. W., & Khanna, M. (2003). Individual differences in working memory capacity predict visual attention allocation. *Psychonomic Bulletin & Review, 10*, 884–889.
Bolton, T. L. (1892). The growth of memory in school children. *American Journal of Psychology, 4*, 362–380.
Broadbent, D. E. (1958). *Perception and communication*. New York: Pergamon Press.
Broadbent, D. E. (1975). The magic number seven after fifteen years. In A. Kennedy and A. Wilkes (Eds.), *Studies in long-term memory* (pp. 3–18). Oxford, England: John Wiley & Sons.
Bunting, M. (2006). Proactive interference and item similarity in working memory. *Journal of Experimental Psychology: Learning, Memory, and Cognition, 32*, 183–196.
Burtis, P. J. (1982). Capacity increase and chunking in the development of short-term memory. *Journal of Experimental Child Psychology, 34*, 387–413.
Case, R. (1972). Validation of a neo-Piagetian mental capacity construct. *Journal of Experimental Child Psychology, 14*, 287–302.
Chalfonte, B. L., & Johnson, M. K. (1996). Feature memory and binding in young and older adults. *Memory & Cognition, 24*, 403–416.
Chen, Z., & Cowan, N. (2005). Chunk limits and length limits in immediate recall: A reconciliation. *Journal of Experimental Psychology: Learning, Memory, and Cognition, 31*, 1235–1249.
Cocchini, G., Logie, R. H., Della Sala, S., MacPherson, S. E., & Baddeley, A. D. (2002). Concurrent performance of two memory tasks: Evidence for domain-specific working memory systems. *Memory & Cognition, 30*, 1086–1095.
Conway, A. R. A., Cowan, N., & Bunting, M. F. (2001). The cocktail party phenomenon revisited: The importance of working memory capacity. *Psychonomic Bulletin & Review, 8*, 331–335.
Conway, A. R. A., Cowan, N., Bunting, M. F., Therriault, D. J., & Minkoff, S. R. B. (2002). A latent variable analysis of working memory capacity, short-term memory capacity, processing speed, and general fluid intelligence. *Intelligence, 30*, 163–183.
Conway, A. R. A., & Engle, R. W. (1994). Working memory and retrieval: A resource-dependent inhibition model. *Journal of Experimental Psychology: General, 123*, 354–373.
Cowan, N. (1988). Evolving conceptions of memory storage, selective attention, and their mutual constraints within the human information processing system. *Psychological Bulletin, 104*, 163–191.
Cowan, N. (1992). Verbal memory span and the timing of spoken recall. *Journal of Memory and Language, 31*, 668–684.
Cowan, N. (1995). *Attention and memory: An integrated framework*. Oxford Psychology Series #26. New York: Oxford University Press.

Cowan, N. (1999). An embedded-processes model of working memory. In A. Miyake and P. Shah (Eds.), *Models of working memory: Mechanisms of active maintenance and executive control* (pp. 62–101). Cambridge, UK: Cambridge University Press.

Cowan, N. (2001). The magical number 4 in short-term memory: A reconsideration of mental storage capacity. *Behavioral and Brain Sciences, 24*, 87–185.

Cowan, N. (2005). *Working memory capacity*. Hove, East Sussex, UK: Psychology Press.

Cowan, N., & AuBuchon, A. M. (2008). Short-term memory loss over time without retroactive stimulus interference. *Psychonomic Bulletin & Review, 15*, 230–235.

Cowan, N., Chen, Z., & Rouder, J. N. (2004). Constant capacity in an immediate serial-recall task: A logical sequel to Miller (1956). *Psychological Science, 15*, 634–640.

Cowan, N., Elliott, E. M., Saults, J. S., Morey, C. C., Mattox, S., Hismjatullina, A., et al. (2005). On the capacity of attention: Its estimation and its role in working memory and cognitive aptitudes. *Cognitive Psychology, 51*, 42–100.

Cowan, N., Elliott, E. M., Saults, J. S., Nugent, L. D., Bomb, P., & Hismjatullina, A. (2006). Rethinking speed theories of cognitive development: Increasing the rate of recall without affecting accuracy. *Psychological Science, 17*, 67–73.

Cowan, N., Fristoe, N. M., Elliott, E. M., Brunner, R. P., & Saults, J. S. (2006). Scope of attention, control of attention, and intelligence in children and adults. *Memory & Cognition, 34*, 1754–1768.

Cowan, N., & Morey, C. C. (2007). How can dual-task working memory retention limits be investigated? *Psychological Science, 18*, 686–688.

Cowan, N., Naveh-Benjamin, M., Kilb, A., & Saults, J. S. (2006). Life-span development of visual working memory: When is feature binding difficult. *Developmental Psychology, 42*, 1089–1102.

Cowan, N., Nugent, L. D., Elliott, E. M., Ponomarev, I., & Saults, J. S. (1999). The role of attention in the development of short-term memory: Age differences in the verbal span of apprehension. *Child Development, 70*, 1082–1097.

Cowan, N., Saults, J. S., & Morey, C. C. (2006). Development of working memory for verbal-spatial associations. *Journal of Memory and Language, 55*, 274–289.

Cowan, N., Wood, N. L., Wood, P. K., Keller, T. A., Nugent, L. D., & Keller, C. V. (1998). Two separate verbal processing rates contributing to short-term memory span. *Journal of Experimental Psychology: General, 127*, 141–160.

Craik, F. I. M. (1983). On the transfer of information from temporary to permanent memory. *Philosophical Transactions of the Royal Society of London, 302*, 341–359.

Craik, F. I. M. (1986). A functional account of age differences in memory. In F. Klix and H. Hagendorf (Eds.), *Human memory and cognitive capabilities: Mechanisms and performances* (pp. 409–421). New York: Elsevier Science Publishers.

Davelaar, E. J., Goshen-Gottstein, Y., Ashkenazi, A., Haarman, H. J., & Usher, M. (2005). The demise of short-term memory revisited: Empirical and computational investigations of recency effects. *Psychological Review, 112*, 3–42.

Dehaene, S., Changeux, J.-P., Naccache, L., Sackur, J., & Sergent, C. (2006). Conscious, preconscious, and subliminal processing: A testable taxonomy. *Trends in Cognitive Sciences, 10*, 205–211.

Delaney, P. F., & Sahakyan, L. (2007). Unexpected costs of high working memory capacity following directed forgetting and contextual change manipulations. *Memory & Cognition, 35*, 1074–1083.

Engle, R. W., Cantor, J., & Carullo, J. J. (1992). Individual differences in working memory and comprehension: A test of four hypotheses. *Journal of Experimental Psychology: Learning, Memory, & Cognition, 18*, 972–992.

Engle, R. W., Sedek, G., von Hecker, U., & McIntosh, D. N. (Eds.) (2005). *Cognitive limitations in aging and psychopathology*. New York: Cambridge University Press.

Engle, R. W., Tuholski, S. W., Laughlin, J. E., & Conway, A. R. A. (1999). Working memory, short-term memory, and general fluid intelligence: A latent-variable approach. *Journal of Experimental Psychology: General, 128*, 309–331.

Ericsson, K. A., Chase, W. G., & Faloon, S. (1980). Acquisition of a memory skill. *Science, 208*, 1181–1182.

Ericsson, K. A., Delaney, P. F., Weaver, G., & Mahadevan, R. (2004). Uncovering the structure of a memorist's superior "basic" memory capacity. *Cognitive Psychology, 49*, 191–237.

Ericsson, K. A., & Kintsch, W. (1995). Long-term working memory. *Psychological Review, 102*, 211–245.

Gathercole, S. E., & Baddeley, A. D. (1993). *Working memory and language*. Hove, UK: Erlbaum.

Glanzer, M., & Cunitz, A. R. (1966). Two storage mechanisms in free recall. *Journal of Verbal Learning & Verbal Behavior, 5*, 351–360.

Glanzer, M., & Razel, M. (1974). The size of the unit in short-term storage. *Journal of Verbal Learning & Verbal Behavior, 13*, 114–131.

Gobet, F., Lane, P. C. R., Croker, S., Cheng, P. C.-H., Jones, G., Oliver, I., et al. (2001). Chunking mechanisms in human learning. *Trends in Cognitive Sciences, 5*, 236–243.

Gold, J. M., Fuller, R. L., Robinson, B. M., McMahon, R. P., Braun, E. L., & Luck, S. J. (2006). Intact attentional control of working memory encoding in schizophrenia. *Journal of Abnormal Psychology, 115*, 658–673.

Gray, J. R., Chabris, C. F., & Braver, T. S. (2003). Neural mechanisms of general fluid intelligence. *Nature Neuroscience, 6*, 316–322.

Grossberg, S. (1978). A theory of human memory: Self-organization and performance of sensory-motor codes, maps, and plans. In R. Rosen and F. Snell (Eds.), *Progress in theoretical biology* (Vol. 5, pp. 500–639). New York: Academic Press.

Guttentag, R. E. (1984). The mental effort requirement of cumulative rehearsal: A developmental study. *Journal of Experimental Child Psychology, 37*, 92–106.

Halford, G. S., Baker, R., McCredden, J. E., & Bain, J. D. (2005). How many variables can humans process. *Psychological Science, 16*, 70–76.

Halford, G. S., Cowan, N., & Andrews, G. (2007). Separating cognitive capacity from knowledge: A new hypothesis. *Trends in Cognitive Sciences, 11*, 236–242.

Hambrick, D. Z., & Engle, R. W. (2001). Effects of domain knowledge, working memory capacity, and age on cognitive performance: An investigation of the knowledge-is-power hypothesis. *Cognitive Psychology, 44*, 339–387.

Hasher, L., & Zacks, R. T. (1988). Working memory, comprehension, and aging: A review and a new view. In G. H. Bower (Ed.), *The psychology of learning and motivation* (Vol. 22, pp. 193–225). San Diego, CA: Academic Press.

Hay, J. F., & Jacoby, L. L. (1999). Separating habit and recollection in young and older adults: Effects of elaborative processing and distinctiveness. *Psychology & Aging, 14*, 122–134.

Heitz, R. P., & Engle, R. W. (2007). Focusing the spotlight: Individual differences in visual attention control. *Journal of Experimental Psychology: General, 136*, 217–240.

Hulme, C., & Muir, C. (1985). Developmental changes in speech rate and memory span: A causal relationship. *British Journal of Developmental Psychology, 3*, 175–181.

Hulme, C., Newton, P., Cowan, N., Stuart, G., & Brown, G. (1999). Think before you speak: Pause, memory search and trace redintegration processes in verbal memory span. *Journal of Experimental Psychology: Learning, Memory, and Cognition, 25*, 447–463.

Hulme, C., & Tordoff, V. (1989). Working memory development: The effects of speech rate, word length, and acoustic similarity on serial recall. *Journal of Experimental Child Psychology, 47*, 72–87.

Jacobs, J. (1887). Experiments on "prehension." *Mind, 12*, 75–79.

Jiang, Y., Olson, I. R., & Chun, M. M. (2000). Organization of visual short-term memory. *Journal of Experimental Psychology: Learning, Memory, & Cognition, 26*, 683–702.

Kail, R., & Salthouse, T. A. (1994). Processing speed as a mental capacity. *Acta Psychologica, 86*, 199–255.

Kane, M. J., Bleckley, M. K., Conway, A. R. A., & Engle, R. W. (2001). A controlled-attention view of working-memory capacity. *Journal of Experimental Psychology: General, 130*, 169–183.

Kane, M. J., & Engle, R. W. (2000). Working-memory capacity, proactive interference, and divided attention: Limits on long-term memory retrieval. *Journal of Experimental Psychology: Learning, Memory, and Cognition, 26*, 336–358.

Kane, M. J., & Engle, R. W. (2003). Working-memory capacity and the control of attention: The contributions of goal neglect, response competition, and task set to Stroop interference. *Journal of Experimental Psychology: General, 132*, 47–70.

Kane, M. J., Hambrick, D. Z., Tuholski, S. W., Wilhelm, O., Payne, T. W., & Engle, R. E. (2004). The generality of working-memory capacity: A latent-variable approach to verbal and visuo-spatial memory span and reasoning. *Journal of Experimental Psychology: General, 133*, 189–217.

Kim, S.-Y., Kim, M.-S., & Chun, M. M. (2005). Concurrent working memory load can reduce distraction. *Proceedings of the National Academy of Science (PNAS), 102*, 16524–16529.

Kynette, D., Kemper, S., Norman, S., & Cheung, H. (1990). Adults' word recall and word repetition. *Experimental Aging Research, 16*, 117–121.

Lavie, N., Hirst, A., de Fockert, J. W., & Viding, E. (2004). Load theory of selective attention and cognitive control. *Journal of Experimental Psychology: General, 133*, 339–354.

Lewandowsky, S., Duncan, M., & Brown, G. D. A. (2004). Time does not cause forgetting in short-term serial recall. *Psychonomic Bulletin & Review, 11*, 771–790.

Logie, R. H., & Gilhooly, K. J. (1998). *Working memory and thinking*. Hove, England: Psychology Press.

Lovett, M. C., Reder, L. M., & Lebière, C. (1999). Modeling working memory in a unified architecture: An ACT-R perspective. In A. Miyake and P. Shah (Eds.), *Models of working memory: Mechanisms of active maintenance and executive control* (pp. 135–182). Cambridge: Cambridge University Press.

Luck, S. J., & Vogel, E. K. (1997). The capacity of visual working memory for features and conjunctions. *Nature, 390*, 279–281.

Lustig, C., May, C. P., & Hasher, L. (2001). Working memory span and the role of proactive interference. *Journal of Experimental Psychology: General, 130*, 199–207.

Mandler, G., & Shebo, B. J. (1982). Subitizing: An analysis of its component processes. *Journal of Experimental Psychology: General, 111*, 1–22.

Marmurek, H. H., & Johnson, N. F. (1978). Hierarchical organization as a determinant of sequential learning. *Memory & Cognition, 6*, 240–245.

Massaro, D. W. (1970). Retroactive interference in short-term recognition memory for pitch. *Journal of Experimental Psychology, 83*, 32–39.

May, C. P., Hasher, L., & Kane, M. J. (1999). The role of interference in memory span. *Memory & Cognition, 27*, 759–767.

Miller, G. A. (1956). The magical number seven, plus or minus two: Some limits on our capacity for processing information. *Psychological Review, 63*, 81–97.

Miller, G. A. (1989). George A. Miller. In L. Gardner (Ed.), *A history of psychology in autobiography* (Vol. VIII, pp. 391–418). Stanford, CA: Stanford University Press.

Miller, G. A., Galanter, E., & Pribram, K. H. (1960). *Plans and the structure of behavior*. New York: Holt, Rinehart and Winston, Inc.

Mitchell, K. J., Johnson, M. K., Raye, C. L., Mather, M., & D'Esposito, M. (2000). Aging and reflective processes of working memory: Binding and test load deficits. *Psychology and Aging, 15*, 527–541.
Miyake, A., Friedman, N. P., Emerson, M. J., Witzki, A. H., & Howerter, A. (2000). The unity and diversity of executive functions and their contributions to complex "frontal lobe" tasks: A latent variable analysis. *Cognitive Psychology, 41*, 49–100.
Morey, C. C., & Cowan, N. (2004). When visual and verbal memories compete: Evidence of cross-domain limits in working memory. *Psychonomic Bulletin & Review, 11*, 296–301.
Morey, C. C., & Cowan, N. (2005). When do visual and verbal memories conflict? The importance of working-memory load and retrieval. *Journal of Experimental Psychology: Learning, Memory, and Cognition, 31*, 703–713.
Mueller, S. T., Seymour, T. L., Kieras, D. E., & Meyer, D. E. (2003). Theoretical implications of articulatory duration, phonological similarity, and phonological complexity in verbal working memory. *Journal of Experimental Psychology: Learning, Memory, and Cognition, 6*, 1353–1380.
Mulligan, N. W., & Lozito, J. P. (2007). Order information and free recall: Evaluating the item-order hypothesis. *Quarterly Journal of Experimental Psychology, 60*, 732–751.
Naveh-Benjamin, M. (2000). Adult age differences in memory performance: Tests of an associative deficit hypothesis. *Journal of Experimental Psychology: Learning, Memory and Cognition, 26*, 1170–1187.
Naveh-Benjamin, M., Cowan, N., Kilb, A., & Chen, Z. (2007). Age-related differences in immediate serial recall: Dissociating chunk formation and capacity. *Memory & Cognition, 35*, 724–737.
Naveh-Benjamin, M., Craik, F. I. M., Guez, J., & Kreuger, S. (2005). Divided attention in younger and older adults: Effects of strategy and relatedness on memory performance and secondary task costs. *Journal of Experimental Psychology: Learning, Memory and Cognition, 31*, 520–537.
Naveh-Benjamin, M., Hussain, Z., Guez, J., & Bar-On, M. (2003). Adult age differences in episodic memory: Further support for an associative-deficit hypothesis. *Journal of Experimental Psychology: Learning, Memory, and Cognition, 29*, 826–837.
Neath, I., Bireta, T. J., & Surprenant, A. M. (2003). The time-based word length effect and stimulus set specificity. *Psychonomic Bulletin & Review, 10*, 430–434.
Oberauer, K. (2002). Access to information in working memory: Exploring the focus of attention. *Journal of Experimental Psychology: Learning, Memory, and Cognition, 28*, 411–421.
Oberauer, K. (2005). Control of the contents of working memory—A comparison of two paradigms and two age groups. *Journal of Experimental Psychology: Learning, Memory, and Cognition, 31*, 714–728.
Pascual-Leone, J. (2005). A neoPiagetian view of developmental intelligence. In O. Wilhelm and R. W. Engle (Eds.), *Understanding and measuring intelligence* (pp. 177–201). London: Sage.
Pascual-Leone, J. A. (1970). Mathematical model for the transition rule in Piaget's developmental stages. *Acta Psychologica, 32*, 301–345.
Pashler, H. (1988). Familiarity and visual change detection. *Perception & Psychophysics, 44*, 369–378.
Posner, M. I., & Konick, A. F. (1966). On the role of interference in short-term retention. *Journal of Experimental Psychology, 72*, 221–231.
Raye, C. L., Johnson, M. K., Mitchell, K. J., Greene, E. J., & Johnson, M. R. (2007). Refreshing: A minimal executive function. *Cortex, 43*, 135–145.
Rosen, V. M., & Engle, R. W. (1997). The role of working memory capacity in retrieval. *Journal of Experimental Psychology: General, 126*, 211–227.
Rosen, V. M., & Engle, R. W. (1998). Working memory capacity and suppression. *Journal of Memory and Language, 39*, 418–436.
Ross-Sheehy, S., Oakes, L. M., & Luck, S. J. (2003). The development of visual short-term memory capacity in infants. *Child Development, 74*, 1807–1822.

Saito, S., & Miyake, A. (2004). On the nature of forgetting and the processing-storage relationship in reading span performance. *Journal of Memory and Language, 50*, 425–443.

Salthouse, T. A. (1985). *A theory of cognitive aging*. Amsterdam: North-Holland.

Salthouse, T. A. (1996). The processing-speed theory of adult age differences in cognition. *Psychological Review, 103*, 403–428.

Saults, J. S., & Cowan, N. (2007). A central capacity limit to the simultaneous storage of visual and auditory arrays in working memory. *Journal of Experimental Psychology: General, 136*, 663–684.

Saxe, M. D., Malleret, G., Vronskaya, S., Mendez, I., Garcia, A. D., Sofroniew, M. V., et al. (2007). Paradoxical influence of hippocampal neurogenesis on working memory. *Proceedings of the National Academy of Sciences (PNAS), 104*, 4642–4646.

Schweickert, R., Guentert, L., & Hersberger, L. (1990). Phonological similarity, pronunciation rate, and memory span. *Psychological Science, 1*, 74–77.

Shah, P., & Miyake, A. (2005). *The Cambridge handbook of visuospatial thinking*. New York: Cambridge University Press.

Slak, S. (1970). Phonemic recoding of digital information. *Journal of Experimental Psychology, 86*, 398–406.

Sperling, G. (1960). The information available in brief visual presentations. *Psychological Monographs, 74*, (Whole No. 498).

Stevanovski, B., & Jolicoeur, P. (2007). Visual short-term memory: Central capacity limitations in short-term consolidation. *Visual Cognition, 15*, 532–563.

Stroop, J. R. (1935). Studies of interference in serial verbal reactions. *Journal of Experimental Psychology, 18*, 643–662.

Taub, H. A. (1974). Coding for short-term memory as a function of age. *Journal of Genetic Psychology, 125*, 309–314.

Towse, J. N., Hitch, G. J., Hamilton, Z., Peacock, K., & Hutton, U. M. Z. (2005). Working memory period: The endurance of mental representations. *Quarterly Journal of Experimental Psychology A: Human Experimental Psychology, 58A*, 547–571.

Treisman, A., & Zhang, W. (2006). Location and binding in visual working memory. *Memory & Cognition, 34*, 1704–1719.

Tuholski, S. W., Engle, R. W., & Baylis, G. C. (2001). Individual differences in working memory capacity and enumeration. *Memory & Cognition, 29*, 484–492.

Tulving, E., & Patkau, J. E. (1962). Concurrent effects of contextual constraint and word frequency on immediate recall and learning of verbal material. *Canadian Journal of Psychology, 16*, 83–95.

Unsworth, N., & Engle, R. W. (2007). The nature of individual differences in working memory capacity: Active maintenance in primary memory and controlled search from secondary memory. *Psychological Review, 114*, 104–132.

Vogel, E. K., McCollough, A. W., & Machizawa, M. G. (2005). Neural measures reveal individual differences in controlling access to working memory. *Nature, 438*, 500–503.

Wechsler, D. (1944). *The measurement of adult intelligence* (3rd edn.). Baltimore, MD: The Williams and Wilkins Company.

Wechsler, D. (1991). *Manual for the Wechsler Intelligence Scale for Children—third edition (WISC-III)*. San Antonio, TX: The Psychological Corporation.

Weiss, V. (1995). Memory span as the quantum of action of thought. *Cahiers de Psychologie Cognitive, 14*, 387–408.

Wheeler, M. E., & Treisman, A. M. (2002). Binding in short-term visual memory. *Journal of Experimental Psychology: General, 131*, 48–64.

Xu, Y., & Chun, M. M. (2006). Dissociable neural mechanisms supporting visual short-term memory for objects. *Nature, 440*, 91–95.

Zelazo, P. D., Craik, F. I. M., & Booth, L. (2004). Executive function across the life span. *Acta Psychologica, 115*, 167–183.

WHAT GOES WITH WHAT? DEVELOPMENT OF PERCEPTUAL GROUPING IN INFANCY

Paul C. Quinn, Ramesh S. Bhatt, and Angela Hayden

Abstract

Pattern perception and organization provide the representations that form the basic processing units in the visual cognition system of adults. This chapter will highlight a line of research investigating the origins and development of such perceptual organization abilities in infants. In particular, the chapter will describe the major theoretical positions on the development of perceptual unit formation and review empirical findings on the operation of a variety of organizational principles that become functional during the first months of life. The results demonstrate that a variety of grouping principles are available for use by infants, although different principles may become functional over different time courses of development, may be governed by different developmental determinants (i.e., maturation vs experience), and not all principles are readily deployed in the manner originally proposed by Gestalt psychologists. The findings also suggest that the principles can yield processing units of an abstract nature and that the operation of the principles can be modulated by top–down influences. © 2008, Elsevier Inc.

THE PSYCHOLOGY OF LEARNING
AND MOTIVATION VOL. 49
DOI: 10.1016/S0079-7421(08)00003-0

I. Introduction

Grouping is considered to be a fundamental perceptual ability in terms of its ability to establish coherence in complex visual scenes (Palmer, 1999). It plays a critical role in generating the representations that form the basic processing units in the visual cognition system of adults. It also serves a cognitive simplification function in terms of reducing the number of things that need our attention (Tversky, 2006). The present chapter will take up the question of how during development human observers come to know which elements of a visual scene should be grouped together to form which objects. The coverage will focus on the theoretical views and empirical evidence addressing the origins and development of perceptual organization abilities in infants. The significance of this body of work is that it provides knowledge about how perceptual units are formed, their nature, and their ontogenesis, as well as how representations of visual pattern information by adults arise from the perceptual units of infants.

Consider the minimal visual display depicted in Fig. 1 in which uniformly black elements of a common shape are presented against a white background. Most adults would perceive the pattern as a whole "triangle," in spite of the fact that there is nothing triangular about the individual elements. One could argue that this perception is hardly surprising given the years of experience with a well-known object that has a name. But this argument begs the developmental question of how a young infant would perceive such a display. Is the display perceived in the initial weeks and months of life as

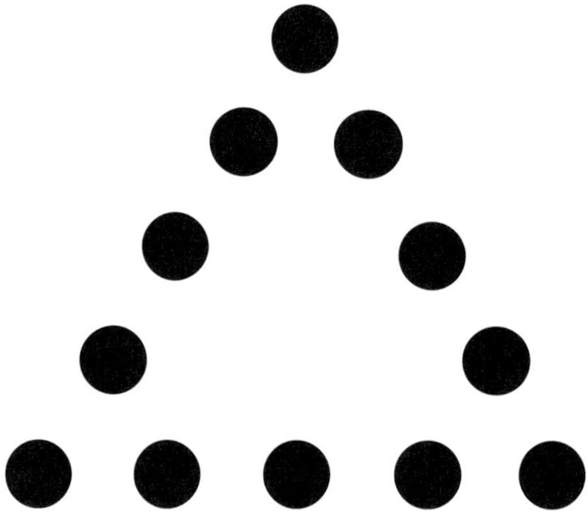

Fig. 1. A pattern of elements that adults organize into a "triangle" form.

black on white—a summation of darkness, a set of dots, a set of spaces between dots, a subset of the dots (enough to represent an angle or corner of the whole form), a single dot, part of a single dot, or the whole form? The question of whether organization of visual pattern information is a starting point for perceptual–cognitive development or whether it is the end product of a slow learning process has been a central concern in perceptual psychology ever since the Gestalt psychologists of the 1920s raised the issue of how we come to know which parts of an image belong together as one object and which belong to different objects (Koffka, 1935; Kohler, 1929; Wertheimer, 1923).

The chapter will begin with a brief description of the major historical positions on how perceptual organization is achieved. This section will be followed by a discussion of some initial empirical work on the problem and its theoretical implications. The chapter will then proceed to a review of recent research examining how infants utilize both classic and modern grouping principles, much of it conducted by members of the authorship team. The conclusion will center on how this new work connects with various aspects of the literature on visual cognition and its development.

II. Historical Views on the Development of Perceptual Organization

A. Hebb

For Hebb (1949), the perception of a whole object was founded in the perception of the individual features of the object and the integration of those perceptions. Perception of wholes was constructed from perceptions of parts. In other words, reality was constructed in the same way that home builders erect houses, piece by piece. Eye movements were an important linking mechanism in Hebb's account of the genesis of perceptual organization—they were used to generate an internal representation of a visual pattern in the same way that an Etch a Sketch toy can be used to plot the outlines of a simple geometric form. As proposed by Hebb, "If line and angle are the bricks from which form perceptions are built, the primitive unity of the figure might be regarded as mortar, and eye movement as the hand of the builder" (p. 83).

If Hebb's (1949) position is taken at face value, then there are serious implications for the development of perceptual organization. In particular, if a young infant was presented with the stimulus in Fig. 1, and the best that infant could do in light of immature eye movements and lack of practice scanning visual patterns would be to fixate the single dot at the lower right corner of the triangle, then the internal representation of the pattern for that particular infant would consist of that single dot. The development of perceptual organization would thus take considerable developmental time and presumably be dependent on the maturation of eye movements that yield more holistic perceptions as visual scanning becomes more systematic. Hebb expresses this idea concisely when he notes that even "simple perceptions" will be "slowly and painfully learned" (p. 77).

B. The Gestaltists

By contrast, the original Gestaltists adopted a nativist stance, contending that perceptual organization was automatic and present even in an initial encounter with a visual pattern. This is so because our perceptual systems are constrained to follow certain grouping principles that operate on the basis of the proximity, similarity, common movement, and good continuation properties of the elements. The perception of one organization over other organizations that are equally physically possible reflects adherence to such grouping principles. As described by Wertheimer (1923), "I see it in this particular combination, this particular segregation; and the sort of combination or segregation in which I see it is not simply up to my choice: it is almost impossible for me to see it in any desired combination that I may happen to choose" (p. 115). Moreover, emphasizing the nativist basis for this organization, Kohler (1929) observes that "sensory units may have acquired names and have become richly symbolic in the context of our knowledge, while existing, nevertheless, as segregated units in the sensory field prior to such accretions" (p. 151). Koffka (1935) seconds this observation with the comment that "Whereas to traditional psychology the articulation of our field into things ... appears as a clear example of experience or learning, our theory considers this articulation as the direct result of the stimulus distribution, that is, as the spontaneous organization aroused by the stimulus mosaic" (p. 209). Finally, in summary form, Kohler concludes that "elementary organization is an original sensory fact" (p. 163).

III. Initial Empirical Efforts and Their Theoretical Implications

A. Salapatek and Eye Movement Recording

At the time that Wertheimer (1923), Kohler (1929), Koffka (1935), and Hebb (1949) were theorizing about the development of perceptual organization, empirical methodologies were not yet available to investigate the perceptual abilities of infants. However, such methods did become available in the 1960s and 1970s, and one technique, in particular, provided some initial data on the debate that had been struck between Hebb and the Gestaltists. Specifically, Salapatek (1975) developed photographic records of infant eye movements while infants were engaged in visual scanning of simple outline figures. Salapatek reported that there was a developmental trend that took place over the first months of life in which scanning was initially limited to single features and gradually expanded to include a set of features and eventually the whole pattern. These eye movement data, considered by themselves, are consistent with a Hebbian account of the development of perceptual organization, although one can question how direct a relation there is between fixation and the window of attention that surrounds the fixation point. That is, if attention is distributed broadly about the fixation point, then it is possible that an infant that fixates the lower right corner of the triangle is actually processing information across the entire portion of the visual field that encompasses the whole pattern. For this reason, a question mark follows what can be concluded from the infant visual scanning patterns, at least as they pertain to the debate over the ontogenesis of perceptual organization.

B. Spelke and Looking-Time Studies

A second source of empirical evidence relevant to the issue of how perceptual grouping emerges comes from behavioral investigations measuring infant looking time to displays of visual elements. These investigations have been able to capitalize on the finding that infants prefer novel stimuli (Fantz, 1964; Slater, 1995). This preference enabled researchers to develop a procedure whereby infants were familiarized with one stimulus and then presented with the familiar stimulus paired with a novel stimulus. A preference for the novel stimulus (not attributable to an a priori preference for that stimulus) implies both memory for the familiar stimulus and the ability to discriminate between it and the novel stimulus. In its simplest form, the procedure could be used to measure, for example, whether infants could discriminate between the "triangle" stimulus shown in Fig. 1 and a stimulus depicting elements with the same shape, size, and number, but arranged in a "square" configuration. Positive evidence in the form of a novelty preference on this task would indicate that infants can discriminate between the two configurations; however, returning to the question at hand, the evidence would not be definitive as to whether infants represented the two patterns as configural wholes because the discrimination could have been featurally based. That is, the infants might simply have differentiated between a diagonal side of the triangle and a vertical side of the square.

To provide behavioral looking-time evidence that can be used to make inferences about the *organization* of infants' representations, researchers have introduced variations in the manner of presenting the familiarization and test stimuli (e.g., testing with two novel stimuli, presenting variants of the familiar stimulus). In a now classic study that followed this general form, one that can be viewed as ushering in the period of modern behavioral work on the development of perceptual organization in infants, Kellman and Spelke (1983) presented 4-month-old infants with a display consisting of a rod partly occluded by a block. The question was whether infants represented the continuity of the rod behind the block based on the Gestalt properties of the visible portions of the rod including their good continuation and similarity of shape and color. To ask this question, after familiarization with the rod–box display, infants were presented with a complete rod and a broken rod. The rationale is that if infants represented the continuity of the rod (i.e., if they had grouped the bottom and top portions of the rod based on their Gestalt qualities), then the infants would respond to the complete rod as familiar and the broken rod as novel. However, if the rod fragments were not grouped together, then the broken rod should be perceived as familiar and the complete rod as novel. The finding was that the infants looked equally to the complete and broken rod displays, a null result that was difficult to interpret. A follow-up experiment was conducted that was a replication of the initial experiment, except that the cue of common motion was added to the visible portions of the rod. In this instance, the infants preferred the broken rod test display, a result indicating that the complete rod had been perceived as familiar and implying that the infants had grouped together the bottom and top portions of the rod.

Unresolved on the basis of the first two experiments of Kellman and Spelke (1983) is the question of the cues that were the basis for the grouping. That is, in the follow-up experiment that included common motion, it could have been the common motion alone that triggered grouping. Alternatively, it could have been the combination of common motion, good continuation, and similarity that was responsible for the grouping. To decide between these possibilities, infants were presented in a third experiment with stimuli that were the same as those used in the second experiment, except that the bottom portion of the rod was replaced with a polygon shape that differed from the top portion of the rod in terms of shape, color, texture, and alignment of its major axis. The finding was that the 4-month-old infants continued to prefer the broken rod, indicating that they had succeeded in grouping the rod with the irregular shape on the basis of common motion information.

Using a similar methodology, Kestenbaum, Termine, and Spelke (1987) reported that same-aged infants perceived the continuity of two adjacent objects as long as the object surfaces were contiguous and even when the surfaces were dissimilar in size, shape, and textural markings. The results of these studies led Spelke (1982) to develop an account of the development of object perception that was in some sense a hybrid model incorporating Gestalt notions of innate organizing principles as well as a role for Hebbian learning based on experience with a structured environment. Specifically,

Spelke argued that infants at birth are constrained by two *core* organizational principles: common movement and connected surface. Adherence to these principles would essentially parse from a visual scene those surfaces that move together and maintain their coherence as they move and grant them the status of objects. The object "blobs" that are the output resulting from observance in accord with the core principles can then be tracked over real time. This type of experience, according to Spelke, allows infants to discover that objects also exhibit other properties including proximity of parts, similarity of surface, and good continuation of contour (see also Brunswik & Kamiya, 1953). In this way, then, what the Gestaltists had taken to be innate organizing principles are by the Spelke account learned through their natural correlation with the common motion and connected surface core principles.

C. Kellman's Take

A different take on the Kellman and Spelke (1983) findings, one that emphasizes biological determinants of development, has been advanced by Kellman and colleagues (Kellman, 1996; Kellman & Arterberry, 1998; Kellman & Shipley, 1991). This account includes two processes, including a "primitive" edge-insensitive process that is presumed to be operational from birth and that utilizes common motion information, and a developmentally later, maturationally determined "rich" edge-sensitive process that becomes available beginning at around 7 months of age and that responds to good continuation information. Thus, according to Kellman, 4-month-olds failed to utilize continuity to organize the static rod–box display in the Kellman and Spelke (1983) study because infants that age lack the edge-sensitive organizing mechanism that is necessary to utilize continuity.

IV. Further Empirical Work on the Classic Grouping Principles

A question that arises from the initial round of behavioral studies investigating infant perceptual organizational abilities concerns the status of grouping principles such as similarity, good continuation, and proximity. While common motion was found to be a more potent determinant of grouping relative to similarity and good continuation in a perceptual display in which the two sources of information were pitted against each other [the rod–polygon experiment of Kellman & Spelke (1983), discussed above], one can ask whether similarity and good continuation might be functional when not in competition with another principle. Moreover, although the principles of similarity and good continuation were not sufficiently strong to provide a basis for grouping when they were the sole sources for organization in the case of partial occlusion with the rod and box display in Kellman and Spelke (1983), it is conceivable that the principles could be functional for displays in which all of the elements are completely visible. In addition, the Kellman and Spelke study investigated only one type of similarity (form), thus leaving unresolved the issue of whether infants might be able to utilize other forms of similarity (e.g., lightness). Furthermore, one other of the classic Gestalt principles, proximity, was not investigated in the Kellman and Spelke experiments, thereby keeping open the question of its functionality.

A. Lightness Similarity

To examine how young infants utilize the classic static Gestalt grouping principles for visual displays consisting of completely visible elements and where other principles are not suggesting an alternative organization, a program of research was undertaken to investigate how infants would respond to arrays of elements that could be organized by one or another principle. An advantage to this approach is that a number of studies assessing use of grouping principles by adults have used such displays, thereby allowing for some level of informed comparison between the two age groups (e.g., Behrmann & Kimchi, 2003b; Ben-Av & Sagi, 1995; Han, Song, Ding, Yung, & Woods, 2001). In the initial study, Quinn, Burke, and Rush (1993) asked whether 3-month-olds could utilize lightness similarity to organize visual pattern information. A schematic of the experimental procedure is depicted in Fig. 2. The familiarization stimuli were columns or rows of squares or

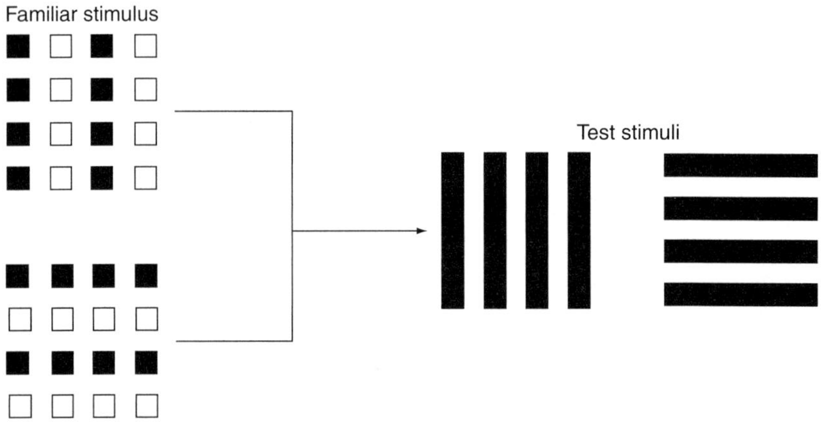

Fig. 2. Familiarization and test stimuli used in the Quinn et al. (1993) study investigating whether 3-month-olds can organize visual pattern information in accord with lightness similarity.

diamonds that could be organized only on the basis of the lightness versus darkness of the elements, and the test stimuli were horizontal versus vertical bars. The rationale is that if the organization in the row and column arrays is apprehended, then infants familiarized with columns should prefer the novel horizontal bars and infants familiarized with rows should prefer the novel vertical bars. These expectations were based on the assumption that the infants would not have an a priori preference for horizontal versus vertical bars. The findings provided positive evidence for the use of lightness similarity: infants preferred the orientation of bars that was oppositely organized relative to the array of elements presented during familiarization, and a control group of infants presented with just the test stimuli and not the familiarization stimuli did not show a differential preference between the two orientations.

Although the results of Quinn et al. (1993) are consistent with the idea that the infants had grouped the individual elements of the arrays into rows or columns based on lightness similarity, they are also consistent with the two other explanations that arise as a consequence of the immature resolution acuity that is present at 3 months of age. Because young infants have at times been characterized as low-pass filters of spatial frequency information (Banks & Salapatek, 1981), it is possible that the loss of high spatial frequency could have been severe enough to cause the individual elements of the displays, both filled and unfilled, to be irresolvable. If this were the case, then the resulting percept would have consisted of two dark vertical or horizontal bars for the column and row displays, respectively. By this account, the differential preferences observed for the test stimuli could simply have been based on infants' abilities to discriminate horizontally versus vertically oriented bars, and infants' utilization of lightness similarity as an organizational principle need not be invoked as the underlying explanation for performance. It is also possible, by the same reasoning, that the loss of high spatial frequency could have produced a less severe resolution deficit, one that would have prevented infants from resolving the unfilled elements, but not the filled ones. In this instance, the familiarization displays could have been organized by infants into two rows or columns of filled elements based on the proximity of the elements. A grouping principle would thus have been the basis for performance, but not the one hypothesized.

To assess the possibilities that infant performance could have been rooted in either orientation discrimination or proximity-based grouping, Quinn et al. (1993) removed from the column and row stimuli all spatial frequencies above 4 cy/deg, the cutoff spatial frequency for 3-month-old infants as estimated from preferential looking measures (Banks & Salapatek, 1978). The resulting pattern is shown in the top panel of Fig. 3. Both the filled and unfilled squares are resolvable, even though some sharpness has been lost, an observation that is confirmed when the squares are changed to diamonds in

Fig. 3. Patterns with spatial frequencies above 4 cycles/degree removed. While the individual elements of the patterns have lost some "sharpness," their shape (square or diamond) remains clearly discernable. From Quinn et al. (1993).

the middle and bottom panels, and the change is readily apprehended. The results of this spatial frequency analysis of the information that should be available to 3-month-olds suggests that the infants had sufficient resolution acuity to perceive the individual elements of the displays and group them into rows or columns based on lightness similarity. This suggestion was subsequently confirmed in a behavioral experiment, in which one group of infants was familiarized with the row or column displays consisting entirely of square or diamond elements (the displays of square elements are those shown in Figs. 4 and 5) and then tested with the familiar array paired with a novel array in the same organization in which either the filled (Fig. 4) or unfilled (Fig. 5) elements were changed (from square to diamond or vice versa). Another group of infants was familiarized with hybrid arrays in row or column organization, either filled squares plus unfilled diamonds or unfilled squares plus filled diamonds, and tested with the familiar array paired with a novel array consisting of entirely square or diamond elements in the same organization. The infants in each group preferred the novel array, irrespective of whether the change occurred for the filled or unfilled elements. Both the spatial frequency analysis and positive discrimination performance in the element change tasks thus support the lightness similarity account.

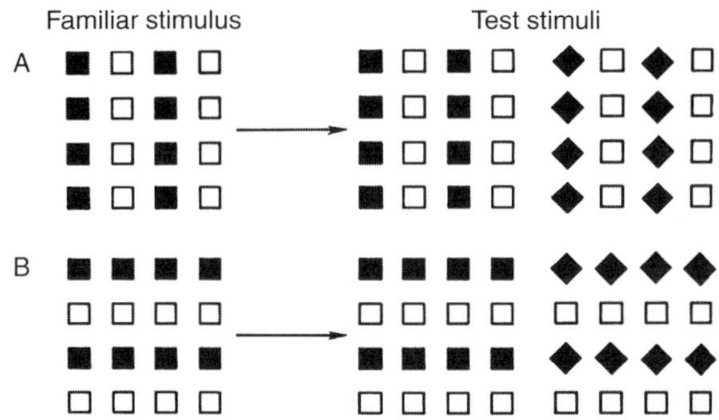

Fig. 4. Familiarization and test stimuli used to assess detection of a change in the dark (filled) elements. From Quinn et al. (1993).

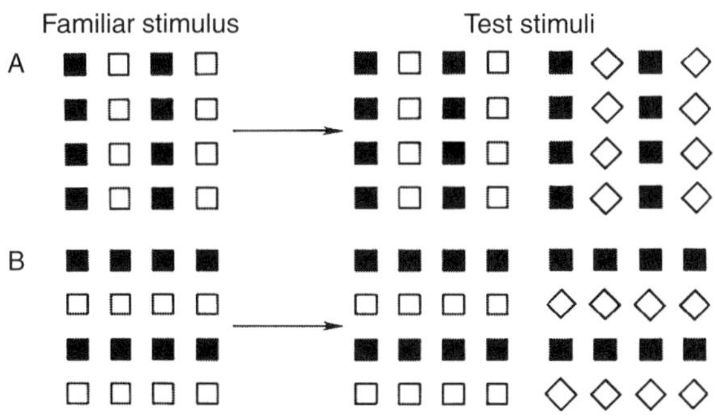

Fig. 5. Familiarization and test stimuli used by Quinn et al. (1993) to assess detection of a change in the light (unfilled) elements.

Convergent evidence for the conclusion that infants can use lightness similarity to organize visual pattern information was obtained in the experimental procedure depicted in Fig. 6. In the top panel, it can be seen that one group of infants was presented with rows or columns of elements and then tested with the familiar array and an array that was rotated by 90° to yield the opposite organization. If infants can use lightness similarity to organize the patterns, the expectation is that this should be an easy discrimination, with the one stimulus represented as "rows" and the other as "columns." In contrast, in the bottom panel, another group of infants was presented with an unorganized array of light and dark elements and then tested with the familiar array and its 90° rotation. The expectation is that this should be a more difficult discrimination for the infants, given the absence of different Gestalts by which to differentiate between the patterns. The results were that infants distinguished between the organized, but not the unorganized, arrays of elements. These findings lend corroborating support to the conclusion that young infants group elements on the basis of lightness similarity and can form "row" versus "column" Gestalts as a consequence of deploying the principle.

B. Good Continuation

A second classic static principle investigated in the same line of studies was that of good continuation (Quinn & Bhatt, 2005a). Adapting a methodology that had been used to investigate good continuation grouping by adults (Prinzmetal & Banks, 1977), infants as young as 3 months of age were administered the experimental procedure depicted in Fig. 7. The displays consisted of a line of distractor circular elements and a target element that was either a square or diamond. Infants were presented with one pattern and

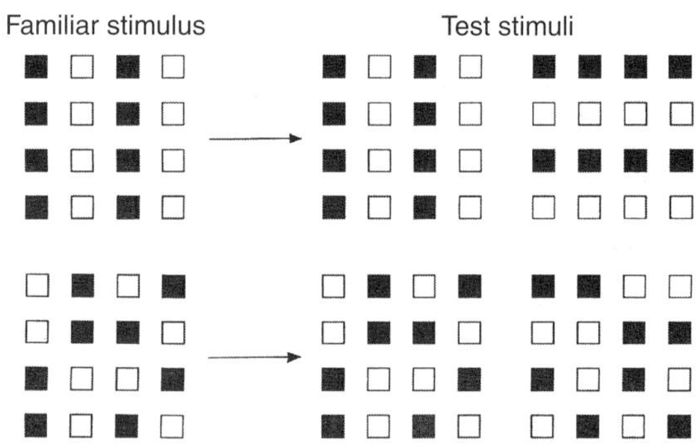

Fig. 6. Illustration of the discrimination task used by Quinn et al. (1993) to test for perceptual organization by lightness similarity.

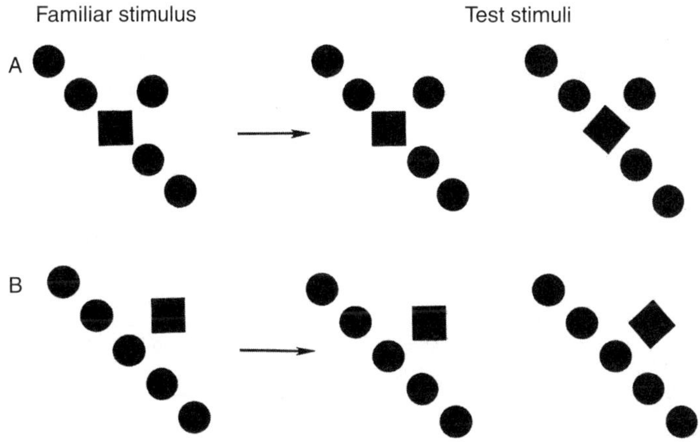

Fig. 7. Examples of the familiarization and test stimuli used in Quinn and Bhatt (2005a). The in-line condition is depicted in Panel A; the off-line condition is shown in Panel B. Experimental design was fully counterbalanced so that for half of the infants in each condition, the target element in the familiar stimulus was a square; for the other half, it was a diamond.

then tested for discrimination between the familiar pattern and a novel one. In the top Panel (A), the target element appeared in line (and thus in good continuation) with the distractor elements, whereas in the bottom Panel (B), the target element was off line with the distractor elements. The expectation is that if infants perceive the patterns in accord with good continuation, then the change in the target element should be more difficult to detect when the target element is in a good continuation relation with the distractor elements. In other words, if good continuation is functional, then the target element would be grouped with the distractors, thus making it less likely that a change in its form would be registered. By contrast, in the off-line condition, the target element would not group with the distractors and would retain its status as an independently processed unit of information, thereby increasing the likelihood that a change in its form would be detected. The findings were that infants preferred the novel test stimulus in the off-line condition, but not in the in-line condition. This evidence suggests good continuation as a second organizational principle that is available to young infants for the grouping of visual elements.

C. Proximity

A third classic static grouping principle investigated in this program of research was that of proximity (Quinn, Bhatt, & Hayden, 2008). As may be observed in Fig. 8, using the same row versus column methodology employed

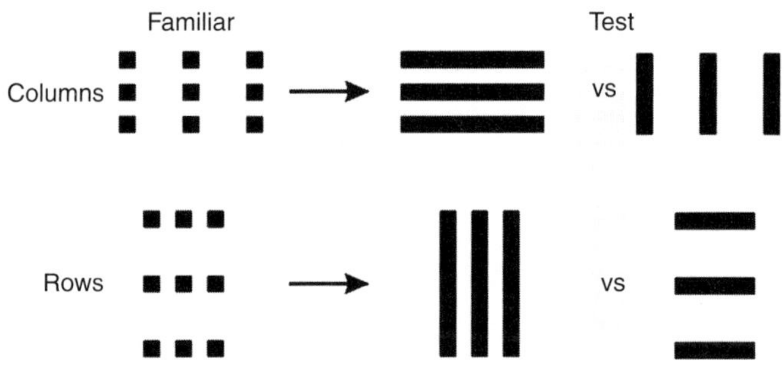

Fig. 8. Familiarization and test stimuli used to determine whether infants adhere to proximity when organizing visual patterns. From Quinn et al. (2008).

by Quinn et al. (1993), 3- to 4-month-old infants were presented with the arrays of elements that could be organized into rows or columns of elements on the basis of proximity, and then tested with horizontal versus vertical bars. The infants preferred the test stimuli with the novel organization, and subsequent control experiments indicated that these preferences could not be attributed to an a priori preference (i.e., the infants did not spontaneously prefer one test stimulus over another when they were presented without a familiarization stimulus) or to an inability to resolve the elements within the rows and columns (i.e., the infants discriminated between arrays where the only difference was whether the arrays consisted of square or diamond elements). The findings suggest that proximity joins lightness similarity and good continuation as a grouping principle that can be used to organize visual pattern information by young infants.

One may ask at this point in the presentation whether the results of the studies investigating use of lightness similarity, good continuation, and proximity by infants are inconsistent with the findings from Kellman and Spelke (1983). The answer is not necessarily, inasmuch as proximity was not investigated in the earlier investigation and lightness similarity was the principle at issue in Quinn et al. (1993), whereas form similarity was the principle examined in Kellman and Spelke. In addition, in the Quinn et al. (1993), Quinn and Bhatt (2005a), and Quinn et al. (2008) studies, all of the elements were completely visible, whereas in the Kellman and Spelke investigation, one object was partly occluded by the other. This last point of comparison would actually be consistent with the possibility that principles such as similarity and good continuation are functional in young infants for displays of completely visible elements, but perhaps not yet operational in cases of partial occlusion, an arguably more complex perceptual display. This observation is in turn suggestive of an ontogenetic trajectory in which infants initially deploy these principles in simple perceptual displays and then with development come to utilize them more powerfully and flexibly so that they can be applied to increasingly more intricate perceptual displays of visual pattern information. A similar claim has been made about the ontogenesis of perceptual categorization, namely, that with development, infants become more skilled at using inherent categorization abilities to represent less well-structured classes of information (Younger & Gotlieb, 1988). And a related conclusion has also been reached about how infants develop physical reasoning skills that are initially applied simply and narrowly, but become more sophisticated and more broadly utilized with development (Baillargeon, 2002).

V. Infants' Use of a Classic Grouping Principle to Organize a More Complex Stimulus

To examine how well infants organize more complex visual configurations that at least begin to approximate the processing demands of more natural scenes where multiple objects with overlapping contours may be depicted, Quinn, Brown, and Streppa (1997) investigated how young infants would represent the pattern shown in Panel A of Fig. 9. This stimulus may present infants with an organizational task that may be thought of as intermediate in difficulty level relative to those used by Quinn et al. (1993) on the one hand and Kellman and Spelke (1983) on the other. That is, given that the stimulus is composed of outline contours that intersect, rather than surfaces that occlude, the stimulus seems intuitively easier to organize than the rod–box display. However, because of the various possible interpretations of pattern in Panel A of Fig. 9, infants are presented with an arguably more difficult organizational task than is the case when a single pattern depicting elements

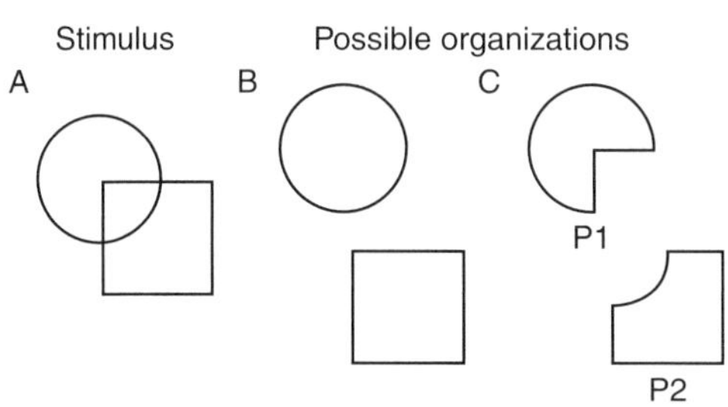

Fig. 9. Intersecting circle–square stimulus in (A) and two possible organizations in (B) and (C). Adherence to the Gestalt principle of good continuation favors organization (B) over organization (C). From Quinn et al. (1997).

that are completely visible is presented. The pattern of intersecting lines must be parsed into a set of primitive contours, and these contours must be organized into coherent representations of whole shapes. For example, adults tend to parse and organize this pattern into the square and circle shapes shown in Panel B of Fig. 9, rather than the pacman shapes shown in Panel C. Presumably adults are following the Gestalt organizational principle of good continuation to represent the pattern information in this manner.

To determine whether young infants would parse and organize the pattern shown in Panel A of Fig. 9 into the square and circle shapes perceived by adults, a group of 3- to 4-month-olds was familiarized in an experiment with the overlapping square–circle configuration and then preference tested with the circle versus the pacman shape shown in the top portion of Panel C (call it P1) and the square versus the pacman shape shown in the bottom portion of Panel C (call it P2). There are at least three ways in which infants may represent the familiar pattern information, each of which would produce a distinct pattern of looking among the test stimuli. First, if infants parse the pattern and organize its contours into the circle and square shapes in accord with the Gestalt principle of good continuation, then the circle and square shapes should be recognized as familiar in preference tests with P1 and P2, and P1 and P2 should be preferred. Second, if infants do not parse the unitary configuration, and the outcome is a representation of an unparsed whole, or if infants parse the configuration into more than one whole, but not the wholes predicted by adherence to good continuation, then one would not expect a consistent preference for P1 or P2 in either test. Third, infants may have spontaneous preferences for certain stimulus features (e.g., curvature, horizontal/vertical line elements) that could eventuate in parsing of the configuration and selective organization of the preferred features into either the circle or square. In this case, one would expect a preference for the pacman shape (P1 or P2) in one or the other preference test, but not both.

The results were that infants preferred the pacman shapes in both preference tests, a pattern of looking that is consistent with the idea that infants had organized the familiar configuration into the circle and square shapes in a manner predicted by adherence to the Gestalt principle of good continuation. Moreover, the findings imply that infant utilization of the classic static grouping principles is not limited to cases of stimuli where all the elements are completely visible, even though they may not be fully operational for even more complex cases involving stimuli depicting partial occlusion.

A potentially informative effect that was observed in Quinn et al. (1997) is that there was a spontaneous preference observed in a control group of infants who were assessed for possible a priori preferences among the test patterns. Specifically, without prior familiarization experience, the P2 shape was significantly preferred to the square. Although the novelty preference for

P2 over the square in the experimental group occurred above and beyond that of the a priori preference for P2 in the control group, it is interesting to consider the possible significance of the spontaneous preference for P2. The critical physical difference between P2 and the square is the presence of a curved contour in P2 and the absence of it in the square. In addition, there is evidence that infants have a spontaneous preference for curved over rectilinear contours (Fantz, Fagan, & Miranda, 1975). It is conceivable that the a priori preference for P2 is more than just a potential confound, a noise factor to be acknowledged, but then ruled out with appropriate statistical tests. The curvature-based preference for the P2 stimulus may help answer the question: How does the infant initially begin to break down a complex stimulus into a set of component contours? More specifically, where on the stimulus does the infant begin the complementary processes of parsing and organization? It may be that spontaneous preferences for some stimulus features over others could play an important "START HERE" role in initiating the parsing process for an unanalyzed configuration that contains a number of diverse features. A curvature preference, combined with a Gestalt principle like good continuation, may have allowed infants to first develop a representation for the circle shape. Once the circle was organized, infant attention may then have been free to explore other portions of the stimulus, thereby allowing for organization of the remaining contours into the square shape.

VI. Infants' Utilization of New Grouping Principles

While the grouping principles discussed thus far have been known to psychologists at least since the pioneering work of the early Gestaltists in the 1920s, the grouping principles that will be examined in this section, uniform connectedness (UC) and common region, were introduced by Palmer and Rock in the 1990s (Palmer, 1992, 1999; Palmer & Rock, 1994; Rock & Palmer, 1990). Although there has been some research aimed at understanding how adults use these principles to group stimuli (e.g., Kimchi, 2000), to our knowledge, the studies to be reviewed in this section are the only ones to directly examine whether infants group visual elements in accord with these principles (although the work of Kestenbaum et al., 1987, is clearly consistent with the idea that infants use a connected surface principle when determining how visual surfaces should be separated into distinct objects).

A. Uniform Connectedness

Rock and Palmer (1990) introduced the principle of UC to refer to the visual system's tendency to group together elements that are connected. They also suggested that "connectedness ... may be the most fundamental principle of grouping yet uncovered" (p. 86), and argued that it is needed to even determine that each local element in a configuration is itself a local entity. To examine whether sensitivity to UC is functional in early infancy, as shown in Fig. 10, infants as young as 3 months of age were habituated to the uniformly connected patterns shown in Panels A or B, and then administered a preference test pairing connected elements (Panel C) with disconnected elements (Panel D) (Hayden, Bhatt, & Quinn, 2006). The rationale is that if the infants organized the habituation patterns on the basis of UC, then they should respond to the connected-element test stimulus as familiar and display a novelty preference for the disconnected-element test stimulus. This is the result that was observed, and a control condition showed that there was no a priori preference for the disconnected-element test stimulus when it was paired with the connected-element test stimulus without a prior habituation stimulus. The findings of Hayden et al. (2006) indicate that infants by 3 months of age are sensitive to UC as an organizing principle. It is the contention of Palmer and Rock (1994) that the operation of UC allows for the delineation of entry-level units that can then be organized into holistic percepts according to other classic grouping principles such as proximity and similarity. By this reasoning, the Hayden et al. data imply that 3-month-olds are able to use UC to identify the entry-level units that are then subject to further perceptual organization.

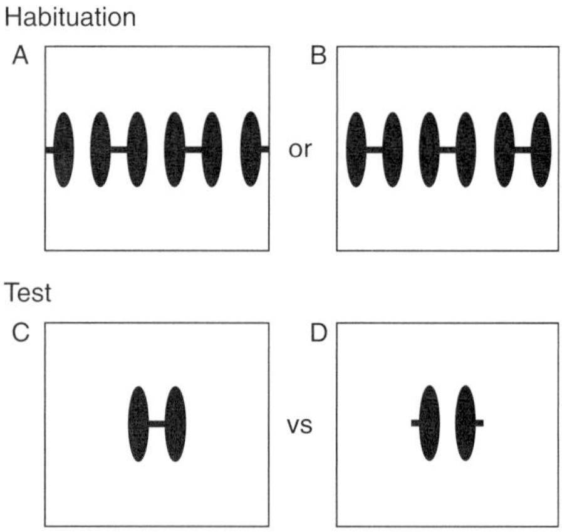

Fig. 10. The stimuli used in Hayden, Bhatt, and Quinn (2006). Infants in the habituation conditions were habituated to the uniformly connected patterns in Panel A or B and tested with the patterns in Panels C and D. Infants in the no-habituation condition were tested with the patterns in Panels C and D without prior exposure to the patterns in Panels A and B.

B. Common Region

The second newer grouping principle investigated was that of common region (Bhatt, Hayden, & Quinn, 2007). This principle proposes that elements within a region are grouped together and are separated from those in other regions (Palmer, 1992). According to Palmer, grouping on the basis of common region helps to "organize texture elements within a contour as going with each other and as belonging to the surface or object that is bounded by the contour" (pp. 445–446). Palmer has also suggested that common region might be a different kind of organizational cue than classic Gestalt cues because here the organization is driven by a characteristic that is external to the elements themselves (see also Beck & Palmer, 2002). That is, the "common region" quality that engenders grouping of the elements is not inherent in the elements themselves. In contrast, other grouping principles, such as similarity, are based on the intrinsic characteristics of the to-be-grouped elements themselves. Palmer thus differentiated between "extrinsic" versus "intrinsic" organizational cues and suggested that common region is an extrinsic cue. This distinction raises the possibility that common region could be a different *kind* of organizational cue than many others, thereby adding to the importance of understanding its emergence in young infants to see if it is somehow unique.

To investigate whether young infants could use common region to organize visual pattern information, 3- to 4-month-olds were familiarized to images with two pairs of shapes, with one pair (say A and B) always located together in a region and the other pair (say C and D) located together in another region (see Fig. 11). The actual location of the individual shapes changed from one trial to the next but the shapes A and B always shared a region while the shapes C and D shared another region. Infants were then tested for their preference between a *within-region* grouping (e.g., AB) versus a *between-region* grouping (e.g., BC; see Fig. 11). The stimulus patterns presented to the infants were such that the physical distance between A and B and between B and C was always the same. In other words, the only difference in the relationships between A and B versus B and C was that the former pair always shared the same region while the latter pair contained shapes from different regions. If the principle of common region is operational in infancy, then the fact that the A and B elements always shared the same region should lead to the grouping of these elements. Thus, infants should find the *within-region* grouping to be familiar and the *between-region* grouping to be novel and discriminate between these patterns during the test. In addition, in a control condition, infants experienced the same habituation and test patterns as in the experimental condition, except for the fact that the stimulus patterns in the habituation phase were not organized into regions (see Fig. 11). Thus, a difference between performances in the experimental versus control conditions would indicate the role of common region as an organizing cue.

It should be noted that the experiment of Bhatt et al. (2007) is a demanding one in that it asks if grouping will carry over to novel regions, given that infants were habituated to vertical regions during habituation and tested with novel horizontal regions. In other words, this experiment gets at the question of whether, when elements that were previously grouped based on a set of regions are subsequently encountered in novel regional configurations, does the visual system expect this grouping to be intact? If grouping and perceptual organization are to be functionally advantageous, they need to allow the world to be organized into meaningful entities that transcend particular situations. For instance, if a perceiver were to be exposed to two standing

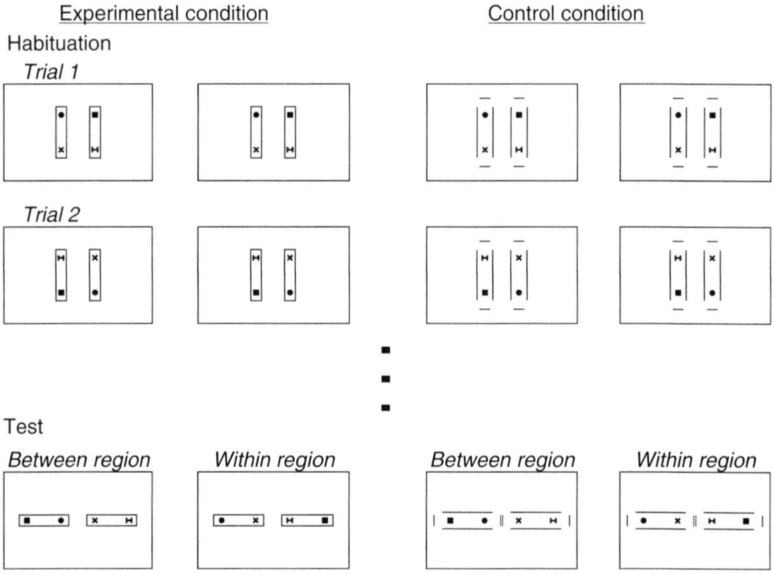

Fig. 11. Examples of the stimuli used in Bhatt et al. (2007). Infants in the *experimental group* were habituated to two pairs of shapes, with one pair sharing a vertical region and the other pair a different vertical region. Infants were then tested for their preference between a pair of shapes that had shared a common region during habitation (*within-region* pair) versus a pair of shapes that had been in different regions during habituation (*between-region* pair) both presented in novel horizontal regions. Infants in the *control group* saw the same kind of patterns, except for the fact that their stimuli did not contain enclosed regions. The habituation patterns and the pairs of shapes that comprised the *within-region* and *between-region* patterns were counterbalanced across infants.

humans and were to associate the individual faces to the individual bodies, then, for this organization to be functional, the perceiver should expect the same grouping to prevail if the humans were now lying down.

The major result from the Bhatt et al. (2007) study was that the infants in the experimental condition exhibited a familiarity preference. Although differentiation of the patterns on the basis of a familiarity preference was unexpected, this result suggests that infants found the grouping of elements from different regions to be different from the grouping of elements that had shared a common region during habituation. In contrast, infants in the control condition failed to exhibit a preference during the test. Moreover, the novelty preference score of the experimental group was significantly different from the novelty preference score of the control group. These results indicate that the infants in the experimental condition organized information based on common region and preferred to look at a familiar grouping, whereas infants in the control condition in which enclosed regions were not present failed to group elements. The findings are also impressive in terms of demonstrating that infants generalize grouping based on the principle of common region to novel regions.

While infants provided evidence of the use of common region to organize information in Bhatt et al. (2007), this conclusion was based on a familiarity preference, that is, a preference for a grouped pattern that was similar to that seen during habituation (combination of elements within the same region) over a grouped pattern that was different from that seen during habituation (combination of elements from different regions). Logically, this result is indicative of the role of common region because any discrimination must have been driven by the status of the grouping based on common region. Infants exhibit a familiarity preference when the stimulus patterns that they are exposed to are complex (e.g., Bhatt, Hayden, Reed, Bertin, & Joseph, 2006; Cohen, 2004; Fiser & Aslin, 2002; Hunter & Ames, 1988; Roder, Bushnell, & Sasseville, 2000), and that may be the reason for the infants' exhibition of a familiarity preference.

As mentioned earlier, Palmer (1992) suggested that common region might be a fundamentally different kind of organizational cue than most classic Gestalt cues because it is an "extrinsic" grouping principle in the sense that the organization of elements is based on external factors (being part of a common region), whereas many other organization cues are intrinsic in the sense that the organization depends upon the characteristics of the elements themselves (e.g., lightness similarity, which depends upon the surface lightness of the elements). The finding from Bhatt et al. (2007) that infants are sensitive to common region suggests, therefore, that the extrinsic nature of common region did not preclude its role as an organizing cue in infancy. In other words, infants, like adults, are not solely dependent upon the intrinsic nature of elements to organize them; they are able to use extrinsic factors such as common region to organize.

Another point of contact between the results of Bhatt et al. (2007) and the larger visual cognition literature concerns the fact that adults organize information based not only on spatial aspects of images but also on objects. Thus, for example, researchers have found that the attentional system of adults can be object based—in the sense that, once attention is directed to a portion of an object, it is easier to move focus to another spot on the same object than an equivalent distance to another object (e.g., Egly, Driver, & Rafal, 1994; Vecera & Behrmann, 2001). Based on these findings, the Bhatt et al. results can be described as indicating that infants are sensitive to changes that cross object boundaries and that they preferentially group features from the same object over features from different objects. This observation in turn raises the question of whether it may be more accurate to classify the Bhatt et al. outcomes as involving object-based processing or region-based processing.

Our inclination is to characterize the Bhatt et al. (2007) investigation as involving the study of common region instead of object-based processing because we view the common region principle as being more basic than the notion of objects. "Objecthood" is a complex construct and assumes the encoding of certain organizational structures such as 3-D shape that may or may not have been attained by the infants in our experiments. In contrast, regional analysis can function at an earlier level of visual processing, perhaps at the level of the 2-D image itself (i.e., before depth and other 3-D information have been processed; see Palmer, 1992). Thus, our view is that it is more conservative to characterize the current research as involving the perception of common regions than of objects. Nevertheless, we believe that further theoretical and empirical analyses of the relations between the notions of common region and object-based processing are necessary for a more comprehensive understanding of perceptual organization and its development.

VII. Classic Grouping Principles Reconsidered: The Special Case of Form Similarity

Although the proposals of Spelke (1982) and Kellman (1996) reviewed at the beginning of the chapter suggested that important cues for grouping and perceptual unit formation were not available to young infants, the results of the last two sections of the chapter have provided evidence that infants as young as 3 months of age can use a variety of static grouping principles, both classic and modern ones, to organize visual pattern information. In particular, the findings indicate that the principles of similarity, proximity, good continuation, UC, and common region are functional in at least some perceptual contexts, and the outcomes of the good continuation and common region studies suggest that the principles may be operative even for visual displays that involve complexities such as parsing patterns with intersecting contours and generalization of elements across novel regions. These data suggest that some level of revision is in order with regard to thinking about the sources of information available to younger infants for perceptual grouping.

Still, it needs to be acknowledged that this chapter has yet to consider the role of form information in perceptual grouping. Form information and its relative lack of availability as an organizing cue to younger infants were central to the proposals of Spelke (1982) and Kellman (1996). Yet, one might ask: Given that lightness similarity was shown to be functional in young infants, why is there a need to show that form similarity is also operational? The answer is that, at least in the adult literature, there is evidence for distinct systems for grouping on the basis of luminance and edge information (Gilchrist, Humphreys, Riddoch, & Neumann, 1997). Also, neuropsychological research indicates that different grouping processes can fractionate across visual agnosic patients; for example, some visual agnosics show intact grouping by lightness similarity, but impaired configuring and shape formation abilities (Behrmann & Kimchi, 2003b). In addition, grouping by lightness similarity has been shown to be superior to grouping by shape similarity in individuals with Williams syndrome (Farran, 2005). These observations raise the possibility that form similarity might behave differently than lightness similarity in early development. It therefore becomes important to ask whether form similarity can serve as a perceptual grouping principle for young infants.

A. Development of Form Similarity: An Age Difference in Performance

The functionality of form similarity in young infants was examined by Quinn, Bhatt, Brush, Grimes, and Sharpnack (2002), who drew upon the row versus column methodology used to investigate lightness similarity and proximity. As can be seen in Fig. 12, 3- to 4-month-olds were familiarized with rows or columns of Xs versus Os, and then tested with horizontal versus vertical bars. The rationale follows that of the earlier lightness similarity and proximity studies: if the infants could group the familiarization stimulus into rows or columns on the basis of form similarity, then they should prefer the novel organization of bars during test. However, the infants did not display such a preference; instead, they divided their attention between the test stimuli. Given that this null result did not provide evidence that infants

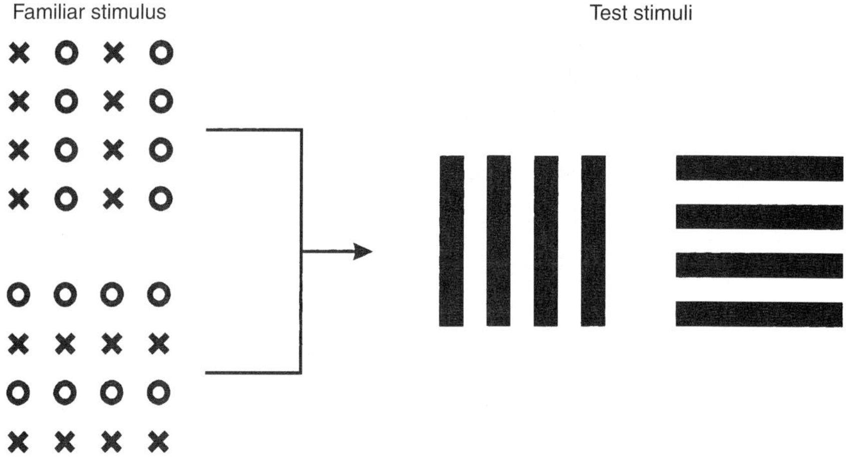

Fig. 12. Examples of the familiarization and test stimuli used in the elements → bars generalization task to test for perceptual organization by form similarity in Quinn et al. (2002).

could group by form similarity, Quinn et al. (2002) asked whether infants might simply need more study time with the familiarization stimulus to organize it. To this end, the initial experiment was repeated, but in this case, with double the familiarization time. Once more, the infants divided their attention between the test stimuli, still not providing evidence of grouping by form similarity.

Given the two null outcomes, Quinn et al. (2002) questioned whether the infants could even discriminate between the X and O elements comprising the rows and columns of the stimulus arrays. If the infants could not differentiate the shapes, then there would be no basis for grouping the elements into larger perceptual units (i.e., rows vs columns). To examine the abilities of the infants to distinguish between the X and O shapes, 3- to 4-month-olds were familiarized with columns or rows of Xs and Os and then given a preference test in which the choice was between the familiar array and a novel array consisting entirely of Xs or Os. Representative experimental sequences are presented in Fig. 13. A separate group of 3- to 4-month-olds was familiarized with a pattern consisting entirely of X or O elements, and then given a preference test pairing the familiar array with a pattern consisting of columns or rows of Xs and Os. For both groups, a preference for the novel array would suggest that the infants had detected and processed the element information within the columns or rows. The infants preferred the novel array indicating that the failure to perform in accord with the form similarity principle was not due to an inability to discriminate between the constituent X and O shapes.

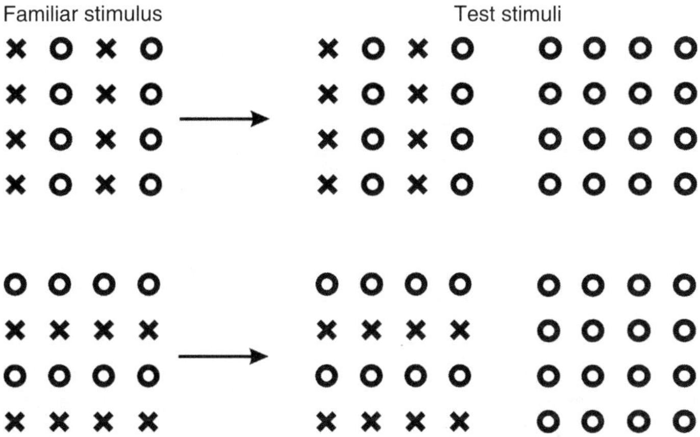

Fig. 13. Examples of the familiarization and test stimuli used to test for discrimination of elements in Quinn et al. (2002).

A further attempt to explore whether 3- to 4-month-olds could, under some set of experimental conditions, be shown to use form similarity was motivated by the possibility that the infants might have organized the arrays into columns or rows of elements, but then had difficulty generalizing their representations of these perceptual units to the bar stimuli presented during the test trials. Although generalization from elements to bars did not impair infants' ability to demonstrate their use of lightness similarity as a grouping principle, it is possible that it could have interfered with infants' ability to demonstrate their use of form similarity. Quinn et al. (2002) therefore assessed 3- to 4-month-olds' ability to use form similarity using the organized versus unorganized discrimination task that was previously used to establish convergent evidence for young infants' use of lightness similarity. As is depicted in Fig. 14, the infants were randomly assigned to one of two discrimination conditions. In the organized discrimination condition (top panel), infants were familiarized with one organized pattern (e.g., columns) and then given a preference test that paired this pattern with its 90° rotation (e.g., rows). In the unorganized discrimination condition (bottom panel), infants were familiarized with a random arrangement of elements and then tested with this pattern and its 90° rotation. The rotation manipulation resulted in a clear, new global identity for the pattern only in the organized discrimination condition, so successful discrimination performance would be expected in this condition if grouping by form similarity were in operation. The major finding was that infants did not prefer the novel stimulus in either condition, thus providing additional evidence indicating that 3- to 4-month-olds do not use form similarity to organize visual pattern information.

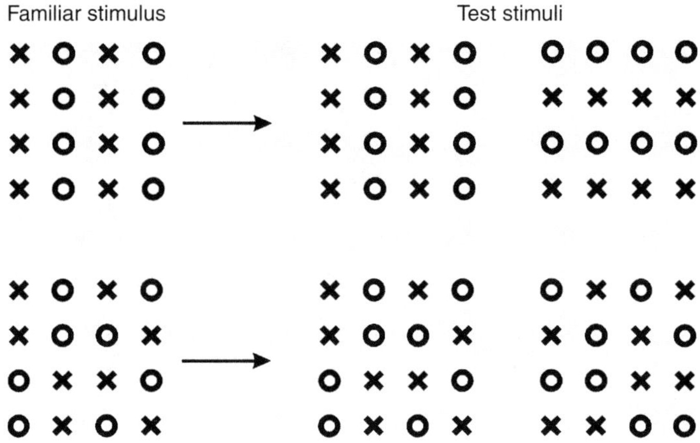

Fig. 14. Examples of the familiarization and test stimuli used in the organized versus unorganized discrimination task to test for perceptual organization by form similarity in Quinn et al. (2002).

With the data thus far described failing to turn up support for young infants' use of form similarity, Quinn et al. (2002) tested older infants, 6- to 7-month-olds, on both the X-O elements → bars generalization task depicted in Fig. 12 and the X-O organized versus unorganized discrimination task shown in Fig. 14. This age group responded to the generalization task and the organized discrimination task by preferring the novel stimulus organization. The combined findings from the two age groups indicate that 6- to 7-month-olds, but not 3- to 4-month-olds, can organize visual patterns in accord with form similarity.

In combination with the outcomes indicating that 3-month-olds can utilize lightness similarity to organize visual pattern information (Quinn et al., 1993), the present findings indicating that only 6- to 7-month-olds can use form similarity are consistent with the earlier accounts of perceptual unit formation which suggested that different Gestalt principles may become functional over different time courses of development. The outcomes are consistent, in particular, with the hypothesized age of onset for the edge-sensitive process (Kellman, 1996), and also with Spelke's (1982) proposal that some Gestalt principles may be learned in a constructivist framework, rather than automatically deployed as originally conceived by the Gestaltists (e.g., Kohler, 1929). The data are additionally consistent with the evidence indicating that adults have independent luminance- and edge-based grouping mechanisms (Gilchrist et al., 1997). They are further in accord with the finding that some visual agnosics show intact lightness similarity grouping, but impaired shape configuring ability (Behrmann & Kimchi, 2003b) and the result that individuals with Williams Syndrome show superior lightness similarity grouping abilities relative to those for form similarity (Farran, 2005). However, as the next section reveals, young infants' inability to use form information to organize visual images is not absolute.

B. Development of Form Similarity: Maturation or Experience?

Given that the Quinn et al. (2002) results showed a later development of form similarity, Quinn and Bhatt (2005b) sought to determine whether this development was driven by maturation or learning. They reasoned that if form similarity is under experiential control, then it might be possible to find a stimulus or a procedural manipulation that would show that 3- to 4-month-olds would organize visual pattern information in accord with form similarity. Alternatively, if infants' use of form similarity is maturationally determined, then methodological variants would not be expected to bring about positive evidence that form similarity is functional in the younger age group. Given that Quinn et al. (2002) found that the X-O form contrast yielded null results with 3- to 4-month-olds, Quinn and Bhatt tested this age group with two other form contrasts, square versus diamond geometric shapes or H versus I letter shapes, on the elements → bars generalization version of the form similarity organization task. The task and the three different form contrasts are depicted in Fig. 15. Neither of the two additional form contrasts was successful in producing a preference for the novel organization; the infants in each case divided attention between the horizontal and vertical bars. This result suggests that young infants' inability to organize by form similarity is not a specific deficit with Xs versus Os, but rather a phenomenon of a more general nature.

A second attempt by Quinn and Bhatt (2005b) to determine if 3- to 4-month-olds could be induced to use form similarity focused not on the use of different stimuli, but rather on the employment of a different familiarization procedure. Specifically, Quinn and Bhatt asked whether variations in the patterns used to depict rows or columns during familiarization would enhance infants' performance in the form similarity task. One may reason that pattern variation will facilitate performance because the invariant organization of the stimuli will be more easily detected against a changing background. In other words, variation might provide infants with the opportunity to form concepts of "rows" or "columns." To investigate this possibility, the elements → bars generalization version of the form similarity organization task that had previously produced null results (when each of the three different form contrasts was presented individually) was administered, but in this instance, with each of the three form contrasts presented

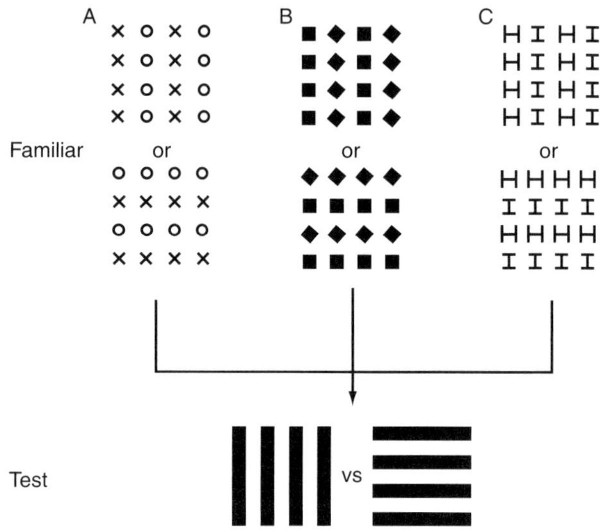

Fig. 15. Familiarization and test stimuli used in Quinn and Bhatt (2005b).

during a single familiarization session. The younger infants now preferred the novel organization of bars. This striking result suggests that 3- to 4-month-olds are capable of using form similarity to organize elements if they are provided with varied examples with which to abstract the invariant arrangement of the pattern. The outcome is theoretically significant because it demonstrates that the ability to use the principle does not have to wait until 6–7 months (cf. Kellman, 1996). The evidence is more consistent with the view that learning may play a role in acquiring some aspects of perceptual organization (Spelke, 1982).

VIII. Lightness Versus Form Similarity: Automatic Versus Constructivist Grouping?

The chapter has thus far documented a developmental difference in the use of lightness and form similarity and has also raised the possibility that grouping by form similarity may occur because of learning taking place via the perceptual experience that accrues during the time course of familiarization. These observations motivated an inquiry into the question of how readily the principles of lightness and form similarity may be deployed. In particular, Quinn and Bhatt (2006) used the row versus column methodology of Quinn et al. (1993, 2002) and Quinn and Bhatt (2005b), except that in this instance, a condition requiring infants to generalize from elements to bars was compared with a condition requiring infants to generalize from bars to elements. That is, one group of infants was familiarized with rows or columns of elements and preference tested with horizontal versus vertical bars, whereas the comparison group tested on the same grouping principle was familiarized with horizontal or vertical bars and preference tested with rows or columns of elements. The lightness similarity version of the bars → elements task is shown in Fig. 16, whereas the form similarity version of this task is depicted in Fig. 17. It is important to mention that in both the lightness and form similarity studies, the familiar stimulus was presented for six 15-s familiarization trials, whereas the test stimuli were presented for two 10-s test trials. The test trials were deliberately kept to few in number and to a short duration to capture a presumed burst of differential responsiveness toward the novel versus familiar stimulus. If there were more test trials or they were made longer in duration, any initial advantage in responsiveness to the novel stimulus could conceivably begin to subside because that stimulus is now becoming familiar.

The rationale behind comparing performance in the elements → bars versus bars → elements versions of the perceptual organization task is that if the Gestalt process that infants use to group by similarity is deployed readily, with the consequence that organization is rapidly apprehended, then one would not expect the nature of the switch from familiarization to test stimuli to affect performance. If, however, Gestalt grouping by similarity occurs less readily, because of learning taking place during the time course of familiarization, then one might expect infants in the elements → bars condition to outperform infants in the bars → elements condition because of the

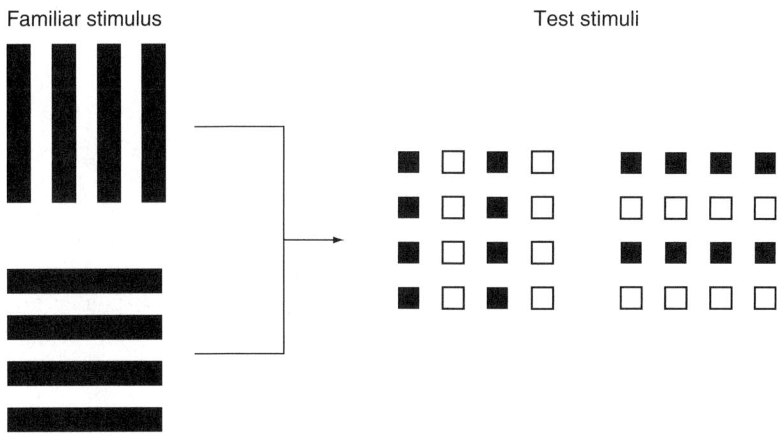

Fig. 16. Illustration of the bars → elements version of the lightness similarity perceptual organization task used in Quinn and Bhatt (2006).

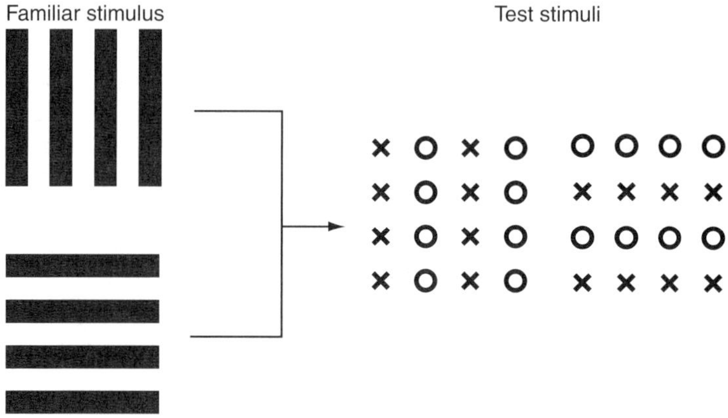

Fig. 17. Illustration of the bars → elements version of the form similarity perceptual organization task used in Quinn and Bhatt (2006).

reduced study time available to process the row versus column stimuli in the bars → elements condition.

Infants in Quinn and Bhatt (2006) were tested at the initial point in developmental time when the principle was shown to be operational for organizing a single visual pattern, 3–4 months for lightness similarity and 6–7 months for form similarity. The results for lightness similarity were that the novel organization was preferred, irrespective of whether infants were familiarized with elements and tested with bars or familiarized with bars and tested with elements. These findings suggest that perceptual organization that occurs via grouping by lightness similarity is readily apprehended. In contrast, in the case of form similarity, the novel organization was preferred only in the elements → bars version of the task. Infants in the bars → elements version of the task divided their attention between the test stimuli. The results indicate that grouping by form similarity was adversely affected by the switch in familiarization and test stimuli, which in turn implies that grouping via form similarity occurs less readily than grouping by lightness similarity. One potential objection to this conclusion is that the type of similarity (lightness vs form) was confounded with age (3–4 months vs 6–7 months). U-shaped patterns of development have on occasion been reported (Siegler, 2004), thereby raising the possibility that older infants might have performed poorly in the bars → elements version of the perceptual organization task, no matter what form of similarity was tested. To respond to this objection, Quinn and Bhatt tested a group of 6- to 7-month-olds on the bars → elements version of the lightness similarity task. The infants performed successfully on the task, thereby weakening an age-based explanation for the performance difference between lightness and form similarity.

The findings of Quinn and Bhatt (2006) imply that lightness and form similarity grouping processes differ qualitatively. That is, lightness similarity grouping processes may be deployed rapidly because they are hardwired. In this view, perceptual organization would be perceived immediately upon presentation with a row or column pattern of light versus dark elements. By contrast, form similarity grouping processes may be learned from perceptual experience. In this account, perceptual organization would be constructed during the course of the familiarization trials. To these observations, one can add the report of Quinn et al. (2008) that young infants performed successfully in a bars → elements version of the proximity organization task shown in Fig. 18. This latter finding suggests that perceptual organization that occurs via grouping by proximity is also readily apprehended. Grouping by proximity thus appears to be more similar to grouping by lightness similarity than grouping by form similarity.

IX. Theoretical Significance and Connections with the Literature

The developmental research highlighted in the present chapter has begun to investigate the origins and development of perceptual unit formation during infancy (Quinn et al., 1993). The data suggest that different organizational principles may become functional over different time courses of development (Quinn et al., 2002), may be governed by different developmental determinants, that is, maturation versus experience (Quinn & Bhatt, 2005b), and that not all principles are readily deployed in the manner originally proposed by Gestalt theorists (Quinn & Bhatt, 2006).

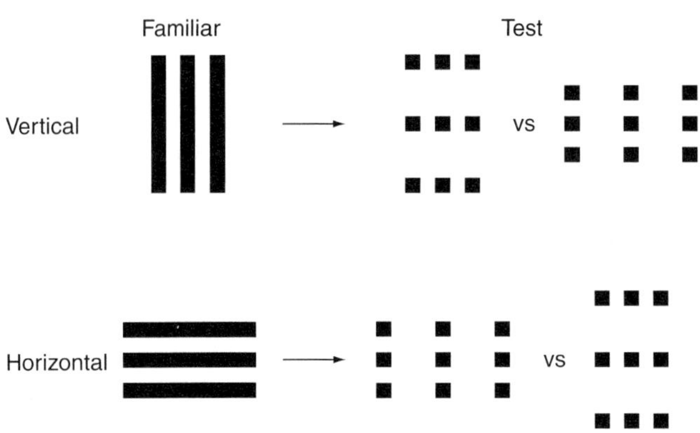

Fig. 18. Familiarization and test stimuli used in the bars → elements version of the proximity grouping task used in Quinn et al. (2008).

A. An Orthogenic Perspective

The findings reviewed are consistent with recent investigations of perceptual grouping in adults that have adopted a microgenetic approach and examined the time course of development of a particular percept (e.g., Kimchi, 2000). The outcomes of these investigations suggest that different grouping principles are differentially powerful or operational at different times in the overall course of processing (Behrmann & Kimchi, 2003a,b). In particular, some forms of perceptual organization occur early in the time course of processing and do not require attention, whereas other forms of perceptual organization occur later in the time course of processing and require attention. This work has led to a newly emerging view that perceptual organization is not a monolithic phenomenon, but rather represents a confluence of multiple processes. The findings that lightness similarity and proximity emerge more readily than form similarity during early development (i.e., in younger infants with just a single example pattern and limited presentation time) suggest a correspondence between what is observed ontogenetically in infants and microgenetically in adults. This correspondence is more generally supportive of an orthogenic approach to understanding perceptual organization (Burack, Enns, Iarocci, & Randolph, 2000; Werner, 1957), one which emphasizes that mechanisms underlying performance become most transparent as they are revealed in the processes of change at different time scales.

B. A Possible Classification Scheme

The empirical coverage in the chapter indicates that good continuation (Quinn et al., 1997; Quinn & Bhatt, 2005a), proximity (Quinn et al., 2008), UC (Hayden et al., 2006), and common region (Bhatt et al., 2007), are all functional in 3- to 4-month-old infants. The early emergence of these principles contrasts with the later emergence of form similarity at 6–7 months when form similarity is investigated under comparable testing conditions (Quinn et al., 2002). The ontogenetic evidence contrasting the relative time course of emergence of the principles of proximity and form similarity in infants is (as noted) consistent with the microgenetic evidence in adults indicating that grouping by proximity occurs more rapidly than grouping by form similarity in the time course of processing (Ben-Av & Sagi, 1995; Han, Humphreys, & Chen, 1999). Taken together, the infant and adult behavioral data are consistent with the classification scheme dividing grouping principles into those that rely on the positioning of the elements versus those that rely on both the positioning and nature of the elements (Pomerantz, 1981, 1983). In particular, good continuation, UC, common region, and proximity are all position-based principles, whereas form similarity also relies on the processing of the shape of the elements being grouped.

C. Relation to the Dorsal–Ventral Debate

The distinction between principles that rely on the positioning of elements versus those that rely on the nature and positioning of elements may cohere with the distinction between dorsal and ventral processing streams (Ungerleider & Mishkin, 1982). It is arguable that positioning-based principles may be mediated by activity in the dorsal stream, whereas principles that additionally rely on information about the nature of the elements may also tap into ventral stream mechanisms. In support of this argument, event related potential (ERP) data from adults indicate that proximity grouping produces relatively more dorsal activation, whereas form similarity grouping produces relatively more ventral activation (Han et al., 2001). Also consistent with this argument is the performance of neuropsychological patient H.J.A. who suffered damage to temporal brain areas in the ventral stream and who displayed intact abilities to organize by proximity, but had difficulties grouping by form similarity (Humphreys, 2003).

If one assumes that the dorsal and ventral processing streams are differentiated during the early months of development (Dobkins, 2005; Johnson & Vecera, 1996), the developmental differences in the emergence of the position-based grouping principles and principles that involve processing of both the position and nature of the elements suggest either that the dorsal stream may develop earlier than the ventral stream or that performance on tasks requiring just a single stream (i.e., dorsal stream) may be superior to that observed on tasks requiring integration of information across the two streams. Additional evidence is consistent with either the former possibility (Kovacs, Kozma, Feher, & Benedek, 1999; Mash, Quinn, Dobson, & Narter, 1998) or the latter possibility (Leslie, Xu, Tremoulet, & Scholl, 1998; Mareschal & Johnson, 2003). It should be acknowledged that this analysis is not without difficulties inasmuch as further data are actually consonant with the proposal that the ventral stream develops prior to the dorsal stream (Braddick, Atkinson, & Wattam-Bell, 2003; Coch, Skendzel, Grossi, & Neville, 2005). Also, the presumed developmentally late integration of dorsal versus ventral processing systems is not in accord with the findings of Bhatt et al. (2007) that even infants as young as 3–4 months of age use common region to group elements by identifying different shapes and tracking their relative locations in regions. Moreover, differences in the timing of emergence and ease of deployment of the principles of lightness versus form similarity (Quinn et al., 2002; Quinn & Bhatt, 2006), two presumed ventral stream attributes, suggest that even development within a stream may not be a unitary phenomenon (see also Atkinson et al., 2004). Developmental differences during the childhood years in the potency of proximity and good continuation, two presumed dorsal stream attributes, are consistent with this suggestion (Rush, 1937).

D. Abstract Units

Two of the findings described in the chapter are noteworthy because they hint that perceptual organizing processes can produce units of processing that have an abstract nature. In Quinn et al.'s (2008) demonstration that proximity is readily apprehended, which was documented by successful performance in the bars → elements version of the proximity grouping task, the generalization from the bars to the familiar organization of elements was accomplished even though the physical dimensions of the bar stimuli were different from those of the element stimuli (see Fig. 18). For example, the vertical (and horizontal) bars were longer and more closely spaced than the columns (and rows) of elements. There was actually more physical overlap between the bars and the elements depicting the novel organization. These results suggest that the units that arise as a consequence of grouping have an abstract quality in terms of their transfer. The findings on the flexible nature of proximity grouping are consistent with those reported by Bhatt et al. (2007) on grouping by common region by infants where it was shown that elements that grouped in one region were also expected to appear together in a differently shaped region. Both sets of outcomes are further consistent with the data of Quinn and Bhatt (2005b) who reported that infants generalized from bars to elements on the basis of form similarity but only when provided with multiple form contrasts depicting a column- or row-like organization. All three studies suggest that the emergent features formed from deployment of perceptual organizational principles are conceptual-like in terms of their generalizability (see also Feigenson & Halberda, 2004).

E. A Model

The experimental outcomes reviewed in the chapter indicate that a wider variety of grouping principles appear to be available to young infants than was anticipated based on the early empirical work conducted with the rod–box display (Kellman & Spelke, 1983). In fact, subsequent work examining how infants respond to the rod–box display is consistent with the proposal to expand the range of unifying cues to which infants are sensitive. For example, the work of Johnson and Aslin (1996) indicates that infants by the age of 4 months may rely on a variety of cues including common motion, depth, accretion and deletion of background texture, color similarity, and good continuation to represent the unity of a partly occluded object. This work led Johnson (1997) to propose a sensory–perceptual threshold model of unit formation. Unit formation in this model is determined by the presence of multiple cues that, when detected from the same display, become sufficient for unit formation. Failures to engage in unit formation may reflect lack of sufficiency of cues, lack of sensitivity to the cues that are available, or both.

This account accords well with our own findings, although given that form similarity requires additional experience to be manifested in infants, it may be important in the further development of this model to determine if the different cues themselves have different thresholds for detection. In addition, given the results of Kellman and Spelke (1983) showing that common motion was more influential than good continuation and similarity, it will also be important to determine if there is a relative weighting of the various cues in the calculation of whether a particular arrangement of elements is above threshold for unity.

In light of a trend in the adult literature to bring together perceptual and conceptual explanations of performance under a common set of operating principles (Barsalou, 1999; Goldstone & Barsalou, 1998), it is worth noting that the sensory–perceptual threshold model for the development of perceptual unit formation (Johnson, 1997) appears to operate via the same general principles as the family resemblance model of object categorization (Rosch & Mervis, 1975). In the family resemblance model, an object does not need to possess a set of defining cues (i.e., singly necessary and jointly sufficient) to be identified as a member of Category A rather than Category B. Instead, if an object has more of the cues that are characteristic of Category A than of Category B, then the object is assigned to Category A. Both the threshold model for perceptual unit formation and the family resemblance model of categorization have in common the idea that when a given stimulus possesses a sufficient subset of some larger set of cues characteristic of a class, then the stimulus will be assigned to that class rather than some other class (whether the classes in question are a single unified element or two disconnected elements in the case of unit formation or Category A vs Category B in the case of categorization). As noted earlier, the function that determines "sufficiency" may not be a simple summation with each cue providing an equal value toward the computation; rather, some cues may carry more weight than others.

F. A Top–Down Contribution

Needham and Baillargeon (1998) form another investigative team that has advanced the idea that there may be a multiplicity of cues available for perceptual unit formation by infants. Some of these cues, like those emphasized earlier in the chapter and highlighted in our own program of research, fall under the heading of configural information (e.g., color, shape, and texture similarity) and may be characterized as bottom–up. Other cues, such as knowledge of particular objects and object kinds, reflect experiential information, and may be thought of as top–down.

A framework for thinking about the relative contributions of bottom–up perceptual process and top–down knowledge access in perceptual organization has been offered by Schyns, Goldstone, and Thibaut (1998). Schyns et al. argue for a flexible system of perceptual unit formation, one in which the features that come to define objects are extracted during the task of concept learning. The idea is that an individual's history of concept formation (i.e., the concepts possessed by an individual at a specific point in time) will affect their subsequent perceptual organization processes.

Quinn and Schyns (2003) undertook a set of experiments to better understand whether the proposed interplay between adherence to Gestalt organizational principles and flexible feature creation would be manifested in young infants. The experiments were designed to answer the following question: Will features that are specified as coherent by Gestalt principles be "overlooked" by young infants if alternative means of perceptual organization are "suggested" by presenting the infants with a category of objects in which the features uniting the objects are "non-natural" in the Gestalt sense? In the first experiment, 3- and 4-month-olds were familiarized with a number of complex figures, examples of which are shown in the top portion of Fig. 19. Subsequently, during a novelty preference test, the infants were presented with the pacman shape paired with the circle shown in the bottom portion of Fig. 19. The infants were found to recognize the circle as familiar as evidenced by their preference for the pacman shape. This finding is consistent with the idea that the infants had parsed the circle from the complex figures in accord with good continuation.

In follow-up experiments, Quinn and Schyns (2003; see also Quinn, Schyns, & Goldstone, 2006) asked whether an invariant part abstracted during category learning would interfere with perceptual organization achieved by adherence to good continuation. The experiments consisted of two parts. In Part 1, the infants were familiarized with multiple exemplars, each marked by an invariant pacman shape, and were subsequently administered a novelty preference test that paired the pacman shape with the circle shape. Examples of the stimuli are shown in Fig. 20. The pacman shape was recognized as familiar as evidenced by a preference for the circle shape. Part 2 of the procedure was then administered and it simply followed the design of Experiment 1. The expectation is that if the category learning from Part 1 of the procedure, in particular, the representation of the invariant pacman shape, can interfere with the Gestalt-based perceptual organization that was observed in Experiment 1, then the preference for the pacman shape that was observed in Experiment 1 should no longer be observed. In fact, if the representation of the pacman shape carries over from Part 1 to Part 2 of the procedure, one would expect the opposite result, that is, the infants should continue to prefer the circle. The latter result is what was observed

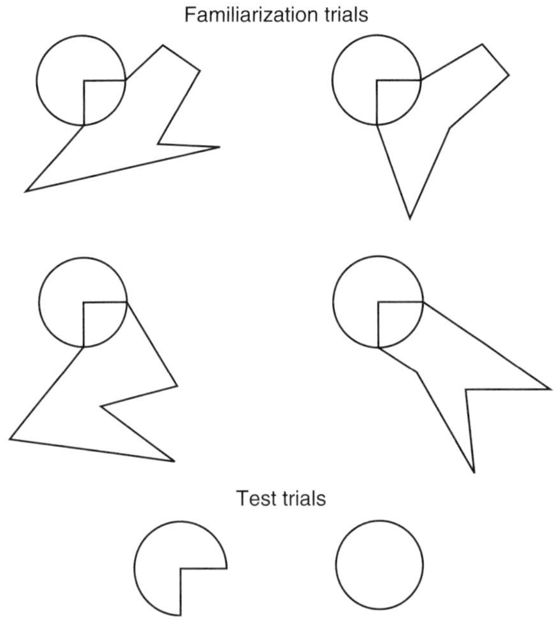

Fig. 19. Examples of the familiarization and test stimuli used in Quinn and Schyns (2003). If the infants can parse the circle from the familiar patterns in accord with good continuation, then they should prefer the pacman shape over the circle during the test trials.

and it suggests that perceptual units formed during category learning can be (1) entered into a perceptual system's working "featural" vocabulary and (2) available to subsequent object recognition processes. The bias set by the Gestalt principle of good continuation might thus be thought of as soft wired in the sense that it is subject to interference. More generally, an individual's history of categorization will affect their subsequent object parsing abilities.

G. Looking to the Future

The research described above indicates that the infants' perceptual world is systematically organized based on both general Gestalt rules and on specific personal experiences. However, much remains unknown about how perceptual organization develops. For instance, although infants as young as 3 months of age may utilize a number of different Gestalt rules to organize, little work has been done to examine how these rules function in relation to each other (cf. Kellman & Spelke, 1983). The complexity of the real world probably implies that Gestalt cues sometimes work in concert and other times in opposition; how infants at different ages deal with the organizational challenges under such diverse conditions needs to be understood.

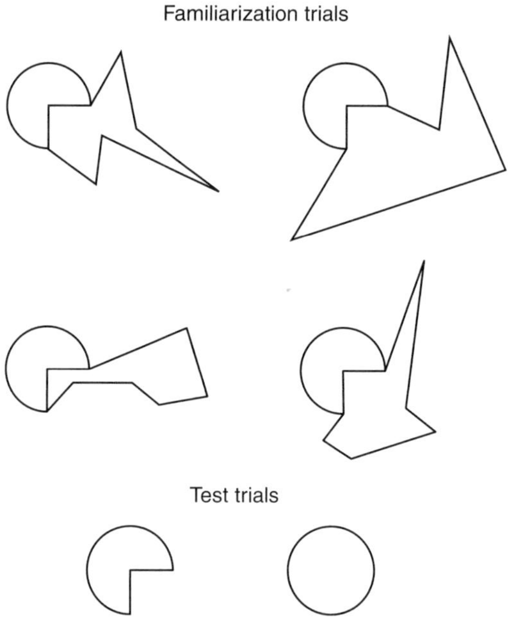

Fig. 20. Examples of the familiarization and test stimuli used in Quinn and Schyns (2003). If the infants can extract the invariant pacman from the familiar patterns, then they should prefer the circle shape over the pacman shape during the test trials.

A comprehensive account of the development of perceptual organization also has to include the relations between bottom–up rule-based organization and top–down experience-based organization (Gerganov, Grinberg, Quinn, & Goldstone, 2007). This will require a systematic analysis of the roles of different kinds of experience on perceptual organization in infancy and an understanding of how these experiences interact with bottom–up processes at different ages. More generally, the separate and interactive roles of experience and maturation have to be studied further in order to understand how the infant perceptual system develops into the adult system.

H. Conclusion

While much remains to be determined about the development of perceptual organization, it seems clear that the present chapter has reported research suggesting that even young infants' interactions with the visual world are guided by a considerable degree of perceptual coherence resulting from adherence to grouping principles that are functional in the first months of postnatal experience. As a consequence, the view expressed in a widely used introductory psychology text from the 1950s, that "With few possible exceptions provided by primitive organization, all perceiving is dependent on past experience—the so called habit factor" (as cited by Zuckerman & Rock, 1957, p. 269), no longer seems tenable.

Acknowledgments

Preparation of this chapter was supported by Grants HD-42451 and HD-46526 from the National Institute of Child Health and Human Development. The authors thank Brian H. Ross for inviting the contribution and providing helpful editorial comments on an earlier draft.

References

Atkinson, J., Wattam-Bell, J., Braddick, O., Birtles, D., Barnett, A., & Cowie, D. (2004). Form vs motion coherence sensitivity in infants: The dorsal/ventral developmental debate continues [Abstract]. *Journal of Vision, 4*, 32a.

Baillargeon, R. (2002). The acquisition of physical knowledge in infancy: A summary in eight lessons. In U. Goswami (Ed.), *Blackwell handbook of childhood cognitive development* (pp. 47–83). Oxford, UK: Blackwell Publishers.

Banks, M. S., & Salapatek, P. (1978). Acuity and contrast sensitivity in 1, 2, and 3-month-old human infants. *Investigative Ophthalmology and Visual Science, 17*, 361–365.

Banks, M. S., & Salapatek, P. (1981). Infant pattern vision: A new approach based on the contrast sensitivity function. *Journal of Experimental Child Psychology, 31*, 1–45.

Barsalou, L. (1999). Perceptual symbol systems. *Behavioral and Brain Sciences, 22*, 577–609.

Beck, D. M., & Palmer, S. E. (2002). Top-down influences on perceptual grouping. *Journal of Experimental Psychology: Human Perception & Performance, 28*, 1071–1084.

Behrmann, M., & Kimchi, R. (2003a). Visual perceptual organization: Lessons from lessons. In R. Kimchi, M. Behrmann, and C. R. Olson (Eds.), *Perceptual organization in vision: Behavioral and neural perspectives* (pp. 337–375). Mahwah, NJ: Erlbaum.

Behrmann, M., & Kimchi, R. (2003b). What does visual agnosia tell us about perceptual organization and its relationship to object perception? *Journal of Experimental Psychology: Human Perception and Performance, 29*, 19–42.

Ben-Av, M. B., & Sagi, D. (1995). Perceptual grouping by similarity and proximity: Experimental results can be predicted by autocorrelations. *Vision Research, 35*, 853–866.

Bhatt, R. S., Hayden, A., & Quinn, P. C. (2007). Perceptual organization based on common region in infancy. *Infancy, 12*, 147–168.

Bhatt, R. S., Hayden, A., Reed, A., Bertin, E., & Joseph, J. E. (2006). Infants' perception of information along object boundaries: Concavities versus convexities. *Journal of Experimental Child Psychology, 94*, 91–113.

Braddick, O., Atkinson, J., & Wattam-Bell, J. (2003). Normal and anomalous development of visual motion processing: Motion coherence and "dorsal stream vulnerability." *Neuropsychologia, 41*, 1769–1784.

Brunswik, E., & Kamiya, J. (1953). Ecological cue validity of "proximity" and other Gestalt factors. *American Journal of Psychology, 66*, 20–32.

Burack, J. A., Enns, J. T., Iarocci, G., & Randolph, B. (2000). Age differences in visual search for compound patterns: Long- versus short-range grouping. *Developmental Psychology, 36*, 731–740.

Coch, D., Skendzel, W., Grossi, G., & Neville, H. (2005). Motion and color processing in school-age children and adults: An ERP study. *Developmental Science, 8*, 372–386.

Cohen, L. B. (2004). Uses and misuses of habituation and related preference paradigms. *Infant and Child Development, 13*, 349–352.

Dobkins, K. R. (2005). Enhanced red/green color input to motion processing in infancy: Evidence for increasing dissociation of color and motion information during development. In Y. Munakata and M. Johnson (Eds.), *Attention and Performance XXI* (pp. 401–423). Oxford: Oxford University Press.

Egly, R., Driver, J., & Rafal, R. D. (1994). Shifting visual attention between objects and locations: Evidence from normal and parietal lesion subjects. *Journal of Experimental Psychology: General, 123*, 161–177.

Fantz, R. L. (1964). Visual experience in infants: Decreased attention to familiar patterns relative to novel ones. *Science, 164*, 668–670.

Fantz, R. L., Fagan, J. F., III, & Miranda, S. B. (1975). Early visual selectivity as a function of pattern variables, previous experience, age from birth and conceptual and cognitive deficit. In L. B. Cohen and P. Salapatek (Eds.), *Infant perception: From sensation to cognition. Basic visual processes* (Vol. 1, pp. 249–345). New York: Academic Press.

Farran, E. K. (2005). Perceptual grouping in Williams syndrome: Evidence for deviant patterns of performance. *Neuropsychologia, 43*, 815–822.

Feigenson, L., & Halberda, J. (2004). Infants chunk object arrays into sets of individuals. *Cognition, 91*, 173–190.

Fiser, J., & Aslin, R. N. (2002). Statistical learning of new visual feature combinations by infants. *Proceedings of the National Academy of Sciences, 99*, 15822–15826.

Gilchrist, I. D., Humphreys, G. W., Riddoch, M. J., & Neumann, H. (1997). Luminance and edge information in grouping: A study using visual search. *Journal of Experimental Psychology: Human Perception and Performance, 23*, 464–480.

Goldstone, R. L., & Barsalou, L. W. (1998). Reuniting perception and conception. *Cognition, 65*, 231–262.

Gerganov, A., Grinberg, M., Quinn, P. C., & Goldstone, R. L. (2007). Simulating conceptually-guided perceptual learning. In D. S. McNamara and J. G. Trafton (Eds.), *Proceedings of the 29th Annual Conference of the Cognitive Science Society* (pp. 287–292). Austin, TX: Cognitive Science Society.

Han, S., Humphreys, G. W., & Chen, L. (1999). Uniform connectedness and classical Gestalt principles of perceptual grouping. *Perception & Psychophysics, 61*, 661–674.

Han, S., Song, Y., Ding, Y., Yung, E. W., & Woods, D. L. (2001). Neural substrates for visual perceptual grouping in humans. *Psychophysiology, 38*, 926–935.

Hayden, A., Bhatt, R. S., & Quinn, P. C. (2006). Infants' sensitivity to uniform connectedness as a cue for perceptual organization. *Psychonomic Bulletin & Review, 13*, 257–271.

Hebb, D. O. (1949). *The organization of behavior*. New York: Wiley.

Humphreys, G. W. (2003). Binding in vision is a multistage process. In R. Kimchi, M. Behrmann, and C. R. Olson (Eds.), *Perceptual organization in vision: Behavioral and neural perspectives* (pp. 377–399). Mahwah, NJ: Erlbaum.

Hunter, M. A., & Ames, E. W. (1988). A multifactor model of infant preferences for novel and familiar stimuli. In L. P. Lipsitt (Ed.), *Advances in child development and behavior* (pp. 69–95). New York: Academic Press.

Johnson, M. H., & Vecera, S. P. (1996). Cortical differentation and neurocognitive development: The parcellation conjecture. *Behavioural Processes, 36*, 195–212.

Johnson, S. P. (1997). Young infants' perception of object unity: Implications for development of attentional and cognitive skills. *Current Directions in Psychological Science, 6*, 5–11.

Johnson, S. P., & Aslin, R. N. (1996). Perception of object unity: The roles of motion, depth, and orientation. *Cognitive Development, 11*, 161–180.

Kellman, P. J. (1996). The origins of object perception. In R. Gelman and T. Kit-Fong Au (Eds.), *Perceptual and cognitive development* (pp. 3–48). San Diego: Academic Press.

Kellman, P. J., & Arterberry, M. E. (1998). *The cradle of knowledge: Development of perception in infancy*. Cambridge, MA: MIT Press.

Kellman, P. J., & Shipley, T. F. (1991). A theory of visual interpolation in object perception. *Cognitive Psychology, 23*, 141–221.

Kellman, P. J., & Spelke, E. S. (1983). Perception of partly occluded objects in infancy. *Cognitive Psychology, 15*, 483–524.

Kestenbaum, R., Termine, N., & Spelke, E. S. (1987). Perception of objects and object boundaries by three-month-old infants. *British Journal of Developmental Psychology, 5*, 367–383.

Kimchi, R. (2000). The perceptual organization of visual objects: A microgenetic analysis. *Vision Research, 40*, 1333–1347.

Koffka, K. (1935). *Principles of Gestalt psychology*. New York: Harcourt, Brace & World.

Kohler, W. (1929). *Gestalt psychology*. New York: Horace Liveright.

Kovacs, I., Kozma, P., Feher, A., & Benedek, G. (1999). Late maturation of visual spatial integration in humans. *Proceedings of the National Academy of Sciences (USA), 96*, 12204–12209.

Leslie, A. M., Xu, F., Tremoulet, P. D., & Scholl, B. J. (1998). Indexing and the object concept: Developing "what" and "where" systems. *Trends in Cognitive Sciences, 2*, 10–18.

Mareschal, D., & Johnson, M. H. (2003). The "what" and "where" of object representations in infancy. *Cognition, 88*, 259–276.

Mash, C., Quinn, P. C., Dobson, V., & Narter, D. B. (1998). Global influences on the development of spatial and object perceptual categorization abilities: Evidence from preterm infants. *Developmental Science, 1*, 85–102.

Needham, A., & Baillargeon, R. (1998). Effects of prior experience on 4.5-month-old infants' object segregation. *Infant Behavior and Development, 21*, 1–24.

Palmer, S. E. (1992). Common region: A new principle of perceptual grouping. *Cognitive Psychology, 24*, 436–447.

Palmer, S. E. (1999). *Vision science: Photons to phenomenology*. Cambridge, MA: MIT Press.

Palmer, S. E., & Rock, I. (1994). Rethinking perceptual organization: The role of uniform connectedness. *Psychonomic Bulletin & Review, 1*, 29–55.

Pomerantz, J. R. (1981). Perceptual organization in information processing. In M. Kubovy and J. R. Pomerantz (Eds.), *Perceptual organization* (pp. 141–180). Hillsdale, NJ: Erlbaum.

Pomerantz, J. R. (1983). Global and local precedence: Selective attention in form and motion perception. *Journal of Experimental Psychology: General, 112*, 516–540.

Prinzmetal, W., & Banks, W. P. (1977). Good continuation affects visual detection. *Perception & Psychophysics, 21*, 389–395.

Quinn, P. C., & Bhatt, R. S. (2005a). Good continuation affects discrimination of visual pattern information in young infants. *Perception & Psychophysics, 67*, 1171–1176.

Quinn, P. C., & Bhatt, R. S. (2005b). Learning perceptual organization in infancy. *Psychological Science, 16*, 515–519.

Quinn, P. C., & Bhatt, R. S. (2006). Are some Gestalt principles deployed more readily than others during early development? The case of lightness versus form similarity. *Journal of Experimental Psychology: Human Perception and Performance, 32*, 1221–1230.

Quinn, P. C., Bhatt, R. S., Brush, D., Grimes, A., & Sharpnack, H. (2002). Development of form similarity as a Gestalt grouping principle in infancy. *Psychological Science, 13*, 320–328.

Quinn, P. C., Bhatt, R. S., & Hayden, A. (2008). Young infants readily use proximity to organize visual pattern information. *Acta Psychologica, 127*, 289–298.

Quinn, P. C., Brown, C. R., & Streppa, M. L. (1997). Perceptual organization of complex visual configurations by young infants. *Infant Behavior & Development, 20*, 35–46.

Quinn, P. C., Burke, S., & Rush, A. (1993). Part-whole perception in early infancy: Evidence for perceptual grouping produced by lightness similarity. *Infant Behavior & Development, 16*, 19–42.

Quinn, P. C., & Schyns, P. G. (2003). What goes up may come down: Perceptual process and knowledge access in the organization of complex visual patterns by young infants. *Cognitive Science, 27*, 923–935.

Quinn, P. C., Schyns, P. G., & Goldstone, R. L. (2006). The interplay between perceptual organization and categorization in the representation of complex visual patterns by young infants. *Journal of Experimental Child Psychology, 95*, 117–127.

Rock, I., & Palmer, S. (1990). The legacy of Gestalt psychology. *Scientific American, 263*, 84–90.

Roder, B. J., Bushnell, E. W., & Sasseville, A. M. (2000). Infants' preference for familiarity and novelty during the course of visual processing. *Infancy, 1*, 491–507.

Rosch, E., & Mervis, C. B. (1975). Family resemblances: Studies in the internal structure of categories. *Cognitive Psychology, 7*, 573–605.

Rush, G. P. (1937). Visual grouping in relation to age. Archives of Psychology. (No. 217).

Salapatek, P. (1975). Pattern perception in early infancy. In L. B. Cohen and P. Salapatek (Eds.), *Infant perception: From sensation to cognition: Vol. 1. Basic visual processes* (pp. 133–248). New York: Academic Press.

Schyns, P. G., Goldstone, R. L., & Thibaut, J. P. (1998). The development of features in object concepts. *Behavioral and Brain Sciences, 21*, 1–54.

Siegler, R. S. (2004). U-shaped interest in U-shaped development—And what it means. *Journal of Cognition and Development, 5*, 1–10.

Slater, A. M. (1995). Visual perception and memory at birth. In C. Rovee-Collier and L. P. Lipsitt (Eds.), *Advances in infancy research* (Vol. 9, pp. 107–162). Norwood, NJ: Ablex.

Spelke, E. S. (1982). Perceptual knowledge of objects in infancy. In J. Mehler, M. Garrett, and E. Walker (Eds.), *Perspectives on mental representation* (pp. 409–430). Hillsdale, NJ: Erlbaum.

Tversky, B. (2006). Gestalts of thought. In L. Albertazzi (Ed.), *Visual thought* (pp. 155–163). Amsterdam, The Netherlands: John Benjamins.

Ungerleider, L. G., & Mishkin, M. (1982). Two cortical visual systems. In D. J. Ingle, M. A. Goodale, and R. J. W. Mansfield (Eds.), *Analysis of visual behavior* (pp. 549–586). Cambridge, MA: MIT Press.

Vecera, S. P., & Behrmann, M. (2001). Attention and unit formation: A biased competition account of object-based attention. In T. F. Shipley and P. J. Kellman (Eds.), *Advances in Psychology: Vol. 130. From fragments to objects—Segmentation and grouping in vision* (pp. 37–69). New York: Elsevier.

Werner, H. (1957). The concept of development from a comparative and organismic point of view. In D. B. Harris (Ed.), *The concept of development* (pp. 125–148). Minneapolis, MN: University of Minnesota Press.

Wertheimer, M. (1923/1958). Principles of perceptual organization. In D. C. Beardslee and M. Wertheimer (Eds.), *Readings in perception* (pp. 115–135). Princeton, NJ: Van Nostrand.

Younger, B., & Gotlieb, S. (1988). Development of categorization skills: Changes in the nature or structure of infant form categories? *Developmental Psychology, 24*, 611–619.

Zuckerman, C. B., & Rock, I. (1957). A reappraisal of the roles of past experience and innate organizing processes in visual perception. *Psychological Bulletin, 54*, 269–296.

CO-CONSTRUCTING CONCEPTUAL DOMAINS THROUGH FAMILY CONVERSATIONS AND ACTIVITIES

Maureen Callanan and Araceli Valle

Abstract

Constructivist theories of cognitive development have considered children as active individuals, learning about the world through observations and interactions with others; development is seen as happening in the mind of the child. Sociocultural theories, in contrast, consider development as embedded in social context, where changing patterns of participation in activities signal change. In this chapter we take seriously the notion of integrating these two approaches, with the aim of moving toward a theory of cognitive development that involves both the active mind of the child and the social embeddedness of developmental change. We discuss findings from three types of studies of development in context—learning object names, understanding symbols, and learning causal explanations for events. We conclude with some potential mechanisms for change in a new integrated theory and propose some questions for future study. © 2008, Elsevier Inc.

THE PSYCHOLOGY OF LEARNING
AND MOTIVATION VOL. 49
DOI: 10.1016/S0079-7421(08)00004-2

I. Introduction

While children's experiences are largely socially embedded, the literature on cognitive development has often considered development as involving change within an individual. In this chapter we take seriously the question of how cognitive development happens in context. In some sense everyone who studies children's thinking considers the context, but we are asking for a much deeper and more careful consideration of what it might mean to see developmental change as embedded in social and cultural contexts. We also ask how taking context seriously might change some of the fundamental assumptions we make about cognitive development. We propose turning the usual assumption about cognitive development on its head and asking how development happens IN and FOR social contexts, rather than how individuals change while being surrounded by social contexts.

Our approach integrates two theoretical frameworks, both of which have been essential to developmental psychology: the constructivist approach and the sociocultural approach. When we discuss the constructivist approach, we mean approaches that were inspired by Piaget's early work but also more recently by scholars such as Henry Wellman, Allison Gopnik, and Susan Gelman, among others. The sociocultural approach includes a range of theories inspired by Vygotsky's work as well as his students such as Leontev, and includes recent theories of Barbara Rogoff, Michael Cole, James Wertsch, and others. We will first contrast these two approaches, then discuss how they might be integrated. Next, we cover three areas of research where we have explored the ways that this integrated theory might be applied. Finally, we draw conclusions about the challenges and promise of this new approach.

A. Contrasting Constructivist and Sociocultural Approaches

The constructivist and sociocultural approaches make incompatible assumptions regarding a number of fundamental questions about the nature and processes of cognitive development. In Table I we summarize some of these important contrasts. In constructivist theories, the child is the unit of analysis, development happens in the mind of the child, and the social context is conceptualized as merely "input" to the process of development. In other words, the social world is seen as peripheral to the real site of development. In contrast, sociocultural approaches conceptualize the unit of analysis for development as the dyad or larger social group, and development is seen as happening within and for activities. Social context is not just an input to the system of interest, it *is* the system—it serves as both the setting and the impetus (or even perhaps the mechanism) of change. All of the actors in

TABLE I

TWO THEORETICAL APPROACHES TO COGNITIVE DEVELOPMENT

	Constructivist approaches	Sociocultural approaches
Relevant theorists	Piaget, Gopnik, Wellman	Vygotsky, Rogoff, Cole, Lave
Unit of analysis	Child	Activity
Site of developmental change	In mind of child	In social activity
Role of social context	"Input" to developing mind	Site/mechanism of developmental change
Notion of child	Little scientist	Social being
Notion of development	Acquiring concepts and theories for goal of better understanding world	"Making sense" to participate effectively in social world (culture)
Positioning of participants	Either actively learning on their own or being taught by another person	Engaged in "being" in activity, which naturally leads to "becoming" more expert
When is social context helpful?	Only useful after relevant developmental changes have already happened (AFTER development)	Helping to produce developmental change (BEFORE development)

the social context (child and adults) act on each other and shape the activity that incorporates the child. These varying assumptions lead to quite distinct views of the child's role in development. While the constructivist might see the child as a little scientist, and development as a process of acquiring new concepts and theories that help the child to better understand the world, the socioculturalist is likely to see the child as first and foremost a social being, and development as "making sense" of things with a central goal of participating effectively in the social world.

Another crucial distinction is between the role of the child—either in teaching/learning or in being/becoming. It seems that constructivists tend to see learning as the result of either "teaching" by the parent (or other), or active exploration by the child. The sociocultural view focuses more on how being in activity leads to becoming more expert in the activity and in related skills. In the case of language learning, for example, taking social context seriously does not necessarily mean looking for teaching behaviors, but rather looking more broadly at how the parent helps the child effectively engage in conversation. A sociocultural view might be that both teaching and learning about object names are unintentional side-effects of mutual efforts to communicate (see Akhtar & Tomasello, 2000).

Finally, an implication of the difference in views about the role of the social context involves the timing of impact on development. Constructivist approaches often seem to make an assumption that input is useful only if certain developmental abilities are in place first. In contrast, a sociocultural argument would be that development happens as a consequence of social interaction. We believe it is worth some careful thought to consider whether development happens as a result of children's participation in these conversations, rather than as a precursor to their occurrence.

Perhaps the most fundamental constructivist assumption that socioculturalists question is the idea that development happens inside the head (or in the privacy of the child's mind). While this has been largely unexamined in much of the cognitive development literature, we see little rationale for accepting the claim so readily. One might argue that the metaphors we use for thinking about the mind may lead us to the assumption. Indeed, the metaphor of the mind as a container is a very common one, documented in the literature on adult thinking about abstract concepts (Gibbs, 1994; Lakoff & Johnson, 1980). Because it is difficult to step out of one's own metaphorical ways of thinking, researchers in cognitive development may have difficulty recognizing this as a cultural metaphor, and even more difficulty thinking outside of it. Taking seriously a sociocultural model requires that we at least consider the possibility that development happens in the dynamic social context of activities, and in the conversations inherent to shared activity, rather than solely in quiet individual reflection.

The contrasting views of the place of social context in development are also of key importance. The word "input," which fits the constructivist model quite well, is an inappropriate description of social context in the sociocultural view. This is much more than just a matter of preferred word choice. The notion of input implies both that the important activity is all in the child's mind and that the environment provides only "inputs" to that system. "Input" also conveys the assumption that the underlying mental structures develop independent of social context; at most social context influences the timing or capacity of these structures. One source of the assumption may be Piaget's (e.g., 1973, 1976) view of cognition as evolving toward an abstract and decontextualized form of thinking, and his conceptualization of the process of cognitive development as similarly decontextualized or independent of the social context in which it occurs. When contemporary constructivists consider social context, they still seem to maintain this idea of decontextualization, insofar as the shared understanding of the meaning of the context/activity to the participants tends not to be a focus. Sociocultural approaches suggest a more radical notion—that the mental structures themselves may be dynamically constructed in the process of social interaction. For example, the type of allowable content for a structure or the linkages among structures might be determined by social experience. In the later sections of this chapter, we will consider some examples of what that type of dynamic and jointly constructed cognitive development might look like.

B. Integrating the Two Approaches

Despite the incompatibility of a number of the assumptions discussed above, our contention is that it may be possible to integrate the constructivist and sociocultural theoretical frameworks. While each approach offers some crucially important perspectives on development, neither seems to provide a full and satisfactory account for the processes of cognitive development. The constructivist view is not a sufficient theory because it takes too narrow a view, with the role of the context being a one-sided "input" to the thinking that goes on in the child's mind. At the same time, the sociocultural view, at least in its contemporary form, seems to us to give short shrift to the important factor of learning within the mind of the child. Taking only the sociocultural view seems to us to leave out the consequences of development beyond those seen in the immediate context; in other words, if all development happens within interactions then how is it that a child takes with her from one experience some "knowledge" or "concepts" that can be built on in new experiences? We see these two views not as competing theories that differ on a key testable claim; rather they are competing perspectives that each offer a view of development, and that each has merit. If we are to truly integrate these theories, then the hard work to be done involves careful analysis of which parts of each theoretical perspective should be integrated into a new theory. Our goal in this chapter is to take some small steps in that direction.

Clearly the ideas we raise regarding integration of constructivist and sociocultural approaches are not entirely new (see, e.g., Bruner, 1990; Goodnow, 1990; Rogoff, 2003; Siegler, 2007). Any overall characterization of a set of theories and research programs as "constructivist" or "sociocultural" is usually misleading and ignores subtle distinctions among individual theories. Indeed, our arguments have much in common with recent arguments by theorists who fall closer to the constructivist side, yet make important claims about socially embedded cognition—for example, Wilson and Keil's (2000) work on the social context of explanation and Harris and Koenig's (2006) work on the notion of "testimony" as a means of development. Further, other theorists more on the sociocultural side have made important arguments about individual learning, most notably diSessa and colleagues' (e.g., diSessa, Gillespie, & Esterly, 2004) work on "knowledge in pieces," and social-pragmatic accounts of language learning by Akhtar and Tomasello (2000) and others (see Bloom, 2000; Clark & Wong, 2002; Diesendruck, 2005; Gelman, Coley, Rosengren, Hartman, & Pappas, 1998). These integration efforts aside, when one considers the basic assumptions in Table I, most researchers seem to fall on one side or the other. We have not yet seen in the literature a careful investigation of these two sets of assumptions with the aim of considering what a truly integrative view would look like.

Our goal, then, is to consider what an integration of the two perspectives would look like and how effectively it would account for data on conceptual changes in children's thinking. Because of this integrative goal, we have focused on children's conversations with parents and others as a setting where thinking takes place in social context. We take conversation not only as a window on children's thinking, but maybe more profoundly, as a window on processes of development. In this chapter we attempt to explore how these two contrasting approaches can be integrated within three different areas of research—sample domains where we have conducted studies in which to explore the integration. The three areas we have chosen are ones where there is solid developmental research and theory taking a constructivist approach. Our strategy, then, has been to ask what kinds of research questions a sociocultural approach would ask about the same domains. And with the data in hand, how we might reinterpret the body of data in that domain with an approach that integrates constructivist with sociocultural accounts. We consider, in sequence, the domains of early word learning, early understanding of symbolic objects, and intuitive causal theories.

II. Studies of Development in Context

A. Learning Object Names

Children's understanding of word meanings, and especially names for objects, has been a basic area of cognitive and language development for decades. While there are a variety of theoretical approaches to these questions, many of the dominant theories in recent years have fallen squarely in the constructivist perspective. For example, one debate within the field focuses on whether there are internal "constraints" or biases that children use in early word learning, and whether these constraints help explain how quickly children are able to make sense of the overwhelming task of learning how spoken words apply to objects—not to mention events, features, and abstract concepts (see Golinkoff, Mervis, & Hirsh-Pasek, 1994; Markman, 1989; Waxman, 1998). Markman (1989) has shown that children seem to expect labels to refer to whole objects ("whole object" constraint), for example, and that they expect that different types of objects should have mutually exclusive names ("mutual exclusivity" constraint).

We have raised the question of whether there might be an alternative explanation for the word learning data that has suggested the existence of internal constraints. While attention to "input" has been an important part of the field of language development for decades (Gleitman, Newport, & Gleitman, 1984; Hoff-Ginsberg & Shatz, 1982; Lieven, 1994), much of this research seems to fall squarely in a constructivist camp (but see Akhtar & Tomasello, 2000). We have undertaken a research program meant to take more seriously the idea that word learning is embedded in the social enterprise of communicating in meaningful everyday activities.

In one set of studies we asked what it would look like to integrate a sociocultural approach with the standard constructivist approach to the study of children's understanding of word meanings. While the constraints view focuses on the ways that children may be preprogrammed to resolve the ambiguity of reference, integrating sociocultural ideas requires us to take seriously the importance of conversation and activities as settings for learning. Taking a particular constraint as our focus, Callanan and Sabbagh (2004) asked whether, rather than constraints in the head, might the patterns of word use in conversation have the potential to lead children to mutually exclusive meanings? To address this question we asked about the conditions under which parents would use multiple names for the same object.

Parents were invited into the lab with their child, ranging in age from 12 to 24 months. They were given several sets of toys, chosen to contrast in ways that might elicit multiple labels (e.g., several different types of trucks), and asked to play with each toy set for a few minutes as they might at home. In our coding we asked about how often parents used multiple names for the same object, and also when they did use two labels we asked about whether they "bridged" the two, providing information about how they are related or why they might both apply (or not apply). Examining parents' conversations with their children in these settings we found that they predominantly used a single name for each object (roughly 75–80% of the time), suggesting that the patterns in how parents name objects may guide children to expect mutually exclusive names. Further, when parents did use two names for an object they were overwhelmingly likely to provide some sort of "bridging" information. Some examples are as follows: "That's a beluga. It's a kind of whale" and "That's either a seal or a walrus." It was quite rare for parents to use two labels with no bridging. Across the different sets of toys, only about 5–6% of the label episodes involved multiple labels without bridging. Interestingly, we also asked parents to fill out MacArthur Vocabulary Checklists for their children, and we found that parents' multiple label use correlated with children's productive vocabulary, even after partialing out labels mothers used that were initiated by their child. Further, the frequency of parents' bridging utterances also correlated with children's language production as measured by the MacArthur scale.

In general then, the majority of objects that parents named in these settings were named with single labels, and when two labels were used they were most often accompanied by clarifying information. With these data we argue that participating in conversation with parents could guide children to expect mutually exclusive names for things. The further finding of correlations between parents' multiple labeling and children's vocabulary supports the idea that participating in these conversations could serve as a potential mechanism for children's developing understanding of words as names for objects.

B. Children's Understanding of Symbolic Objects

Another area of intense research in recent years has been the development of children's understanding of external representations, or representational objects. Led by DeLoache and her colleagues (DeLoache, 2002; DeLoache & Burns, 1994; Troseth & DeLoache, 1998) a large body of research has accumulated, documenting the early development of children's ability to search for a hidden object using a scale model, a photograph, or a videotaped action. Children succeed in these tasks at different ages depending on the type of representational object, as well as other key features of the task. DeLoache's compelling explanation has to do with the development of "dual representation," an ability to think of an object as both an object in its own right (e.g., a dollhouse) and as a representation for something else (e.g., a scale model of a larger room). In all of this work there is an expectation that what development consists of is the acquisition of an internal capacity that was not present earlier.

In our research we again asked whether there is evidence to support a sociocultural account of this developmental change. We wondered if it is possible that participation in activity and conversation might serve as the mechanism for children's changing understanding of representational objects. Soennichsen and Callanan (2008) investigated (1) how parents naturally talk about representations and (2) how parents' ways of discussing representational events might impact children's learning (see also Callanan, Jipson, & Soennichsen, 2002). We focused in particular on how parents talk about video as a representational medium and on children's understanding of video. DeLoache and her colleagues (Troseth & DeLoache, 1998) find that children begin to show evidence of understanding video images as representations of real objects between the ages of 2 and 3 years.

In our first study we explored parents' conversations about video in a children's museum context. Two exhibits that we studied included video representations of objects as well as the actual objects that were pictured in the video images. In one of these exhibits, for example, a model train was mounted with a video camera, and the video taken by the train was simultaneously presented on a screen inside a large booth shaped like a train engine. Objects around the track (e.g., model trees, model houses) could be viewed on their own, and their images could also be viewed on the video monitor. We coded parents' talk to 2-, 3-, and 4-year-old children. In talking about the exhibit, parents were very likely to name the objects as well as their video images. Labels for the referent objects were especially likely in speech to 2-year-olds—parents of 2-year-olds named the real objects shown in the video an average of 4 times, which was significantly more often than for parents of 3-year-olds (who named the objects an average of 2 times), and parents of 4-year-olds (who named the objects an average of 1 time).

Somewhat surprisingly, parents were much less likely to offer explanations about the connection between the real object and its video image than to merely label the objects. In many of the labeling episodes it appeared that parents were merely trying to clarify the link between the specific object (e.g., a toy house) and its representation (its image on the video screen). Our guess is that the parents either might assume that children know the general link between objects and their video representation, or that they might not think about that general link at all. In labeling the objects though, it seemed that parents were merely helping their child to see where the real version of the particular video-pictured object was in this situation. Whether or not adults are able to give a deep explanation of symbolic representation in video, they simply recognize the link between object and image in this instance. If they think their child is not understanding the link between the video and the objects, they may help them to make that specific connection. An important question that remains is whether this sort of conversational talk helps children to come to understand the symbolic nature of video.

We attempted to begin to address this question of impact in a second study, this time using an experimental method with 2-year-old children. In three conditions, we recreated the different types of strategies parents used in the museum—Labeling and Explaining—and added a Control condition. Comparing these three conditions allowed us to ask whether children seemed to be learning about the video representation from these different types of talk. Intriguingly, the finding was that children in the Labeling condition, where the experimenter labeled objects as parents had done in the museum, were more likely to succeed on one of DeLoache's hiding tasks than were children in the other two groups. In fact, 75% of the 2-year-olds in the Labeling condition succeeded on the first trial of finding a hidden object after seeing it hidden on video. As in DeLoache's earlier work, only 25% of the children in the Control condition were successful. And in the Explanation condition, 50% of the children were successful (which was not significantly different from the Control condition).

That this brief intervention could influence children's performance on a task that is demonstrably difficult for this age group is quite surprising. We interpret these data as consistent with the idea that participating in conversation with parents can serve as a potential mechanism for children's developing understanding of objects as representations. Troseth (Troseth, 2003; Troseth, Casey, Lawver, Walker, & Cole, 2007) has additional data that supports the idea that children's experiences with parents around video may support their developing understanding of dual representation. What our study adds is information about actual conversational patterns used by parents when talking with children about these objects.

While a purely sociocultural account of this phenomenon might not specify what is going on in the child's head as a result of these conversations, we are interested in considering this question. DeLoache's explanation—that failure on the search tasks indicates that a child lacks the ability to think of an object as both an object in itself and a representation of another object—leaves open the question of what actually gets added in the mental representations that allows children to reach this understanding. The missing piece may be a link from the model to the object it is modeling. And we argue that this is exactly what parents seem to be elaborating in the examples above. What parents may be doing, then, is helping children to build initial links between referent objects and representations (such as video images), for a particular situation. While only a first step, this guidance may be crucial in allowing the child to create the mental architecture that is necessary to understand dual representation.

C. Causal Understanding and Explanations

Finally, a third domain we consider is children's intuitive theories about the world. A number of scholars have proposed "theory theory" as a general framework, acknowledging the very active role that children take in their own thinking and noting the strong evidence that children often have a very coherent understanding of the world, even when it differs from the adult view (Carey, 1985; Gopnik & Wellman, 1994). As compelling as these arguments are, consideration of the possible integration of the sociocultural approach with the constructivist approach requires that we attend to a number of critiques asking whether theories are stable structures that are found "in the head." Nelson and her colleagues (Nelson, Henseler, & Plesa, 2000) argue that the theory notion seems too static and individualistic to account for the situated, dynamic, and socially embodied nature of thinking. Lillard (1997) argues that there are questions about the universalist assumptions often

TABLE II

SAMPLE "WHY" QUESTIONS FROM DIARY STUDIES (FROM CALLANAN, PEREZ-GRANADOS, ET AL., 2008)

Where does the sky end? (5 years; 6 months)
How come fish are in the water and they don't drown? (4;8)
Why do we dream? (5;8)
Why are the clouds painted black? (3;8)
Why do people get cancer? (5;4)

made (at least implicitly). And data from Medin, Atran, Waxman, and their colleagues suggest that there are profound variations in children's categorizing and reasoning depending on cultural experiences (Ross, Medin, Coley, & Atran, 2003; Waxman & Medin, 2007). In a series of different projects we have explored children's explanatory conversations with parents and others as a social and pragmatic activity that can help us to consider the social context of causal thinking.

In our research we have used a number of different methods to attempt to uncover explanatory conversations in naturalistic settings. We have used diary study methods (Callanan & Oakes, 1992; Callanan, Perez-Granados, Barajas, & Goldberg, 2008), and natural observation, as in the museum study mentioned earlier (Callanan & Jipson, 2001; Callanan et al., 2002), as well as focused observation in more structured tasks. Two examples of this third method are a study of conversations about growth (Jipson & Callanan, 2003) and a study of conversations about earthquakes (Callanan, Valle, & Azmitia, 2007).

Some examples of children's questions found using the diary method are presented in Table II (Callanan & Oakes, 1992), and examples of explanatory conversations from a variety of studies are shown in Table III (Callanan, Frazier, Gorchoff, Esterly, & Martin, 2008; Callanan, Valle, et al., 2007). It may be obvious from these examples that parents' comments are often very different from what a scientist might say. And yet, our sense is that the sorts of everyday explanatory talk presented in these examples may contribute to children's developing "theories" in at least two ways. First, domain-specific vocabulary may help children to learn how adults in their community carve up the world into meaningful domains. Second, hearing the causal explanations parents give, and coconstructing such explanations (when they are a bit older), may help children to develop and revise causal theories.

One example of a study that addresses the domain-specific vocabulary point is a study of children's understanding of growth (Jipson & Callanan, 2003).

TABLE III

Samples of Explanatory Talk from Family Conversations

Child (3 years): Mommy, I always ask why. Why do I always ask why?

Parent: Because you are curious about things.
Child: What is curious?
Mother: "Curious" means you want to know more about something and you are interested and want to understand.
(from Callanan & Oakes, 1992)

Parent (to 4-year-old):
What causes an earthquake? . . . There's parts of the earth that are called plates and it's sort of like the plates we eat off of. And you know what sometimes happens? Sometimes the plates decide to go in different directions.
(from Callanan, Valle, et al., 2007)

Sample explanations from museum visits:
(from Callanan, Frazier, et al., 2008)

Explaining science principles
For example, "When the light is brighter on one side it makes the cat disappear."

Explaining how exhibit works
For example, "If you turn this knob the globe will move."

Using analogies
For example, "That's how the flower would look to a mouse."

Parents and children were asked to discuss a number of sequences of pictures that showed objects increasing or decreasing in size. Parents tend to reserve the use of the word "grow" for biological changes in size (a plant getting larger) and to use different wording for an inanimate object (a balloon getting larger). When children used the word "grow" in nonbiological settings, parents often commented in ways that might steer children away from using the word in this less conventional (but perfectly understandable) way. For an example, see the child's use of "grow" to describe the moon in Table IV. Note that while this parent's explanation for the changing shape of the moon is not necessarily correct by astronomers' standards, the point here is that the parent is subtly guiding the child toward an understanding of "grow" as referring to certain specific kinds of increases in size.

Another example of how parent–child conversation may guide children's understanding of the language used in a domain comes from a study of mental state language by Sabbagh and Callanan (1998). In this study,

TABLE IV

EXAMPLE OF PARENT'S RESPONSE TO CHILD'S USE OF "GROW" FOR NONBIOLOGICAL ENTITY (FROM JIPSON & CALLANAN, 2003)

Parent: Yeah, it's a full moon. Do you know why it's getting bigger?
Child: Because it's growing.
Parent: It's growing? Does this grow like mushrooms grow?
Child: Uh. Yeah.
Parent: It grows in the dirt? I've never seen the moon in the dirt! No, the moon is up in the sky!
Child: Yeah. Why did they grow up?
Parent: The earth is blocking it. It's a shadow so it gets bigger and bigger.

parent–child book reading sessions were analyzed for parents' and children's use of mental state language. One analysis looked at parents' responses when children used the phrase "I don't know." While nobody would argue that this phrase is evidence that children understand mental states (e.g., see Shatz, Wellman, & Silber, 1983), it was intriguing to find that when children said "I don't know" parents were very likely to respond in one of two ways. First, parents were more likely to use mental state terms following "I don't know" than they did following children's mental state terms in general. Second, children's "I don't know" utterances were likely to be followed by what we coded as "helping" comments, that is, comments offering help to find out information that one doesn't know. For example, if a child answered "I don't know" when asked what happened to the snowman, a helping comment might be "let's look back and see if we can find out where he went." We argue that these responses by parents, whether or not they are consciously planned, provide potentially important information for children.

The developmental sequence apparent in the example from the Sabbagh and Callanan (1998) study is particularly interesting. What we see happening is that children are participating in activities, using words that they have heard before but about which they are likely to have little deep understanding. In other words, children use the phrase "I don't know" in a routinized way well before they begin to speak about mental terms in meaningful ways. By virtue of using these words, however, children are (inadvertently) creating opportunities for their parents to provide guidance about what that phrase "I don't know" actually means. And so, perhaps children's act of taking up parts of these conversations is what allows them to begin to come to understand more about the mind. This account has much in common with sociocultural approaches such as Lave and Wenger's (1991) notion that when learners engage in "legitimate peripheral participation" they begin to master the knowledge and skills at the center of the activity. Similarly, the classic notion of "prolepsis," which comes out of Vygotsky's theory, suggests that parents treat their children "as if" they understand them, and that this process may actually create understanding in the child (see Stone, 1993). We return to these ideas in the concluding section of this chapter.

The second point about how family conversation may guide children's developing "theories" has to do with causal explanation. As Keil (2006) argues, causal explanation is a social action, not equivalent to internal thoughts about causality. By engaging with explanation in social settings, children likely come to understand many of the ways that people in their community, or at least their family, make links between causes and effects of everyday events. Over a number of different studies, we have explored the kinds of causal explanations that parents and children discuss in a number of settings. In diary studies we find that parents are extremely likely to provide causal answers when children ask "why" questions (Callanan & Oakes, 1992; Callanan, Perez-Granados, et al., 2008). While visiting museums, parents sometimes provide causal information about how an exhibit works, or about the scientific principle involved in the exhibit (Crowley, Callanan, Jipson, et al., 2001; Crowley, Callanan, Tenenbaum, & Allen, 2001). In general, we find in this work that explanations in the midst of family conversation tend to be brief, mundane, and embedded in the activity. Crowley and Galco (2001) discuss these as "explanatoids" or "just-in-time" explanations. One might argue that these explanations are not very much like the ones that you would find in science classrooms when a teacher is attempting to communicate a new scientific principle to children. And yet, Keil's arguments about explanatory depth suggest that these sorts of "shallow" explanations may be the norm for human thinking in action (Keil, 2006; Wilson & Keil, 2000).

Thus far we have paid little attention to cultural variation in family conversations, and yet this is a crucial question. If social experiences have a potential role in children's conceptual development then variation must be considered. In our lab we have some relevant data regarding how families from different communities engage in explanation. In one study, Tenenbaum and Callanan (2008) looked at parents' explanations in two groups of families of Mexican descent—one group of parents had "basic schooling" (average of 9 years or less) and the other group had "high schooling" (at least high school graduation). In a museum setting, the two groups of parents differed in how often they gave scientific explanations to their children, with the higher schooling parents using more explanations. However, the museum setting seemed a very different experience for the two groups—many of the basic schooling parents had never been to a museum, and their focus was on "how to do a museum" rather than on science content. In support of this account, we found in a subsequent home task that the two groups of parents did not differ in the frequency of explanations they gave. Both the cultural context of the family and the immediate context of the task are clearly important determiners of the nature of conversation.

In another study, Valle (2005) asked parents and children to discuss conflicting claims, for example, the advantages and disadvantages of food additives. She found that parents varied in their tendency to focus on scientific evidence—and that this variation was related to parents' college major and/or occupation. Parents who studied engineering were especially likely to focus on evidence in discussing the conflicting claims with their children. Parents with humanities backgrounds focused on other methods, such as intuition or religion, for evaluating the claims. Parents with science backgrounds mentioned both evidence-based methods and alternative methods equally. These findings suggest that children in different families and/or communities are likely to hear different kinds of discussions about how to figure out the causes for complex events. A great deal of further research is needed to determine what impact these variations have for children's conceptual development.

We interpret these data as suggesting that participating in conversation with parents is a potential mechanism for children's developing understanding of domains and causal connections (often called intuitive theories). But we are also persuaded by those who question the notion of "theory" as a description of children's conceptual development. We are struck by the variation in children's thinking within a domain but across activities, an important point emphasized by Siegler (2007). For example, in their fascinating work on children's mental models of the earth, Vosniadou and Brewer (1992) showed that classifying children as "having" a particular model involves summarizing across what is usually a diverse set of answers and choosing the model that is most characteristic. Were we to take the variability more seriously, might we be inclined to consider children's thinking as more a matter of variable on-line answers rather than more stable models or theories (diSessa et al., 2004; Siegler, 2007)? Perhaps the notion of "theory" is less appropriate as a description of how children are thinking, yet more appropriate when applied to the researcher's generalization across multiple opportunities for children to think about a topic.

III. Conclusions About Cognitive Development in Context of Conversations

With these three example domains, we have attempted to begin to integrate constructivist and sociocultural approaches, and to ask how children's participation in everyday conversations may be the impetus for important developmental changes in language and conceptual development. There is still much more to learn, however, about what these everyday conversations might tell us about children's developing word meanings and "theories."

One problem with testing the effects of conversation on children's thinking is that we do not expect immediate effects on children's conceptual development based on a simple experience, which makes it difficult to come up with effective methods and assessment tools. There is a need for new methods and tools of analysis for this new approach.

Another issue is the common critique of contextual approaches—that children cannot make use of information from others unless they have already developed the relevant concept. But, the question we raise is whether the reverse is possible. Might children instead learn concepts and theories through their participation in these social interactions? With the three examples in the preceding pages we present data that could plausibly be interpreted as linking such participation with particular aspects of conceptual development. Further elaboration on possible mechanisms for such change is clearly needed.

We propose two possible mechanisms for how cognitive developmental change may happen in the context of conversation and activity. The first is a type of incidental learning– for example, a sequence where the child uses language that they do not fully understand, but that fits the situation (e.g., "I don't know"), and the parent responds *as if* the child understands the underlying concept, but needs clarification about the particular situation. What may follow is that as a result of cumulative "situated" explanations, the child may come to understand the concept. So, for example, parents responding to children's "I don't know" phrases by using complex mental state language may actually be guiding the children to understand more about mental states. This notion of treating children "as if" they understand is related to the idea of "prolepsis" discussed by Vygotskian theorists (see Bruner, 1990; Cole, Matusov, Wertsch, others).

The second proposed mechanism involves a kind of more explicit teaching. Here the child may ask "why" questions or use theory-laden words in an unconventional way (e.g., "the moon grows"), and the parent provides an explanation or clarifies conventional boundaries on the use of the word. From cumulative "situated" explanations, the child's understanding of the domain and/or relevant causes may begin to change.

These speculated mechanisms need further thought and analysis, and additional mechanisms are certainly possible as well. Other challenging problems also remain to be dealt with. For example, our reliance on language as a measure of thought is potentially problematic. Also, as discussed earlier, methods that better suit the theory need to be developed (see also Matusov, 2007).

In general, however, we believe that these studies of conversation offer some hope of integrating the sociocultural and constructivist approaches to children's conceptual development. We hope that the suggestions of plausible mechanisms for cognitive developmental change may spur further thought and analysis, and that raising questions about whether development occurs only in the head may lead to new consideration of untested assumptions.

References

Akhtar, N., & Tomasello, M. (2000). The social nature of words and word learning. In R. M. Golinkoff, *et al.* (Eds.), *Becoming a word learner: A debate on lexical acquisition* (pp. 115–135). New York: Oxford University Press.

Bloom, P. (2000). *How children learn the meanings of words*. Cambridge, MA: MIT Press.

Bruner, J. (1990). *Acts of meaning*. Cambridge, MA: Harvard University Press.

Callanan, M., Frazier, B., Gorchoff, S., Esterly, J., & Martin, J. (2008). Gender revisited: Family conversations about science in an "Alice's Wonderland" exhibit. Manuscript in preparation.

Callanan, M., Jipson, J., & Soennichsen, M. (2002). Maps, globes, and videos: Parent-child conversations about representational objects. In S. Paris (Ed.), *Perspectives on object-centered learning in museums* (pp. 261–283). Mahwah, NJ: Lawrence Erlbaum Associates.

Callanan, M., & Oakes, L. (1992). Preschoolers' questions and parents' explanations: Causal thinking in everyday activity. *Cognitive Development, 7*(2), 213–233.

Callanan, M., Perez-Granados, D., Barajas, N., & Goldberg, J. (2008). *Everyday conversations about science: Questions as contexts for theory development.* Manuscript under review.

Callanan, M., & Sabbagh, M. (2004). Multiple labels for objects in conversations with young children: Parents' language and children's developing expectations about word meanings. *Developmental Psychology, 40*, 746–763.

Callanan, M., Valle, A., & Azmitia, M. (2007). Expanding studies of family conversations about science through video analysis. In R. Goldman, B. Barron, and R. Pea (Eds.), *Video research in the learning sciences*. Mahwah, NJ: Erlbaum.

Callanan, M. A., & Jipson, J. L. (2001). Explanatory conversations and young children's developing scientific literacy. In K. S. Crowley, C. Schunn, and T. Okada (Eds.), *Designing for science: Implications from everyday, classroom, and professional settings* (pp. 21–49). Mahwah, NJ: Lawrence Erlbaum Associates.

Carey, S. (1985). *Conceptual change in childhood.* Cambridge, MA: Bradford Books.

Clark, E. V., & Wong, A. D. W. (2002). Pragmatic directions about language use: Offers of words and relations. *Language and Society, 31*, 181–212.

Crowley, K., Callanan, M., Jipson, J., Galco, J., Topping, K., & Shrager, J. (2001). Shared scientific thinking in everyday parent-child activity. *Science Education, 85*(6), 712–732.

Crowley, K., Callanan, M. A., Tenenbaum, H. R., & Allen, E. (2001). Parents explain more often to boys than to girls during shared scientific thinking. *Psychological Science, 12*, 258–261.

Crowley, K., & Galco, J. (2001). Everyday activity and the development of scientific thinking. In K. S. Crowley, C. Schunn, and T. Okada (Eds.), *Designing for science: Implications from everyday, classroom, and professional settings* (pp. 393–413). Mahwah, NJ: Lawrence Erlbaum Associates.

DeLoache, J. S. (2002). The symbol-mindedness of young children. In *Child psychology in retrospect and prospect: In celebration of the 75th anniversary of the Institute of Child Development* (pp. 73–101). Mahwah, NJ: Lawrence Erlbaum Associates.
DeLoache, J. S., & Burns, N. M. (1994). Early understanding of the representational function of pictures. *Cognition, 52*(2), 83–110.
Diesendruck, G. (2005). The principles of conventionality and contrast in word learning: An empirical examination. *Developmental Psychology, 41*, 451–463.
diSessa, A., Gillespie, N., & Esterly, J. (2004). Coherence versus fragmentation in the development of the concept of force. *Cognitive Science, 28*, 843–900.
Gelman, S. A., Coley, J. D., Rosengren, K., Hartman, E., & Pappas, T. (1998). Beyond labeling: The role of parental input in the acquisition of richly structured categories. *Monographs of the Soceity for Research in Child Development*. Serial No, 253, Vol. 63, No. 1.
Gibbs, R. W. (1994). *The poetics of mind: Figurative thought, language, and understanding*. Cambridge: Cambridge University Press.
Gleitman, L. R., Newport, E., & Gleitman, H. (1984). The current status of the motherese hypothesis. *Journal of Child Language, 11*(1), 43–79.
Golinkoff, R. M., Mervis, C., & Hirsh-Pasek, K. (1994). Early object labels: The case for a developmental lexical principles framework. *Journal of Child Language, 21*(1), 125–155.
Goodnow, J. J. (1990). The socialization of cognition: What's involved?. In J. W. Stigler, R. A. Shweder, and G. H. Herdt (Eds.), *Cultural psychology: Essays on comparative human development* (pp. 259–286). New York: Cambridge University Press.
Gopnik, A., & Wellman, H. (1994). The theory. In L. Hirschfeld and S. Gelman (Eds.), *Mapping the mind: Domain specificity in cognition and culture* (pp. 257–293). New York, NY: Cambridge University Press.
Harris, P. L., & Koenig, M. A. (2006). Trust in testimony: How children learn about science and religion. *Child Development, 77*, 505–524.
Hoff-Ginsberg, E., & Shatz, M. (1982). Linguistic input and the child's acquisition of language. *Psychological Bulletin, 92*(1), 3–26.
Jipson, J., & Callanan, M. (2003). Mother-child conversation and children's understanding of biological and nonbiological changes in size. *Child Development, 74*, 629–644.
Keil, F. C. (2006). Explanation and understanding. *Annual Review of Psychology, 57*(1), 227–254.
Lakoff, G., & Johnson, M. (1980). *Metaphors we live by*. Chicago/London: University of Chicago Press.
Lave, J., & Wenger, E. (1991). *Situated learning: Legitimate peripheral participation*. Cambridge, UK: Cambridge University Press.
Lieven, E. (1994). Crosslinguistic and crosscultural aspects of language addressed to children. In C. Gallaway and B. J. Richards (Eds.), *Input and interaction in language acquisition* (pp. 56–73). Cambridge: Cambridge University Press.
Lillard, A. (1997). Other folks' theories of mind and behavior. *Psychological Science, 8*, 268–274.
Markman, E. M. (1989). *Categorization and naming in children: Problems of induction*. Cambridge, MA: MIT Press.
Matusov, E. (2007). In search of "the appropriate" unit of analysis for sociocultural research. *Culture & Psychology, 13*(3), 307–333.
Nelson, K., Henseler, S., & Plesa, D. (2000). Entering a community of minds: "Theory of Mind" from a feminist standpoint. In P. Miller and E. Kofsky Scholnick (Eds.), *Toward a feminist developmental psychology* (pp. 61–83). Florence, KY: Taylor & Francix.
Piaget, J. (1973). *The child and reality: Problems of genetic psychology*. Oxford, England: Grossman.

Piaget, J. (1976). *The grasp of consciousness: Action and concept in the young child.* Oxford, England: Harvard University Press.
Rogoff, B. (2003). *The cultural nature of human development.* New York: Oxford University Press.
Ross, N., Medin, D., Coley, J., & Atran, S. (2003). Cultural and experimental differences in the development of folkbiological induction. *Cognitive Development, 18*(1), 25–47.
Sabbagh, M., & Callanan, M. (1998). Metarepresentation in action: 3-, 4-, and 5-year-olds' developing theories of mind in parent-child conversations. *Developmental Psychology, 34*, 491–502.
Shatz, M., Wellman, H., & Silber, S. (1983). The acquisition of mental verbs: A systematic investigation of the first reference to mental state. *Cognition, 14*(3), 301–321.
Siegler, R. S. (2007). Cognitive variability. *Developmental Science, 10*, 104–109.
Soennichsen, M., & Callanan, M. (2008). *Children's emerging understanding of video as a symbolic medium: The role of parent-child conversation.* Manuscript under review.
Stone, C. A. (1993). What is missing in the metaphor of scaffolding? In E. Forma, N. Minick, and C. A. Stone (Eds.), *Contexts for learning: Sociocultural dynamics in children's development* (pp. 169–183). New York, NY: Oxford University Press.
Tenenbaum, H. R., & Callanan, M. A. (2008). Parents' science talk to their children in Mexican-descent families residing in the USA. *International Journal of Behavioral Development, 32*(1), 1–12.
Troseth, G., Casey, A., Lawver, K., Walker, J., & Cole, D. (2007). Naturalistic experience and the early use of symbolic artifacts. *Journal of Cognition and Development, 8*, 309–331.
Troseth, G. L. (2003). TV guide: Two-year-old children learn to use video as a source of information. *Developmental Psychology, 39*, 140–150.
Troseth, G. L., & DeLoache, J. (1998). The medium can obscure the message: Young children's understanding of video. *Child Development, 69*(4), 950–965.
Valle, A. (2005). *How do you know? Communicating ideas about science and scientific reasoning in parent-child conversations.* Unpublished doctoral dissertation University of California, Santa Cruz.
Vosniadou, S., & Brewer, W. (1992). Mental models of the earth: A study of conceptual change in childhood. *Cognitive Psychology, 24*(4), 535–585.
Waxman, S., & Medin, D. (2007). Experience and cultural models matter: Placing firm limits on childhood anthropocentrism. *Human Development, 50*(1), 23–30.
Waxman, S. R. (1998). Linking object categorization and naming: Early expectations and the shaping role of language. In D. Medin (Ed.), *The Psychology of Learning and Motivation: Advances in Research and Theory* (Vol. 38, pp. 249–291). San Diego, CA: Academic Press.
Wilson, R. A., & Keil, F. C. (2000). The shadows and shallows of explanation. In F. C. Keil and R. A. Wilson (Eds.), *Explanation and cognition.* Cambridge, MA: MIT Press.

THE CONCRETE SUBSTRATES OF ABSTRACT RULE USE

Bradley C. Love, Marc Tomlinson, and Todd M. Gureckis

Abstract

We live in a world consisting of concrete experiences, yet we appear to form abstractions that transcend the details of our experiences. In this contribution, we argue that the abstract nature of our thought is overstated and that our representations are inherently bound to the examples we experience during learning. We present three lines of related research to support this general point. The first line of research suggests that there are no separate learning systems for acquiring mental rules and storing exceptions to these rules. Instead, both items types share a common representational substrate that is grounded in experienced training examples. The second line of research suggests that representations of abstract concepts, such as *same* and *different* that can range over an unbounded set of stimulus properties, are rooted in experienced examples coupled with analogical processes. Finally, we consider how people perform in dynamic decision tasks in which short- and long-term rewards are in opposition. Rather than invoking explicit reasoning processes and planning, people's performance is best explained by reinforcement learning procedures that update estimates of action values in a reactive, trial-by-trial fashion. All three lines of research implicate mechanisms of thought that are capable of broad generalization, yet inherently local in terms of the procedures

THE PSYCHOLOGY OF LEARNING
AND MOTIVATION VOL. 49
DOI: 10.1016/S0079-7421(08)00005-4

0079-7421/08 $35.00

used for updating mental representations and planning future actions. We end by considering the benefits of designing systems that operate according to these principles.

I. Introduction

We live in a world consisting of concrete experiences. Moment to moment, we learn and make decisions based on these experiences. Given this characterization of our environment, it is unclear what would constitute a true abstraction, let alone how we could acquire and retrieve such knowledge based on the sensory cues provided by the environment. After all, we are situated in the same world as pigeons, grasshoppers, and newborn humans, not in a platonic realm of universals that exist independently of the particulars of our concrete experiences.

This view of our environment has strong implications for theories of learning and representation. It predicts that our knowledge structures are updated in a moment-to-moment fashion, instead of being calculated as global statistics or parameters. Observed ordering effects in learning support this view (Clapper & Bower, 1994; Medin & Bettger, 1994). Our view also predicts that it is not possible to acquire true abstractions. Even when people seem to have acquired and successfully applied an abstraction, we predict that the concrete basis of this behavior should become apparent on closer inspection. Following this view, findings in category learning demonstrate that experienced examples influence classification decisions in rule-governed tasks. For example, similarity effects exert themselves even when people apply explicit rules (Allen & Brooks, 1991) and exemplar frequency affects performance in seemingly rule-based tasks (Nosofsky, 1991; Rouder & Ratcliff, 2006).

In light of these findings, one reasonable position is that there is both an abstract and concrete basis to cognition. Dual processing theories are prevalent in cognitive science (Ashby & Maddox, 2005; Sloman, 1996). Sloman (1996) distinguishes between a fast associative system that operates according to similarity to past experiences and an analytical system that is slower and more deductive in nature. Reasoning fallacies, such as the conjunctive fallacy (Tversky & Kahneman, 1983) and susceptibility to framing effects (Tversky & Kahneman, 1981), are attributable to associative processes, whereas the ability to appreciate and overcome these pitfalls is attributable to the analytical system.

One fundamental challenge for dual accounts is establishing the necessity of the abstract system. Adapting to the local statistics of the environment, calculating similarities, and forming analogies to past examples offer substantial reasoning abilities without invoking rule systems (Forbus, Gentner, & Law, 1994; Ross & Kennedy, 1990). It is not clear that non-rule-based systems are inferior in terms of the range of problems that can be successfully addressed. Accounting for human-level competency might not require positing rule-based systems. For example, language is often viewed as a uniquely human competence, but even in this domain arguments regarding the necessity of rule systems are common. For example, the language processing literature offers ample examples of debates between proponents of single and dual accounts for domains like the past tense (Pinker & Prince, 1988; Rumelhart & McClelland, 1987). Challenges to these dual route accounts bring into question the necessity of positing abstract rule-based processes and representations.

In this chapter, we argue that the prevalence of abstract representations in cognition is overestimated. We do not argue that people cannot create or follow sequences of rules. For example, baking a cake according to a recipe involves executing an algorithm that was constructed by another human. Instead, we argue that seemingly abstract rule representations are built on and are intimately linked to concrete experiences. We predict that our representations never fully transcend these concrete experiences that they are built on and, therefore, are not truly abstract in nature. Upon closer inspection, the messy underpinnings of these seemingly abstract rules are revealed.

We offer three supportive cases drawn from our own research. In each case, seemingly abstract processes and representations appear to govern performance, but on closer examination performance is instead governed by incremental learning processes operating over experienced examples. We offer model-based explanations for all three cases considered. Each model learns on a trial-by-trial basis by adjusting its memory representations based on the current example. These learning mechanisms do not follow from a rational analysis in that they update their category estimates based on local statistics from the immediate context (e.g., the discrepancy between the current memory representation of a category and the current stimulus).

In the first case study, we consider how people learn and apply rules, as well as encode exceptions to rules. We find evidence that people do not posses separate rule and exception systems, but instead rely on a single cluster system that is intimately influenced by the concrete details of the training set. Even when subjects mentally rehearse rules, much like a baker following a recipe step-by-step, recognition performance following learning reveals that the representation of rules is intimately linked to the distribution of experienced examples.

In the second case study, we extend this analysis to abstract rules in which the acquired rules are not bound by concrete stimulus aspects. For example, abstract notions like *same* and *different* do not range over specific stimulus properties, like *has blue eyes* or *has two wheels*. For example, two identical wheelbarrows are the same as are two identical comets, and this notion of sameness is not based on a shared property spanning wheelbarrows and comets. We find evidence that such seemingly abstract notions are rooted in experienced exemplars. Analogy to these stored exemplars enables seemingly abstract rule performance, but the concrete substrate enabling this performance can be seen by considering stimulus probes that fall in between relational categories. The results from these probes reveal a family resemblance structure to abstract concepts that is rooted in experienced exemplars.

In the final case study, we examine how people learn to reason about rewards in a dynamic decision task that puts short- and long-term rewards in opposition. People's representation of the underlying system, which can be manipulated by introducing perceptual cues, strongly constrains performance. People eventually gain an understanding of the dynamics of the system, but the trajectory of learning implicates, as in the previous two cases, a trial-by-trial learning mechanism that makes local updates to estimates of the value of particular actions. All three cases suggest that our abstract knowledge supervenes on concrete representations and processes.

II. When Rules Are Not Rules: Rule-Plus-Exception Category Learning

In our first case study, we consider how people acquire rules and master exceptions to these rules in category learning tasks. The results we review suggest that even when people explicitly acquire and apply a rule, closer inspection of the data reveals a strong dependency on the concrete examples experienced during training. Recent studies in human rule-plus-exception learning strongly suggest that people do not fully abstract away the details of the training set when acquiring rules. Rather than propose a dual system model to account for these results, we propose a clustering model. This model does not contain a rule route, but nevertheless explains rule-like behavior, as well as subtle, but diagnostic, deviations from rule-like behavior that will be discussed later in this section.

Proposals for category representation are diverse, ranging from exemplar based (Medin & Schaffer, 1978) to prototype based (Smith & Minda, 1998) and include proposals between these two extremes (Love, Medin, & Gureckis, 2004). Determining the best psychological model can be difficult as one model may perform well in one situation but be bested by a competing model in a different situation. One possibility is that there is not a single "true" model.

In category learning, this line of reasoning has led to the development of models containing multiple learning systems. These more complex models hold that category learning behavior reflects the contributions of different systems organized around discrepant principles that utilize qualitatively distinct representations. The idea that multiple learning systems support category learning behavior enjoys widespread support in the cognitive neuroscience of category learning (see Ashby & O'Brien, 2005, for a review and Nosofsky & Zaki, 1998, for a dissenting opinion). Multiple systems models typically include a rule system.

Multiple system models of category learning detail the relative contributions of the component learning systems. The relative contributions can depend on the circumstances. For example, ATRIUM (Erickson & Kruschke, 1998) contains a rule and exemplar learning system. Which system is operable is determined by a gating system, allowing different classification procedures to be applied to different parts of the stimulus space. For example, familiar items could be classified by the exemplar system, whereas rules could be applied to unfamiliar items. The power to apply qualitatively different procedures to different stimuli is the hallmark of multiple systems models.

Proposing multiple systems begs the questions of how many systems are present and how do they interact. Are there two, three, or thirty-four systems? Do some systems combine outputs whereas others shunt each other? These questions are not trivial to answer. For example, a two system model may suffice for one data set, but a new manipulation could provide evidence for a third system. As systems propagate, the complexity of the overall system dramatically increases. Building in this degree of complexity complicates model evaluation.

Instead of proposing a complex model of category learning containing multiple systems, we advocate a complex systems approach to category learning modeling in which multiple learning systems emerge from a flexible and adaptive clustering mechanism's interactions with the environment. We evaluate the hypothesis that a relatively small set of learning principles can effectively "grow" knowledge structures that satisfy the needs that multiple systems models are intended to address. Our proposal does not require positing a separate rule route and instead maintains some details about the experienced examples. The forces of trial-by-trial learning grow knowledge structures that approximate abstract rules, but are in fact more consistent with human performance.

A. Past Work and Current Challenges

Previous work with the SUSTAIN model, which is the precursor to the model that we introduce here, has partially delivered on the promise of flexibly building needed knowledge structures. SUSTAIN is a clustering model that starts simple and recruits clusters in response to surprising events, such as encountering an unfamiliar stimulus in unsupervised learning or making an error in supervised learning (cf. Carpenter & Grossberg, 2003). Surprising events are indicative that the existing clusters do not satisfy the learner's current goals and that the model should grow new knowledge structures (i.e., clusters). These clusters are modified by learning rules that adjust their position to center them amidst their members. Dimension-wide attention is also adjusted to accentuate stimulus properties that are most predictive across clusters.

Although simple, these growth dynamics allow SUSTAIN to address a wide range of human learning data across various paradigms including unsupervised, inference, and classification learning (Love et al., 2004). Depending on the circumstances of the learning situation (i.e., depending on what the task stresses and target categories), SUSTAIN can evolve clusters that resemble prototypes, exemplars, or rules (Love, 2005). Careful behavioral experiments support the conclusion that SUSTAIN is not merely mimicking these other models, but that human learners' and SUSTAIN's representations are in accord (Sakamoto & Love, 2004). Importantly, SUSTAIN's clusters maintain a great deal of information about the experienced exemplars and their distributions of feature values. Although some abstraction occurs when items cluster together, the degree of information preservation appears to be in accord with human learners and is to some extent dictated by the nature of the task and domain. In summary, SUSTAIN accounts for both classical studies of category learning and the more contemporary work that suggests that conceptual organization is determined by the interplay of information structures in the environment and task pressures or goals (Markman & Ross, 2003).

Despite these successes, considerable challenges remain. Two basic challenges are (1) to formalize the notion of a goal or task pressure and specify how such factors direct learning and (2) to endow learning models with the flexibility to develop representations that approach the range, and richness of the representations that human learners build when learning from examples.

Although SUSTAIN made strides in capturing the influence of goals, its notion of goal is underdeveloped. In particular, SUSTAIN is sensitive in an all-or-none fashion to whether a particular stimulus dimension is queried (e.g., an unknown perceptual feature or category label). Ideally, the notion of goal would be more encompassing and continuous to capture all possible cases from pure classification learning in which the only goal is to predict category membership to pure unsupervised learning in which the goal is to predict every feature (i.e., to capture the correlational structure of the environment in an unbiased fashion). Importantly, the formal notion of goal should directly affect the recruitment and modification of clusters in a principled way. Learning rules should update clusters to reflect the goal measure, and clusters should be recruited in light of how well the current clusters satisfy the current goal measure.

In regards to the second basic challenge, current models like SUSTAIN are too limited in terms of the range of knowledge structures they can construct. For instance, SUSTAIN's attentional mechanism accentuates certain features that are predictive in the current task, but is constrained such that every cluster is focused on the same set of properties. In contrast, people stress different properties in different domains. For example, when shopping for clothing, color is important, but when shopping for a computer the type of processor is important (a feature not even relevant to clothing). To evolve these kinds of knowledge structures and to apply different "procedures" to different parts of the stimulus space as multiple systems models do, each cluster needs to be able to accentuate the features that satisfy the learning goals for the stimulus aspects it represents. A related challenge is storing information and capturing regularities at different scales ranging from very specific (e.g., Jim's dog Fido) to very broad (e.g., living things). To address these issues, clusters need to fine tune their level of specificity to satisfy the goal measure. As in the case of adjusting attention at the individual cluster level, adjusting specificity at the individual cluster level allows for different criteria to be applied to different parts of the stimulus space, as in multiple systems models.

The model that is introduced in the next section, CLUSTer Error Reduction (CLUSTER), meets these stated challenges. CLUSTER incorporates a formal goal measure that directs cluster development. CLUSTER has sufficient flexibility to evolve conceptual structures (i.e., clusters) that reflect key aspects of human knowledge representation. After introducing the model, a supportive simulation will be discussed. The simulation illustrates how CLUSTER can evolve cluster organizations that serve the functions of multiple systems. Importantly, CLUSTER does not posit a separate rule system and maintains key aspects of the training examples that allow it to capture human performance. Finally, we will consider how CLUSTER is consistent with cognitive neuroscience findings advocating multiple memory systems, and briefly discuss work that is being done to further develop and verify the model. The mathematical details of the model are presented in Love and Jones (2006).

B. Overview of CLUSTER

CLUSTER is an autoassociative model of human category learning in which the "hidden" layer consists of clusters (see Fig. 1). A cluster is a bundle of related features. A presented stimulus activates the existing clusters, which

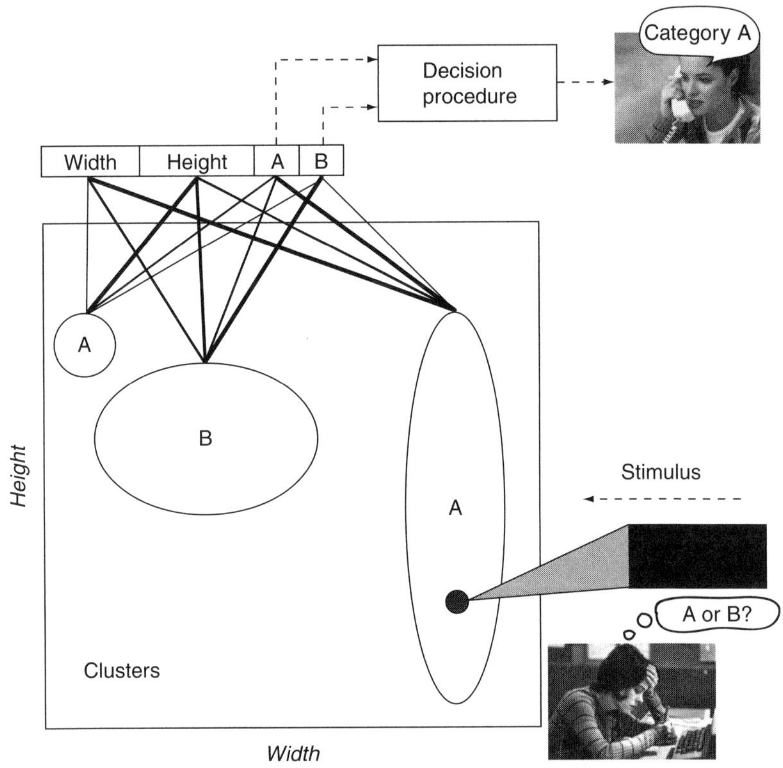

Fig. 1. CLUSTER is an autoassociative learning model in which the hidden layer consists of clusters that adjust their position, attention, and association weights to minimize an error term that reflects the learner's goals. In the illustrated example, three clusters have been recruited and the model is being asked to infer the category label. The different shape of each cluster indicates its unique attention profile. The thickness of the links from each cluster to the output layer reflect the strength of the association weights. The input layer, which mirrors the output layer, is not shown. Instead, each cluster's position is shown geometrically for the width and height dimensions. Category dimensions are indicated by the labels A and B.

pass their activation to the output layer via connection weights. Like other autoassociative models (e.g., Kurtz, 2007), CLUSTER attempts to replicate the input layer at the output layer and in the process develops internal representations that seize on key regularities.

CLUSTER differs from other autoassociative models in a critical way. The error term that CLUSTER minimizes does not uniformly weight reconstruction error equally across features. Instead, each feature's error is weighted according to its goal relevance. For example, pure classification learning places all the error term weighting on the category label features and error associated with reconstructed perceptual features is disregarded (as in most category learning models). At the other extreme, pure unsupervised learning weights the reconstruction error uniformly across features (as in most auto-associative models). CLUSTER can capture every conceivable case in between these extremes, which is critical as the extremes are likely caricatures that do not correspond to human learning (e.g., people incidentally learn about feature correlations in classification learning and place more importance on predicting certain features in unsupervised learning).

The error term (with goal weights on each feature) reflects the discrepancy between what CLUSTER predicts and what is observed. Importantly, discrepancies for features that are goal-relevant are weighted more highly and, therefore, have more influence on learning. To satisfy this goal, clusters adjust their position, attention, and weights to minimize the error term through gradient descent learning. Thus, depending on the goal weights, different cluster organizations will emerge. Unlike most models, each cluster can adjust its own attention to minimize error and attention does not sum to a fixed number (i.e., clusters can vary in overall attention or specificity). These changes allow additional flexibility for clusters to emphasize different features and to vary in specificity (e.g., a specific dog vs dogs in general). Although in Fig. 1 grouping of features implies dimensional structure, CLUSTER departs from the majority of models that utilize selective attention mechanisms (e.g., Nosofsky, 1986) in that it does not assume a dimensional structure. Not assuming dimensional structure allows for additional flexibility (e.g., the presence or absence of red can be critical to a cluster, whereas the presence or absence of blue can be somewhat irrelevant).[1]

CLUSTER begins with one cluster centered on the first training example, and recruits additional clusters when the existing clusters are not supportive of the current goal. Each newly recruited cluster is centered on the current stimulus. Like CLUSTER's other operations, the algorithm for cluster recruitment is consistent across all induction tasks (there are no special cases). Despite its consistency across situations, CLUSTER retains the flexibility to build representations that capture many of the competencies of human learners without proposing distinct learning systems. CLUSTER is highly principled (all of its operations are tied to the goal-weighted error term), but minimal structure is built into the model. Instead, CLUSTER evolves the knowledge structures needed to solve the current task.

[1] Interestingly, in cases in which contrasts are consistent (e.g., when red is present, blue is absent, and vice versa), CLUSTER attends equally to the contrasting features within each cluster. Thus, CLUSTER may prove to provide some insight into how dimensional structure arises.

C. Illustrative Simulation

Findings from previous studies exploring rule-plus-exception learning have been problematic for exemplar models and have been used to support multiple systems models, like the RULEX model of category learning (Nosofsky, Palmeri, & McKinley, 1994). RULEX proposes that rule-following items are captured by a rule system whereas exception items reside in an exemplar store. Interestingly, both SUSTAIN and CLUSTER can account for such findings (e.g., Palmeri & Nosofsky, 1995). Such fits alone cast doubt on the necessity of rule systems. Here, we go farther and present more challenging findings that establish that human rule-plus-exception learning is inconsistent with rule-plus-exception models, but does follow from CLUSTER. We demonstrate that CLUSTER can accommodate such findings by applying different procedures to different parts of the stimulus space and in fact provides an account superior to RULEX's.

To test between this dual route account (i.e., rules and exceptions) and a clustering account, Sakamoto and Love (2004) revisited the rule-plus-exception design with the twist that one rule was twice as frequent as the other. Subjects sequentially classified stimulus items into categories A and B and received corrective feedback. Each category was defined by a rule (e.g., if large, then A; if small, then B). Additionally, each category contained an exception (e.g., a small member of A; a large member of B). Table I provides the design details of Sakamoto and Love's variation in which one experienced category had twice as many rule-following items as the contrasting category. Because subjects reason from stimulus dimensions to categories in classification learning, the exception in the smaller category violates the more frequent rule in Table I (i.e., if value 1 on the first stimulus dimension, then A). Following learning, recognition memory was assessed. In contrast to RULEX's predictions (across all explored parameter values), the exception violating the more frequent rule was better remembered than the exception violating the less frequent rule (see Fig. 2). This result is surprising given that the "rules" during learning were cued on the screen and that subjects reported internally rehearsing these rules. The fact that the item violating the more salient or frequent rule was remembered better than the other exception is evidence that the mental substrate of rule-plus-exception learning does not consist of separate rule and exception routes.

CLUSTER was applied to the data to illustrate its ability to "evolve" multiple systems. Each stimulus dimension shown in Table I and category membership were represented by 2 features for a total of 12 features. In contrast to RULEX (which requires eight parameters to CLUSTER's seven for the simulation), multiple sets of parameters replicated the basic pattern of results, indicating that these findings follow from CLUSTER's

TABLE I

THE ABSTRACT STIMULUS STRUCTURE FOR SAKAMOTO AND LOVE'S (2004) EXPERIMENT 1 IS SHOWN

Learning items	Dimension values	Novel items	Dimension values
Category A			
→ A1	21112	N1	11221
A2	12122	N2	12112
A3	11211	N3	12221
A4	12211	N4	12212
A5	11122	N5	12222
A6	12111	N6	21221
A7	11222	N7	22112
A8	11212	N8	22221
A9	12121	N9	22212
Category B		N10	22222
→ B1	11121		
B2	22122		
B3	21211		
B4	22211		
B5	21122		

Items A1 and B1 (indicated by the arrows) violate the imperfect rule of the first stimulus dimension. subjects completed 10 training blocks where each block consisted of each item below presented in a random order. Following learning, items A1–5 and B1–5 were paired with all combinations of novel foils that matched on the first dimension in forced choice recognition. The actual stimuli were simple geometric figures. for example, for some subjects the first dimension was size with a 1 indicating a small figure and 2 indicating a large figure.

basic operation and that additional work is necessary to establish default parameters for CLUSTER. These and other model evaluation issues, such as consideration of nested models within CLUSTER's formalism, are topics currently being intensely pursued, but are set aside here in favor of demonstrating CLUSTER's promise to evolve multiple learning systems. Here, we focus on the results and rationale, rather than the details of the simulations. Readers interested in the details of the simulations are directed to Love and Jones (2006).

Using these parameters, CLUSTER was simulated 10,000 times, adopting methods paralleling the human study (e.g., 10 blocks of training) and the results were averaged. CLUSTER correctly predicts that the exceptions are recognized best with the exception from the small category recognized better (.88 vs .80) than the exception from the large category. Rule items from the small and large categories are recognized at similar rates (.58 vs .59, respectively). In summary, CLUSTER's predictions matched the basic pattern observed in human subjects (see Fig. 2).

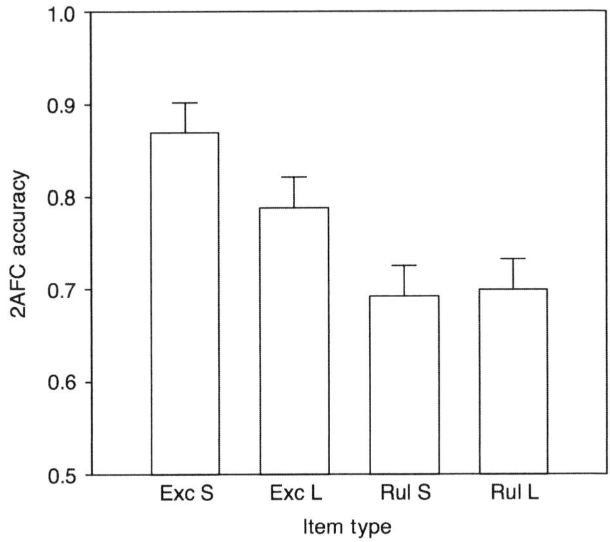

Fig. 2. Mean accuracies in the recognition phase of Sakamoto and Love's (2004) Experiment 1 are shown along with 95% within-subjects confidence intervals (see Loftus & Masson, 1994). Exc S are the exception of the small category, Exc L are the exception of the large category, Rul S are the rule-following items of the small category, and Rul L are the rule-following items of the large category.

CLUSTER recruited 11.4 clusters on average (the median was 11) to represent the 14 training items. The number of clusters recruited followed a normal distribution with solutions ranging from 4 to 23 clusters with a standard deviation of 2.3. Every solution examined involved devoting at least one cluster to encoding each exception with many simulations devoting multiple clusters to each exception. Because CLUSTER is a distributed model and its predictions for an item depend on the responses of all clusters, an analysis of the four item types was conducted that factored in all clusters.

One explanation for CLUSTER's ability to accommodate the results is that it increased attention for clusters playing prominent roles in coding the exceptions, particularly for nonrule stimulus features. Encoding these items at a different specificity than rule-following items would help reduce confusions between these items and rule-following items, resulting in both reduced error during training and in enhanced recognition for exceptions. The pressure to enhance attention should be greatest for the exception violating the more frequent rule as every rule-following item from the contrasting category provides an impetus to enhance attention. This process is illustrated and explained in greater detail in Fig. 3.

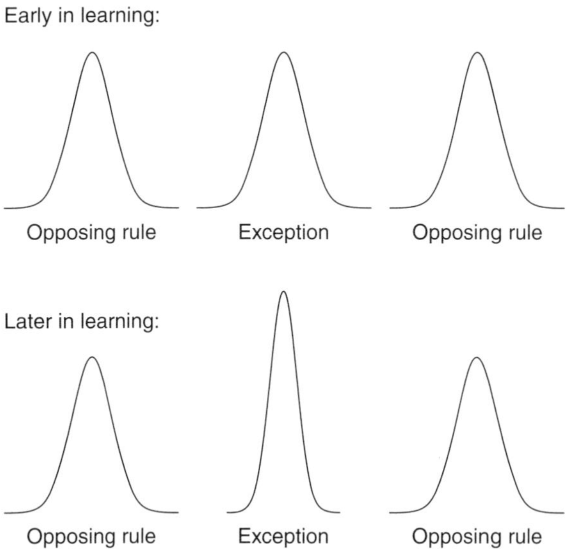

Fig. 3. Better recognition of exceptions in CLUSTER is driven by two factors. The first factor (shown in the top panel) is that exception items elicit surprise and are subsequently encoded by their own recruited cluster. In contrast, clusters responding to rule-following items tend to encode for multiple items, which leads to the loss of some item individuating information that in turn reduces later item recognition. The second factor is that the tuning or specificity of exception-encoding clusters tends to become peaked in order to reduce confusion with rule-following items from the opposing category. This process is illustrated in the bottom panel. Every time a cluster encoding a rule-following item from the contrasting category is activated, the cluster encoding the exception from the opposing category is inappropriately activated as this cluster tends to be similar to rule-following items from the contrasting category but votes for the opposite response. This inappropriate activation of the exception cluster leads to error and the tuning of the exception cluster increases to reduce this error by limited generalization or coactivation. Increasing the exception cluster's tuning boosts recognition of that exception item. This process is more pronounced for exception clusters that are more confusable with rule-following items from the contrasting category because of either the numerosity of these rule-following items (e.g., Sakamoto & Love, 2004) or because of their high similarity to the exception cluster (e.g., Sakamoto & Love, 2006). Both of these findings are inconsistent with rule-based accounts of rule-plus-exception learning.

To evaluate this explanation, following training, study items were presented to CLUSTER and a weighted sum of attention to nonrule features was calculated by multiplying each cluster's sum of attention for nonrule features by its activation. Then, these products were summed and normalized by dividing by the sum of all cluster activations. The results for items of the same type were averaged. The mean results for the four item types (averaged over 10,000 simulations) are 1.36, 1.32, 1.28, and 1.29 for exceptions from the small category, exceptions from the large category, rule items from the small category, and rule items from the large category, respectively. As predicted, these sums perfectly track item recognition. Exceptions (particularly the exception violating the more frequent rule) were stored as "hot spots" of focused activity, whereas clusters coding for rule items were more broadly tuned and were less apt to code item specific differences. Distinct representations emerge for the item types.

CLUSTER provides a similar account of related data sets in which exception memory was manipulated by varying the similarity between exception types and contrasting rule items instead of manipulating rule token frequency (Sakamoto & Love, 2006). SUSTAIN cannot account for these data. The Sakamoto and Love (2006) studies demonstrate that enhanced recognition of exceptions violating frequent rules is not due to frequency per se. Instead, increased confusions in memory enhance exception encoding (see Fig. 3). Sakamoto and Love (2006) equated the frequency of each rule and instead varied how similar rule-following items were to the exception from the opposing category. The more similar the exception, the more the specificity of the exception increased to offset confusions with rule-following items from the contrasting category. This enhancement boosted recognition. These results provide further support that one learning system underlies rule-plus-exception learning, and that there is not a separate rule system governing performance.

D. Discussion

Human learners display flexibility in how they represent category information that outstrips the capacities of traditional single system models. In response, the field has developed multiple system models that are themselves not without problems. These multiple system models often contain a separate rule system. One such model, RULEX, could not account for the results presented here despite its complexity. Here, we pursue a theoretical approach that diverges from straightforward single system models and multiple system models—knowledge structures evolve as needed to satisfy the learner's goals.

CLUSTER embodies this third position. CLUSTER has a formally defined notion of goal that spans induction tasks, recruits clusters when existing clusters fail to support the learner's goals, and adjusts clusters' positions, attention, and association weights to reduce goal mismatch. These operations are sufficient to apply different procedures to different parts of the stimulus space, as multiple systems models do.

How do we reconcile our position with impressive evidence from cognitive neuroscience that multiple systems underlie human category learning performance? We do not deny that multiple learning systems underlie human category learning. A nonexhaustive list of systems includes a dopaminergic procedural learning system, a working memory system engaging cortical–thalamic loops, and a PFC-hippocampal-perirhinal learning system. The last system is marked by its flexibility and is adept at creating new conjunctive representations that link features (i.e., clusters). SUSTAIN (the precursor to CLUSTER) is readily put in correspondence with this learning circuit and has successfully simulated populations with hippocampal deficits by reducing the model's ability to form new clusters (Love & Gureckis, 2007). CLUSTER likely corresponds to the hippocampal system as well. We believe that a fast learning hippocampal system is shadowing the other learning systems. For instance, the literature is replete (including Sakamoto & Love, 2004) with cases in which learners are clearly applying a rule stored in working memory, but are nevertheless storing additional information about rule-following examples. Critically, we believe our empirical studies and simulations demonstrate that positing multiple systems is not enough in itself to explain human behavior. We believe that at least one of the systems posited must have the ability to build new representations flexibly in response to a learner's goals, like CLUSTER does.

The proposal that CLUSTER relates to a learning circuit involving the hippocampus is consistent with our position that experienced examples exert an influence on performance following learning, as opposed to experienced examples being completely abstracted away by a rule representation. The hippocampal memory system is closely tied to episodic memory, which requires memory for experienced examples. Love and Gureckis's (2007) account of CLUSTER and the hippocampal system posits that every semantic memory begins as an episodic memory (surprising events are stored as separate clusters). Although recruited clusters can be activated and modified by subsequent events, in many cases clusters will retain some information about the original episode.

Of course, much work remains to be done. Efforts are underway to apply CLUSTER to all the studies to which SUSTAIN has been applied. The results so far are promising. Additionally, we are applying CLUSTER to studies exploring how people partition knowledge and appear to apply different procedures depending on context (e.g., Yang & Lewandowsky, 2004). Finally, CLUSTER has been successfully applied to Kruschke's (1993) filtration and condensation tasks that were intended to demonstrate the necessity of dimensional attention (CLUSTER has cluster and feature-specific attention). Although CLUSTER does not have a built in notion of dimensional attention, dimensional attention emerges (i.e., there is advantage for aligning all clusters along the same contrasting features) much like how what looks like multiple learning systems emerges out of the Sakamoto and

Love (2004) simulations. While CLUSTER itself is still evolving, it appears it has the necessary constraints built in to account for human learning and no more. CLUSTER demonstrates that learning can be both intimately tied to the specifics of the training examples (in terms of presentation order, numerosity, similarity relations, etc.) and display the kinds of flexibility that human learners show. This flexibility outstrips multiple system models consisting of separate rule systems.

III. Learning Abstract Rules from Examples

The previous section suggested that people do not use mental rules to capture rule-like regularities defined over stimulus features. This section makes a bolder claim. Here, we claim that similar mechanisms rooted in concrete examples can explain our ability to acquire and apply seemingly abstract rules or concepts. Abstract rules are not defined over any particular set of stimulus properties. In the introduction, the concepts same and different were provided as examples of abstract rules. To provide another example, Chomsky (1957) described the rules of language as being abstract in nature. According to Chomsky, transformative and generative rules govern whether a sentence is grammatical. On this view, the set of grammatical sentences in a language is infinite and no specific set of features (e.g., "The" appears before "boy") can be used to classify sentences as grammatical or ungrammatical. The difficulty in imagining how such a complex and abstract concept could be acquired is one of the motivating pillars of the nativist position.

In this section, we argue that humans can learn seemingly abstract concepts by making analogy to concrete exemplars. Our view predicts that abstract concepts should display a family resemblance structure (cf. Rosch & Mervis, 1975) determined by similarity to stored exemplars. Evidence of such similarity effects would suggest a concrete basis to abstract concepts. To support our conjecture, we present an exemplar model of category learning that can learn seemingly abstract concepts by analogy to stored exemplars. To foreshadow our simulation results, the model, Building Relations through Instance Driven Gradient Error Shifting (BRIDGES), accounts for the acquisition of seemingly abstract concepts and correctly predicts that these concepts have a family resemblance structure rooted in experienced examples.

Exemplar models of category learning hold that all abstraction or generalization occurs through similarity-based activations of concrete examples. In contrast, CLUSTER formed abstractions directly in memory in the form of clusters. We will consider the relationship between CLUSTER and BRIDGES in the General Discussion. In exemplar models like BRIDGES, each experienced instance is stored in memory. When a new item is encountered, the similarity between the item and each exemplar in memory is calculated. The stimulus is predicted to belong to the category with the greatest sum of pairwise similarity (Medin & Schaffer, 1978). Thus, exemplar models clearly link experienced events to later generalization.

BRIDGES is derived from ALCOVE (Kruschke, 1992), a connectionist-based exemplar model of classification. ALCOVE learns to weight different aspects of the exemplars differently when calculating similarity. Through a process of trial-by-trial backpropagation of error, when computing the similarity between stimuli and exemplars, ALCOVE learns to ignore those aspects of the stimuli that are not predictive of correct classification. ALCOVE learns to generalize over the irrelevant features. When first learning about mammals, fur, or giving birth to live young might be considered important, but with enough experience possession of a mammary gland will become the sole predictor of category membership. Thus, ALCOVE can exhibit abstract behavior. However, ALCOVE, like many models of learning, is limited to only learning regularities over features.

BRIDGES generalizes ALCOVE by extending the notion of attention shifting and similarity to include relational match. The model supports the notion that analogy to stored experiences and attention shifting are the only attributes required of a model to appreciate abstract relationships. Furthermore, by incorporating ALCOVE's attentional shifting mechanisms into BRIDGES, we forward an explanation of how perceived similarity can change over the course of learning as more predictive stimulus properties are accentuated. Such attentional shifts will prove useful in demonstrating how seemingly abstract understandings can arise from analogies to concrete experiences.

Numerous accounts of how people detect and grade these analogical similarities exist (Connectionist Analogy Builder (CAB), Larkey, & Love, 2003; LISA, Hummel, & Holyoak, 1997; SME, Falkenhainer, Forbus, & Gentner, 1989). Most approaches assume that an analogy is a mapping from items in one domain to items in another domain (Gentner, 1983). The differences between the various models occur in how the domains are represented and exactly how the mapping process progresses. Although we illustrate BRIDGES using a variation of the theory behind the Structure-Mapping Engine (SME), other methods for detecting analogical fit could have instead been implemented. In fact, BRIDGES is readily implemented using radically different match procedures, such as transformation approaches. The transformation account holds that one analog is transformed into the other over a series of steps until they match (Hahn, Chater, & Richardson, 2003). The fewer the steps and the smaller their cost, the higher the resulting similarity is. Learning would progress in much the same way with attention shifting to more predictive transformations.

Structure mapping holds that people encode stimuli (e.g., objects, scenes, events) in terms of predicate representations that capture relations among entities (e.g., Revolves(planets,sun)). Relations can serve as arguments to other relations (e.g., Causes(GreaterMass(sun,planets), Revolves(planets, sun))). Structure mapping posits that people align structured representations to find the most satisfying correspondences. Satisfying correspondences are those that map elements playing identical roles in corresponding relations. Higher-order relations (i.e., relations serving as arguments to other relations) can serve to disambiguate and strengthen candidate mappings between analogs. In the solar system/atom example, an analogical sounds alignment places the sun in correspondence with the nucleus and the planets in correspondence with the electrons. Sounder mappings lead to increased perceived similarity (Gentner & Markman, 1997).

A. Abstraction Through Attention Shifting

By bridging the work from analogy to category learning, the BRIDGES model is able to demonstrate relational abstraction by extending the traditional definition of similarity used in category learning to make use of analogical alignment. For any given comparison between a stimulus and a stored exemplar, BRIDGES considers all of the possible one-to-one mappings between the stimulus and each exemplar.[2] For each exemplar, similarity is determined according to a difference measure that incorporates notions of featural and relational mismatch (see Fig. 4). A relational mismatch of 1 occurs when a relation does not exhibit parallel connectivity[3] (i.e., the mapped entities play different roles in their respective relations, see the right panel of Fig. 4). A featural mismatch of 1 occurs when nonidentical entities or entities containing mismatching features are mapped to one another (see the right panel of Fig. 4). As Fig. 4 illustrates how these two measures can be at odds.

Both types of mismatch are weighted by attention weights and the sum of these attention weighted mismatches yields an overall differences measure that is inversely proportional to similarity. The mapping that maximizes similarity (i.e., minimizes attention weighted difference) is chosen. These exemplar similarity values serve as exemplar unit activations and are passed across association weights to category units (e.g., predator and prey).

[2] Models of analogical alignment avoid this exhaustive search by using heuristics to guide the mapping process. BRIDGES could be extended to incorporate these shortcuts, but instead we focus on the basic ideas underlying BRIDGES.

[3] Systematicity has been left out as a constraint because it falls out as a natural consequence of parallel connectivity (Larkey & Love, 2003).

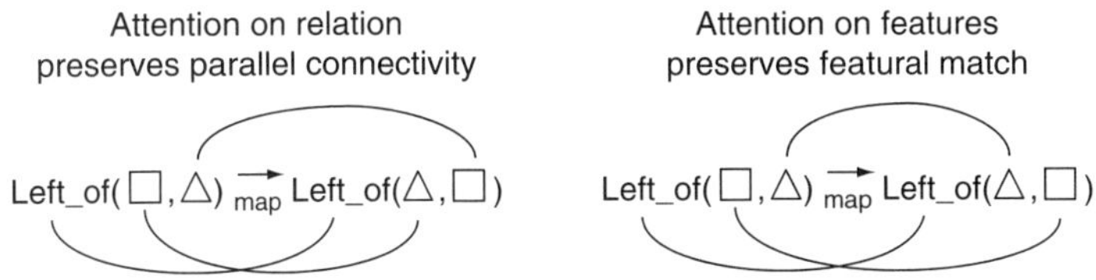

Fig. 4. There are two possible ways to map the elements in these corresponding relations. The example on the left preserves parallel connectivity by mapping elements that play the same role in each relation to one another. This solution is high in relational match, but low in featural match because the corresponding elements differ in shape features. The situation is reversed in the mapping shown in the right example. Attention weighting of mismatches determines which of these two possible mappings will be preferred by BRIDGES. BRIDGES chooses the mapping that minimizes attention-weighted mismatch.

The stimulus tends to be classified into the category whose unit has the greatest activation.

After feedback is provided, attention weights and association weights between exemplars and category units are adjusted to reduce error. Changes in attentional weights can lead to different future mappings. When attention shifts away from features and toward relations, parallel connectivity (i.e., analogical match) is stressed over featural similarity and BRIDGES demonstrates abstract understanding of a domain. Conversely, when featural matches lead to successful predictions, attention shifts toward features and BRIDGES is governed by featural similarity. When relational information is not discriminative or present, BRIDGES reduces to the standard ALCOVE model. A complete formalism for BRIDGES can be viewed in Tomlinson and Love (2006).

B. Relations Without Rules

Marcus, Vijayan, Bandi Rao, & Vishton (1999) found that infants could discriminate between abstract patterns or grammars of speech sounds. Importantly, this discrimination could not be accomplished by any weighting of phonetic features. Because featural regularities could not be leveraged to discriminate between grammars, Marcus et al. proposed that infants utilized variable binding in conjunction with algebraic rules to master such learning tasks.

We posit, based on evidence provided by BRIDGES, that infants do not use algebraic rules. Instead, the rule-like behavior arises from a comparison process between stimuli and previous exemplars coupled with a learned attention shift away from the concrete features of the stimuli to the relations within the stimuli.

In Marcus et al. (1999), 7-month-old infants were exposed to sentences that followed either an AAB pattern or an ABB pattern. The sentences were made up of simple monosyllable sounds (words) such as "GA TI TI." After training on one of the patterns, the infants were tested with novel phonemes following the same patter or the opposite pattern (e.g., "BA BA GU"). The researchers found that 15 of the 16 infants were able to distinguish between the two grammars using novel phonemes.

BRIDGES was fit to the study. Each sentence (e.g., "GA TI TI") was represented as an exemplar. BRIDGES's exemplar representation for "GA TI TI" is shown in Table II. Each syllable is represented as an entity involved in a type-token relation with an abstract representation of the type. Each syllable's position in the speech stream is encoded by a positional feature. These syllables have a number of phonetic features that are not represented in these simulations. Not including such features follows Marcus et al.'s presumption that no significant regularities exist across these features. Importantly, including uncorrelated features does not alter the pattern of our simulation results.

Critically, relational information was included in BRIDGES's representations. BRIDGES makes a distinction between tokens and types. In effect, we assume that infants have developed categories of speech sounds (Eimas, Siqueland, Jusczyk, & Vigorito, 1971). These type relations allow for abstract patterns to be uncovered through analogy to stored exemplars as one type of sound can be mapped to another.

Following Love et al. (2004), unsupervised learning was modeled by a network consisting of a single category output unit with a target value of 1 for all stimuli. In effect, this category unit is a familiarity detector. Association and attention weights in the model were learned which uncovered the underlying regularities across the sentences to yield consistently high familiarity (i.e., high output values for the category unit).

During habituation, the 16 unique sentences were presented three times each to BRIDGES and stored as exemplars. On each presentation, association and attention weights were updated. Though not critical, we assumed

TABLE II

BRIDGES'S REPRESENTATION OF "GA TI TI"

Entities	Features	Relations
GA_1	Position (GA_1) = 1	Type of (GA_1, GA)
TI_1	Position (TI_1) = 2	Type of (TI_1, TI)
TI_2	Position (TI_2) = 3	Type of (TI_2, TI)

that the saliency of positional features is sufficiently great to constrain the mapping process (i.e., words in sentences align temporally). Besides position (which does not discriminate between grammars), no regularities across features or entities existed. However, parallel connectivity was perfect for members of the same grammar. For instance, "GA TI TI" is isomorphic to "LI NA NA" in that all token and types in the type relation (see Table II) can be mapped to one another and preserve parallel connectivity. This degree of perfect match caused BRIDGES to shift attention to the type relation. This shift makes BRIDGES sensitive to the underlying grammar and immune to changes of the phonemes, rendering novel sentences following the original grammar somewhat familiar. Sentences not following the learned grammar can be mapped to the stored exemplars, but parallel connectivity is violated making these items less familiar and resulting in greater looking time as infants dishabituate.

BRIDGES was able to learn to discriminate between abstract patterns on the basis of analogical similarity. Storing concrete exemplars, shifting attention, and analogical matching are sufficient to show generalization to novel items. BRIDGES's success calls into question Marcus et al.'s (1999) claim that algebraic rules underlie infant performance. However, BRIDGES's success is attributable to its ability to bind arguments to relations, which is consistent Marcus et al.'s claim that infants bind variables.

Marcus (1999) has criticized other accounts (Seidenberg & Elman, 1999) of these results for including a same/different detector. The BRIDGES simulations do not explicitly label speech sounds as identical, rather the model assumes that infants can categorize speech sounds, as embodied by the type/token distinction. BRIDGES's solution does not hinge on a same detector. In fact, the patterns that can be discriminated by analogical mapping (even in simple domains in which only the type relation is present) are more encompassing than the concepts *same* and *different*. The analogical mapping process in these simulations aligned the current stimulus to stored exemplars—BRIDGES did not label words within sentences as same or different nor did it shift attention to a same feature. Abstract responding arose through analogy to stored exemplars and attention shifting from concrete features to relations.

C. Graded Responses as Similarity

One of the key assumptions of BRIDGES is that the basis for understanding abstract relations is similarity based and therefore inherently graded. The design of the Marcus et al. study did not allow for assessment of this possibility because stimuli were either grammatical or ungrammatical. According to BRIDGES, learners can both respond abstractly (i.e., generalize to featurally novel stimuli) and show evidence for the influence of past examples. If BRIDGES is correct, category membership in relationally defined categories is graded as it is in natural categories (Rosch & Mervis, 1975).

To evaluate BRIDGES's predictions, we will consider results from a series of studies exploring how pigeons and humans learn notions of same and different. To illustrate how BRIDGES learns the concepts same and different, we applied BRIDGES to Young and Wasserman's (1997) study demonstrating that pigeons can learn to discriminate between arrays of same and different icons. To foreshadow, Young and Wasserman's results indicate that pigeons can master a notion of same and different that cannot be explained by featural similarity. At the same time, the pigeons are sensitive to the particular examples they experienced during training and display a graded notion of same and different. Although fascinating, it would be easy to dismiss these results as relevant to pigeon cognition, but not human cognition. However, later work found the same pattern of performance with human subjects (Castro, Young, & Wasserman, 2006; Young & Wasserman, 2001). Humans as a group are slightly more deterministic than pigeons, but this group difference is within the range of individual differences. The bottom and top 20% of humans clearly bracket the mean performance of pigeons.

In Young and Wasserman (1997), pigeons learned to respond differentially to displays containing 16 identical and 16 different icons. On each trial, the 16 icons were randomly placed within a 5×5 grid. The pigeons were reinforced for pushing a green button when presented with a same stimulus and a red button when presented with a different stimulus. Training consisted of blocks of 16 same stimuli and 16 different stimuli in a random order. An identical set of icons was used to form stimuli for both the same and different items, making it impossible to correctly associate an icon or icon feature with a response. The pigeons were trained until 80% accuracy and then tested.

The test phase consisted of intermediate stimuli that were somewhat similar to both the same and different stimuli experienced in the training phase. Some examples of the intermediate stimuli are shown in Fig. 5. These stimuli can be viewed as forming a continuum between the pure same stimuli (all 16 icons identical) and the pure different stimuli (all 16 icons different) used during the training phase. The pigeon's performance in these intermediate conditions, as well as BRIDGES's predictions, is shown in Fig. 6.

Like the Marcus et al. (1999) simulations, we adopted a minimal approach to stimulus representation in fitting the BRIDGES model. Each stimulus's icon was represented as an entity. Each of the 16 entities participated in a type relation as in the Marcus et al. simulations (see Table II).

Through training BRIDGES discovered analogical mappings among presented stimuli and exemplars stored in memory that correctly predicted the label for the training stimuli. For example, consider aligning a stimulus

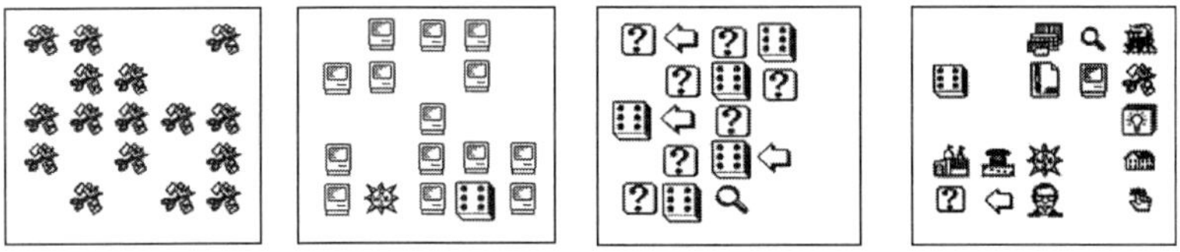

Fig. 5. Pigeons were trained on pure same or different stimuli like those shown on the far left and far right. At test, intermediate cases between pure same and different stimuli were shown like the middle two stimuli.

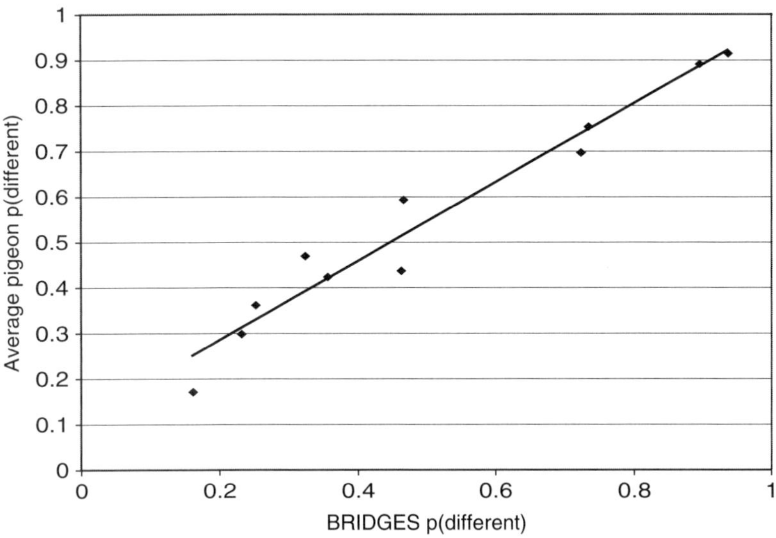

Fig. 6. The results from Young and Wasserman's (1997) studies and BRIDGES's predictions are shown. The 11 intermediate conditions form a continuum between pure same and pure different stimuli. Figure 5 provides two examples of such intermediate cases. Detailed descriptions of these intermediate can be found in Young and Wasserman (1997).

containing 16 squares to another stimulus containing 16 triangles. Each triangle entity is put into correspondence with a square entity. This results in a perfect feature mismatch, but parallel connectivity is preserved. Within each type relation, the type triangle maps to the type square. This alignment leads to attention shifting toward the type relation and away from the entities. In contrast, only 1 out of 16 type relations will exhibit parallel connectivity when aligning a different stimulus with a same stimulus. Thus, it is straightforward for BRIDGES to discriminate between same and different stimuli in the absence of featural support, by learning to pay attention to the number of type relations that match between the stimuli.

BRIDGES used the same similarity measure with the intermediate stimuli during testing. For example, the second stimulus from the right in Fig. 5 would result in 7 of 16 (seven identical icons) relational matches to each same exemplar and 4 of 16 (four distinct icon types) relational matches to each different exemplar. Similarity-based activations are not all or none and these intermediate cases activate stored examplars to varying degrees, leading to gradation in response. This gradation of response almost exactly matches the responding of the pigeons to the intermediate stimuli ($R^2 = .95$).

This simulation demonstrates how abstract concepts can be acquired through storage and analogy to concrete examples. BRIDGES's excellent fit of the intermediate conditions is a natural consequence of similarity-based processing. Like natural categories, BRIDGES predicts that relational categories have a graded structure.

D. Discussion

By combining insights from the category learning and analogy literatures, BRIDGES provides an account of how people and animals can gain abstract understandings of domains based solely on experience with concrete instances. BRIDGES's power arises from using a notion of similarity informed by work in both analogy and category learning. Structural alignment processes allow BRIDGES to appreciate analogical similarities, while attention shifting modifies BRIDGES notion of similarity over the course of learning. Integrating these mechanisms allows BRIDGES to grasp abstract patterns by shifting attention to relations which drive the alignment process.

In the supportive simulations, BRIDGES offered an explanation of how infants become sensitive to abstract grammars and how people and pigeons develop the concepts of same and different irrespective of a stimulus's features. BRIDGES's exemplar-based representation of experienced examples and trial-by-trial error-driven learning were sufficient to capture seemingly abstract concepts. Consistent with the stance that abstract concepts are similarity based, the relational concepts same and different display graded membership like natural categories.

BRIDGES is not the first model to use analogical alignment to support category learning. SEQL can acquire category structures through a process of repeated abstraction of a structured category representation and has been successfully applied to the infant grammar learning studies considered here (Kuehne, Gentner, & Forbus, 2003). While SEQL stresses building abstract representations, abstraction in BRIDGES arises from shifting attention. Some relative strengths of BRIDGES are that it extends an existing model of category learning (ALCOVE is a special case of BRIDGES) and incorporates attentional mechanisms.

One challenge for BRIDGES is incorporating new relational information into its exemplar representations. Although BRIDGES can learn relational concepts, BRIDGES is not yet able to incorporate acquired relations directly into its exemplar representations (see Doumas & Hummel, 2005, for an example of a predicate discovery system).

IV. Learning to Reason About Rewards in Dynamic Environments

The previous examples demonstrate how abstract rule-like behavior may be rooted in concrete experience. As a final example, we examine how people learn to control a dynamic system that continually evolves in response to their ongoing interaction. Like the categorization studies reviewed above, these experiments and simulations emphasize the way people learn (what appear to be) abstract rules that help them achieve their current goal. However, like our previous simulations, we will show how this rule-like behavior may emerge, not from abstract reasoning processes, but through simple trial-by-trial updates of concrete task representations.

A. Learning in Dynamic Tasks

Flexible adaptation to our environment requires us to learn in a variety of ways. Fortunately, a teacher is often times available to provide us with corrective feedback or instruction (i.e., supervised learning). However, in other situations we must discover for ourselves the relevant contingencies in the world through trial and error. For example, many video games require players to discover sequences of actions that allow them to advance to a new level through trial-and-error learning. In a set of recent studies (Gureckis & Love, 2008a,b), we have examined how people discover response strategies that maximize their long-term benefit in an interactive task environment where the structure of rewards continually change in response to the actions of the individual (see Berry & Broadbent, 1988, or Stanley, Mathew, Russ, & Kotler-Cope, 1989, for a similar approach).

In our task (called the "Farming on Mars" task), subjects are given a cover story about controlling two fictitious farming robots on a distant planet in order to generate oxygen for future human inhabitants. On each trial, subjects are asked to make repeated choices between these two alternatives (i.e., robots) with the goal of maximizing the rewards (i.e., oxygen) they receive over the entire experiment. On any given trial, one robot always generated more oxygen than the other. However, each time the subject selects this more attractive alternative, the long-range expected utility of both robots is lowered on the following trial. Thus, the strategy which provides the most reward over the entire experiment is to choose what appears to be the immediately inferior robot on every trial. Critically, the nature of this contingency is only revealed to subjects through their ongoing interaction with the system (i.e., responses and associated rewards) and subjects must learn for themselves how to maximize their earnings.

The conflict between short- and long-term rewards in our task is relevant to many realworld decision making situations. For example, drug addicts are often unable to overcome the desire for an immediate high despite the long-term consequences to their health. Interestingly, a number of studies that have examined choice behavior in tasks where short- and long-term rewards conflict have found that both humans and other animals often fail to inhibit the tendency to select an initially attractive option even when doing so leads to lower rates of reinforcement overall, a phenomena referred to as melioration (Herrnstein, 1991; Herrnstein & Prelec, 1991; Neth, Sims, & Gray, 2006; Tunney & Shanks, 2002). This pattern of results appears at odds with rational accounts, which dictate that decision makers follow a strategy that maximizes their long-term expected utility (see Tunney & Shanks, 2002, for a similar discussion). However, the rational account fails to specify how this optimal strategy should be determined in an unknown environment.

Indeed, one interesting question concerns the process by which learners arrive at effective strategies in these kinds of highly interactive and dynamic tasks. By one account, subjects reason in an abstract way about the contingencies in the task and effortfully evaluate the costs and benefits of various choice strategies. Such a strategy might involve explicit planning and sequencing of future choices, as well as evaluation of candidate plans through hypothesis testing. Instead, we propose that people engage in a trial-by-trial value estimation procedure using reinforcement learning. Success under this scheme is closely linked to people's representation of the underlying state of the system, which can be inferred from perceptual cues in the environment. Here, as in our previous examples, abstract behavior appears to emerge naturally from a learning process which is more directly grounded in concrete experience.

B. Bootstrapping Abstract Strategies from Concrete Cues

In one set of experiments (Gureckis & Love, 2008b), we evaluated how subjects use cues about their current state to support their learning and decision making abilities. The term state simply refers to a discrete situation that a situated agent may be in with respect to their environment. For example, a state might correspond to an agent being in a particular location in a maze. For agents interacting in an unknown environment, successful identification of the current state can provide important source of information that can help structure their behavior. For example, when an agent determines they are in a particular location in a maze, they can use that knowledge to help determine which direction to head next in order to increase the chances of successful escape. While representations of the current state can help determine which actions to take in particular situations, identifying task-relevant states in an unknown environment can be challenging. For example, in a maze it is often possible to arrive at physically different locations which are perceptually identical (e.g., two hallways which have the same configuration of doorways and junctions). In this case, the agent must deal with the problem of perceptual aliasing (McCallum, 1993; Whitehead & Ballard, 1991), where multiple percepts may map onto a single state or situation in the world.

Determining the mapping from observations in the world to relevant task states about which the agent can learn is often a nontrivial problem. For example, in the standard version of the Farming on Mars task, successive states of the task environment are not clearly distinguished from one another. Figure 7 and the associated caption describe the payoff structure of the basic version of the task. Note that each time a player makes a choice, the underlying state of the task system can change so that reward possibilities on the next trial are different than they were on the previous trial. However, no discriminative cues are available about how the current state of the system has changed as a result of the agents actions. As a result, functionally distinct task states which lead to different rewards tend to alias together, making it difficult for the learner to detect the subtle contingency between their past actions and future rewards. Indeed, one hypothesis tested in our studies is that the aliasing of functionally distinct task states might partially explain why subjects seem to prefer short-term, melioration strategies.

We consider how to limit this aliasing and encourage learners to adopt useful representations of the state structure of the task. Subjects in our experiment were assigned to one of three conditions which provided different kinds of perceptual cues about the current state of the Mars farming system. In the no-cue condition, subjects were tested in the simple two-choice task described above and were given no additional information. Subjects in this condition were susceptible to perceptual aliasing of successive task states as there was no discriminative information available to indicate how the task environment was changing in response to the learners' actions. In two other conditions (the shuffled-cue and consistent-cue conditions) subjects display was augmented to include a row of indicator lights. Only one of these lights was active at any point in time, the position of which correlated with the current state of the system.

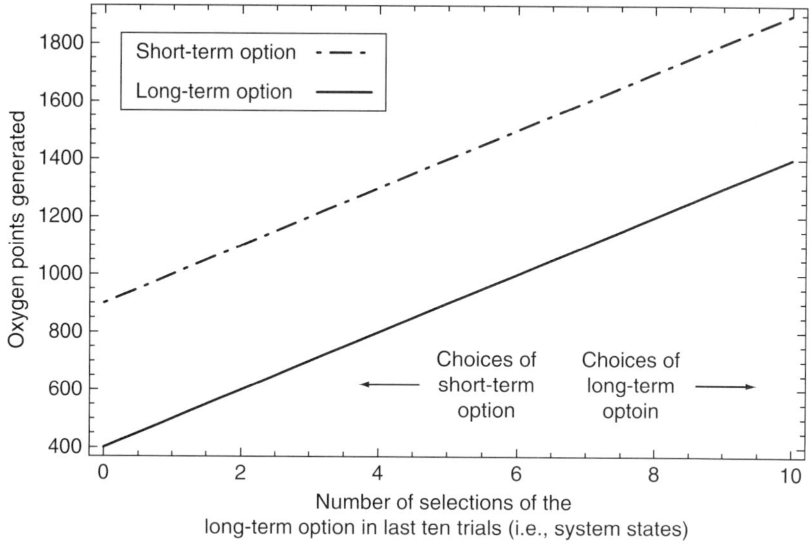

Fig. 7. The payoff structure for the Farming on Mars task used in Gureckis & Love (2008b, Exp. 1). Unknown to subjects, one option (i.e. robot) always generates more oxygen than the other on any given trial. For example, at the midpoint along the horizontal axis, selecting the more immediately productive option (referred to as the short-term option) would generate 1300 oxygen units, whereas selecting the other option (referred to as the long-term option) would generate only 800 oxygen units. However, each time the short-term option is selected, the expected output of both options is lowered on the following trial (i.e., the state of the system shifts to the left). Selections of the long-term option behave in the opposite fashion. The current state of the system (i.e., position along the horizontal axis) depends on the number of long-term selections subjects make over the preceding ten trials. Note that the reward received from repeatedly selecting the long-term option exceeds that from always selecting the short-term option (i.e., the highest point of the long-term option curve is above the lowest point for the short-term option curve). As a result, the optimal strategy is to select the long-term option on every trial, even though selecting the short-term option would earn more on any single trial.

In the consistent-cue condition, the indicator lights were organized in a regular fashion such that the active light moved one position either to the left or to the right as the state was updated. In other words, the light veridically represented the current position of the task environment along the horizontal axis in Fig. 7. In this condition, neighboring states in the task corresponded to neighboring positions of the indicator light. The shuffled-cue condition also featured indicator lights, but the relationship between neighboring states was obscured by randomly assigning each state to a particular light. In the shuffled-cue condition, the position of the light was still perfectly predictive of the underlying state of the farming system, but the relationship between successive states and the magnitude of the reward signal was less obvious because neighboring states are unlikely to have neighboring indicator lights (e.g., the lit indicator could "jump" as one moves from state to state). We predicted that systematic cues which afford generalization between successive states (such as those in the consistent-cue condition) would be most effective for learning as they allow experience in one state to be easily generalized to related states. Note that the addition of the perceptual cue in the consistent-cue and shuffled-cue conditions does not render the task trivial—subjects still need to learn that the short-term option yields less reward over the course of the experiment than the long-term option to excel at the task.

Figure 8 shows the basic pattern of results from Experiment 1 of Gureckis and Love (2008b). In the no-cue condition, subjects had no strong preference for either option (the proportion of trials in which the long-term maximizing response was selected was .52). In contrast, subjects in the consistent-cue condition made significantly more selections of the long-term, reward-maximizing option (.76) compared to either the shuffled-cue (.57) or no-cue conditions. This pattern of results suggests that an important factor limiting performance in the standard version of the task is in identifying the current task state. When given a simple cue which reflected the underlying state of the system (the purpose of which was never explicitly explained), subjects performance drastically improved. Note that the advantage for state information also extends to the shuffled-cue condition. Subjects in this condition started out with a tendency to select the short-term, impulsive option, but later switched to moderately favor the long-term, maximizing-response option. However, subjects' performance appears to benefit most in the consistent-cue condition where the dynamics of the state indicator cue were consistent with the true underlying structure of successive task states.

In summary, subjects in our experiment generally failed to find a reward maximizing strategy unless they were given cues about the current state of the task environment. These results are particularly interesting, given previous work showing that across a variety of manipulations designed to encourage long-term responding, subjects seem to prefer suboptimal strategies (Neth et al., 2006; Tunney & Shanks, 2002). Across the three experimental conditions, subjects' task was held constant. The only difference concerned the presence and dynamic structure of cues that reflected of the underlying state of the task environment. Subjects's learning abilities appear to bootstrap off these concrete perceptual features. Without cues, learners had difficulty constructing an abstract representation of the task dynamics which impaired their ability to detect the relationship between their actions and future rewards. The ability to effectively discover and use an abstract rule may first depend on identifying the correct mental representation of the task environment, which itself maybe tied to concrete, perceptual aspects of the learning environment.

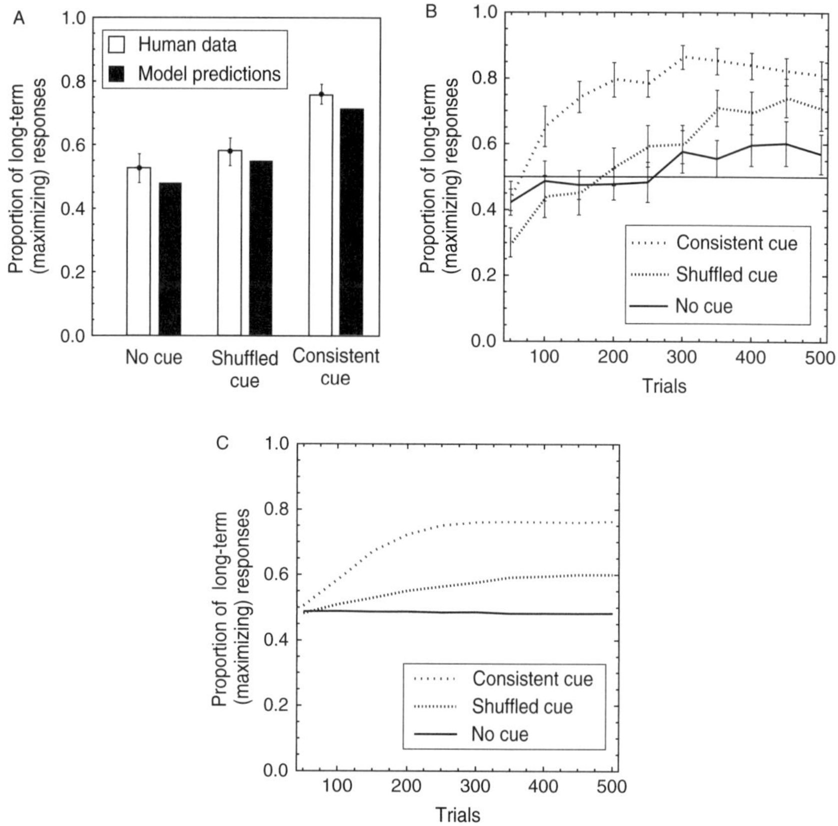

Fig. 8. Overall results of Experiment 1 and accompanying simulations from Gureckis and Love (2008b). Panel A shows the average proportion of maximizing response made throughout the experiment as a function of condition for both human subjects and the model. Panel B presents performance curves for human subjects calculated as the average proportion of maximizing responses considered in blocks of 50 trials at a time for all three condition. Error bars are standard errors of the mean. Panel C shows the same performance curves for the model.

The time course of learning in the task reveals interesting details about the way that subjects learned about the reward contingencies in the task. In all three conditions, subjects started out with a bias toward the short-term impulsive option, but gradually increased the proportion of trials on which they selected the long-term option (Fig. 8B). The specific shape of this pattern (early melioration followed by a gradual shift toward maximizing) suggests that subjects incrementally explored the task environment. Early in learning and prior to much exploration, subjects settled on a suboptimal short-term strategy. However, later in the task, as random, exploratory actions accumulated performance gradually improved. Closer analyses of individual subjects response trajectory showed that the shift from short- to long-term responding was in most cases gradual, taking place over a period of 100 or more trials.

C. Using Reinforcement Learning to Model Task Performance

In order to understand the cognitive processes that underlie performance in the task we developed a simple computational model within the Reinforcement Learning (RL) framework (Sutton & Barto, 1998). RL is an agent-based approach to learning through interaction with the environment. In recent years, RL has attracted considerable attention based on its success in both practical applications (such as flying helicopters, Bagnell & Schneider, 2001, and teaching computers to play backgammon, Tesauro, 1994), and in the modeling of biological systems (Daw & Touretzky, 2002; Montague, Dayan, & Sejnowski, 1996; Montague, Dayan, Person, & Sejnowski, 1995; Schultz, Dayan, & Montague, 1997; Suri, Bargas, & Arbib, 2001). What makes RL an interesting tool for understanding higher-level cognition is the fact that it details how situated learners can bootstrap effective behavioral strategies through self-guided interactions with an unknown environment.

A key feature of the simple RL models considered here is their ability to develop strategies that take into account delayed outcomes. However, unlike classical planning methods from artificial intelligence, our model can learn what appear to be far-sighted strategies in an incremental, trial-by-trial fashion. Our account is fundamentally shortsighted and reactive: The agent's only goal is to greedily choose whichever action is estimated to be best on each trial. However, through a trial-by-trial update procedure the model is able to learn estimates which reflect the long-term value of actions. Through a simple bootstrapping procedure (related to the well-known temporal-difference algorithm, Sutton & Barto, 1998), immediate online experience is passed backwards to adjust the estimates of previous executed actions. Through a combination of learning, exploration, and bootstrapping, globally optimal rule-like behavior can emerge in the model through direct error-driven learning. In the interest of brevity, we refer the reader to Gureckis and Love (2008b) for the mathematical details of the model, and instead elaborate three psychological principles that motivate the model.

1. *Principle 1: Learning Depends on Subjects' Mental Representation of the Task*

On each trial, the model assumes that people attempt to choose the actions (or robot) that they estimate will earn the most reward over the long run. To do this, the model maintains estimates the long-term value of selecting a particular action *a* in state *s*, as *a* value referred to as *Q*(*s*, *a*) (or more generally a *Q*-value). Note, however, that because the estimate of any action depends on the current task state, *s*, subjects' identification of the true state of the environment plays a fundamental role in learning. Indeed, the model's estimate of the *Q*-value of a particular action on any trial is a simple linear function of the current input cues (which correspond to the indicator lights presented to subjects in the task). The model attempts to learn the mapping between input cues and the *Q*-values associated with each state using a simple single-layer network (Widrow & Hoff, 1960). Changing the types of input cues the model is given modulates the ability of the model to learn the appropriate representation of the state structure of the task and ultimately influences its ability to uncover an optimal response strategy.

2. *Principle 2: Learning Involves Taking into Account Future Rewards*

Each time an action is selected, the model updates its current estimate of the corresponding *Q*-value according to the temporal-difference error between the reward received as a result of that action and a current estimate of the future reward available from the following state-action pair. The model's asymptotic estimate of the value of each action depends on the relative weight given to immediate versus delayed rewards. In our model, the degree to which learners value short- or long-term rewards is determined by a simple discounting parameter (γ). When $\gamma = 0$, the learning procedure in the model reduces to the standard delta rule (Rescorla & Wagner, 1972; Wagner & Rescorla, 1972; Widrow & Hoff, 1960). Under these conditions, the model strongly favors immediate rewards (and thus predicts melioration behavior in the Farming on Mars task). As the value of γ increases, the model gives more weight to future rewards, eventually allowing it to favor selections of the long-term robot.

3. *Principle 3: Learning Involves Balancing Between Exploration and Exploitation*

Successful behavior in an unknown environment requires learners to balance the exploration of unknown alternatives versus the exploitation of resources or strategies that are known to be productive. In order to capture this tradeoff in the model, the estimated values of each state-action pair are input to a probabilistic choice mechanism that generates a final choice (Luce, 1959). Early in the task, this choice function favors exploration of actions which may appear to be less profitable. However, overtime the operation of this choice mechanism becomes more deterministic capturing the intuition that early in the experiment subjects are more willing to explore different alternatives, but later their behavior shifts to exploit the known resources they have uncovered.

In our simulations, the model was treated as an active participant in the Farming on Mars task and was given the same number of trials as human subject in which to explore the operation of the system and to uncover the optimal strategy. On each simulated trial the model selected either the short- or long-term option, the appropriate rewards were delivered, and the current state of the task system was updated. Through its ongoing experience the task, the model learns estimates of the value of choosing either the short- or long-term option via an adaptive learning procedure described above (Sutton & Barto, 1998).

Changing the types of cues the model is given about the current state of the system modulates the representation of the task that the model utilizes and ultimately influences its ability to uncover the optimal strategy. In simulations of the no-cue condition, the model (like human subjects) was given no discriminative information about the current task state. As a result, the model was forced to treat the task as consisting of just one, highly aliased state. In the consistent-cue condition, the model was presented with a set of input units that distinctly encoded the current position of the indicator light on the display. The input representation given to the model roughly matches the input provided to subjects, and allowed prediction and generalization between nearby states. Finally, in the shuffled-cue simulations, the input to the model was erratic. In some cases, there were source of predictability that the model could take advantage of, but in others the input cues could be misleading or force the model to become trapped in local, suboptimal solutions.

Figure 8A and C show the basic pattern of results. Using a single set of parameters across all three conditions the model was able to provide an excellent fit to the data. While the best fit parameters used to generate the learning curves in Fig. 8 tended to emphasize considerable exploration early on (thus the near-chance responding in the first few trials of the task), many other parameter combinations allowed the model to capture the trial-by-trial dynamics of human performance curves. For example, after a few early selections and prior to much exploration of the system, the model generally favored the short-term strategy of selecting the impulsive option on each trial. However, after a short period of time following this impulsive strategy, the continued accumulation of exploratory decisions eventually helps to shift the model toward a reward maximizing strategy.

Critically, learning in the model takes the form of trial-by-trial updates to estimates of the long-term value of each action in each possible state. In each state, the model is biased to choose the action whose estimated earnings are highest. However, there is no global representation in the model that represents a general rule about how to behave. Instead, performance is heavily tied to moment-to-moment estimates of estimated values of particular actions. In addition, our simulations show that learning critically depends on the structure of cues in the environment, which, in turn, structure the model's mental representation of the task. In the no-cue condition, the model fails to show any learning because all states collapse together. Building from this representation, the model has trouble developing a strategy which favors either option. In contrast, in the shuffled-cue and consistent-cue conditions, the structure of concrete, perceptual information in the environment helps to provide a framework for interpreting and integrating feedback.

D. Discussion

The experimental and simulation results reviewed in this section suggest that reasoning about complex systems can be accomplished through concrete means. All three conditions in our experiment involved the same reward structure, but subjects' performance across conditions varied as a function of the perceptual cues provided. We had success in helping subjects enrich their representation of the task environment by providing perceptual cues which reflected the underlying task state.

Overall, our results suggest that debates about rationality or optimality may be ill conceived. Learning in our task appears optimal with respect to the representation the learner adopts of the task environment which may or may not be congruent to the actual environment dynamics. The ability to approach the true "optimal" depended on the structure of concrete cues about system state in the environment. In this sense, abstract performance was shown to depend on concrete features of the environment.

Finally, our results show that subjects' ability to learn an effective control strategy is well accounted for by a simple RL learning based on trial-by-trial learning updates and simple task representations. Unlike other methods, the RL agent simulations did not explicitly plan, but instead reasoned in a reactive manner. Rather than engage in hypothesis testing strategies, the RL agent estimated the value of possible options by trial-by-trial updates. In addition, we offer a novel take on previous findings showing that humans and other animals prefer impulsive, short-term gains over higher utility future outcomes by suggesting that some of these failures may actually derive from how learners represent the relevant states and dynamics underlying their environment (as opposed to a failure in the ability to properly discount future outcomes).

V. General Discussion

When observing a complex system, it is tempting to ascribe sophisticated intentions and abilities. For instance, people sometimes believe machines, like personal computers and cars, are conspiring against them. The job of the cognitive psychologist is to observe the most complex of machines and entertain theories of how it works. Perhaps it is not surprising that many researchers believe humans possess transcendent and abstract thinking abilities. After all, humans appear to acquire abstract understandings of domains and reason in ways that indicate a deep understanding. In this chapter, we argued through three cases that, while humans can perform impressively and demonstrate broad generalization, our performance is intimately tied and colored by the concrete examples we experience during learning. In effect, we never fully transcend our training set.

In the first case study, we examined how people appear to acquire and apply rules. One popular account proposes multiple systems in which one system applies abstract rules and another system stores items that violate these rules (e.g., Nosofsky et al., 1994).

Instead, we found evidence for a single system in which both rule-following and rule-violating items are stored in a common substrate. Recognition performance for stimuli that violated rules indicated that the rules themselves were rooted in experienced examples. In particular, items that violated more frequent rules were remembered better. This effect was also found in studies that manipulated the similarity of rule-following items to exceptions from the opposing category. The results from both manipulations were explained by a clustering model that sharpened its memory representations for exception items in order to reduce confusions with rule-following items from the opposing category. The more extreme the confusions (because of either numerosity or similarity relations), the greater the enhanced memory for exception items. These results are both supportive of a clustering model that updates its representation by trial-by-trial learning, and inconsistent with dual route models that posit an abstract rule system. In summary, even when people mentally rehearse and consciously apply rules, the concrete details of the training examples affect performance.

The second case study makes a much stronger claim—abstract concepts and rules (i.e., concepts not reducible to a finite set of features) are in fact grounded in experienced examples. A model that stored each example in memory as an exemplar and made analogies to these stored exemplars was able to learn seemingly abstract concepts. In the first simulation, the model, BRIDGES, successfully simulated infant learning of abstract rules consisting of sound patterns. The model learned to extend the pattern to novel cases by making analogies to previous cases. This simulation alone provides a powerful existence proof that abstract rules may not be necessary. The second simulation tested a key prediction of BRIDGES that membership in seemingly abstract concepts is graded and determined by the similarity to stored examples. Data exploring how pigeons (and humans) learn the concepts of same and different were supportive of this prediction. After initial training on pure cases of the two concepts, intermediate cases partially activated exemplars from both concepts leading to graded responding. The exact nature of this gradient was predicted by BRIDGES notion of exemplar similarity, which incorporates a notion of analogical match.

In the final case study, we considered how people reason about rewards in dynamic environments in which learner's actions affect the underlying state of the system (e.g., much like how humans affect the climate). This study brings our analysis closer to the kinds of learning problems that people face in their daily lives. In these situations, do people reason explicitly about system dynamics, form a plan for future actions, and test hypotheses about the nature of the underlying system? While climatologists might undertake such analyses, our results indicate that nonexperts learn about such systems by exploring myopically and adjusting estimates of future rewards in a trial-by-trial fashion.

People's performance was consistent with simple reinforcement learning models that incrementally learn about rewards and use these tentative estimates of reward to bootstrap learning the long-term value of particular actions. People's performance was consistent with simple reinforcement learning models. These models incrementally learn about reward. Current estimates of future reward are used to bootstrap improved estimates of the long-term value of particular actions. While reinforcement learning models may appear to follow farsighted strategies, they are essentially reactive and do not explicitly plan ahead. Such models are exquisitely sensitive to how the state of the system is represented. Human subjects also proved to be sensitive to state representation. When human subjects were given a consistent cue to the underlying state of the system, they were able overcome an option that was more attractive in the short term and instead learned to prefer the option that was optimal in the long term.

These three cases demonstrate the power and richness of learning systems that learn by exposure to concrete examples. All three case studies involve fairly sophisticated and adaptive behaviors. The three models reach human proficiency in each case and correctly predict the idiosyncrasies of human behavior. These idiosyncrasies arise from our concepts being rooted in experienced examples and updated by incremental learning processes. One general lesson from these studies is that one should be cautious in making claims about the representational machinery needed to capture human behavior.

The three case studies we considered here each invoke a different model-based explanation. One key question is whether the models from the three case studies are the same in some sense. Certainly, the models differ in their details, but all three models learn incrementally, are myopic, are bound by experienced examples, and do not engage in hypothesis testing. Numerous relations exist among the three models. The BRIDGES model from the second case study generalizes ALCOVE, which itself is conceptually related to the CLUSTER model from the first case study. Work is currently underway on a version of BRIDGES that, instead of exemplars, represents concepts by clusters that are recruited in response to surprising events as in SUSTAIN and CLUSTER. Matt Jones and the first author have developed a reinforcement learning version of the CLUSTER model. This model offers a connection to the reinforcement learning model showcased in the third case study. One exciting possibility is incorporating analogical notions of similarity into reinforcement learning models. Doing so would enable generalization across analogical states, which could greatly speed learning. All three models considered here incorporate error terms that are minimized. Although all three models are distinct, common themes emerge and avenues for unifying these three models are within reach.

One common theme that emerges across models is that details of the training set are retained. Humans appear to operate in a similar fashion. One question is why would evolutionary processes or within individual learning processes settle on such a solution. One answer is robustness. Grounding performance and generalization in concrete cues present in the environment is a conservative strategy that increases system robustness and stability. Models grounded in these details are less likely to become decoupled from environmental feedback and run amok. Also, details that appear irrelevant at the current moment may prove critical in the future. The complexity and dynamic nature of our environment might dictate such learning mechanisms.

Our discussion has been titled in favor of single system models over multiple system models, particularly in regards to multiple system models containing a rule route. To clarify our stance, we are not opposed to multiple system proposals in general, but we do believe that successful multiple system proposals will be bounded by experienced examples. Of course, proposing multiple systems does not in itself guarantee success. The second case study makes this point by demonstrating that existing dual system accounts do not account for human rule-plus-exception learning behavior. We take our results to indicate that models must be both adaptable and grounded in experienced examples, like the CLUSTER model. We are agnostic about whether such proposals are best described as single or multiple learning system models.

One strength of our theoretical outlook is that it does not demand leaps of imagination to accept. In contrast, we do not see in principle how the human brain could acquire truly abstract representations given that our perceptions and actions are embedded in a noisy world of concrete examples. Evoking a nativist position does not solve the conundrum, as abstract representations would need to be learned over evolutionary time and must be retrieved within the individual's life via perceptual cues in the environment. Our account also has the advantage of not being at odds with sensible intuitions about ontogenetic and phylogenetic continuity. We predict that other species (e.g., pigeons) are cleverer than we expect and that the abstract nature of our own thought is overstated.

Acknowledgments

This work was supported by AFOSR grant FA9550-04-1-0226, ARL grant W911NF-07-2-0023, and NSF CAREER grant 0349101 to B.C. Love.

References

Allen, S. W., & Brooks, L. R. (1991). Specializing the operation of an explicit rule. *Journal of Experimental Psychology: General, 120*, 3–19.

Ashby, F., & O'Brien, J. B. (2005). Category learning and multiple memory systems. *Trends in Cognitive Sciences, 9*, 83–89.

Ashby, F., & Maddox, W. (2005). Human category learning. *Annual Review of Psychology, 56*, 149–178.

Bagnell, J. A., & Schneider, J. (2001). Autonomous helicopter control using reinforcement learning policy search methods. In *International Conference on Robotics and Automation.* (pp. 1615–1620). IEEE press.

Berry, D. C., & Broadbent, D. E. (1988). Interactive tasks and the implicit-explicit distinction. *British Journal of Psychology, 79*, 251–272.

Carpenter, G., & Grossberg, S. (2003). Adaptive resonance theory. In M. Arbib (Ed.), *The handbook of brain theory and neural networks* (pp. 87–90). Cambridge, MA: MIT Press.

Castro, L., Young, M. E., & Wasserman, E. A. (2006). Effects of number of items and visual display variability on same-different discrimination behavior. *Memory & Cognition, 34*(8), 1689–1703.

Chomsky, N. (1957). *Syntactic structures*. The Hague/Paris: Mouton.

Clapper, J. P., & Bower, G. H. (1994). Category invention in unsupervised learning. *Journal of Experimental Psychology: Learning, Memory, & Cognition, 20*, 443–460.

Daw, N., & Touretzky, D. (2002). Long-term reward prediction in td models of the dopamine system. *Neural Computation, 14*, 603–616.

Doumas, L. A. A., & Hummel, J. E. (2005). A symbolic-connectionist model of relational discovery. In *Proceedings of the Twenty-Seventh Annual Conference of the Cognitive Science Society*. Hillsdale, NJ: Erlbaum.
Eimas, P., Siqueland, E., Jusczyk, P., & Vigorito, J. (1971). Infant speech perception. *Science, 171*(3968), 303–306.
Erickson, M. A., & Kruschke, J. K. (1998). Rules and exemplars in category learning. *Journal of Experimental Psychology: General, 127*, 107–140.
Falkenhainer, B., Forbus, K. D., & Gentner, D. (1989). The structure mapping engine: Algorithm and examples. *Artificial Intelligence, 41*, 1–63.
Forbus, K. D., Gentner, D., & Law, K. (1994). MAC/FAC: A model of similarity-based retrieval. *Cognitive Science, 19*, 141–205.
Gentner, D. (1983). Structure-mapping: A theoretical framework for analogy. *Cognitive Science, 7*, 155–170.
Gentner, D., & Markman, A. B. (1997). Structure mapping in analogy and similarity. *American Psychologist, 52*, 45–56.
Gureckis, T., & Love, B. C. (2008a). Solving partially observable markov decision processes via reinforcement learning. Manuscript under review.
Gureckis, T., & Love, B. C. (2008b). Short term gains, long term pains: Reinforcement learning in dynamic environments. Manuscript under review.
Hahn, U., Chater, N., & Richardson, L. B. (2003). Similarity as transformation. *Cognition, 87*, 1–32.
Herrnstein, R. (1991). Experiments on stable suboptimality in individual behavior. *The American Economic Review, 81*(2), 360–364.
Herrnstein, R., & Prelec, D. (1991). Melioration: A theory of distributed choice. *The Journal of Economic Perspectives, 5*(3), 137–156.
Hummel, J. E., & Holyoak, K. J. (1997). Distributed representations of structure: A theory of analogical access and mapping. *Psychological Review, 104*, 427–466.
Kruschke, J. K. (1992). ALCOVE: An exemplar-based connectionist model of category learning. *Psychological Review, 99*, 22–44.
Kruschke, J. K. (1993). Human category learning: Implications for backpropagation models. *Connection Science, 5*, 3–36.
Kuehne, S., Gentner, D., & Forbus, K. (2003). Modeling infant learning via symbolic structural alignment. In *Proceedings of the twenty-second annual conference of the Cognitive Science Society*. Hillsdale, NJ: Erlbaum.
Kurtz, K. J. (2007). The divergent autoencoder (DIVA) model of category learning. *Psychonomic Bulletin & Review, 14*(4), 560–576.
Larkey, B. L., & Love, B. C. (2003). CAB: Connectionist Analogy Builder. *Cognitive Science, 27*, 781–794.
Loftus, G. R., & Masson, M. E. J. (1994). Using confidence intervals in within-subject designs. *Psychonomic Bulletin & Review, 1*, 476–490.
Love, B. C. (2005). Environment and goals jointly direct category acquisition. *Current Directions in Psychological Science, 14*, 195–199.
Love, B. C., & Gureckis, T. M. (2007). Models in search of a brain. *Cognitive, Affective, & Behavioral Neuroscience, 7*, 90–108.
Love, B. C., & Jones, M. (2006). The emergence of multiple learning systems. *Proceedings of the Cognitive Science Society*. Mahwah, NJ: Erlbaum.
Love, B. C., Medin, D. L., & Gureckis, T. (2004). SUSTAIN: A network model of human category learning. *Psychological Review, 111*, 309–332.
Luce, R. D. (1959). *Individual choice behavior: A theoretical analysis*. Westport, CT: Greenwood Press.

Marcus, G. F. (1999). Do infants learn grammar with algebra or statistics? Response to seidenberg & elman, eimas, and negishi. *Science, 284*, 436–437.

Marcus, G. F., Vijayan, S., Bandi Rao, S., & Vishton, V. (1999). Rule learning by seven-month-old infants. *Science, 283*(5298), 77–80.

Markman, A. B., & Ross, B. H. (2003). Category use and category learning. *Psychological Bulletin, 129*, 592–613.

McCallum, R. (1993). *Overcoming incomplete perception with utile distinction memory.* In *the proceedings of the Tenth International Machine Learning Conference (ML'93).* Amherst, MA.

Medin, D. L., & Bettger, J. G. (1994). Presentation order and recognition of categorically related examples. *Psychonomic Bulletin & Review, 1*, 250–254.

Medin, D. L., & Schaffer, M. M. (1978). Context theory of classification learning. *Psychological Review, 85*, 207–238.

Montague, P., Dayan, P., Person, C., & Sejnowski, T. (1995). Bee foraging in uncertain environments using predictive hebbian learning. *Nature, 377*(6551), 725–728.

Montague, P., Dayan, P., & Sejnowski, T. (1996). A framework for mesencephalic dopmaine system based on predictive hebbian learning. *Journal of Neuroscience, 16*(5), 1936–1947.

Neth, H., Sims, C., & Gray, W. (2006). Melioration dominates maximization: Stable suboptimal performance despite global feedback. In R. Sun and N. Miyake (Eds.), *Proceedings of the 28th annual meeting of the Cognitive Science Society.* Hillsdale, NJ: Erlbaum.

Nosofsky, R. M. (1986). Attention, similairty, and the identification-categorization relationship. *Journal of Experimental Psychology: General, 115*, 39–57.

Nosofsky, R. M. (1991). Typicality in logically defined categories: Exemplar similarity versus rule instantiation. *Memory & Cognition, 19*, 131–150.

Nosofsky, R. M., Palmeri, T. J., & McKinley, S. C. (1994). Rule-plus-exception model of classification learning. *Psychological Review, 101*(1), 53–79.

Nosofsky, R. M., & Zaki, S. F. (1998). Dissociations between categorization and recognition in amnesic and normal individuals. *Psychological Science, 9*, 247–255.

Palmeri, T. J., & Nosofsky, R. M. (1995). Recognition memory for exceptions to the category rule. *Journal of Experimental Psychology: Learning, Memory, & Cognition, 21*, 548–568.

Pinker, S., & Prince, A. (1988). On language and connectionism: Analysis of a parallel distributed processing model of language acquisition. *Cognition, 28*, 73–193.

Rescorla, R., & Wagner, A. (1972). A theory of pavolvian conditioning: Variations in the effectiveness of reinforcement and non-reinforcement. In A. Black and W. Prokasy (Eds.), *Classical conditioning ii: Current research and theory* (pp. 64–99). New York: Appleton-Century-Crofts.

Rosch, E., & Mervis, C. B. (1975). Family resemblences: Studies in the internal structure of categories. *Cognitive Psychology, 7*, 573–605.

Ross, B. H., & Kennedy, P. T. (1990). Generalizing from the use of earlier examples in problem solving. *Journal of Experimental Psychology: Learning, Memory, & Cognition, 16*, 42–55.

Rouder, J. N., & Ratcliff, R. (2006). Comparing exemplar- and rule-based models of categorization. *Current Directions in Psychological Science, 15*, 9–13.

Rumelhart, D. E., & McClelland, J. L. (1987). Learning the past tense of English verbs: Implicit rules or parallel distributed processing? In B. MacWhinney (Ed.), *Mechanisms of language aquisition* (pp. 195–248). Hillsdale, NJ: Erlbaum.

Sakamoto, Y., & Love, B. C. (2004). Schematic influences on category learning and recognition memory. *Journal of Experimental Psychology: General, 33*, 534–553.

Sakamoto, Y., & Love, B. C. (2006). Vancouver, Toronto, Montreal, Austin: Enhanced oddball memory through differentiation, not isolation. *Psychonomic Bulletin & Review, 13*, 474–479.

Schultz, W., Dayan, P., & Montague, P. R. (1997). A neural substrate of prediction and reward. *Science, 275*, 1593–1598.

Seidenberg, M., & Elman, J. (1999). Do infants learn grammars with algebra or statistics? *Science, 284*(5413), 433.

Sloman, S. A. (1996). The empirical case for two systems of reasoning. *Psychological Bulletin, 119*, 3–22.

Smith, J. D., & Minda, J. P. (1998). Prototypes in the mist: The early epochs of category learning. *Journal of Experimental Psychology: Learning, Memory, & Cognition, 24*, 1411–1430.

Stanley, W., Mathew, R., Russ, R., & Kotler-Cope, S. (1989). Insight without awareness: On the interaction of verbalization, instruction, and practice in a simulated process control task. *Quartley Journal of Experimental Psychology, 41A*(3), 553–577.

Suri, R., Bargas, J., & Arbib, M. (2001). Modeling functions of striatal dopamine modulation in learning and planning. *Neuroscience, 103*, 65–85.

Sutton, R., & Barto, A. (1998). *Reinforcement learning: An introduction*. Cambridge, MA: MIT Press.

Tesauro, G. (1994). TD-Gammon, a self-teaching backgammon program, achieves master-level play. *Neural Computation, 6*(2), 215–219.

Tomlinson, M., & Love, B. C. (2006). *From pigeons to humans: Grounding relational learning in concrete examples. Proceedings of the Twenty-First National Conference on Artificial Intelligence* (AAAI-2006).

Tunney, R. J., & Shanks, D. R. (2002). A re-examination of melioration and rational choice. *Journal of Behavioral Decision Making, 15*, 291–311.

Tversky, A., & Kahneman, D. (1981). The framing of decisions and the psychology of choice. *Science, 211*, 453–458.

Tversky, A., & Kahneman, D. (1983). Extension versus intuitive reasoning: The conjunction fallacy in probability judgment. *Psychological Review, 90*, 293–315.

Wagner, A., & Rescorla, R. (1972). Inhibition in pavlovian conditioning: Application of a theory. In R. Boake and M. Halliday (Eds.), *Inhibition and learning* (pp. 301–336). London: Academic Press.

Whitehead, S., & Ballard, D. (1991). Learning to perceive and act by trial and error. *Machine Learning, 7*(1), 45–83.

Widrow, B., & Hoff, M. (1960). Adaptive switching circuits. *Institute of Radio Engineers, Western Electronic Show and Convention Record, 4*, 96–104.

Yang, L. X., & Lewandowsky, S. (2004). Context-gated knowledge partitioning in categorization. *Journal of Experimental Psychology: Learning, Memory, & Cognition, 30*, 1045–1064.

Young, M. E., & Wasserman, E. A. (1997). Entropy detection by pigeons: Response to mixed visual displays after same-different discrimination training. *Journal of Experimental Psychology: Animal Behavior Processes, 23*, 157–170.

Young, M. E., & Wasserman, E. A. (2001). Entropy and variability discrimination. *Journal of Experimental Psychology: Learning, Memory and Cognition, 27*(1), 278–293.

AMBIGUITY, ACCESSIBILITY, AND A DIVISION OF LABOR FOR COMMUNICATIVE SUCCESS

Victor S. Ferreira

Abstract

People talk to be understood, and so they should produce utterances that are easy for their listeners to understand. I begin this chapter by describing evidence showing that speakers rarely avoid sentences that are ambiguous, even though ambiguity is a factor that is well known to cause difficulty for listeners. Instead, speakers seem to choose utterances that are especially easy for them to say, specifically by producing more accessible, easy-to-think-of material sooner, and less accessible, harder-to-think-of material later. If speakers produce utterances that are easy to say but not utterances that are easy to understand, how is it that we understand each other? A third line of evidence shows that even when sentences are structurally ambiguous, they are likely to include enough information for comprehenders to figure out what they mean. This suggests that speakers produce ambiguous utterances simply because they can—because the grammar of their language will only let them produce utterances that are unambiguous enough to be understood most of the time anyway. And so, we understand each other because speakers produce utterances efficiently even if they are not optimally understandable;

THE PSYCHOLOGY OF LEARNING
AND MOTIVATION VOL. 49
DOI: 10.1016/S0079-7421(08)00006-6

addressees do what they need to understand their speakers; and the grammar makes sure everything works out properly.

I. Introduction

When someone speaks, it is usually with the goal of being successfully understood. Such successful communication comes from a particular division of labor between speaker and listener. A speaker can expend little effort when constructing an utterance ("the thing"), leaving much of the burden for understanding to his or her listener. Or, speakers can work harder ("the red Honda on your left"), leaving less work for their addressees. The question of interest here is, given the cognitive capabilities of speakers and listeners, and the nature of the languages they speak, what is the *actual* division of labor that leads to the communicative success we experience everyday?

To understand the division of labor for communicative success, we must understand the behavior of speakers: Why do speakers produce utterances in the ways that they do? Producing an utterance involves a sequence of processing steps. First, a speaker must settle upon the meaning they wish to express. This meaning is a nonlinguistic entity, and is often termed a *message*. The message is fed to a set of processes that are collectively termed *grammatical encoding*. Here, we focus on two aspects of grammatical encoding: Speakers must choose the words that describe the people, places, things, actions, and so forth in their messages, and they must arrange those words into grammatical sequences that convey who did what to whom. Grammatical encoding processes feed their products into articulatory processes, which direct muscle movements that cause the now linguistically encoded messages to be presented as perceptible signals to an addressee.

Interestingly, grammatical encoding often involves choices: A speaker can express a given message with different words or with different arrangements of words. Barry Bonds hit his 762 (and counting) home runs with a "bat" or with a "baseball bat." If a particular acquaintance ran a 26.2-mile event, it could be described as "Steve ran a marathon" or "a marathon was run by Steve." These choices are interesting because as far as production is concerned, they are a valuable resource—the flexibility to say "bat" or "baseball bat," or "Steve ran a marathon" or "a marathon was run by Steve" can be exploited to achieve different goals. One general goal such flexibility can be exploited to achieve is to make comprehension easier, if speakers say "baseball bat" or "a marathon was run by Steve" when the alternative would be harder to understand. If this is what speakers do, then the division of labor for communicative success is such that speakers have to work to produce optimally comprehensible utterances. A different general goal that the flexibility in production can be exploited to achieve is to make production easier, if speakers say "baseball bat" or "a marathon was run by Steve" when the alternative would be more difficult to produce. If this is what speakers do, then the division of labor for communicative success is such that speakers do not have the responsibility of crafting especially easy-to-understand sentences; rather, speakers should produce utterances quickly and efficiently, and addressees simply need to do what is necessary to understand those sometimes suboptimal utterances.

In my lab, we have explored these issues mostly by investigating a rather useful sentence structure termed a *sentence-complement structure*, as in "I saw that Steve ran a marathon." In sentence-complement structures, a main verb like "see" takes an *embedded-clause* argument (a full sentence, at least including a subject and verb) like "Steve ran a marathon." Critically, sentence-complement structures allow speakers to mention or omit a "that," termed a *complementizer*, immediately after the main verb: "I saw *that* Steve ran a marathon" or "I saw Steve ran a marathon." The mention versus omission of the optional "that" is subtle, and likely has very little effect on the meaning of the sentences (though some speculations have been offered—e.g., Bolinger, 1972; Thompson & Mulac, 1991; Yaguchi, 2001). As such, this optional "that" is very useful; if its mention is weakly (or not at all) determined by meaning, then its mention can only be determined by grammatical encoding proper. Thus, by investigating why speakers mention the optional "that," we can determine how grammatical encoding processes use a source of flexibility to achieve communicative success, and in particular, whether this flexibility is exploited to produce easier-to-understand sentences or easier-to-produce sentences. The former possibility I term *listener-centered grammatical encoding*, and the latter I term *speaker-centered grammatical encoding*.

II. Listener-Centered Grammatical Encoding: "That" as Disambiguator

The primary job of the language comprehension system is to try to recover the words speakers used and how those words are arranged, so that it can in turn recover the message the speaker intended. Accordingly, any property of an utterance that hinders this recovery process challenges the comprehension system and thus threatens communicative success. A primary hindrance to such recovery is *ambiguity*—when a given linguistic utterance is able to convey more than one meaning. The newspaper headline, "Hospital sued by seven foot doctors" is ambiguous, because it can mean that seven podiatrists sued a hospital, or that some very tall doctors sued a hospital.

A specific kind of ambiguity that can be especially disruptive is termed a *temporary ambiguity* or a *garden path*; this is when the first part of an utterance seems to convey one meaning that is then rendered impossible by the remainder of the utterance. Take the sentence, "The reporter believed the president lied." The beginning of the sentence—"the reporter believed the president ..." implies that "the president" is the direct object of the verb "believed" (which suggests that the reporter thought the president to be honest). Upon being presented with the word "lied," however, it becomes apparent that the reporter in fact did not believe the president at all; rather, the reporter believed a fact about the president—that the president was not honest. With this interpretation, "the president" is not the direct object of "believed," but instead is the subject of the verb "lied"—what is termed an *embedded subject*. Generally speaking, when hearing ambiguous fragments like "the reporter believed the president," comprehenders tend to adopt a direct-object interpretation of "the president" because it is simpler (Frazier & Fodor, 1978) and more common (MacDonald, Pearlmutter, & Seidenberg, 1994). Then, when "the president" turns out to be an embedded subject, this original direct-object interpretation must be discarded and the correct embedded-subject interpretation recovered. This garden path represents a notable disruption to the comprehension process, as has been documented in hundreds of experiments exploring language comprehension (for reports on this specific kind of garden path, see F. Ferreira & Henderson, 1990; Trueswell, Tanenhaus, & Kello, 1993).

Because garden paths seem to pose measurable difficulties for comprehenders, if speakers design utterances to be maximally comprehensible, they should avoid them. In fact, the optional "that" is capable of allowing speakers to avoid just this ambiguity. Specifically, in the fragment, "The reporter believed *that* the president ...," the above-noted garden path is absent, because "the president" cannot be interpreted as a direct object. Rather, the "that" is a strong signal that the subsequent noun phrase is an embedded subject. Upon being presented with "lied," addressees do not have to discard an incorrect interpretation, and can maintain their (ultimately correct) original embedded-subject interpretation. As a result of the mention of the optional that, comprehension proceeds more smoothly. Indeed, the optional "that" in sentence-complement structures are sufficiently disambiguating that they are typically used as control conditions in studies looking at this ambiguity.

This analysis raises an interesting question, however: If "that" can disambiguate structures for addressees, why do speakers leave them out at all? From the perspective of listener-centered grammatical encoding, the answer might be that some structures are unambiguous even without the optional "that." Take the sentence, "The reporter believed I had lied." Even though this utterance omits the optional "that," the resulting structure does not include a garden path. This is because "I" is a subject pronoun and so can only be interpreted as a subject (to be a direct object, the fragment would have to be "the reporter believed me ..."). Overall, this analysis thus brings us to a specific prediction: If the grammatical-encoding process uses the flexibility available to it to craft utterances that are optimally comprehensible, then speakers should use "that" more in just those sentences that otherwise would include garden paths.

A. Pronoun and Verb-Suffix Ambiguity

Ferreira and Dell (2000) explored this question in six experiments (three of which will be discussed at this point). In Experiment 1, we had speakers produce sentences like, "The coach knew (that) I missed practice" and "The coach knew (that) you missed practice." In the former sentence, the embedded subject is the unambiguous subject pronoun "I," and so this sentence is unambiguous even when it does not include the optional "that." In the latter sentence, the embedded subject is an ambiguous pronoun "you," which can either be a direct object ("The coach knew you well") or an embedded subject ("The coach knew you missed practice"). Thus, the latter sentence requires the optional "that" to not include a garden path. We asked 96 subjects to each produce 48 such critical sentences. To get speakers to produce these sentences, we presented them as part of a memory task. Subjects read and encoded into memory these critical sentences, along with one or two filler sentences. Then, speakers were prompted (in an unpredictable order) to produce each sentence back. It is well known that memory for the specific forms of sentences is poor (e.g., Sachs, 1967); instead, people largely remember the meaning or "gist" of a sentence, and upon recall, regenerate the sentence from that gist (for especially convincing evidence on this front, see Lombardi & Potter, 1992). In the original sentences that speakers encoded into memory, half had the optional "that" and half did not (counterbalanced with all other factors). Across all experiments, speakers' memory for the originally presented "that" was ~65%; though significantly better than chance, this level of memory for the "that" leaves plenty of room for other factors—for example, the potential ambiguity of the eventual sentence—to influence the use or omission of the "that." And so, if grammatical encoding is listener centered, we should see that speakers mention "that" in their recalled sentences more when they would otherwise cause a garden path—"the coach knew (that) you missed practice"—compared to when they would not—"the coach knew (that) I missed practice."

The results for this experiment (as well as two follow-up experiments) are shown in Fig. 1. The graph plots along the horizontal axis the percentage of "that" speakers produced in sentences that were unambiguous regardless of inclusion of "that" (top bar) or that are disambiguated with the "that"

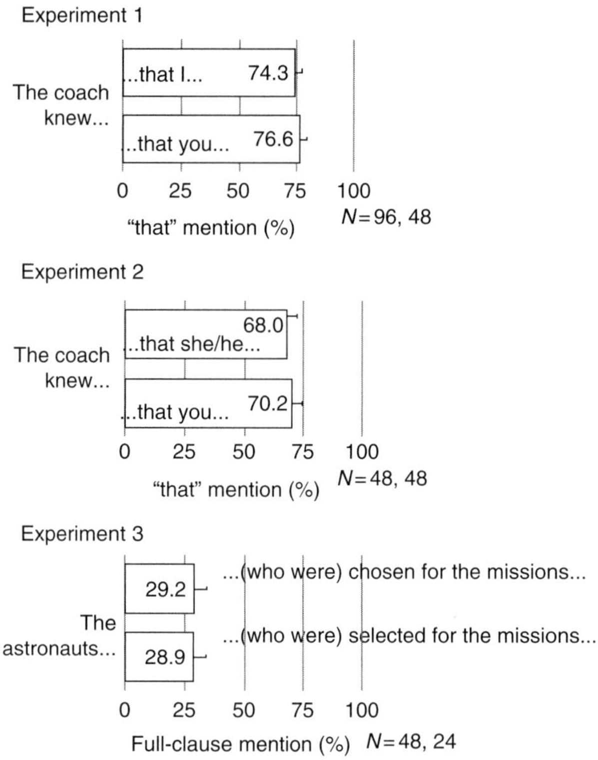

Fig. 1. Percentage of sentences with optional "that" and full relative clauses produced in unambiguous and ambiguous sentence structures. Data from Ferreira and Dell (2000).

(bottom bar). Speakers barely produced "that" more often (by 2.3%) in sentences that would otherwise be ambiguous. Despite testing 96 subjects each producing 48 sentences (yielding a 95% confidence interval of the difference of ±3.1%), this 2.3% difference was not significant. Figure 1 also reports the results of Experiment 2, which replicated Experiment 1, only replacing the pronoun "I" (which is unambiguously a subject) with the pronouns "she" and "he" (which are also unambiguously subjects). This experiment was conducted because the first-person pronoun "I" might be special in some way, and so the third-person pronouns "she" and "he" could make for a tighter comparison to "you." Experiment 2 again revealed a small (2.2%) difference, which (despite testing 48 subjects each producing 48 critical sentences, yielding a confidence interval of ±4.3%) was not significant.

At this point, a concern was that though the above-described garden path caused by sentence-complement structures is well attested, it is relatively weak.

And so, perhaps the reason that only small nonsignificant tendencies to avoid garden paths with sentence-complement structures were observed is because sentence-complement structures only cause small garden paths. If this is correct, then if we ask speakers to produce sentences that could include more disruptive garden paths, they should avoid them more consistently. Experiment 3 (also shown in Fig. 1) assessed this possibility. Here, speakers produced sentences that could include the well-known *reduced relative* garden path, as in the celebrated example "The horse raced past the barn fell" (Bever, 1970). In reduced relatives, the first verb ("raced") is initially interpreted as a main verb ("the horse raced past the barn quickly"). However, this verb is not the main verb, but is instead part of a relative clause that modifies the subject noun. Speakers can avoid this disruptive garden path by producing optional material before the ambiguous verb—"the horse *that was* raced past the barn fell." If grammatical encoding is listener centered—if speakers use syntactic flexibility to avoid garden paths—this optional material should be used in sentences that would otherwise cause disruptive garden paths.

To test this, speakers produced sentences that require the optional material to avoid the garden path, like, "The astronauts (who were) selected for the missions made history," as well as sentences that do not include a garden path even without the optional material, like "The astronauts (who were) chosen for the missions made history." In the latter sentence, the first verb has an unambiguous "-en" suffix that requires it to be part of a relative clause, blocking the main verb interpretation (for evidence, see Trueswell, Tanenhaus, & Garnsey, 1994). The prediction is that if speakers only weakly (and nonsignificantly) avoided garden paths in the first two experiments because the sentence-complement garden paths are only mildly disruptive, they should produce the optional material (yielding a *full relative clause*) significantly more often in ambiguous ("selected") than unambiguous ("chosen") relative clause structures, because these structures are more profoundly disruptive. Results showed that if anything, the nonsignificant differences observed in Experiments 1 and 2 are eliminated with the more disruptive garden path (with a 0.3% difference in the wrong direction; Experiment 3 tested 48 subjects each producing 24 critical sentences, yielding a confidence interval of ±5.1%).

In sum, the first three experiments in Ferreira and Dell (2000) provided no evidence that speakers use "that" as a disambiguator, in turn suggesting that grammatical encoding is not listener centered. However, it is important to recognize that Ferreira and Dell established a quite specific test for ambiguity avoidance, namely, whether speakers produced "that" more in sentences that were ambiguous, relative to sentences that were disambiguated either by specific features of pronouns (that "you" is ambiguous whereas "I" is not) or verb suffixes (that "-ed" is ambiguous whereas "-en" is not). Speakers' mention of "that" may in fact be generally sensitive to the potential ambiguity of their utterances, but it just happens to be insensitive to the disambiguating properties of pronouns or verb suffixes.

B. Plausibility and Verb Bias

Ongoing research in my lab is assessing the effect of two other factors that are known to be relevant to ambiguity. Both factors, originally explored in comprehension research by Susan Garnsey and her colleagues (Garnsey, Pearlmutter, Myers, & Lotocky, 1997) are continuous in nature, increasing or decreasing the degree to which sentence-complement structures are ambiguous. One factor is *plausibility*. This refers to real-world knowledge, in this case, regarding whether the ambiguous noun phrase can be reasonably interpreted as a direct object. For example, in "The talented photographer accepted *the money* could not be spent yet," "the money" is an embedded subject that seems plausible as a direct object—it is something a talented photographer would reasonably accept. But in "The talented photographer accepted *the fire* could not be prevented," "the fire" is a less plausible direct object—it is something that a talented photographer would be less likely to accept. Ambiguous noun phrases that are plausible direct objects are more ambiguous, because they encourage the ultimately incorrect direct-object interpretation of the ambiguous fragment. In fact, Garnsey et al. (1997) showed that such plausibility can affect comprehension, such that ambiguous sentences (ones without the "that") took longer to read when the ambiguous noun phrase was a more plausible direct object. The question for language production, then, is whether speakers say the optional "that" more in sentences that have embedded subjects that are more plausible as direct objects; if so, this would be evidence for listener-centered grammatical encoding.

The second factor explored in these experiments (also following Garnsey et al., 1997) was *verb bias*. This refers to how often in everyday language use particular verbs are used in particular ways. Here, this refers to whether the main verb in a sentence-complement structure more often is followed by a direct object, an embedded clause, or some other type of linguistic constituent. For example, "accepted" in "The talented photographer *accepted* the fire could not be prevented" is a verb that commonly occurs with a direct object, compared to "announced" in "The proud mother *announced* the flowers would be delivered soon." Verbs like "accepted" that commonly occur with direct objects make sentence-complement structures more ambiguous, because again, they more encourage the ultimately incorrect direct-object interpretation. Again, this was shown by Garnsey et al. (1997), in that comprehenders took longer to read ambiguous sentence-complement structures with verbs that had a direct-object verb bias, compared to ones with verbs that had a sentence-complement verb bias or that were "equibiased," which were midway between these extremes. The question for production is whether speakers say optional "that" more in sentences including verbs with direct-object verb bias, compared to in sentences including verbs that have sentence-complement verb bias (and sentences with equibiased verbs should be in between).

Three experiments (two of which will be discussed at this point) assessed whether plausibility and verb bias affect speakers' mention of the optional "that" in sentence-complement structures. The first experiment used a memory-based sentence production procedure much like that used by Ferreira and Dell (2000). The second experiment used what has been called a "Post-to-Times" task (Bradley, Fernandez, & Taylor, 2003). Here, speakers are given a pair of simpler sentences, and asked to combine them into a single more complex sentence that expresses about the same amount of information. (Subjects are given a cover story that they are practicing to adapt stories from the New York Post, which by reputation uses simpler language, to be published in the New York Times, which by reputation uses more complex language, thus giving the procedure its name.) Here, speakers were given simpler sentences like, "The talented photographer accepted something," and "The money could not be spent yet," and were asked to combine them; sentence-complement structures ("The talented photographer accepted (that) the money could not be spent yet") were the overwhelmingly common product of such combination.

Figure 2 reports the results of both experiments. Experiment 1 included an equibiased verb-bias condition that Experiment 2 did not, because Experiment 2 had speakers produce more sentences in the two more extreme verb-bias conditions. Considering plausibility first, it is evident that in both experiments, speakers had no consistent tendency to use "that" more in sentences with embedded subjects that were more plausible as direct objects (open bars) than in sentences with embedded subjects that were less plausible as direct objects (grey bars). In contrast, verb bias did have a consistent and predicted effect on "that" mention: Speakers said "that" most in sentences that included verbs that more often take direct objects (the top sets of bars in both graphs), least in sentences that least often take direct objects (the bottom sets of bars in both graphs), and (in Experiment 1) sentences with equibiased verbs were between these extremes (the middle set of bars in the top graph).

What do these results mean? First, when the plausibility of a sentence magnified ambiguity, speakers failed to avoid that ambiguity any more often. Note that plausibility was a very reasonable factor that might have caused ambiguity avoidance. Because plausibility is grounded in real-world

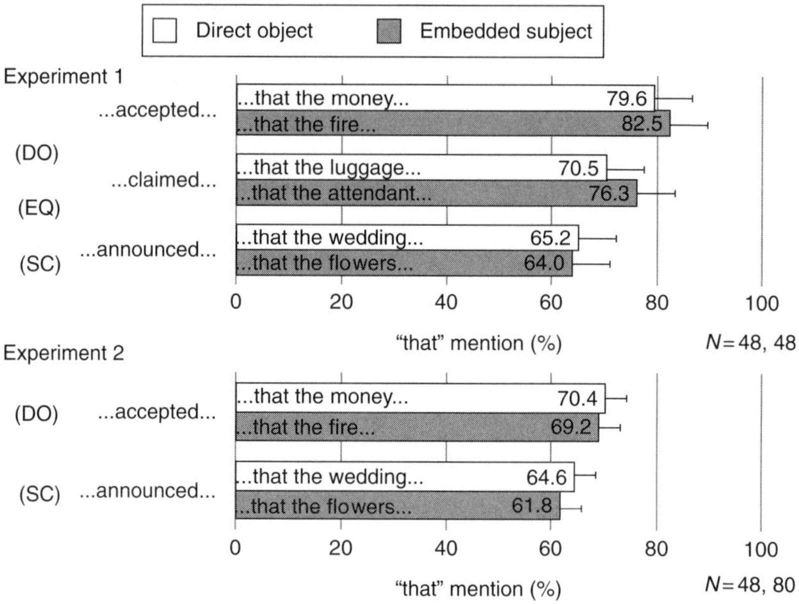

Fig. 2. Percentage of sentences with optional "that" produced in sentences with direct-object biased (DO), equibiased (EQ), and sentence-complement biased (SC) verbs (on vertical axes) and embedded subjects that were plausible (white bars) or implausible (dark bars) as direct objects. Data from in-progress experiments.

knowledge (rather than, say, the ambiguity of a pronoun or a verb suffix), it is something that speakers should have intuitive access to. Furthermore, the plausibility of a sentence fragment—essentially, an aspect of the meaning of that sentence fragment—is available to speakers before they choose particular sentence structures. (In the terms used above, plausibility is a feature of messages, which serve as input to grammatical encoding.) Thus, in terms of intuitiveness to speakers and processing flow, plausibility could have readily influenced speakers' choices about sentence structure. Yet it did not.

On the other hand, verb bias did affect "that" mention in a manner predicted by a listener-centered grammatical-encoding mechanism—speakers said "that" more often in sentences including verbs that commonly occur with the incorrect direct-object interpretation. Why might verb bias have exerted this effect, when other factors (pronoun or verb-suffix ambiguity, or plausibility) did not? One possibility is that verb bias may represent a more static or fixed information source regarding the strength of an ambiguity, relative to other sources of information. That is, plausibility is highly contextual, in that a given sentence may be differently plausible in different contexts or contingent upon very diverse properties of that sentence. Similarly, the ambiguity of a pronoun or verb suffix is likely not usually relevant to its interpretation (most pronouns and verbs are likely produced in unambiguous contexts). Verb bias, on the other hand, is more consistent: Any sentence-complement structure with a particular verb will be more or less ambiguous depending upon verb bias every single time. This may allow the production system to employ a more "brute force" ambiguity avoidance strategy: With verbs that are misleading because of their verb bias, use "that" more often.

A different possibility, of course, is that the effect of verb bias is not due to its effect on ambiguity at all, but rather is due to some other factor that also varies with verb bias. The third experiment in this project distinguishes these possibilities, and is discussed further below.

Thus far then, not much evidence suggests that grammatical encoding is listener centered (except possibly for the effect of verb bias just discussed). However, an important feature of the experiments presented so far is that isolated speakers (speakers did not speak to any actual person in the experiments) produced isolated sentences (the sentences were not part of a discourse or conversation). Of course, the whole point of listener-centered grammatical encoding is that speakers produce sentences that are easy *for a listener*. If speakers are not addressing an actual listener, why avoid ambiguity?

This is not to say that the evidence cited thus far is wholly uninformative. The experiments in Ferreira and Dell (2000) and the in-progress experiments just described used memory-based production and Post-to-Times tasks because they were designed to assess the reasonable possibility that speakers might *automatically* avoid ambiguities during production. Such automatic ambiguity avoidance appears not to hold. Still, an interesting alternative possibility is that listener-center grammatical encoding is only invoked as a kind of speech register—that when a speaker produces natural sentences for an actual listener, she or he might better avoid ambiguity.

C. Speaking to Listeners

One experiment in Ferreira and Dell (2000), Experiment 6, was designed to assess part of this issue. Speakers still produced isolated sentences from memory, but this time to actual addressees (who were themselves real experimental participants, not confederates). Addressees were instructed to listen to speakers' utterances and rate them for how easy they were to understand, and speakers were instructed to maximize these clarity ratings. Speakers produced four different types of sentences, varying in terms of whether the main subject and embedded subject was "I" or "you":

(1) I knew (that) I would miss the flight.
(2) I knew (that) you would miss the flight.

(3) You knew (that) I would miss the flight.
(4) You knew (that) you would miss the flight.

(The reason these four sentence types, in particular, were elicited is described further below.) Without the optional "that," of these four sentence types, only (2) includes a garden path. Sentences like (1) and (3) do not include a garden path because the embedded subject pronoun "I" cannot be an object (as was the case for Experiment 1 of Ferreira & Dell, described above). Sentences like (4) do not include a garden path for more complex reasons. In particular, the embedded subject "you" cannot be interpreted as a direct object in the same clause as another phrase before it referring to the same entity; instead, such a pronoun would have to be reflexive ("You knew yourself ..."). This implies that when both the main and embedded subjects are "you," a comprehender can be certain that the pronoun is an embedded subject even without the "that." And so, because only sentences like (2) contain an ambiguity, if speakers use "that" to avoid ambiguity, they should say them more in sentences like (2), compared to the other three sentence types.

Figure 3 reveals results from this experiment, when speakers addressed addressees (top graph) and when they did not (bottom graph). Speakers did not produce "that" most in ambiguous sentences like (2). In fact, they

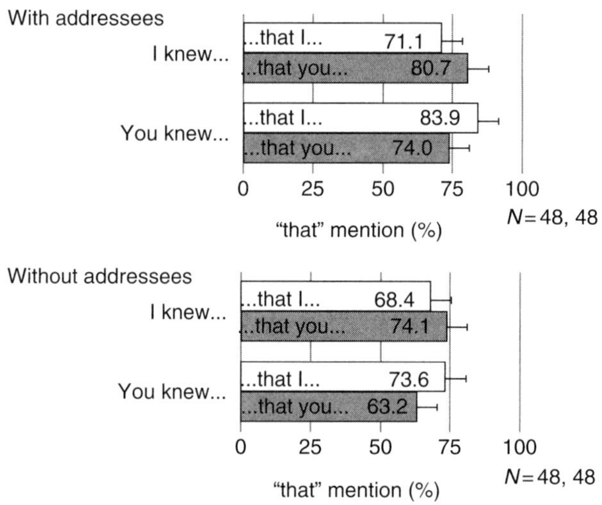

Fig. 3. Percentage of sentences with optional "that" produced in sentences with different main and embedded subjects with addressees (top graph) or without (bottom graph). Data from Ferreira and Dell (2000).

produced "that" just as often in sentences like (3), even though such sentences had "I" as embedded subjects and so were unambiguous. Furthermore, the same pattern is observed regardless of whether speakers addressed an actual addressee (top panel) or not. Speakers did say "that" overall more when addressing real addressees (by about 7%), however, they increased "that" mention just as much in unambiguous sentences like (1), (3), and (4) as in unambiguous sentences like (2). Thus, it appears that addressing an actual person by itself is not enough to cause grammatical encoding to be listener centered, at least in terms of avoiding ambiguity.

However, though Ferreira and Dell's (2000) Experiment 6 assessed the possibility that speakers might avoid ambiguity more when addressing a real addressee, it was still the case that Ferreira and Dell's speakers produced isolated sentences—individual sentences from memory, rather than sentences that were part of a discourse or conversation. Ongoing work with Melanie Hudson is exploring whether speakers might avoid ambiguity more effectively when producing conversationally situated sentences to real addressees. To get speakers to produce sentences like (1) –(4) above, pairs of experimentally naïve subjects were told that they would read each other passages that included statements describing one of them observing one of them behaving in some manner, and then a question asking what kind of emotion that behavior might correspond to. For example, one subject would ask the other (from a script), "You notice I am stamping my feet. What do you believe about me?" The other subject was asked to answer in a complete sentence, and so might say something like "I believe (that) you are angry." We then manipulated who did the observing and who did the behaving, and so elicited all sentence types (1) through (4) above. For example, an answer to "I notice I am smiling from ear to ear. What do I believe about myself?" would be something like, "You believe you are ecstatic." (We began the experiment by describing a theory of emotion to subjects suggesting that we may not always have direct access to our emotional states, so that sometimes, we infer even our own emotional states based on our behaviors. This allowed responses like "I believe (that) I am ecstatic" and "you believe (that) you are ecstatic" to seem reasonable.)

Figure 4 reports the results of two experiments using this methodology. The first graph reports results from the just-described basic paradigm. If speakers use "that" to disambiguate otherwise ambiguous sentences, as a listener-centered grammatical-encoding mechanism would predict, they should say "that" most in sentences like "I believe (that) you are angry." Rather, we observed that speakers produced "that" *least* in such sentences. The bottom graph reports results from another experiment in which on some filler trials, subjects answered questions that elicited responses like

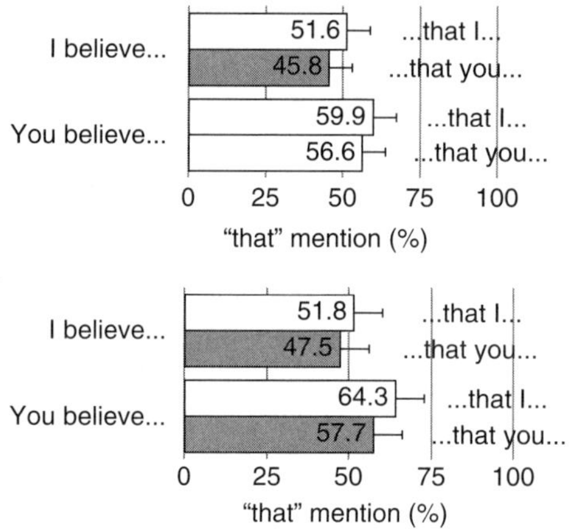

Fig. 4. Percentage of sentences with optional "that" produced by speakers in interactive dialogue in sentences with different main and embedded subjects in a basic referential communication paradigm (top graph) and when fillers included direct objects (bottom graph). Data from in-progress experiments.

"I believe you," in which the pronoun "you" was a direct object. This assessed the possibility that speakers failed to avoid ambiguity in the first experiment because all responses in the experimental situation were sentences with "you" as embedded subjects, possibly making such embedded subjects effectively unambiguous. Still, the observed result was that speakers said "that" least often in the ambiguous case. In sum, these experiments provide no evidence that speakers avoid ambiguity more effectively when producing communicatively situated sentences for actual addressees. (It is worth noting that though the data reported in Fig. 4 shows speakers mentioning "that" least in ambiguous sentences, the pattern is rather unlike that revealed by Ferreira & Dell Experiment 6 that was just discussed, despite the fact that the same sorts of sentences were produced in the studies. This point is considered further below.)

To sum up: Through the mention of the optional "that," grammatical-encoding processes have the opportunity to produce less ambiguous, easier-to-understand utterances to addressees. A series of investigations looking at this possibility revealed little evidence that grammatical encoding processes do this, however. Speakers did not use "that" more in sentences that were ambiguous because they include an ambiguous pronoun; they did not produce disambiguating full relative clauses more in sentences that had ambiguous verb suffixes; they did not produce "that" more in sentences that had real-world meaning that encouraged an incorrect interpretation; and they did not say "that" more often in ambiguous compared to unambiguous sentences when addressing real addressees, even in naturalistic, interactive conversational settings. One effect suggests ambiguity avoidance: Speakers did say "that" more in sentences that include verbs that commonly occur with the misleading direct-object interpretation, compared to in sentences that include verbs that commonly occur with the intended embedded-subject interpretation, an effect that is explored further below.

The weight of this evidence suggests that grammatical encoding is not listener centered—that when speakers have flexibility in how to express a message, they do not choose a form that is easier for their listener to comprehend. This suggests that the division of labor for communicative success may be such that speakers use flexibility to produce easy-to-formulate sentences. Evidence for this is discussed next.

III. Speaker-Centered Grammatical Encoding: "That" as Syntactic Pause

Of course, speakers have the job not only of saying things their addressees can understand (even if as suggested by the evidence in the previous section, perhaps not things their addressees can *optimally* understand), but also to say things quickly and efficiently. In fact, such an "efficiency mandate" is likely very important—it is not clear that a speaker who takes an inappropriately long time to craft a perfect utterance benefits the communicative process more than a speaker who gets his or her utterance out quickly, even if that utterance is not perfect. This is closely related to what Clark (1996) calls the *temporal imperative*—speakers are responsible for the time that they use in a conversation, and so need to use that time judiciously (despite what many of us may think during faculty meetings). The experiments reviewed next were designed to assess whether speakers use syntactic flexibility to promote such efficiency of production.

A. Accessibility-Sensitive Production

One strategy that has been argued to promote the efficiency of production is based on a kind of first-in-first-out principle (Bock, 1982). The idea is that a major challenge to efficient production is variability in retrieving from memory the words to be included in a sentence; some words are retrieved quickly, whereas others are retrieved more slowly. Meanwhile, utterances are largely sequential structures—sentences are produced one word after another in certain constrained orders. An *in*efficient production strategy would be to commit to producing a word at a particular point in a sentence irrespective of when it is retrieved from memory. For example, if speakers commit to producing a word early in a sentence that is difficult to retrieve, the production of the whole sentence will need to wait until the retrieval of that word is complete. More efficient would be for speakers to produce sentences such that easy-to-retrieve material is positioned early in the sentence whereas hard-to-retrieve material is positioned later. If easy-to-retrieve material is positioned early, the production of the sentence can begin sooner, whereas delaying the mention of hard-to-retrieve material to later in the sentence buys time for the successful retrieval of that material. This strategy is here termed *accessibility-based* syntactic production: Choose syntactic structures that allow more accessible material to be mentioned sooner.

The classic experimental demonstration of accessibility-based syntactic production comes from Bock (1986). She investigated the influence of *priming* on sentence production, that is, the fact that people retrieve words from memory more quickly when they previously process related words. On target trials in Bock's experiment, speakers described simple line-drawn scenes that allowed for active- and passive-structure descriptions like "lightning is striking the church" or "the church is being struck by lightning." Before describing such pictures, speakers heard and repeated individual words that were similar in meaning to one element of the picture or another, thereby priming the names of such elements—for example, "thunder" (priming "lightning") or "worship" (priming "church"). Results showed that speakers used active or passive sentence structures in order to position the primed word earlier in their sentences, so that they tended to say "lightning struck the church" when they previously heard and repeated "thunder," but "the church was struck by lightning" when they previously heard and repeated "worship." This is accessibility-based sentence production: Speakers chose sentence structures that allowed accessible material to be spoken sooner.

Critical for present purposes is that accessibility-based sentence production might affect not just the choice between an active versus passive structure, but also the mention of the optional "that." The optional "that" itself should be especially easy to retrieve for production: It is very common (the 17th most frequent word in the language, according to the CELEX database, Baayen, Piepenbrock, & van Rijn, 1993), it has a simple sound structure, and its production may even come essentially "for free" as part of a syntactic selection process (V. S. Ferreira, 2003). This implies that when speakers mention an easy-to-retrieve "that," they delay the retrieval and production of the subsequent material. Thus, if accessibility-based syntactic production applies to "that" mention, speakers should mention "that" when the retrieval of the subsequent material is more difficult (thereby mentioning difficult-to-retrieve material later), and they should omit "that" when the retrieval of subsequent material is easier (thereby mentioning easy-to-retrieve material sooner).

Is "that" mention in fact sensitive to the accessibility of sentence material in this fashion? Current evidence is consistent with this. Above, I described Experiment 6 from Ferreira and Dell (2000), in which speakers produced sentences like the following (repeated from above):

(1) I knew (that) I would miss the flight.
(2) I knew (that) you would miss the flight.
(3) You knew (that) I would miss the flight.
(4) You knew (that) you would miss the flight.

In the description above, it was noted that sentences like (2) are ambiguous whereas sentences like (1), (3), and (4) are not. However, sentences (1) through (4) also vary in a way that likely affects accessibility. In particular, in sentences (1) and (4), the main and embedded subjects are identical: They are the same word, referring to the same entity (they are *coreferential*, linguistically speaking). The fact that the embedded subject is identical to the main subject in these sentences should make retrieval of that main subject easier: When speakers need to produce the embedded subject, they simply need to repeat a word they used two or three words previously. In contrast, in sentences (2) and (3), the main and embedded subjects are different words referring to different entities (they are not coreferential). This implies that retrieval of the embedded subject should be more difficult in these sentences, because a speaker cannot simply repeat a word retrieved two or three words previously. Thus, if "that" mention is accessibility based, speakers should say the "that" less in sentences like (1) and (4), compared to in sentences like (2) and (3).

This was tested first in Experiment 4 of Ferreira and Dell (2000). (Note that Experiment 6, reported above, was a replication of Experiment 4 manipulating the presence of an addressee.) The result of Experiment 4 is shown in the top graph in Fig. 5. Speakers indeed produced "that" less in sentences like (1) and (4), in which the embedded subject is identical to the main subject, compared to in sentences like (2) and (3), in which the embedded subject differs from the main subject. Reinspection of Fig. 3 above reveals that the same pattern was also observed in Experiment 6, regardless of whether speakers addressed addressees. This suggests that speakers mention "that" in response to the accessibility of the material in their sentences. This should make production easier, in turn suggesting that the grammatical-encoding process operates in a speaker-centered rather than listener-centered way.

Of course, it is possible that the repetition (or coreferentiality) manipulated in Experiments 4 and 6 of Ferreira and Dell (2000) affected "that" mention for reasons other than accessibility. However, other experiments provide converging evidence that accessibility indeed affects "that" mention

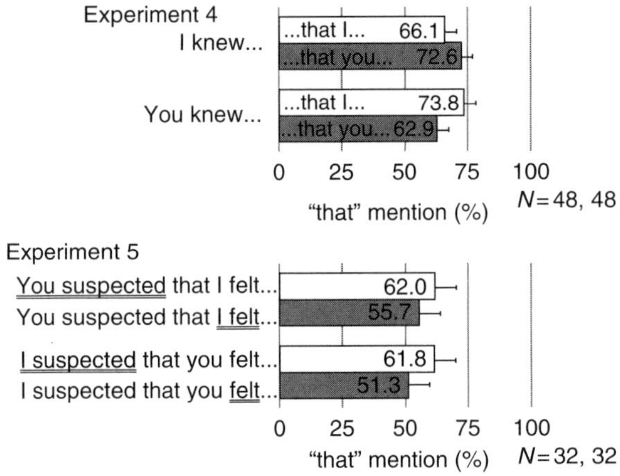

Fig. 5. Percentage of sentences with optional "that" produced by speakers under different conditions of greater or lesser accessibility. In the bottom graph, underlining indicates material used as the recall prompt in the memory-based sentence-production task. Data from Ferreira and Dell (2000).

in the predicted manner. Experiment 5 in Ferreira and Dell assessed the effect of accessibility directly. Speakers were presented with sentences like "I suspected (that) you felt uncomfortable" in a memory-based task. The primary manipulation was of the cue used to prompt production of the critical sentence. Specifically, speakers were cued to produce critical sentences either with the main subject and verb of the sentence ("I suspected") or with the embedded subject and verb ("you felt"). When cued with the embedded subject and verb, the retrieval of that embedded subject and verb should be especially easy—after all, the material is literally given to speakers. If "that" mention is sensitive to the accessibility of subsequent material, speakers should say the "that" less when cued with the embedded subject and verb ("I felt")—the material after that "that"—compared to when cued with the main subject and verb ("I suspected")—the material before the "that." The bottom graph in Fig. 5 shows that in fact, when prompted with the embedded subject and verb, speakers say "that" significantly less often than when prompted with the main subject and verb, as predicted by an accessibility-based syntactic production mechanism (the experiment included yet one more manipulation of ambiguity, illustrated in the graph, just to give the ambiguity-avoidance prediction one more chance; once again, ambiguity was uninfluential).

More converging evidence that accessibility per se affects "that" mention comes from a study by Ferreira and Firato (2002). There, we explored the effect of *proactive interference* on sentence production. Proactive interference refers to difficulty retrieving information from memory because of previous memory retrievals, which is greater to the extent that the current and previously retrieved material is more similar. For example, imagine someone attempted to retrieve the lists of words "author, poet, biographer, *writer*" and "author, poet, biographer, *golfer*." Because "writer" is more similar in meaning to "author," "poet," and "biographer" than "golfer" is, "writer" should be relatively harder to retrieve from memory. In fact, in a list-recall experiment, Ferreira and Firato revealed just this effect. Now, consider sentences (5) and (6) below:

(5) The author, the poet, and the biographer recognized (that) the *writer* was boring.
(6) The author, the poet, and the biographer recognized (that) the *golfer* was boring.

If speakers are asked to remember and produce these sentences, because "writer" should be harder to remember in sentence (5) than "golfer" is in sentence (6), speakers should be more likely to produce "that" in (5) than in (6). (Note that materials were counterbalanced so that for a different group of subjects, "golfer" was presented with three semantically similar words and "writer" with three semantically different words.) Figure 6 reports the results of the experiment. Speakers in fact did produce "that" more in sentences with embedded subjects that were similar in meaning to main subjects, compared to in sentences with embedded subjects that were different in meaning to the main subjects. This fits with an accessibility-based prediction, assuming that the similar embedded subjects elicited greater proactive interference. Interestingly, not only did speakers say "that" more in sentences like (5)

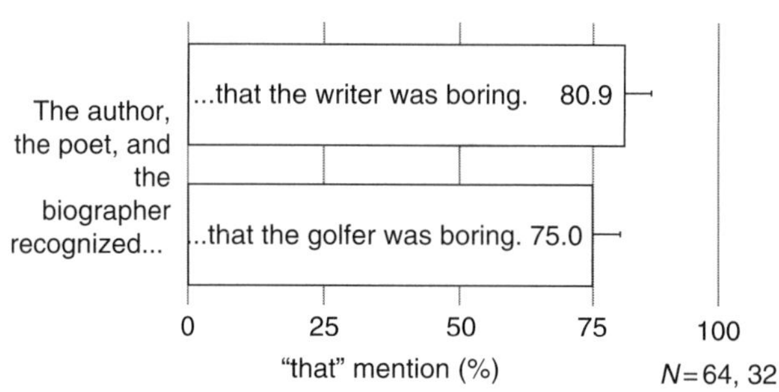

Fig. 6. Percentage of sentences with optional "that" produced by speakers when embedded subjects suffered from more (top bar) or less (bottom bar) proactive interference. Data from Ferreira and Firato (2002).

(with similar-meaning embedded subjects), but they also produced more disfluencies in sentences like (5), such as "ums," "uhs," repetitions, restarts, and so forth. This is consistent with the claim that similar-meaning embedded subjects engendered proactive interference and so greater retrieval difficulty.

B. Other Production-Based Influences

Two results that were presented in the experiments described above assessing listener-centered grammatical encoding were left hanging, and at this point can be resolved. First, the experiments that manipulated plausibility and verb bias revealed that though ambiguity as magnified by plausibility failed to influence "that" mention, ambiguity as magnified by verb bias did. In particular, speakers produced "that" more in sentences with verbs that commonly took direct objects compared to in sentences with verbs that commonly took embedded clauses. The ambiguity-avoidance explanation emphasizes that verbs that commonly take direct objects encourage an incorrect direct-object interpretation and so can use the "that" as a disambiguator, whereas verbs that rarely take direct objects do not encourage an incorrect direct-object interpretation and so do not need the "that" as a disambiguator. There is another explanation for this effect, however. One could equally emphasize the complementary characterization: Verbs that commonly take direct objects rarely take embedded clauses, and so may be hard to produce as embedded-clause structures, whereas verbs that rarely take direct objects commonly take embedded clauses, and so may be easy to produce as embedded-clause structures. If we assume that in general, when production is more difficult, speakers use strategies that make production easier, then speakers should use "that" more in sentences with direct-object biased verbs, but not because the ambiguity of the direct-object biased verbs, but because producing embedded-clause structures with verbs that rarely take embedded-clause structures is more difficult.

A third experiment in this series was conducted to test this possibility. Here, sentences with three types of verbs were compared: Verbs that commonly take direct objects ("Jenny *anticipated* (that) the turn would be extremely sharp"), verbs that commonly take embedded clauses ("Kevin assumed (that) the blame was going to head his way"), and verbs that commonly take neither (because they take other sorts of arguments instead; "Amy confirmed (that) the rumor had been passed on to others"). If speakers say "that" more in sentences with verbs that commonly take direct objects because of the ambiguity that is encouraged by such verbs, then they should say "that" less in verbs that take neither direct objects nor embedded clauses; because such verbs rarely take direct objects, they do not encourage ambiguity, and so do not require the "that" as disambiguator. But if speakers say "that" more in sentences with verbs that commonly take direct objects because it is harder to produce embedded-clause structures with such verbs (because speakers produce embedded-clause structures with direct-object biased verbs less), then speakers should also say "that" often with verbs that take neither direct objects nor embedded clauses, because verbs that take neither type of argument are rarely produced with embedded-clause structures and so should also be harder to produce. Figure 7 reports the results of a Post-to-Times experiment testing these predictions. Speakers produced "that" often both in sentences with verbs that commonly take direct objects and in sentences with verbs that take neither direct objects nor embedded clauses, relative to sentences with verbs that commonly take embedded subjects. Thus, speakers say "that" less only in sentences with verbs that are usually produced with embedded clauses; how commonly verbs take direct objects was irrelevant. This suggests that difficulty of production and not ambiguity is why speakers say "that" more in sentences with direct-object biased verbs. Thus, the only suggestion above that speakers avoid ambiguity appears in fact not to be about ambiguity, but rather, about difficulty of production. This is further evidence that grammatical encoding operates in a speaker-centered rather than listener-centered way.

The second hanging result was from the experiments investigating interactive dialogue. It was noted that though speakers said "that" least in sentences that would otherwise be ambiguous (disconfirming an ambiguity-avoidance prediction), the results of the experiments were different from that observed in Ferreira and Dell (2000). That is, Ferreira and Dell found that when pronouns were repeated (or coreferential), speakers said "that" less than when pronouns were unrepeated (see Figs. 3 and 5). In contrast, the experiment investigating interactive dialogue found two main effects: Speakers said

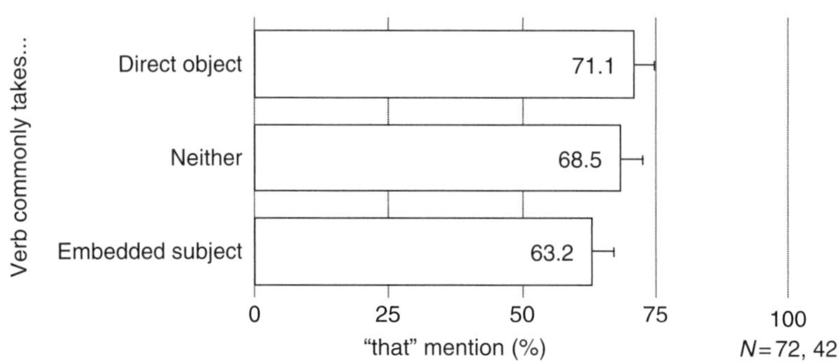

Fig. 7. Percentage of sentences with optional "that" produced by speakers in sentences with verbs that commonly take direct objects (top bar), embedded subjects (bottom bar), or neither (middle bar). Data from in-progress experiment.

"that" less when the main subject was "I" than when the main subject was "you," and speakers said "that" less when the embedded subject was "you" than when the embedded subject was "I" (see Fig. 4). Why did these two sets of experiments observe different results despite the similarity of the materials?

Here, it turns out to be important exactly how sentences are elicited for production, because retrieval difficulty can manifest in different ways depending on exactly how speakers generate the material to be produced. In memory-based sentence production (Ferreira & Dell, 2000), what is likely especially difficult to remember are all of the words (and their meanings) in a sentence. If a pronoun is repeated, it means that there is one fewer word (or referent) to keep track of, which should make retrieval of sentence material easier. In the interactive dialogue situation, however, speakers did not have to hold sentences in memory. Instead, speakers had to generate sentence content by answering their partners' questions concerning which emotion might correspond to a particular observed behavior. This implies that in the interactive dialogue situation, factors that make it easy or hard to think of which emotion corresponds to particular behaviors should determine retrieval difficulty.

In particular, consider the difference between sentences with "I" versus "you" main subjects: "I believe (that) you are angry" versus "You believe (that) you are angry." To produce the first sentence, a speaker must take his or her own perspective ("If I noticed my partner stamping her feet, what emotion would I believe that corresponds to?"). To produce the second sentence, a speaker must take his or her partner's perspective ("If my partner noticed herself stamping her feet, what emotion would she believe that corresponds to?"). The latter process—taking someone else's perspective—is likely more difficult than the former process—taking one's own perspective. So, speakers may have said "that" more in sentences with "I" as a main subject compared to in sentences with "you" as a main subject because the sentences with "I" as a main subject were easier to produce. The difference between sentences with "I" versus "you" as embedded subjects is more subtle (and the effect of the embedded subject is less stable), but here, it may be that it is more difficult to attribute an emotion to oneself (based on observing a behavior) than it is to attribute an emotion to others. This reasoning is based on the well-known *actor–observer discrepancy* in the domain of attribution, whereby people make so-called dispositional attributions (attributions about someone's personality) less to themselves (when they are actors) than to others (when they observe others behaving). Thus, speakers may say "that" less when "you" is the embedded subject because it is easier to think of what emotion might correspond to a behavior when evaluating others' behavior, whereas when "I" is the embedded subject, it is more difficult to think of what emotion might correspond to one's own behavior.

Two experiments sought to confirm this explanation. In one, a third party was introduced to the dialogue situation, namely, the experimenter. Now, subjects could say any of the nine sentences, "I/you/she believe (that) I/you/she is angry," with "she" referring to the experimenter. If the above explanation is correct, "she" should pattern with "you" both as main and embedded subjects (it should be just as difficult to adopt the experimenter's perspective as the speakers' partners' perspective, and it should be just as easy to attribute an emotion to the experimenter as it is to attribute an emotion to one's partner). In fact, the results exhibited a pattern very much like this. In a second experiment, the specific sentences speakers produced in the original experiment (with the results reported in Fig. 4 above) were taken, cleaned up (removing "ums" and so forth), and then given to an independent group of 48 subjects to produce from memory. If the above explanation is correct, then when speakers produce the sentences from memory, the original pattern observed in Ferreira and Dell should return, with "that" produced less when the pronouns were repeated. This prediction was confirmed. Note that this latter result demonstrates an important point, because it shows that "that" mention is not tied to the linguistic properties of speakers' utterances—the same set of sentences exhibited very different patterns of "that" mention when produced from memory, versus when produced in interactive dialogue. This suggests that "that" mention is sensitive to the cognitive states of speakers—in particular what causes greater versus less retrieval difficulty—rather than to the features of speakers' sentences per se.

In sum, the weight of the evidence reviewed thus far suggests that speakers do not use the flexibility that is available to them (in the form of being able to use or omit an optional "that") to produce easier-to-comprehend sentences; instead, they use that flexibility to produce easier-to-produce sentences. This portrays a grammatical-encoding process that is speaker centered and not listener centered. Why might this be the case? A general answer to this question comes from Levinson (2000). He notes that for a variety of reasons, production is likely to be more difficult than comprehension. If so, then communication as a whole would proceed more efficiently if speakers are freed to produce utterances as efficiently as they can, even if the utterances are missing some information or are not optimally comprehensible. Then, given listener's relatively smaller communicative burden, they can bring a powerful inferencing process to bear on the suboptimal utterances they are presented with, filling in missing information or plowing through relatively difficult-to-understand structures. The data presented here are consistent with this general picture. However, this analysis begs the question of why producing an easier-to-comprehend sentence is difficult in the first place. Next, we consider ambiguity avoidance in particular, and why it might hard for producers to do.

IV. Why Do Speakers Not Avoid Ambiguity?

Alhough it is sometimes claimed that speakers should (Grice, 1975) or in fact do avoid ambiguity (e.g., Haywood, Pickering, & Branigan, 2005; Temperley, 2003), it often seems that frank ambiguities go unnoticed even by comprehenders, let alone by speakers. Groucho Marx's famous line, "I once shot an elephant in my pajamas" is likely not humorous to those who first hear it until he follows it up with, "how he got in my pajamas I'll never know." The likely frequency with which ambiguity goes unnoticed suggests an important fact: Detecting ambiguity is often difficult (and interestingly, may not threaten successful communication—more on that below).

Why might it be difficult to detect ambiguity? The forms of ambiguity that have been considered thus far are termed *linguistic* ambiguities. They occur because accidents in the language or limitations of linguistic encoding (i.e., how particular features of meaning are mapped onto words and structures) cause a linguistic utterance to be interpretable in (at least) two otherwise unrelated ways. "I once shot an elephant in my pajamas" is ambiguous because the order of words in a sentence does not completely determine the syntactic structure of that sentence, and so "in my pajamas" can be syntactically interpreted as modifying the verb (meaning that the shooting happened while in pajamas) or as modifying the noun (meaning that the elephant was in pajamas). The same holds for "the reporter believed the president . . .," though only temporarily. A simpler form of linguistic ambiguity occurs with *homophones*: Words with different meanings that happen to sound the same, like "bat" (which can either refer to an instrument for hitting baseballs or cricket balls, or a flying mammal). In this case, it was simply an accident of English that two distinct meanings are sometimes expressed with identical-sounding words.

Now, consider what a speaker must do to detect that "bat" is ambiguous, given how production processes in general operate. A speaker begins with some meaning they wish to express—say, the meaning of a flying mammal. The speaker then must formulate a linguistic description for that meaning: the word "bat." Then, the speaker must assess that linguistic description for whether it could be interpreted in some other way—a way that the speaker does not intend to express, and that is not systematically related to the meaning that the speaker does intend to express. This process describes a kind of "production U-turn": To detect ambiguity, speakers must take a meaning, formulate a candidate expression, and compare it back against meaning (*other* meanings) to determine whether it is ambiguous. Like a U-turn in real life, executing such a U-turn would seem inefficient and difficult.

A. Avoiding Lexically Ambiguous Descriptions

Ferreira, Slevc, and Rogers (2005) sought to determine what conditions must hold for speakers to be able to successfully carry out this "production U-turn." They tested speakers in a *referential communication task*, where they were presented with four line drawings, and were asked to describe one or more of them so that an addressee could pick them out. On critical trials, speakers were asked to describe *target* objects that could be labeled with homophone names, for example, a flying mammal. On some critical trials, such targets were presented in contexts that created linguistic ambiguity, because one of the three other objects in the display, termed the *foil* object, was the homophone counterpart of the target object, and so could be described with the same name. For example, the flying mammal was accompanied by a baseball bat (along with two other unrelated objects, like a swan and a magician), so that "bat" could legitimately describe either object. On other trials, targets were presented in control contexts, where all three other objects in the display were completely unrelated to the target (so a flying mammal was accompanied by a goat, a swan, and a magician). The question of interest was, under what circumstances could a speaker detect that a description like "bat" might be ambiguous? To the extent that speakers can detect ambiguity, they should use potentially ambiguous bare homophone labels like "bat" less in ambiguous contexts (when the flying mammal is accompanied by a baseball bat) than in control contexts.

A first experiment confirmed that speakers are able to avoid linguistic ambiguities at all. When speakers were presented with the display of four pictures, they saw an arrow indicating the target picture, which they were to describe as soon as they saw the arrow. On half of trials, this arrow appeared simultaneously with the pictures; on the other half of trials, the pictures appeared and remained on the screen for 5 s before the arrow appeared, giving speakers a lengthy preview of the whole display. The results, shown in the top panel of Fig. 8, reveal that speakers were able to avoid ambiguity (by avoiding a bare homophone description) 22% more often with preview than without. Furthermore, without preview, speakers hardly avoided ambiguity at all, using potentially ambiguous bare homophone labels (like "bat") only 11% less often in ambiguous contexts compared to in control contexts.

So, when under time pressure, speakers do not avoid ambiguity very well. But, when given enough time (5 s—an eternity to a system that can produce words at a rate of 3–4/s), speakers can avoid linguistic ambiguities. The question of interest is, what does it take for speakers to, in fact, do so? The answer to this question should give us insight into what sorts of processing steps are necessary for speakers to make the "production U-turn" described above. The starting point for the remaining experiments, which were

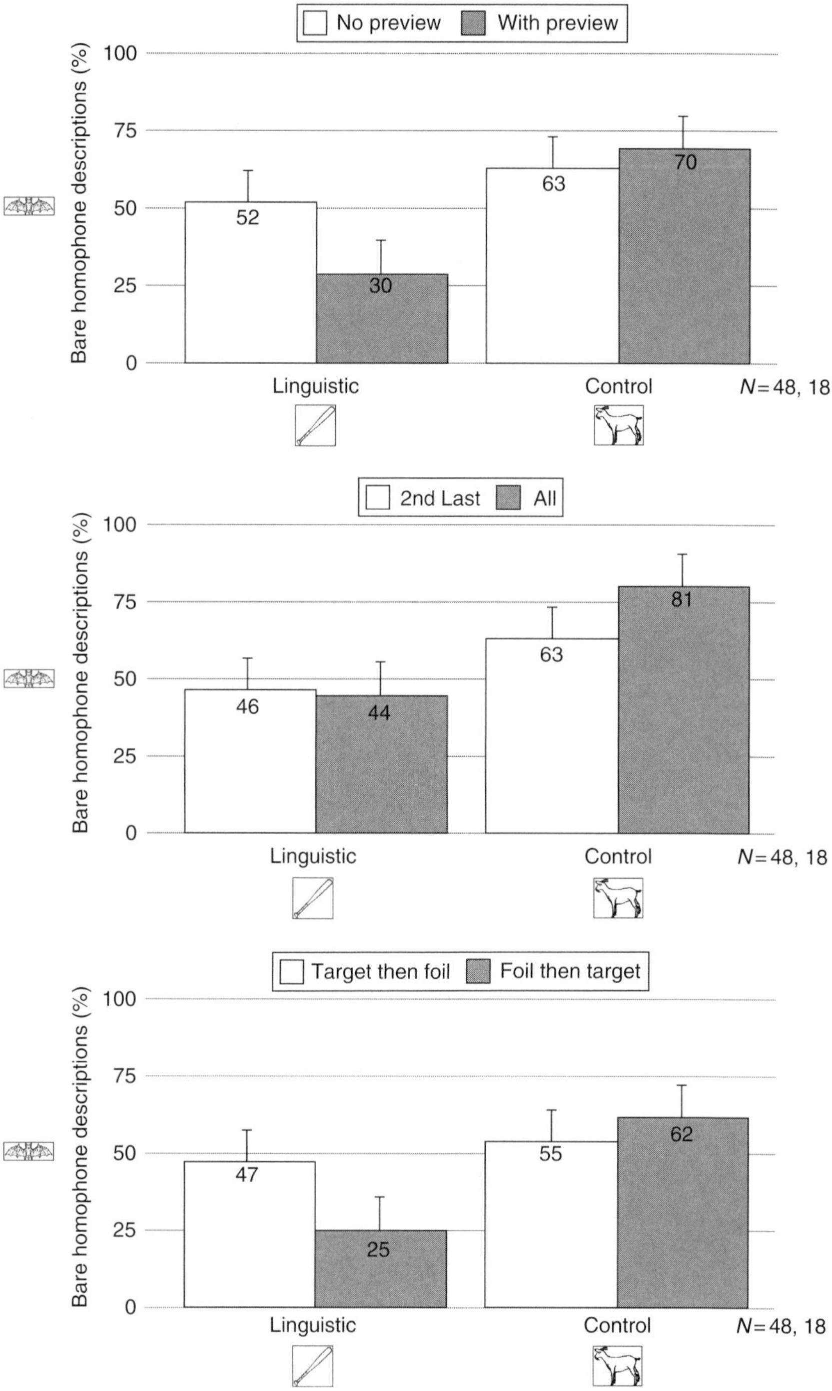
No preview
With preview
Bare homophone descriptions (%)
100
75
50
25
0
52
30
63
70
Linguistic
Control
N=48, 18
2nd Last
All
46
44
63
81
Target then foil
Foil then target
47
25
55
62

designed to answer this question, was that speakers must somehow "activate" the foil object—they must somehow access the representation of the baseball bat in a way that allows it to be recognized as describable by the same name ("bat") as the target object. Or, put another way, perhaps what was happening without preview in the top graph of Fig. 8 is that speakers did not have the resources to process the baseball bat sufficiently to detect that it could be described by the candidate description "bat," whereas with preview, speakers were able to do something more with the foil object that allowed its threat of ambiguity to be detected. The crucial question is, what specifically could speakers do with preview that they could not do without preview?

The simplest possibility is that without preview, speakers simply did not see or attend to the foil objects at all—that when the arrow appeared simultaneously with the pictures, speakers looked at the arrow, then immediately directed their attention to the target, describing it with a bare homophone label like "bat" while remaining wholly oblivious to the ambiguity caused by the foil. Perhaps if speakers simply could look at or draw their attention to the foil before initiating description of the target, the threat caused by that foil could be appreciated. A more extensive possibility is that looking at or drawing attention to the foil object is not sufficient to recognize its ambiguity-causing potential. Rather, perhaps speakers need to process the foil in a way that involves naming it, or applying an "intention to speak" to the object. The idea is that if speakers need to name not just the target (the flying mammal) but also the foil (the baseball bat), this should compel them to recognize that "bat" is a description that could apply to both objects.

To assess this, the task was modified so that instead of an arrow appearing that indicated the target object, a dot appeared and bounced from object to object in the display. On all critical trials, the dot appeared and bounced from a filler object (the swan) to the target object (the flying mammal) to the foil object (the baseball bat), so that the target object was always indicated second last and the foil object last. On noncritical trials, the dot would appear and sometimes bounce to just two objects and other times would bounce to all four objects, so speakers could never anticipate how many objects would be indicated in total. On half of all trials, the speaker was instructed to name only the second-last indicated object (which on critical trials was in fact the target object). Note that overall, speakers cannot know until all dots have bounced which the second-last object is (because two, three, or four objects

←

Fig. 8. Percentage of bare homophones produced under linguistic ambiguity and control conditions with and without preview (top graph), when ambiguity-causing foils were only looked at or were about to be named (middle graph), and when ambiguity-causing foil was named after or before target (bottom graph). Data from Ferreira et al. (2005).

could be indicated in total). This means that on these second-last trials, speakers had to look at all indicated objects, including the foil object, before knowing which the target object was. On the other half of trials, speakers had to name all indicated objects. This means that speakers had to prepare to name not just the target object (which was the second-last description to be provided), but also the foil object (which was the last description to be provided), all in a fluent utterance [by saying something like "swan, (flying) bat, and (baseball) bat"]. So here, speakers described target objects under circumstances where speakers have applied an "intention to name" to the ambiguity-causing foil, and in fact, will describe it with the words that immediately follow the target description. The question of interest is, is looking at the foil object enough to cause speakers to appreciate that it causes ambiguity? If so, then speakers should avoid ambiguity effectively in the second-last condition—about as effectively as they did with preview in the first experiment. Or, is looking not enough—do speakers have to look at and prepare to name the foil object to recognize that it causes ambiguity? If so, then performance in the second-last condition should pattern as in the no-preview condition (with speakers barely avoiding bare homophone ambiguous descriptions), whereas productions in the *all* condition should include bare homophone productions less often (about as rarely as speakers did with preview).

The middle graph in Fig. 8 reports the results. Speakers produced bare homophone labels 46% of the time when instructed to name only the second-last-indicated picture, and they produced bare homophone labels 44% of the time when instructed to name all indicated pictures. Thus, they did not avoid ambiguous descriptions any better when applying an "intention to name" to the ambiguity-causing foil, compared to when they just had to look at that ambiguity-causing foil. However, consider speakers' overall performance relative to the first experiment (top graph): Speakers in Experiment 2 only avoided ambiguity 7% better than speakers in Experiment 1 did *without* preview (52% vs 45%). That is, looking at foils, or looking at and preparing to name foils (with the very next words that a speaker is about to produce) allowed for only a small amount of additional ambiguity detection (compared to, say, the effect of full preview, which was 22–52% vs 30%). This places quite serious limits on speakers' ability to detect ambiguity—they only weakly detected that a description like "bat" is ambiguous, even when they are just about to describe another object that such a description is ambiguous with respect to.

[Two quick notes about this experiment: First, performance differed quite strongly between conditions in the control condition. This reveals a puzzling observation: Speakers were better able to detect that a potentially ambiguous description like "bat" was *not* a threat in the all condition compared to in the second-last condition—they used descriptions like "bat" when ambiguity was not at issue more in the all instruction condition. Why this was observed is unclear. Second, this experiment also included two addressee conditions: speakers addressed either a real addressee who was asked to indicate with pen and paper which objects were described and in which order or addressees were hypothetical. Qualitatively, subjects performed the same in these two cases, though they did use bare homophone descriptions less overall—even in the control condition—when addressing real addressees, likely because they adopted a strategy of being over descriptive (describing the flying mammal with expressions like, "the animal bat with its wings open," providing far more information than is needed to distinguish the target from the foil).]

The performance in this experiment surprised us. How could speakers not effectively avoid ambiguous labels like "bat," even when they were just about to describe two consecutive but distinct objects that could be described with "bat"? When we inspected speakers' actual utterances, it turned out that they frequently produced utterances like "swan, bat, and baseball bat"—in other words, they described the target object with an ambiguous label ("bat"), but then they described the foil object with an unambiguous label ("baseball bat"). On the basis of performance in another condition, we knew speakers did not consider this descriptive strategy to be optimal. That is, when we gave speakers displays with two identical objects that differed only in (say) size, like with a bigger and smaller flying mammal, speakers never produced utterances like "swan, bat, and bigger bat," instead nearly always producing utterances like "swan, smaller bat, and bigger bat." This shows that speakers avoid ambiguity with their first description when they can. Thus, the preponderance of utterances like "swan, bat, and baseball bat" led us to conclude that speakers could avoid ambiguity largely after the fact—that only once speakers were about to use the same label to describe two different referents were they able to recognize the ambiguity of that label. Two final experiments, the results of one of which are shown in the bottom of Fig. 8, confirm that this is the case. Speakers described displays with bouncing dots, but this time, either the target object was indicated before the foil, or the target was indicated after the foil. Speakers were instructed to always describe all objects, so that they either described targets before foils (like in the experiment shown in the middle graph) or after foils. As shown in the graph, speakers described targets with potentially ambiguous bare homophone labels much less often when they described targets after foils than when they described targets before foils. Concretely, speakers produced utterances like "swan, bat, and flying bat" when they described targets after foils, but they produced utterances like "swan, bat, and baseball bat" when they described targets before foils (like they did in the previous experiment). This confirms that speakers can only maximally avoid ambiguity after the fact: Once they have formulated and described one object with a potentially ambiguous label, and they are about to apply that same label to another object—once they are about to say "swan, bat, and . . ."—they can recognize that the label can actually apply to two different objects.

These results provide insight into how speakers do the "production U-turn" noted above that is necessary to detect ambiguity. In fact, the results suggest that to maximally avoid ambiguity, speakers do not do the U-turn at all. They can only apply formulation processes in the forward direction, first formulating a description for one meaning ("bat" for the flying mammal), then once they are about to formulate that same description for another meaning ("bat" for the baseball bat), they can detect the possibility of the same label applying to both meanings. Note that the ambiguity caused by homophones is tightly circumscribed: The whole ambiguity exists with just one (often short) label. The ambiguity caused by syntactic indeterminacies—for example, "I once shot an elephant in my pajamas"—is much more extended in time, and thus is likely even harder to appreciate with this "apply production processes to two separate meanings" strategy.

B. Other Evidence for Ambiguity Avoidance

All of this said, some reports have suggested that speakers produce utterances in certain ways in order to avoid ambiguity. It may be, however, that more production-centered forces or simpler strategies are at work in these reported situations. For example, Temperley (2003) suggested that speakers' use of optional "that" in object-relative clauses like "the lawyer *that* companies hire..." is motivated by ambiguity avoidance, because in part of a corpus of utterances, "that" is more common when without the "that," the sequence could be interpreted as a single noun phrase. So, "the lawyer companies hire..." could be interpreted as a noun phrase (including the compound noun "lawyer companies") followed by a main verb "hire," in a fragment like "the lawyer the companies hire . . .," the "that" is not needed for disambiguation, because "lawyer the companies" cannot be interpreted as a single noun phrase. However, this pattern could also be explained by accessibility: In "the lawyer the companies hire...," the "the" in "the companies"—the word after the optional "that"—is likely easier to retrieve from memory than "companies" is immediately after the optional "that" in "the lawyer companies hire..." If the "the" is easier to retrieve, it will be ready for production sooner, and so should be uttered sooner, and so the "that" is omitted.

In another report, Haywood et al. (2005) showed that speakers mentioned optional "that" more in sentences that would be ambiguous given a current nonlinguistic context compared to the same sentences when the nonlinguistic context eliminated the ambiguity. However, it may be that the contexts that tolerated the ambiguity were perceptually conspicuous in a manner that has been shown to affect production irrespective of ambiguity per se (Kraljic & Brennan, 2005). If so, then the pattern would be consistent with speakers trying to produce utterances that are easier to understand, but not in response to ambiguity per se; rather, they could be sensitive to an ambiguity-independent factor that is correlated with actual linguistic ambiguity.

Finally, Snedeker and Trueswell (2003) showed that speakers modified the prosody (rhythm and pitch) of their sentences to avoid ambiguity. However, only speakers who were consciously aware of the ambiguity avoided it. This raises the possibility that such avoidance may have been closely tied to the experimental context in which it was assessed.

To sum up, given what speakers must do to detect ambiguity, it is not surprising that they do not do so. Speakers have difficulty formulating a candidate description of an utterance and then doubling back, comparing it to some open-ended set of unrelated and unintended alternative meanings an addressee may light upon. This may seem to raise a troubling prospect: If speakers have great difficulty detecting (and therefore avoiding) ambiguity, how do we understand one another at all?

V. How Ambiguous Is Language Really?

The question of the actual potential ambiguity of language was addressed by work by Doug Roland and colleagues (Roland, Elman, & Ferreira, 2006). We took the British National Corpus, which includes over 100 million words (and is thus a large corpus), and used an automatic procedure to parse it into grammatically structured sentences. Although automatic parsing is not flawless (a point I return to shortly), given the size of the corpus, we assumed that the power that would come from having a large number of observations would outweigh the noise added by having some inaccurate parses in the database. We then extracted from the corpus all sentences that began with a noun phrase, a verb, and then a noun phrase, such as "The old man felt the restaurant bill . . .," which in principle could be analyzed either as a subject-verb-direct-object sequence or as a subject-verb-embedded-subject sequence. We then removed any fragment that included disambiguating information, such as direct object pronouns like "me" (and note too that no sequences included the disambiguating "that"). This left ~250,000 structurally ambiguous noun-phrase-verb-noun-phrase sequences; of these, the automatic parsing procedure analyzed about 182,000 as subject-verb-direct-object sequences and about 68,000 as subject-verb-embedded-subject sequences. We measured any relatively easily measurable property of each part of these sequences, including the length of the first and second nouns and noun phrases (in characters, since that was readily available and should be highly correlated with any other measure of length), the frequency of the first and second nouns and noun phrases (based on counts of the words in the British National Corpus itself), and an approximation of the semantic content of the two nouns and noun phrases (based on Latent Semantic Analysis, Landauer & Dumais, 1997). We also took into account the specific verb that was in the sequence. These statistics for each sequence was entered into a kind of regression model (a logistic regression model) whereby the structure of the sequence—whether it was a subject-verb-direct-object sequence versus a subject-verb-embedded-subject sequence—was predicted from the length, frequency, semantics, and verb statistics. In everyday terms, this procedure boils down to assessing whether readily available properties of structurally ambiguous sequences (how long and common parts of the sequences are, the semantic properties of parts of the sequence, and which verb is involved) can provide good information about what the actual structure of the sequence is.

In fact, the regression model was highly successful at predicting the estimated structure (as determined by the automatic parse) of the otherwise structurally ambiguous sequences, as about 86% of all such sequences were accurately predicted to be either subject-verb-direct-object sequences versus subject-verb-embedded-subject sequences. However, it turns out that the performance of the regression model was even better than this. Recall that the automatic procedures used to parse large corpora such as these are imperfect. When we sampled sentences from our parsed observation set at random, and determined their actual structure by hand, it turned out that about 10% of the sentences were incorrectly categorized, so that either a subject-verb-direct-object sequence was analyzed as a subject-verb-embedded-subject sequence or vice versa. This means that 10% of sentences could not have been accurately predicted in the first place. So, of the 90% of sentences that the regression model had a chance to accurately predict the structure of, it got 86% of them right.

It is important to note that it has not been shown that language comprehenders are in fact sensitive specifically to the factors that we measured. Still, this result suggests that in principle, language may in fact be massively *un*ambiguous. If language comprehenders are sensitive to readily accessible properties of the utterances they are presented with, including how long parts of those utterances are, how frequent the words in parts of those utterances are, certain coarse meaning properties of parts of those utterances, and what verb is being used, then *even when those utterances are structurally ambiguous*, comprehenders can still determine the correct structure of those utterances in a very large percentage of cases. This brings the analyses presented here full circle: The question we started out with was, do speakers use certain linguistic devices, especially the mention of the optional "that," to avoid presenting comprehenders with ambiguous structures. The bulk of the evidence suggested that speakers in fact do not do this. Now we see why this may be the case: Speakers do not use certain linguistic devices to structurally disambiguate their sentences because their sentences likely are not ambiguous to comprehenders in the first place. In the overwhelming majority of cases, even when speakers leave out the "that," addressees have all the information they need to be able to correctly determine the structures of the utterances they are presented with. When this observation is combined with the one from the previous section, that it is likely very tricky for speakers to detect (let alone avoid) ambiguity, it does not seem surprising at all that a communicative system would operate in this fashion.

VI. Why Are Speakers' Utterances so Unambiguous?

The analysis in the preceding section could be seen as pinning communicative success rather too heavily on good fortune. Speakers' utterances happen to have enough information so that even when they are structurally ambiguous, addressees can figure out what their intended structure is. Presumably, if this were not the case—if speakers produced impoverished structurally ambiguous utterances—communication would be hindered. So, what ensures that speakers provide their addressees with rich enough utterances so that those utterances can be easily understood?

The answer to this question is: the grammar of language. In general, the grammar of a language describes the rules or guidelines that distinguish well-formed from ill-formed utterances. In English, our grammar dictates that "Steve ran a marathon" is grammatical, but "ran Steve marathon a" is not. A rich controversy in the study of language concerns where the "problem space" of the grammar comes from—what makes it so that the world's languages realize certain grammatical possibilities rather than others (specifically debating whether some innate or genetic component is necessary to explain the structure of this problem space). However, setting aside that thorny problem, another question is, what determines what part of the problem space is carved out by a particular language's grammar? So, for example, in English, our grammar has settled (at least for now) on the prescription that in many structures, the complementizer "that" is optional. Why does the grammar permit that optionality?

To explore this issue, consider a more extreme example. One of the general (and graded) ways that the world's languages are categorized is as *fixed* versus *free word order*. English is a fixed word-order language, because the roles of subject, object, and so forth are determined by relative order information. For example, in an active transitive sentence like "Steve bought a present," the noun phrase before the verb ("Steve") is the subject and the noun phrase after the verb ("present") is the object. If these are reversed—"The present bought Steve"—a very different meaning is conveyed. Japanese is a free word-order language, because noun phrase arguments can be more freely ordered, so that, for example, in an active transitive sentence, the subject can precede or follow the object. The reason this is so is because the roles of subject, object, and so forth in free word-order languages are generally conveyed by suffixes or *case markers*. For example, "Steve-ga purezento-o katta" means "Steve bought a present"; the case marker "ga" indicates that "Steve" is the subject of the sentence; and the case marker "o" indicates that "purezento" is the object. Because the case markers convey subject and object roles, "purezento-o Steve-ga katta," with the object before the subject, also means "Steve bought a present."

What is worth noting is that few (if any) languages exist that have relatively free word order and do not use case markers to indicate grammatical roles like subject and object. The reason such an arrangement is so unusual is that any language that permitted free ordering of arguments and did not have case marking would be rampantly (and likely fatally) ambiguous. In such a language, in the sentences "Steve teased Kim" and "Kim teased Steve," one person (Steve or Kim) should clearly be the subject (the teaser) and the other the object (the one being teased); obviously, this is not the case. And so, grammars of languages use one device or the other (word order or case marking) to disambiguate what would otherwise be impossibly ambiguous utterances. Considering the optional "that" again, this analysis suggests that the reason English permits the "that" to be optional is because in the heavy majority of utterances in which it could be left out, those utterances still have plenty of information for addressees to still efficiently determine speakers' intended structure, consistent with the Roland et al. (2006) results described above. (In this vein, it is interesting to note that one place where the "that" is obligatory is where it would be consistently misleading, namely, in noun phrases with active subject-relative clauses like "the book that fell on the floor ..." Without the "that," the noun phrase would be "the book fell on the floor," which presumably nearly always will be interpreted as a subject-main-verb sequence.)

This general framework thus suggests that it is not the job of speakers to ensure that the sentences they produce are sufficiently unambiguous that they can be efficiently understood. That job belongs to the grammar of the language speakers speak, by only allowing speakers to have options that most of the time (often enough so that communication is not broadly hindered) include enough information so that addressees can efficiently understand them. By restricting speakers' grammatical options just to those that are relatively likely to succeed, the flexibility that comes from having those options can be exploited for the other important communicative imperative: Speakers should choose options that allow them to produce sentences most efficiently. If an option that is more efficient for speakers happens to be less efficient for addressees, that is likely acceptable—because the grammar generally would not allow options that are too ambiguous, addressees should have the resources available to easily enough understand the less-than-optimally-comprehensible utterance.

(An interesting question is, how languages might come to allow only those options that are not generally too ambiguous. It seems a likely candidate mechanism is language acquisition, and the related mechanisms of language change. That is, aspects of a language that are too ambiguous to use are likely too ambiguous to learn as well. If language learners do not pick up on aspects of grammars that are too ambiguous, those aspects would get filtered out, leaving only those aspects that are sufficiently unambiguous. These speculations go beyond the scope of the current presentation, but may be an interesting basis for future research.)

VII. Conclusion: A Division of Labor for Communicative Success

Together, all of these considerations suggest a rather tidy division of labor for communicative success. This division involves three parties: Speakers, addressees, and the grammar of the language they speak. The division is:

Grammar: Allow for a space of possible utterances within a particular language that given the information at addressees' disposal, can be easily enough understood most of the time.

Speakers: Exploit the flexibility within the space of possible utterances defined by the grammar to optimize the efficiency of the formulation and articulation process.

Addressees: Do the work necessary to understand the utterances that your speakers produce.

This division is useful, because it helps to frame our explanations for why speakers or listeners seem to adopt particular linguistic strategies, or why the grammar might have the features that it does. For example, it is often claimed that certain patterns found in language are motivated by an imperative to make comprehension more efficient. Take *heavy NP shift*, referring to the fact that noun phrase objects can be moved from their typical locations when they are especially long (or *heavy*): "I drove to the store *the car that was old and falling apart*" (cf. "I drove to the store *the car*."). Why is shifting a noun phrase in this manner more acceptable when it is heavy? One explanation

(Hawkins, 1994) can be motivated by comprehension preferences: Without the shift, the heavy noun phrase delays the presentation of any part of the subsequent prepositional phrase ("to the store"). When that prepositional phrase is eventually presented, a listener must recall over a now long interval of time and material what the verb was that the preposition modified. By shifting the heavy noun phrase to later in the utterance, the prepositional phrase is presented immediately after the verb it modifies, and the heavy noun phrase object itself is presented relatively sooner after the verb (because the prepositional phrase is shorter). The current framework, by contrast, compels a different explanation: Perhaps speakers tend to shift heavy noun phrases until later because they take longer to formulate (i.e., they are relatively less accessible), and so by delaying their mention, more accessible material (the shorter prepositional phrase) can be mentioned sooner, and speakers can buy time to formulate the more difficult heavy noun phrase (see also Wasow, 1997; Yamashita & Chang, 2001). Note that this latter explanation, by appealing to speakers' preferences rather than listeners' preferences, also does not need to explain how it is that speakers—the creators of the heavy-NP shift pattern—encode comprehension preferences that are sufficiently subtle that they take many sentences to describe in a paper like this. In short, the division of labor for communicative success proposed here suggests that language researchers should not be too quick to posit explanations for patterns of language use in terms of what is easy for comprehenders. Such explanations are less parsimonious compared to explanations in terms of production efficiency (because they must also describe how it is that speakers know what is efficient for comprehenders, a challenge analogous to the above question of how speakers can detect ambiguity), and they overlook the very important mandate speakers have to produce utterances efficiently.

Overall then, the body of work reviewed in this chapter suggests that communication succeeds because speakers do what they need to do to produce utterances efficiently, addressees do what they need to do to understand what their speakers are saying, and the grammar makes sure that it all works out.

References

Baayen, R. H., Piepenbrock, R., & van Rijn, H. (1993). *The celex lexical database*. Philadelphia: Linguistic Data Consortium.

Bever, T. G. (1970). The cognitive basis for linguistic structures. In J. R. Hayes (Ed.), *Cognition and the development of language*. New York: John Wiley.

Bock, J. K. (1982). Toward a cognitive psychology of syntax: Information processing contributions to sentence formulation. *Psychological Review, 89*, 1–47.

Bock, J. K. (1986). Meaning, sound, and syntax: Lexical priming in sentence production. *Journal of Experimental Psychology: Learning, Memory, and Cognition, 12*, 575–586.

Bolinger, D. (1972). *That's that.* The Hague: Mouton.

Bradley, D., Fernandez, E. M., & Taylor, D. (2003). *Prosodic weight versus information load in the relative clause attachment ambiguity.* Paper presented at the CUNY Conference on Human Sentence Processing, Boston, MA.

Clark, H. H. (1996). *Using language.* Cambridge, England: Cambridge University Press.

Ferreira, F., & Henderson, J. M. (1990). Use of verb information in syntactic parsing: Evidence from eye movements and word-by-word self-paced reading. *Journal of Experimental Psychology: Learning, Memory, and Cognition, 16*, 555–568.

Ferreira, V. S. (2003). The persistence of optional complementizer production: Why saying "that" is not saying "that" at all. *Journal of Memory and Language, 48*(2), 379–398.

Ferreira, V. S., & Dell, G. S. (2000). Effect of ambiguity and lexical availability on syntactic and lexical production. *Cognitive Psychology, 40*(4), 296–340.

Ferreira, V. S., & Firato, C. E. (2002). Proactive interference effects on sentence production. *Psychonomic Bulletin & Review, 9*, 795–800.

Ferreira, V. S., Slevc, L. R., & Rogers, E. S. (2005). How do speakers avoid ambiguous linguistic expressions? *Cognition, 96*, 263–284.

Frazier, L., & Fodor, J. D. (1978). The sausage machine: A new two-stage parsing model. *Cognition, 6*, 291–325.

Garnsey, S. M., Pearlmutter, N. J., Myers, E., & Lotocky, M. A. (1997). The contributions of verb bias and plausibility to the comprehension of temporarily ambiguous sentences. *Journal of Memory and Language, 37*, 58–93.

Grice, H. P. (1975). Logic and conversation. In P. Cole and J. L. Morgan (Eds.), *Syntax and semantics: Speech act* (Vol. 3, pp. 41–58). New York: Academic Press.

Hawkins, J. A. (1994). *A performance theory of order and constituency.* Cambridge, England: Cambridge University Press.

Haywood, S. L., Pickering, M. J., & Branigan, H. P. (2005). Do speakers avoid ambiguity during dialogue? *Psychological Science, 16*, 362–366.

Kraljic, T., & Brennan, S. E. (2005). Prosodic disambiguation of syntactic structure: For the speaker or for the addressee? *Cognitive Psychology, 50*, 194–231.

Landauer, T. K., & Dumais, S. T. (1997). A solution to Plato's problem: The latent semantic analysis theory of acquisition, induction and representation of knowledge. *Psychological Review, 104*(2), 211–240.

Levinson, S. C. (2000). *Presumptive meanings: The theory of generalized conversational implicature.* Cambridge, MA: MIT Press.

Lombardi, L., & Potter, M. C. (1992). The regeneration of syntax in short-term memory. *Journal of Memory and Language, 31*, 713–733.

MacDonald, M. C., Pearlmutter, N. J., & Seidenberg, M. S. (1994). The lexical nature of syntactic ambiguity resolution. *Psychological Review, 101*(4), 676–703.

Roland, D. W., Elman, J. L., & Ferreira, V. S. (2006). Why is *that*? Structural prediction and ambiguity resolution in a very large corpus of English sentences. *Cognition, 98*, 245–272.

Sachs, J. S. (1967). Recognition of semantic, syntactic, and lexical changes in sentences. *Psychonomic Bulletin, 1*, 17–18.

Snedeker, J., & Trueswell, J. C. (2003). Using prosody to avoid ambiguity: Effects of speaker awareness and referential context. *Journal of Memory & Language, 48*(1), 103–130.

Temperley, D. (2003). Ambiguity avoidance in English relative clauses. *Language, 79*, 464–484.

Thompson, S. A., & Mulac, A. (1991). The discourse conditions for the use of the complementizer *that* in conversational English. *Journal of Pragmatics, 15*, 237–251.

Trueswell, J. C., Tanenhaus, M. K., & Garnsey, S. M. (1994). Semantic influences on parsing: Use of thematic role information in syntactic ambiguity resolution. *Journal of Memory and Language, 33*, 285–318.

Trueswell, J. C., Tanenhaus, M. K., & Kello, C. (1993). Verb-specific constraints in sentence processing: Separating effects of lexical preference from garden-paths. *Journal of Experimental Psychology: Learning, Memory, and Cognition, 19*, 528–553.

Wasow, T. (1997). End-weight from the speaker's perspective. *Journal of Psycholinguistic Research, 26*, 347–361.

Yaguchi, M. (2001). The function of the non-deictic that in English. *Journal of Pragmatics, 33*(7), 1125–1155.

Yamashita, H., & Chang, F. (2001). "Long before short" preference in the production of a head-final language. *Cognition, 81*, B45–B55.

LEXICAL EXPERTISE AND READING SKILL

Sally Andrews

Abstract

This chapter overviews a research program assessing the lexical expertise hypothesis of reading skill which assumes that the critical, specific determinant of written language proficiency is an "expert lexicon" characterized by precise, redundant, lexical representations that support efficient, autonomous, lexical retrieval (Perfetti, 1992). Evidence for the precision and redundancy of skilled readers' lexical representations is provided by investigations of the masked priming and rhyme judgment performance of university student readers categorized on reading comprehension and spelling performance. Lexical experts, defined by the combination of good reading and good spelling, were more efficient at lexical classification and more sensitive to orthographic–phonological relationships, but less susceptible to priming and interference from orthographically similar stimuli. Further experiments used rapid serial visual presentation sentence paradigms to investigate functional autonomy of skilled readers' lexical retrieval. Better readers were more efficient at selecting the sentence-congruent meaning of a homographic word in a probe memory task but less susceptible to biasing sentence context when the task required accurate identification of sentence-incongruent words and nonwords. These findings support the view that better readers' higher

THE PSYCHOLOGY OF LEARNING
AND MOTIVATION VOL. 49
DOI: 10.1016/S0079-7421(08)00007-8

quality lexical representations allow them to more effectively integrate bottom–up and top–down information and tailor their processing to task demands.

I. Introduction

Exactly a century ago, Huey (1908) declared that understanding skilled reading would be the "acme of psychologists' achievements" because it would provide insight into one of the most remarkable feats of the human mind. Literate adults have a vocabulary of over 50,000 words and can read text for comprehension at a rate of at least 300 words a minute. The speed and efficiency of the process is astounding given the complexity of the processes involved in translating the inkmarks that comprise text into the rich sophisticated meanings that readers extract from them. Words are composed from a finite array of letters which are, themselves, composed from a small set of features; words are therefore necessarily visually confusable with each other. Moreover, the relationships between visual word forms and meaning are essentially arbitrary: words that look the same do not usually have any semantic relationship. Reading also requires highly sophisticated perceptuo-motor control of the eye movements required to extract information from text (Rayner, 1998). In spite of the complexity of the perceptual and cognitive operations required to achieve the task of reading, it occurs seamlessly and effortlessly. The reader usually has no awareness of the operations required to identify words, only of the final outcome—comprehension of the text.

Speech comprehension clearly shares many of these characteristics, and arguably represents an even more amazing perceptual feat because of the variability in the input and the listener's lack of control over the rate at which it is processed. However, what distinguishes reading is that it demonstrates "cultural engineering" rather than the "biological preparation" that underlies speech processing (Carr, 1999). Written languages were only invented by our species 5–10,000 years ago, and literacy remains a far from universal human skill. Learning to read also clearly depends on environmental input. In contrast to spoken language acquisition, which develops spontaneously in all neurologically intact children who are exposed to human language, relatively independently of environmental variations, the acquisition of reading for any individual usually requires explicit instructions and supervised practice. Consistent with the view that learning to read is not "natural" in the same sense as learning to understand speech, up to 30% of children have difficulty learning to read despite normal schooling (Byrne, Deleland, & Fielding-Barnsley, 2002).

The broad aim of the research program overviewed in this chapter is to specify what is unique about reading that makes it difficult for some children to learn and contributes to individual differences in written language skill. The approach I have been using focuses on *skilled* reading—what defines a highly skilled reader and how do these attributes contribute to their reading skill? My goal is to elaborate and validate a particular hypothesis about the cognitive determinants of highly skilled reading by investigating individual differences in performance on reading-related tasks in adults of at least average reading competence.

This is the opposite of the more traditional "cognitive correlates" methodology for investigating individual differences in reading which has focused on determining what distinguishes poor readers from those who have successfully acquired the skill to identify the deficits responsible for poor readers' failure to acquire effective reading. Despite a plethora of research comparing poor readers with age-matched competent readers and with younger children of an equivalent reading level, many ambiguities remain regarding the causal status of the multiple deficits observed in poor readers (e.g., Blachman, 1997). Rather than indicating the causes of reading failure, differences between good and poor readers might be the consequence of failure to acquire proficient reading skills or of lack of exposure to written language. They may also reflect compensatory strategies adopted to deal with either the causes or consequences of reading problems. Reflecting this variety of causal hypotheses, comparisons of poor and competent readers have yielded different outcomes depending on exactly how poor reading is defined, and whether and how it is established that the individual's deficits are specific to reading (Rack, Snowling, & Olsen, 1992).

The focus on predicting expert performance may avoid some of the problems associated with comparing average and poor readers. Reviews of how individual differences are affected by increasing expertise (Ackerman, 1987) suggest that individual differences tend to converge with practice and expertise, at least when the task depends on consistent stimulus–response mapping relationships (Shiffrin & Schneider, 1977). The task of translating visual symbols into their phonological and semantic referents clearly satisfies this condition. Expertise in lexical retrieval may, therefore, be associated with a more uniform and predictable set of processes than the deficits that define the lower end of the reading continuum.

The specific hypothesis motivating this research program is that the crucial determinant of highly skilled written language processing is "*lexical expertise*," defined by the quality of orthographic representations and the autonomy of the lexical retrieval procedures that operate on them (Perfetti, 1992). Skilled readers retrieve the meanings of words so quickly and autonomously that the outcome of lexical access is determined primarily by "bottom–up," perceptual information and only minimally influenced by context.

My empirical approach to this question indexes lexical expertise by measuring both reading and spelling. This definition has external validity because reading comprehension and spelling performance are two of the major behavioral indicators of effective written language processing. However, it is also theoretically motivated by evidence that differences in spelling ability among good readers reflect variations in the quality of lexical representations (e.g., Frith, 1980, 1985; Perfetti, 1992). The next section of the chapter reviews evidence from the literature on both developmental and skilled reading populations relevant to defining and assessing the quality of lexical representations, and reports examples of the empirical methods I have been using to assess lexical expertise. The final section is concerned with the consequences of lexical expertise, and summarizes research investigating how autonomous lexical processing contributes to reading comprehension.

II. Defining and Assessing Lexical Expertise

A. The Development of Reading Skill

Systematic cognitive psychological research over the past three decades has made considerable progress toward understanding the basic processes required to learn to read and how they develop in successful early readers. One influential characterization of reading acquisition distinguishes three major developmental steps referred to as the "logographic," "alphabetic," and "orthographic" stages (Frith, 1985). At the logographic stage, children identify individual words using salient, distinctive features that vary from word to word. Transition from the logographic to the alphabetic stage occurs when the memory demands of the child's increasing vocabulary renders logographic cues unreliable. It also depends critically, on "phonological awareness": the ability to explicitly separate and manipulate the phonological constituents of words. However, phonological awareness is not a unitary construct and itself depends on a number of prerequisite capabilities. The precise set of causal relationships between this cluster of skills therefore remains a focus of debate and ongoing research (e.g., Blachman, 1997; Castles & Coltheart, 2004). Nevertheless, recognition that phonological awareness is a crucial prerequisite for successful reading has led to the development of effective methods for detection, assessment, and remediation of early reading problems (e.g., Blachman, 1997).

The question of how children progress from the alphabetic to the orthographic stage of reading has received less attention, yet it is this latter stage that supports expertise in reading. The "orthographic stage" of developmental reading models refers to children's transition to a fluent word identification strategy that does not rely on the explicit phonological recoding strategies that define alphabetic processing. Phonemic awareness appears to be a necessary but not sufficient condition for fluent orthographically based reading: Children with low levels of phonological awareness experience difficulty learning to read, but not every child with high phonological awareness becomes a good reader. Measures of orthographic sensitivity account for variance in the word recognition efficiency of both children and adults that is independent of variability due to phonological awareness (Stanovich, Cunningham, & West, 1998). This evidence suggests that children who achieve phonological awareness may have to pass another "cognitive 'sticking point' where reading acquisition can run aground" (Stanovich, 1992) that is reflected in a failure to make the transition to a fully efficient orthographic approach to reading. However, apart from the obvious conclusion that development of efficient orthographic processing requires exposure to written text and practice of reading skills (Stanovich et al., 1998), the developmental reading literature provides little definitive insight into exactly what is required to develop fluent orthographic processing.

This is partly because of ambiguities in the definition of "orthographic processing." Some researchers define it as sensitivity to regularities of orthographic structure (e.g., Vellutino, Scanlon, & Tanzman, 1994) while others identify it with word-specific orthographic knowledge (e.g., Szeszulski & Manis, 1990). Both definitions have problems. Assessing word-specific knowledge with tasks like the widely used orthographic choice task (e.g., choose which is the word: *rane* or *rain*) seems to be circular because it essentially uses the ability to identify words as a predictor of word identification ability (Vellutino et al., 1994). However, measures of sensitivity to orthographic regularities (e.g., does *beff* or *ffeb* look more like a word) might be a consequence rather than a cause of orthographic learning. Contradicting this interpretation, there is evidence that both English- and French-speaking children are sensitive to the frequency and legality of letter combinations in their respective languages within the first year of reading instruction (Cassar & Treiman, 1997; Pacton, Perruchet, Fayol, & Cleeremans, 2001). However, systematic longitudinal investigations are necessary to determine whether orthographic sensitivity is a unique predictor of subsequent skill in word identification (Castles & Nation, 2006).

Similar ambiguities attend the evidence about the role of reading practice. There is clear evidence that measures of "print exposure" contribute to predicting visual word recognition skill over and above contributions from measures of phonological and orthographic processing skill (e.g., Stanovich & West, 1989). But, does exposure to print promote orthographic learning or do more effective orthographic readers tend to expose themselves to more print?

In addition to considering differences in children's cognitive capabilities at different stages of reading acquisition, some developmental theories also take an item-based perspective (Ehri, 1992, 2005; Perfetti, 1992; Perfetti & Hart, 2001; Share, 1995, 2004) which emphasizes the processes involved in creating and refining lexical representations. Share (1995, 2004) has focused on how young readers use phonological skills as "self-teaching mechanisms" to develop orthographic representations of novel words. Perfetti (1992) and Ehri (1992) have attempted to characterize the changes that occur in the lexical representations of individual words as the reader shifts from relying on logographic to alphabetic cues, and finally develops a "high-quality" representation (Perfetti, 1992) that "amalgamates" orthographic and phonological knowledge to yield orthographic representations that are "paved by phonology" (Ehri, 2005).

Item-based approaches to the development of reading skills highlight the dynamic nature of the word recognition system in developing readers. Children acquire new written words at an extremely rapid rate (Allington, 1984). Their lexical system must therefore consist of representations that vary in their quality due to differences in both how frequently they have been encountered and how "difficult" they are to learn. Differences between the accuracy and efficiency of word identification for different stimuli will, therefore, occur at the intraindividual level, as well as being affected by between-individual differences in reading-related skills. Consistent with this prediction, Castles, Davis, and Forster (2003) reported that 3rd grade children showed priming between similar words that was not evident in adult readers. When the same children were retested 2 years later on the same items, they showed less priming than they had in 3rd grade. These results are consistent with the progressive "fine-tuning" of lexical representations over development.

Acknowledging intraindividual differences in the quality of representations for different words exacerbates the problems associated with relying on developmental evidence to draw conclusions about the determinants of reading skill. An alternative approach to understanding the later stages of development of reading is to focus on clearly specifying what skilled readers do and then work backwards to determine how these outcomes could have been achieved.

B. Lexical Retrieval in Skilled Readers

Insight into the outcome of successful reading acquisition is provided by the large body of evidence on visual word recognition in skilled adult readers. Despite ongoing debate about a variety of levels of the skilled reading process (e.g., see Andrews, 2006a), most models share the assumption that the basic cognitive architecture of the language system consists of a set of encapsulated modules that operate autonomously and independently of general cognitive processes and strategies (Fodor, 1983). Arguments focus on exactly how these modules are organized and interact with each other and why they are organized that way. These arguments can be quite heated and relate to very fundamental philosophical principles—like those between the proponents of symbolic "dual route" models and Parallel Distributed Processing (PDP) models of visual word recognition (e.g., Rastle & Coltheart, 2006; Seidenberg & Plaut, 2006). But they do not necessarily have important implications for understanding how lexical retrieval contributes to reading comprehension (Andrews, 2006b) because they share the assumption that lexical retrieval processes are functionally, if not structurally, modularized from the processes involved in comprehension so that word identification is "minimally constrained by semantic context" (Perfetti, 1992). The encapsulation of lexical retrieval processes facilitates reading comprehension because it allows the readers' limited attentional and computational resources to be allocated to the integrative and elaborative processes required for comprehension (Andrews, 1992, 2006b).

Perfetti (1992) identified two critical features of the "expert representation system" that supports skilled reading: the "quality" of lexical representations; and the autonomy of retrieval procedures. The quality of representations is defined by the principles of "precision" and "redundancy." Precise representations are fully rather than partially specified so that the input features fully determine the representation to be activated and afford fast activation of a single correct representation with minimal activation of competing candidates. With increasing exposure, representations are becoming more redundant because orthographic and phonological features of words are "amalgamated" (Ehri, 1992), which further facilitates discrimination between similar words. Once lexical representations become sufficiently precise and redundant, they can be activated by visually presented words deterministically and without any requirement for contextually based prediction.

The specificity of retrieval made possible by the development of quality lexical representations provides the basis for development of "a context-free autonomous lexicon" (Perfetti, 1992). This conceptualization of word recognition as encapsulated and context independent might be seen to be incompatible with the flexibility of interpretation essential to skilled comprehension, but Perfetti argues that the "impenetrability" of lexical knowledge to input other than the precise features specifying known words yields more efficient reading because it ensures that, during the early stages of identifying a word, activation due to the actual input dominates over activation due to previous context, expectations etc. These top–down processes exert their influence on the *outputs* of the identification process.

The notion of lexical autonomy clearly overlaps with the well accepted assumption that word identification is "automatic" as indexed by phenomena such as the Stroop effect (McLeod, 1991), but the terms are not synonymous. Autonomy does not entail resource-independence (Logan, 1992)—processing is ballistic and resistant to interference, but that does not necessarily mean it is resource-free (Kahneman & Treisman, 1983).

C. Investigating the Quality of Lexical Representations

One source of evidence for the precision and redundancy of skilled readers' lexical representations comes from the rapidly accumulating body of evidence obtained using the masked priming paradigm. A commonly used version of this procedure, developed by Forster and Davis (1984), presents a forward mask (usually a set of hash marks, ####), followed by a brief duration lower case prime, and then the upper case target, which is usually presented until subjects must make a lexical decision response. With prime durations of 50 ms or below, subjects are usually unaware of the presence or identity of the prime and the change in letter case is argued to reduce or eliminate perceptual contributions to priming (Forster, Mohan, & Hector, 2003). Forster and Davis's (1984) original demonstration of the paradigm revealed two critical characteristics of masked repetition priming that appeared to distinguish it from unmasked priming: Masked priming was insensitive to word frequency and absent for nonwords. This led them to conclude that masked priming indexes the extent to which the prime "opens" or preactivates the lexical representation for the target word. Despite challenges to Forster and Davis's (1984) empirical criteria and interpretation of masked priming (e.g., Bodner & Masson, 2001), their paradigm has become a major vehicle for investigating the early processes involved in lexical retrieval (see Kinoshita & Lupker, 2003).

The results obtained using the masked priming paradigm have revealed the remarkable precision of skilled readers' lexical processing. Randomly selected samples of university student readers tested in a range of languages and countries show highly consistent effects of masked primes of which they are completely unaware. Forster et al. (2003) describe five classes of priming that have been demonstrated with this paradigm. Direct repetition primes typically yield a priming effect roughly equivalent to the prime duration, suggesting that word identification is mediated by abstract letter representations that are insensitive to the case difference between the prime and target (Forster et al., 2003) Smaller, but robust, effects are observed for "form primes" that are one letter different from the target (e.g., *aptitude ATTITUDE*) as well as for "transposed-letter" (TL) primes that differ from the target in the order of letters (e.g., *slat SALT*; Andrews, 1996; *jugde JUDGE*;

Perea & Lupker, 2003a,b). Evidence that priming from one-letter different neighbors is restricted to target words with few neighbors (Forster, Davis, Schocknecht, & Carter, 1987) is consistent with the view that lexical representations become more finely tuned for words that have many lexical "neighbors" (Andrews, 1997) rendering them less vulnerable to being activated by words with overlapping letters. Semantic priming has also been observed in the masked priming paradigm, at least for strong associates (e.g., Sereno, 1991). More robust effects are found for morphologically related words, even when they differ in phonology (e.g., *keep KEPT*; e.g., Forster et al., 1987).

The masked priming effects described so far compare related primes with all-letter different primes. They demonstrate that unselected samples of skilled readers are sensitive to the overall similarity of masked primes to target words, but they do not calibrate the *degree* of orthographic precision of skilled readers' representations. More refined evidence on this issue is provided by recent applications of the masked priming paradigm directed toward distinguishing between different models of how letters are coded by skilled readers during the early stages of lexical retrieval. Perea and Lupker (2003a,b) reported that TL primes yielded significantly faster classification of word targets than primes that replaced two letters (e.g., *jugde JUDGE* vs *juphe JUDGE*), and that associative priming from a TL prime (e.g., *jugde COURT*) was significantly greater than from a prime that replaced a single letter (e.g., *judpe COURT*). Such findings provide strong evidence against the "slot coding" letter schemes implemented in many computational models of visual word recognition which assume that the letters of a word are coded by position-specific letter detectors.

1. Letter Coding in Skilled Readers

McClelland and Rumelhart (1981) used the slot coding method in their seminal Interactive Activation (IA) computational model of visual word recognition, and it was incorporated and extended in later models such as Grainger and Jacob's (1996) Multiple Readout Model (MROM) and Coltheart et al.'s (2001) Dual Route Cascade (DRC) model. Slot coding schemes predict that similarity is a function of the number of shared letters in the same position and therefore cannot explain why TL primes, which swap the position of two letters, should be more effective than a prime that *replaces* two letters of the target, since both share N-2 position-specific letters with the target word (Perea & Lupker, 2003a).

There are other reasons to challenge slot coding schemes. Assuming that letter codes are position-specific carries implications for similarity relationships between words. Moreover, IA and MROM both assume that letter codes are also length-specific which means that words of different lengths (e.g., *can*, *cane*, *candy*; *art*, *tart*, *start*) are not at all similar. Coltheart et al.'s (1993, 2001) version of the slot coding scheme, as implemented in DRC, addressed this problem by using a single set of letter slots for all word lengths. However, their decision to align words of different lengths from their initial letter means that the model is only sensitive to similarity between different-length words that share initial, not final, letters. This contributes to the model's difficulty in simulating people's robust sensitivity to "body"[1] similarity across words of different lengths (e.g., Andrews & Scarratt, 1998).

The more general problem with slot coding schemes is what Plaut, Seidenberg, McClelland, and Patterson (1996) referred to as the "dispersion problem": they do not allow generalization from a letter, or letter-combination, in one position to the same letter(s) in another position. Models that rely only on position-specific slots are unable to show position or context invariance (Davis, 1999) and therefore cannot recognize familiar units in a different within-word position, like *house* in *doghouse*. People are clearly capable of identifying the constituents in familiar compound words like *doghouse*, and seem to do so as part of their normal recognition process (e.g., Andrews, 1986; Andrews, Miller, & Rayner, 2004). They are also easily able to interpret novel compounds like *dogwalker* or *doghole* (Libben, 2006). Recognition of the significance of these issues has generated a new wave of research about input coding issues in visual word identification and generated a number of alternative models of letter coding. Attempting to distinguish between these alternatives is a major focus of current empirical research (Davis & Bowers, 2006).

The significance of these issues in the present context derives from their implications for defining and investigating lexical precision. The available evidence shows that unselected samples of skilled readers have developed lexical representations that yield differential priming as a function of the precise pattern of overlap between the identity and order of letters in prime and target indicating that they rapidly extract very refined information about internal word structure. The lexical quality hypothesis predicts that the performance of "lexical experts" in the masked priming paradigm should reveal particularly precise representations

2. *Assessing Lexical Expertise*

Consistent with Perfetti's (1992) claim that spelling provides the best index of lexical quality, I have been using the combination of proficient reading comprehension and good spelling to define lexical expertise. My students

[1] The term "body" refers to the orthographic equivalent of a word's rime—the vowel and final consonant(s) of a monosyllabic word.

and I have developed measures of reading and spelling that consistently correlate with performance in a variety of language processing tasks, and have now accumulated these measures for a normative sample of over 500 undergraduate university students. The *Reading Comprehension* test we have developed was based on the ACER Cooperative Reading Comprehension Test, which was developed in the 1960's for Australian tertiary students. It consists of short passages followed by three to six multiple-choice questions assessing understanding of each passage. Participants are given 10 min to complete as many items as they can. To minimize effects of speed/accuracy bias on performance, the final measure of reading comprehension subtracts the number of errors from the number of correctly answered questions. The *Spelling Dictation* test consists of 20 words, previously found to be spelt correctly by 15–93% of Australian university students (Burt & Tate, 2002). Each word is read aloud twice, and included in a sentence, and participants write down the word's spelling. *Spelling Recognition* is assessed using a test list of 44 correctly spelt words and 44 misspelt words (half phonologically plausible). Participants are required to circle the misspelt words. The two spelling tests yield correlations of about 0.7 in our normative sample, so they are standardized and averaged to provide a composite measure of spelling. This spelling measure has a correlation of 0.35 with reading comprehension in our normative sample. This is considerably lower than that reported in unselected populations (e.g., Ehri, 2005), presumably reflecting the restriction of range in this sample of skilled readers, but provides the opportunity to identify individuals who are discrepant on these abilities. Our research program has so far focused principally on differences between Good Readers/Good Speller (GRGS) and Good Readers/Poor Spellers (GRPS).

3. *Using Masked Priming to Investigate Lexical Quality*

The approach I have been using to assess differences in the quality of skilled readers' lexical representations is illustrated by an unpublished experiment conducted as part of a senior undergraduate practical class. The participants were 116 students who were monolingual English speakers or had learned English as a second language before the age of seven. Those with a passage comprehension score above the average for the whole group ($N = 54$) were subdivided according to spelling ability. The GRGS group had a mean spelling score at least 0.5 standard deviations above the mean for the total sample; the remainder of the above average readers were classified as GRPS. This yielded two groups who were equivalent in standardized reading comprehension score (0.75 and 0.73, respectively) but significantly different in spelling ability (standarized total spelling scores of 1.0 and −0.15, respectively). The two

TABLE I

Word Target Stimulus Conditions (and Examples) for the Masked Priming Lexical Decision Task

	Prime condition			
	Repetition	Similar O + P	Similar O only	Unrelated
Prime	burden	berden	barden	automatic
Target	BURDEN	BURDEN	BURDEN	BURDEN
Prime	automatic	ortomatic	cetomatic	burden
Target	AUTOMATIC	AUTOMATIC	AUTOMATIC	AUTOMATIC

groups' performance in a masked priming lexical decision task was compared to assess their relative sensitivity to different forms of prime-target similarity.

The design of the masked priming task is summarized in Table I. The base stimuli were a set of 144 words between 6 and 10 letters long and of moderate frequency of occurrence (10–60 per million; Baayen, Piepenbrock, & van Rijn, 1993) that contained a letter or grapheme that is phoneme–grapheme inconsistent in English, that is, corresponds to a sound that can also be spelled in a different way (e.g., the *ur* sound in *nursery* is often spelled as *er*). For each word, two orthographically similar nonword primes were constructed: *Similar O + P* primes were pseudohomophones, that is, could be pronounced identically with the target; *Similar O only* primes differed from the target by the same number of letters in the same positions and were pronounceable, but did not sound exactly like the target. Unrelated prime conditions were created by remixing repetition primes and targets for subsets of stimuli to create an unrelated word prime that controlled for the lexical status of the repetition primes.

Word targets were intermixed with legal nonword targets preceded by primes that differed from their targets on the same dimensions as the primes from the word conditions so that prime-target similarity was not correlated with target lexicality. Counterbalanced stimulus lists rotated prime-target combinations across the different conditions such that each list contained only one instance of each word target, but across lists all target words occurred in all four prime conditions. Each trial consisted of a 500 ms forward mask, #########, which was replaced by the lower case prime stimulus for 50 ms, followed by the target word or nonword in upper case for 500 ms. Participants were instructed to use key press responses to classify the upper case target stimuli as words or nonwords. No mention was made of the prime stimuli.

Average reaction times (RT) to word targets in each prime condition are presented in Fig. 1 separately for the two reading/spelling groups. The GRGS

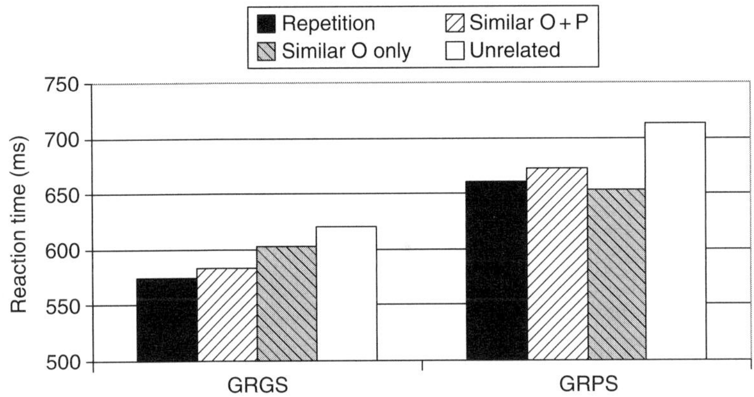

Fig. 1. Average reaction times (RT) for Good Readers/Good Spellers (GRGS) and Good Readers/Poor Spellers (GRPS) for target words in each priming condition.

group classified word targets significantly more quickly, $F(1, 51) = 6.45$, $p < .01$, and more accurately, $F(1, 51) = 5.90$, $p = .02$, than the GRPS group. They were also faster at classifying nonwords than poorer spellers, $F(1, 51) = 5.45$, $p = .02$. The better overall lexical decision performance demonstrated by the GRGS group is consistent with the hypothesis that accurate spelling, in conjunction with good reading comprehension, indexes high-quality lexical representations that support efficient word identification. The greater efficiency of the GRGS group is particularly noteworthy given that the two groups were very well matched on reading comprehension ability and that the "poor" spelling groups performed at an average level compared to other university students.

Comparisons of the prime conditions averaged over groups showed significantly faster responses for all three types of related primes by comparison with the unrelated condition, $F(1, 51) = 37.65, 22.10, 21.10$, respectively, all $p < .001$, but the magnitude and pattern of the priming effects on word classification time differed between the groups (see Fig. 1). The two spelling groups showed equivalent repetition priming effects, $F(1, 51) = 0.20$, $p = .7$, but they differed significantly in the effects of the two types of similar primes on classification time. The GRGS group benefited more from primes that were both phonologically and orthographically similar to the target word than from primes that were only orthographically similar, while the GRPS group showed the opposite pattern, $F(1, 51) = 4.54$, $p = .03$. Poorer spellers also showed a significantly larger RT priming effect in the Similar O only condition, relative to the unrelated control, than better spellers, $F(1, 51) = 5.30$, $p = .03$.

The pattern of word priming is consistent with the assumption that lexical experts, defined by accurate spelling in combination with effective reading, have more redundant lexical representations than above average readers who are poorer at spelling. Good spellers showed significantly stronger priming from a prime that was phonologically as well as orthographically similar to the target than a prime that was similar only orthographically, and primes that were only orthographically similar to the target yielded less priming than they did for poor spellers. This is consistent with Perfetti (1992) and Ehri's (1992) characterization of the tuning of lexical representations in which orthographic knowledge is constrained and shaped by existing phonological knowledge. Lexical experts have developed precise lexical representations that are relatively invulnerable to activation from other words that are only visually similar, but remain sensitive to orthographic overlap that is related to phonology. Poorer spellers appear to be sensitive to perceptual/orthographic independently of its relationship to phonology.

4. *Using Rhyme Judgments to Index the Utility of Redundant Lexical Codes*

The differential masked priming from O + P similar and O only similar primes shown by GRGS readers supports the view that expert lexical representations (Perfetti, 1992) amalgamate orthography with phonology (Ehri, 2005). The functional advantage of amalgamation is that it affords quick retrieval of phonological codes for the service of comprehension. A recent Honours research project conducted in my laboratory by Jolyn Hersch investigated the utility of these redundant lexical codes by comparing the performance of GRGS and GRPS subgroups using a rhyme judgment task.

Participants were selected on the basis of reading comprehension scores above the mean of a sample of 350 students. The GRGS group ($n = 15$) had total spelling scores at least 0.5 standard deviations above the normative mean while the GRGS group ($n = 15$) had spelling scores at least 0.5 standard deviations below the mean. Participants were also assessed on a sentence processing span measure of working memory based on that of Daneman and Carpenter (1980). To assess individual differences in print exposure they were also administered an Australian adaptation of the author recognition test developed by Stanovich and West (1989) consisting of a list of the names of 20 well-known authors interspersed with 20 foil names. Table II presents means for both groups on the various measures. In addition to the significantly higher spelling scores expected from the method of classifying participants, the GRGS group also demonstrated significantly higher scores on the author recognition test than the GRPS group, $F(1, 28) = 8.88, p < .01$, but the groups did not differ in working memory performance, $F(1, 28) = 0.28, p = .60$.

TABLE II

AVERAGE STANDARD SCORES ON THE TESTS OF READING COMPREHENSION AND SPELLING, AND ON TESTS OF WORKING MEMORY (MAXIMUM SCORE = 56) AND AUTHOR RECOGNITION (MAXIMUM SCORE = 40) FOR THE TWO READING/SPELLING GROUPS TESTED IN THE RHYME JUDGMENT TASK

	Reading comprehension	Spelling	WM reading span	Author recognition
GRGS	0.68	1.00	38.80	12.67
GRPS	0.81	−1.13	36.80	7.00

GRGS, Good Readers/Good Spellers; GRPS, Good Readers/Poor Spellers.

The rhyme judgment task was modeled on one used by Weber-Fox, Spencer, Cuadro, and Smith (2003) which orthogonally manipulated orthographic and phonological similarity between cue and target words. Target words were preceded by cues that both rhymed and shared an orthographic body (R + O + pairs e.g., *bull full*), rhymed but had a different body (R + O − pairs e.g., *wool full*), did not rhyme but shared an orthographic body (R − O + pairs e.g., *dull-full*), or shared neither rhyme nor body (R − O − pairs e.g., *worm full*). The same 48 high-frequency (average = 199/million) target words were paired with four different cues, which were also of high frequency, to form the four conditions. Counterbalanced stimulus lists were constructed that presented each target word twice accompanied by different cues; across lists all targets appeared in all cue conditions.

The most marked group differences occurred in the accuracy data which are presented in Fig. 2. The GRGS group was significantly more accurate in judging rhyme than the GRPS group, $F(1, 28) = 19.51$, $p < .001$. Average error rate was significantly higher for pairs that were incongruent in the relationship between rhyme and orthography (R + O − and R − O +) than for congruent pairs, $F(1, 28) = 92.53$, $p < .001$, and this difference was significantly greater for the GRPS than the GRGS group, $F(1, 28) = 8.53$, $p < .01$. The differential effect of congruency on good and poor spellers was due to nonrhyming pairs, $F(1, 28) = 13.77$, $p < .001$, the magnitude of the difference between R + O + and R + O − pairs did not significantly differ between the groups, $F(1, 28) = 1.44$, $p = .24$.

These findings converge with those of the masked priming experiment described earlier in suggesting that good readers who are also good spellers have more effectively amalgamated orthographic and phonological information. These redundant codes allow them to more effectively retrieve the phonological information required to make accurate rhyme judgments. In particular, they make them less vulnerable to interference from orthographic

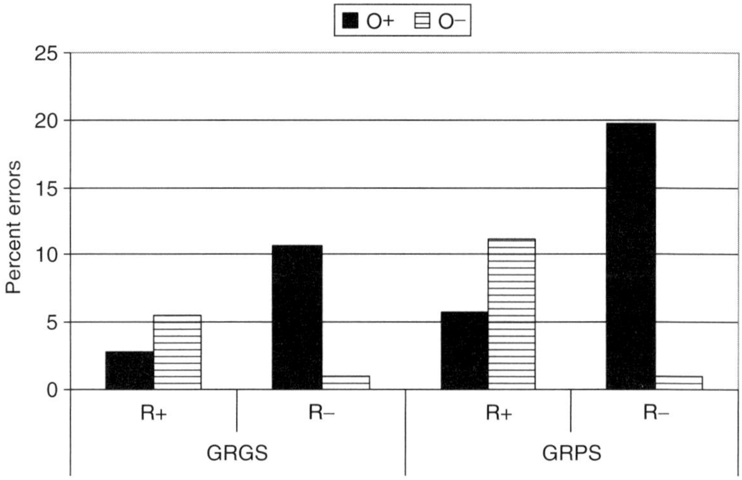

Fig. 2. Average error rates for Good Readers/Good Spellers (GRGS) and Good Readers/Poor Spellers (GRPS) in the rhyme judgment task as a function of the relationship between the rhyme (R) and orthographic body (O) of the word pairs.

similarity that is not correlated with phonology. This parallels the reduced masked priming for O only primes shown by the GRGS group relative to good readers who are poorer spellers.

To provide more refined insight into the basis of the differences between the groups' rhyme-judgment accuracy, regression analyses were conducted predicting accuracy for incongruent pairs from measures of reading, spelling, working memory, and print exposure, as assessed by author recognition accuracy. The complete set of variables accounted for 39% of variance in a simple regression analysis, but the only predictor that accounted for a significant proportion of unique variance was spelling ($p = .03$). Since spelling was highly correlated with scores on the author recognition test ($r = .56$), step-wise regressions were conducted to assess the unique contributions of spelling and print exposure. Reading comprehension and working memory accounted for only 1% of variance when entered in the first step of the analysis. Print exposure and spelling both yielded significant increments in R^2, of .26 and .35, respectively, when added in the second step. Spelling also accounted for a significant 12% of additional variance when added after print exposure, but print exposure did not contribute unique variance over and above spelling (R^2 change $= .03$, $p = .51$). The same was true for a measure of phonological awareness obtained from a phoneme deletion task modeled on Castles, Holmes, Neath, and Kinoshita (2003). Phoneme deletion accuracy accounted for 31% of variance in rhyme judgment accuracy.

Adding spelling contributed an additional 14% of unique variance ($p = .02$) but, when phoneme deletion was added after spelling, it accounted for a nonsignificant 9% of unique variance ($p = .15$).

Thus spelling performance is the strongest predictor of rhyme judgment accuracy and contributes additional variance over and above measures of reading comprehension, working memory, print exposure, and phonological awareness. This is consistent with the prediction derived from the lexical quality hypothesis that lexical expertise, defined by good spelling in conjunction with good reading, is associated with amalgamated lexical representations that afford efficient retrieval of phonological codes. The fact that spelling ability accounts for variance over and above both phoneme deletion and author recognition performance, suggests that something more than phonological awareness and practice is required to develop precise lexical representations. I will discuss the implications of these findings for understanding the architecture of the skilled reading system in the final section of the chapter after considering how effective high-quality representations contribute to "real reading."

III. Lexical Expertise and Reading Comprehension

The evidence discussed so far has been concerned with recognition of isolated words. But the critical prediction of the lexical quality hypothesis is that high-quality representations facilitate reading comprehension. Thus, Perfetti's (1992) "restricted interactive" model of reading comprehension assumes that, although semantic and syntactic information can, in principle, interact with the results of perceptual levels of analysis to facilitate word identification, skilled readers identify most words automatically on the basis of perceptual features alone. Lexical retrieval is "minimally constrained by semantic context" (Perfetti, 1992) and at least functionally, if not structurally, modularized from the processes involved in comprehension (Andrews, 2006b).

The assumption that lexical retrieval and comprehension are functionally modular is well accepted in the cognitive psychological literature, and is used to justify a focus on investigating processing of individual words (Andrews, 2006a), but the evidence remains equivocal. Early cross--modal priming data for ambiguous homographic words (e.g., *bug*, *park*, *bank*) presented in sentences favoring one of their meanings was interpreted as supporting the modular account by showing that both meanings are initially activated, even when they are not contextually appropriate (Swinney, 1979). However, subsequent evidence has revealed that context can exert a strong influence on lexical retrieval of ambiguous words (Tabossi & Zardon, 1993). In addition to empirical contradictions, there are also theoretical questions about the clarity and testability of the modularity hypothesis. Modular accounts *do* allow for contextual influences on lexical retrieval because lexical representations can be "primed" by previous semantic context, increasing the probability and speed of retrieval when they are subsequently presented for identification (Neely, 1977). Such priming provides a mechanism for "top–down" influences on lexical processing that arise within the lexical system itself, rather than from direct on-line interaction between context and lexical retrieval.

Further complexity is introduced by hybrid frameworks. For example, Potter, Moryadas, Abrams, and Noel's (1993) "modular interactive" model assumes that lexical retrieval is autonomous and entirely data driven, but yields a *set* of candidates weighted for their match with the sensory input, that interact with contextual information to select the correct word. These forms of interaction between contextual and data-driven information are conceptually distinct from on-line interaction between bottom–up and top–down knowledge during word identification, but the distinctions can become subtle. The critical issues about the relationship between lexical retrieval and comprehension is not *whether* data-driven, bottom–up processing interacts with context and background knowledge—the final interpretation of text obviously requires both—but exactly when and how they are combined (Bond & Andrews, 2008).

The integrative processes required for comprehension have usually been attributed to a limited-capacity working memory system (Baddeley, 1990) but Potter (1999) argued that the conventional view of this system, which relies heavily on phonological, sequential processing, and the rehearsal mechanisms of the articulatory loop, is "unsuited for conceptual processing that takes place within a second of the onset of a stream of stimuli: It takes too long to be set up, and it does not represent semantic and conceptual information directly" (Potter, 1999, p. 14). She reviewed a variety of evidence implicating a "conceptual short-term memory" (CSTM) system that "leads to the retrieval of additional relevant information from LTM . . . and the formation of new links among concurrently active concepts . . . guided by parsing mechanisms of language . . . and by higher-level knowledge." "Well-connected structures" formed in CSTM are potentially consolidated in LTM while information that is not so incorporated is rapidly forgotten. CSTM processes operate very quickly: "the whole cycle—identification of stimuli, memory recruitment, structuring, consolidation, and forgetting of nonstructured material—may occur in less that 1 sec when ... reading a sentence" (Potter et al., 1993, p. 156).

Most of the evidence for CSTM derives from the "RSVP" paradigm in which a sequence of items—letter, pictures, and words—is presented in a single location at rates of 5–12 items per second. Under these conditions, people can accurately recall *sentences* up to 14 words long at RSVP rates that allow recall of only 2 or 3 items from scrambled sentences or unrelated word lists (Potter, 1999). This level of recall considerably exceeds the 7 ± 2 span conventionally attributed to short-term memory and suggests that "representations of words . . . [are] bound into . . . syntactic and conceptual structures . . . built on the fly" (Potter, Stiefbold, & Moryadas, 1998, p. 26). In contrast to the standard assumption that sentence recall relies on a verbatim record of the sentence stored in working memory, Potter and Lombardi (1990) argue that the conceptual or propositional representations created in CSTM allow participants to regenerate the sentence "using normal speech production processes to express the propositional structure" (p. 27). Recall tends, nevertheless, to be close to verbatim because recently activated lexical representations and syntactic structures are more likely to be selected in the regeneration process (Potter, 1999).

Further evidence for the on-line conceptual processing attributed to CSTM is provided by a Double Word Selection variant of the RSVP task (Potter et al., 1998) in which participants select the contextually appropriate member of a pair of items presented within an RSVP sentence (e.g., *Kate saw the* ***river/color*** *of the rainbow after the storm*). Despite their success at recalling the sentence including the appropriate pair member, even when the context determining selection followed rather than preceded the item pair, participants were very poor at recalling the unselected word. These findings support the modular interactive model's assumption that an initial, bottom–up process produces a set of weighted lexical candidates based on the perceptual evidence from the stimulus and passes this information to a second stage in which contextual evidence is used to select the single candidate which best fits the semantic constraints, while maximizing consistency with the perceptual weightings. Rachel Bond and I have recently reported strong evidence for this account of the relationship between the processes involved in lexical retrieval and sentence comprehension by combining the Double Word Selection task with manipulations designed to investigate Repetition Blindness (Bond & Andrews, 2008).

A. Using RSVP Sentence Processing to Investigate the Autonomy of Lexical Processing

I have recently begun to apply RSVP sentence processing procedures to investigate differences in more and less skilled readers' reliance on bottom-up and top–down processes during sentence processing. One approach to this issue uses effects of lexical ambiguity to provide evidence about the autonomy of lexical retrieval: if lexical retrieval operates autonomously, driven by bottom–up analysis, then both meanings of lexically ambiguous words (e.g., *bat*, *ball*) should be activated, even in contexts that favor one meaning (e.g., *They danced all night at the ball*). As discussed previously, the available evidence on this question using unselected samples of skilled readers is equivocal (e.g., Swinney, 1979; Tabossi & Zardon, 1993). This may, in part, be due to individual differences in lexical expertise.

Gernsbacher, Varner, and Faust (1990) used RSVP sentence processing to investigate individual differences in sensitivity to lexical ambiguity in good and poor adult readers categorized on measures of reading and listening comprehension. They were presented with RSVP sentences that were completed with an ambiguous or nonambiguous word (e.g., *He dug with a spade/shovel*) at about 300 ms/word followed by probe words that had to be judged for its relatedness to the sentence. The critical data were provided by probe words that were related to the sentence-incongruous meaning of the homograph (e.g., *ace*). Gernsbacher et al. (1990) found that, when probe words were presented immediately after the sentence, both skilled and unskilled readers were slower to classify probes related to the sentence-incongruous meaning of the homograph, but if probes were delayed by 1 s, this was true only for poorer readers. Gernsbacher et al. (1990) concluded that skilled readers are faster to suppress irrelevant associations. Her data also support a modular account of sentence processing because they imply that initial lexical activation is not influenced by context. However, Gernsbacher's use of an explicit semantic judgment task means that her results may reflect differences in the comprehension strategies used by good and poor readers. Gernsbacher and Faust (1991) found that good and poor comprehenders benefited equally from a congruous sentence context and argued that this shows that their slower rejection of sentence-incongruent words is not due to problems in sentence comprehension per se, but they never directly compared better and poorer comprehenders performance for sentence-congruent and -incongruent words under identical conditions.

1. Lexical Ambiguity Effects on Probe Memory for RSVP Sentences

To address these issues, I used a probe memory task instead of a meaning judgment and included probe words that were related to both the sentence-congruent and sentence-incongruent meaning of a sentence-final homograph. Participants were presented with an RSVP sentence followed by a probe word and instructed to decide whether the word appeared in the sentence. Rather than requiring deliberate processing of sentence meaning, which may be affected by better readers' more effective comprehension strategies, this task provides an indirect assessment of the effect of sentence

TABLE III

EXAMPLES OF THE PLAUSIBLE SENTENCES AND PROBE WORDS DEFINING THE THREE CRITICAL EXPERIMENTAL CONDITIONS OF THE PROBE MEMORY TASK

	Probe absent		
	Related		
	Congruous	Incongruous	Unrelated
They were still dancing at the end of the ball	WALTZ	THROW	DARE
The crowd cheered when he caught the ball	THROW	WALTZ	DARE
The roof was supported by a strong beam	STEEL	GLOW	STORM
The animal's eyes shone in the torch beam	GLOW	STEEL	STORM

Any participant saw only one probe word with each sentence, but across participants all probes occurred with all sentences.

context. The stimulus materials were constructed around 48 homographic words with two distinct meanings (e.g., *ball, beam, bridge, ring, seal*). For each word, two sentences were created, one favoring each of the separate meanings, and three Probe words were selected, one related to each homograph meaning and one unrelated to either meaning. The critical conditions, depicted in the Table III, are those in which the probe word is absent from the sentence: slower responses to words related to both the context-incongruous and context-congruous meaning of the ambiguous final word would imply that both meaning were activated, while differences between responses to congruous and incongruous probes index the influence of sentence context. A second version of each pair of sentences was created by rearranging target words across sentences to create implausible sentences but only the results for plausible sentences are reported here. In addition to the 48 critical sentences, each list contained 30 sentences in which the Probe word was present in the sentence.

Sentences were presented one word a time at a rate of 300 ms/word ms followed by a probe word for 500 ms, presented in upper case 2 lines below the position in which the sentence had appeared. As in Gernsbacher's (Gernsbacher and Faust, 1991; Gernsbacher et al., 1990) experiments, probe words were presented at either a short (0 ms) or long (1000 ms) delay after the final word of the sentence. Participants were told to respond as quickly as possible by pressing one key if the probe word had been in the sentence and another if it had not.

The participants were undergraduate psychology students who completed the experiment as part of a practical class. Better readers were defined as those with a passage comprehension score at least 0.5 standard deviations above the mean of the sample of 98 participants monolingual or early bilingual English speakers, while poor readers were those with a passage comprehension score at least 0.5 standard deviations below the mean for the whole sample. Fifteen participants from each delay condition were selected for each reading ability group.

Figure 3 presents the average RT for "no" responses to the different probe types separately for better readers (left panel) and poorer readers (right panel). Better readers responded considerably faster than poorer readers, $F(1, 56) = 35.34$, $p < .001$, and they also showed a different pattern of performance across the probe conditions. Better readers were slower to reject congruous probe words than unrelated words, $F(1, 56) = 27.92, p < .001$, but showed no such delay for incongruous compared to unrelated probe words ($F < 1$). This was true for both short- and long-delay conditions. Poorer readers showed the same pattern in the long-delay condition: Responses for congruous words, $F(1, 28) = 12.71, p < .01$, but not incongruous words ($F < 1$) were longer than those to Unrelated probes. But in the short-delay condition they were significantly slower to respond to both congruous, $F(1, 28) = 6.23$, $p = .01$, and incongruous, $F(1, 28) = 5.84$, $p = .02$, probes than to Unrelated probe words.

These data contrast with Gernsbacher's (Gernsbacher and Faust, 1991; Gernsbacher et al., 1990) findings using a meaning judgment task for incongruent probes. She found that both better and poorer comprehenders were slower to reject words related to the sentence-congruent meaning as being

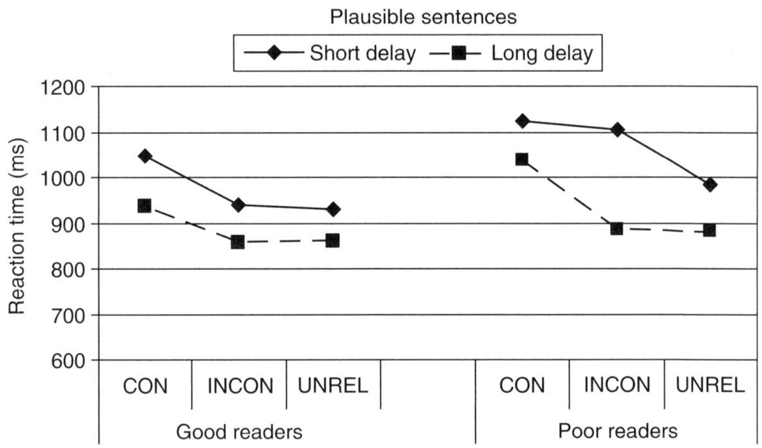

Fig. 3. Average reaction time for probe memory responses to plausible sentences as a function of delay between the sentence and the probe word and whether the probe word was related to the sentence-congruent meaning of the homographic word (CON), the sentence incongruent meaning (INCON) or unrelated to either meaning (UNREL).

related to the sentence at short delays, but only poorer comprehenders continued to show this interference at a long delay. In our data, poorer readers showed a pattern similar to Gernsbacher et al.'s (1990) better readers in the sense that they showed interference for both congruous and incongruous meanings at short delays, but appear to have suppressed this meaning in the long-delay condition. But our better readers never showed interference for the sentence-incongruous meaning, even at the short delay. According to Gernsbacher's framework, this implies that our good readers demonstrate such fast suppression of the sentence-irrelevant meaning that they do not show interference even when the probe is presented immediately after the final word of the sentence.

Potter's (1999) modular interactive framework suggests a somewhat different interpretation. Highly skilled readers may be less susceptible to activation of the sentence-irrelevant word because their efficient lexical retrieval of the earlier words in the sentence allows information in CSTM to contribute to very rapid selection between coactivated lexical candidates, such as the two representations of a homographic word. Probes that are congruent with the sentence are difficult to reject because they are compatible with the information activated in CSTM by previous words in the sentence but probes related to the incongruent meaning are not.

This interpretation of the differences between the processes underlying performance of better and poorer readers in the probe memory task may seem to conflict with my claim that skilled reading relies on a modular lexical retrieval system that is impervious to context. Skilled readers show more contextually sensitive lexical retrieval, even at short delays, potentially indicating that they rely more heavily on top–down context than less skilled readers, or at least are able to use it more quickly. The critical question is whether sentence context exerts a direct effect on lexical processing or influences processes that operate on lexical output. According to the modular interactive framework, lexical retrieval of a particular word is data driven, but the outputs of the retrieval process will enter CSTM and retrieve information from LTM. CSTM processes will bind together coherent information but provide less effective support for unrelated information. Thus, context can influence which outputs of the lexical system remain active but does not directly determine what enters CSTM in the first place. Clearly, this is a fine distinction which requires more direct support.

2. *Word and Nonword Conversion Effects for RSVP Sentences*

More direct evidence about the relative reliance on bottom–up and top–down information of better and poorer readers is provided by a recent unpublished Honours project conducted in my laboratory by Stephen

Laurent using the "nonword conversion task," another RSVP paradigm introduced by Potter et al. (1993). In this paradigm, RSVP sentences are presented in which the correct target word (e.g., *belly*) is sometimes replaced with a similar word or nonword (e.g., *The overweight man had a big belly/bully/bally and red cheeks*). Potter et al. (1993) found that participants often converted an incongruent word or nonword to the target word, even when the distinguishing context followed the target, and that such conversion occurred more frequently for nonwords than for similar words. They also showed that the effects were due to a combination of sentential and lexical bias because conversion effects were larger for sentences, like that above, in which both sentential and lexical context favors *belly* over *bully* and *bally*, than in sentence in which lexical context favored the word that was incongruent with the sentence (e.g., *The overweight man was a big bully/belly/bally and had red cheeks*).

To investigate whether better and poorer readers differ in the sensitivity to sentence and/or lexical context Laurent's experiment compared performance in this nonword conversion task for better and poorer university student readers selected on the same criteria as the probe memory experiment. He created sentences like the examples in the previous paragraph in which the sentential and lexical context either matched or mismatched in their support for one of the target words (presented in bold):

Match: *The girl was captured and subjected to violent* ***rape****/tape/dape*
I got some strange audio magnetic effects when I replayed the ***tape****/rape/dape*
Mismatch: *Luckily for the girl, the act of violence was captured on* ***tape****/rape/dape*
I got some strange audiomagnetic effects when I replayed the ***rape****/tape/dape scene*

The sentences were presented using the RSVP procedure at a rate of 150 ms/word. Counterbalanced lists ensured that any participant only saw each sentence once, but across all lists, each sentence appeared equally often with a congruous word, incongruous word, or nonword target (e.g., *rape/tape/dape*). Instructions and practice trials alerted participants to the presence of similar word and nonword items and emphasized that their task was to report exactly what they saw, even if the sentence did not make sense.

Better and poorer readers showed generally similar patterns of performance across the conditions, but better readers were significantly more accurate in reporting target stimuli, $F(1, 34) = 15.3$, $p < .001$, than poorer readers, particularly the incongruous words and nonwords, $F(1, 34) = 7.10$, $p < .01$. This is summarized in Fig. 4 which presents an index of sentential bias for the incongruous and nonword conditions calculated as the proportion of intrusions of the sentence-congruous word relative to correct target

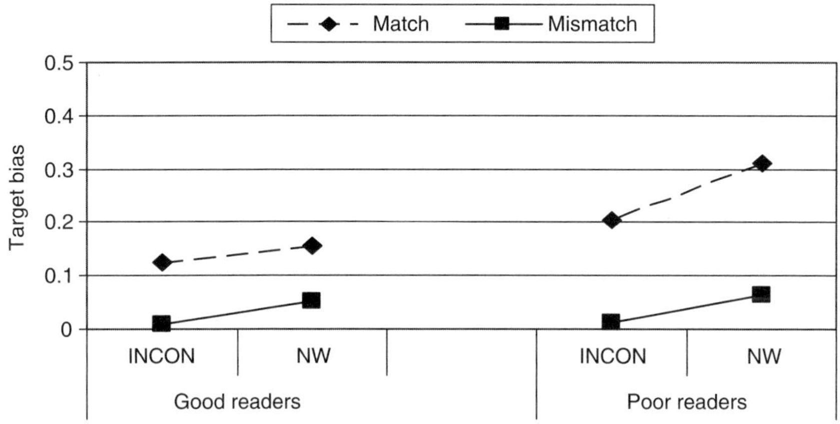

Fig. 4. Average measures of the bias to report the sentence-congruent target word when recalling sentences containing either a similar word incongruent with the sentence (INCON) or a similar nonword (NW).

reports, to control for differences between the overall accuracy of the better and poorer readers. Poorer readers were significantly more likely to "convert" the incongruous stimulus into the sentence appropriate word than better readers, $F(1, 34) = 9.2$, $p < .01$, and this difference was entirely due to the Match sentences, $F(1, 34) = 10.3$, $p < .01$, in which lexical context was consistent with the sentence context. Consistent with Potter et al.'s (1993) results, both better and poorer readers showed a stronger bias to mistakenly report the sentence-congruent word when the presented stimulus was a nonword rather than a word, $F(1, 34) = 10.2$, $p < .001$.

Thus, in task conditions where they were instructed to report "exactly what they saw" even if it was semantically incongruous, better readers were more faithful to the perceptual input and less influenced by sentence context than poorer readers. This is consistent with the assumption that their high-quality lexical representations allow them to more effectively retrieve the exact stimulus they were shown, even when it was inconsistent with the sentential and lexical context. These results contrast with those of the probe memory experiment, where the better readers were more sensitive to sentence context than the poorer readers, as demonstrated by selective interference for sentence-congruent word, even at short delays. Processing the gist of the sentence would benefit the probe memory task by increasing participants' ability to maintain the sentence until the probe word was presented, but have the disadvantage of making it more difficult to reject probe words that were related to the meaning of the sentence as a whole. In combination, the data for the two experiments suggest that more skilled readers are more effective than less skilled readers at both lexical retrieval and contextual integration and also more capable of tailoring their processing to the specific task demands. Their higher quality lexical representations allow them to more effectively use perceptual input to retrieve the lexical codes for individual words under the pressured conditions created by RSVP presentation. This fast efficient lexical retrieval also allows them to rapidly retrieve and integrate semantic information to facilitate comprehension.

IV. Conclusions

The broad aim of the ongoing research program that I have sketched in this chapter is to provide direct evidence of the contribution of lexical expertise to skilled reading and to use this evidence to more precisely define the architecture of the skilled reading system.

Section II focused on defining the "high-quality" lexical representations that are assumed to be the outcome of reaching the orthographic stage of reading development. A vast body of evidence investigating visual word identification in unselected samples of university students has shown that skilled readers are exquisitely sensitive to the internal structure of words suggesting that they do not simply treat words as collections of individual letters. Skilled readers are sensitive to complex interactions between letter identity and sequence that cannot be captured by models that only code letter identity and position (e.g., Davis & Bowers, 2006). The masked priming and rhyme judgment data reported in II.C.3 and II.C.4 extend these findings by showing systematic variation within the population of skilled readers consistent with differences in the precision and redundancy of their lexical representations. Higher spelling ability was associated with sensitivity to more abstract relationships between orthography and phonology and reduced sensitivity to visual or orthographic similarity per se. This is consistent with the view that lexical experts, categorized by the combination of good reading and spelling, have more precise orthographic representations that reflect experience with the grapheme–phoneme relationships embodied in the words of their vocabulary. These amalgamated representations are more resistant to activation by masked primes that are similar only orthographically, and less vulnerable to interference from orthographically similar words in the rhyme judgment task.

Kristi Paul, a doctoral research student working in my laboratory, is extending the masked priming approach to investigate differences in sensitivity to transposed letter (TL) similarity as a function of reading and spelling ability. Consistent with the masked priming data reported in II.C.3, she found that a

GRGS group showed significantly less priming from orthographically similar primes by comparison with repetition primes than groups of poorer spellers (Paul & Andrews, 2007). In this case, the similar primes were a combination of TL and one letter different replacement letter (RL) primes. GRGS subjects also showed less interference for TL nonwords (e.g., *JUGDED*) relative to RL nonwords (e.g., *JUDPED*) than poor spellers. These findings suggest that, as well as being more sensitive to orthographic–phonological redundancy, expert lexical representations more precisely represent the identity and sequence of orthographic units in words.

This evidence that lexical experts are sensitive to multiple levels of orthographic and phonological similarity is broadly consistent with the assumptions of PDP models of visual word recognition which assume that, through repeated exposure to words, the connections between the elements of the orthographic, phonological, and semantic networks that make up the lexical system come to reflect covariations between words at a range of levels and grain sizes (e.g., Seidenberg & McClelland, 1989). Since the structure of PDP networks is learned through exposure to words, individuals will differ in the precise structure of their lexical network (Zevin & Seidenberg, 2006), and the extent of reading experience will contribute to the degree of refinement of lexical networks across individuals.

One critical assumption of the PDP framework that seems incompatible with the lexical framework that I have elaborated is the assumption that there are no word specific-representations: Words are represented by distributed, overlapping patterns of activity rather than by "explicit structural entities such as logogens or localist word units" (Plaut, 1997, p. 785). Such a notion seems incompatible with the proposal of orthographically precise word-specific representations that can be "passed on" to higher levels of processing. Although the assumption of distributed word-level representations has been strongly emphasized by advocates of the PDP framework as one of the critical features distinguishing it from symbolic dual route models, they also acknowledge that implemented PDP models are only approximations, particularly with respect to their assumptions about the "inputs and outputs of the model ... [such as] the form of input processes generated by earlier, upstream processes, and about how the model's output representations are used by later downstream processes" (Seidenberg & Plaut, 2006, p. 37). Implemented PDP models have finessed a number of questions about letter coding by assuming localist codes corresponding to onset, vowel, and coda units (Plaut et al., 1996), without specifying how they are learned through exposure. They have also focused on individual word recognition with little consideration of how the outcomes of word recognition are used for comprehension. I have argued elsewhere (Andrews, 2006b) that, even if representations are spatially distributed, there may still be a discrete point of "lexical closure" when the lexical system settles on a single candidate. That is, lexical processing may be temporally encapsulated, even in the absence of modular lexical structures.

Such a proposal is not necessarily incompatible with the principles of PDP frameworks. This is exemplified by a recent adaptation of the PDP framework that has modified the full interactivity of the original model to more accurately simulate the developmental sequence of children's learning about words. Children have developed a large vocabulary of spoken word forms before they are exposed to written language. Kello (2006) describes a model that takes account of this developmental sequence by pretraining connections between phonological and semantic networks and then mapping orthography directly onto the hidden units linking phonology and semantics, rather than through the separate orthography–semantics and orthography–phonology networks assumed by the original "triangle" PDP models (e.g., Plaut et al., 1996). Kello argues that this "shared route architecture" (see Fig. 5) is efficient because "reading requires a mapping [of orthography] to sound and meaning" (2006, p. 52). He has also shown that, even though the model has a single route from orthography to phonology, it can simulate the dissociations between naming performance for regular words, exception words, and nonwords that have been argued to demonstrate independent lexical and sublexical routes (Coltheart et al., 2001) by manipulating the "input gain" at encoding (Kello, 2003; Kello & Plaut, 2003).

Kello (2006) reports recent extensions of this "junction model" of the lexical system to a large, realistic vocabulary of over 45,000 monosyllabic

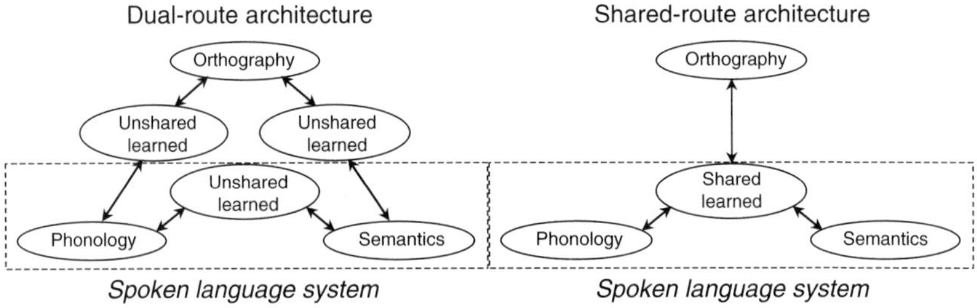

Fig. 5. Diagrams comparing dual-route and shared-route architectures. The well-known triangle model is used to illustrate the theoretical commitments that apply more generally to dual-route architectures. The shared-route architecture is implemented in the junction model of lexical processing. The outlined portions represent the spoken language parts of these architectures, which are presumably in place prior to the development of the written language parts. (From Kello, 2006).

and multisyllabic words. The expanded model uses localist lexical codes to mediate between distributed networks of orthographic, phonological, and semantic units. The use of localist codes is partly a simplification to make it feasible to train the model with such a large vocabulary, but Kello also argues that localist codes have the advantage of being able to capture both systematic mappings (like those between orthography and phonology) and relatively arbitrary mappings (like those between phonology and semantics). In Kello's initial implementation, the localist codes are prespecified, but future developments of the model will train localist codes using algorithms like those applied in adaptive resonance theory (Grossberg, 1987). Such learned localist codes combine the benefits of learning and generalization of distributed representations with the advantages of localist coding (Davis, 1999, p. 2000).

Kello's (2006) model also captures an important difference between learning to read and learning to speak (Carr, 1999): "Children are wired for sound, but print is an optional accessory that must be painstakingly bolted on" (Pinker, 1997, p. ix). The junction model's assumption that orthography is mapped to phonological units that have already been shaped through spoken language acquisition captures the "bolting on" of Pinker's metaphor, and also assigns orthography particular significance in the structuring of lexical knowledge.

The assumption that skilled reading relies on an encapsulated lexicon of visual word forms is supported by recent brain-imaging data that has demonstrated an isolable system in left pre-striate cortex that is selectively activated by words and well-structured nonwords, but not by nonlinguistic or poorly structured linguistic stimuli, which appears to serve as the "primary gateway between the visual system and core components of the preexisting language apparatus" (Carr, 1999, p. 479). Critically, in the present context, the brain region identified with the VWFS appears to play a greater role in the processing of competent readers than disabled readers.

According to Pugh et al.'s (2001) review of a range of neuropsychological and neuroimaging evidence, successful reading relies on two consolidated left hemisphere (LH) posterior systems, a temporo-parietal area that "performs the function of learning to decode print for normally developing young readers" and the extrastriatal VWFS region that "develops with reading experience into a system that recognizes printed words in a fast, automatic manner" (Pugh et al., 2001, pp. 246–247). Disabled readers, by contrast, appear to use compensatory strategies that rely on bilateral activity in the inferior frontal gyrus and in right hemisphere posterior sites homologous to the VWFS. The increased involvement of VWFS as readers acquire increasing proficiency is consistent with the hypothesis that skilled reading relies on the efficient lexical retrieval afforded by high-quality orthographic representations.

Kello's (2006) junction model combines the learning of principles of PDP frameworks with the assumption of localist codes that mediate between different levels of representation to provide a theoretical framework that is compatible with the functions attributed to the VWFS. He argues that a mediating level of localist representation reflects "a more general principle of junctions [that] provides a way to think about cognitive representations that emerge from the demands of perception and action" in complex dynamic systems that rely on the "confluence of competitive and cooperative interactions" (p. 72). This is similar to the metaphor of a "pivot" that I have used to describe the relationship between lexical retrieval and reading: "whatever the 'grain size' of linguistic knowledge in general, there is a functional level at which lexical knowledge acts in a 'localist' manner . . . because words serve as an interface or 'pivot' for reading comprehension" (Andrews, 2006b, p. 319) which summarizes the outcomes of lexical processing and provides the building blocks on which comprehension processes operate.

Orthographic word forms may play a particularly important role in "deep" orthographies like English in which the "morphophonemic" writing system (Chomsky & Halle, 1968) captures morphological relationships that are not evident in phonology (e.g., *heal/healthy*; *sign/signature*). These attributes of the language may encourage the extraction of multiletter units and contribute to the encapsulation of orthographic word forms. But words may be the building blocks of skilled reading in many languages because of the critical role they play in eye movements during reading. For example, the E–Z Reader model of eye movements (Rayner, Reichle, & Pollatsek, 2006) assumes that "attention is allocated serially: to only one word at a time" (p. 126) and that the outcome of lexical retrieval processes determine the timing of saccades and of shifts of attention. Serial word-by-word processing is argued to be crucial to comprehension because readers need to "get the word order straight" (p. 140) in order to successfully construct meaning. The CSTM system proposed by Potter et al. (1993) plays a critical role in this process by providing the bridge between activated lexical forms and the stored knowledge that give meaning to those concepts.

Thus, there is a wide variety of reasons for believing that reading is "all about words" (Andrews, 2006b). Precise, redundant lexical representations facilitate effective reading comprehension by ensuring that skilled readers' bottom–up processing effortlessly retrieves the correct lexical forms which, in turn, make available the appropriate semantic and syntactic information for effective comprehension. Detailed investigations of lexical experts will further contribute to refining our understanding of the nature and determinants of high-quality lexical representations and the role they play in skilled reading comprehension.

Acknowledgments

The research reported in this chapter was supported by the Australian Research Council. I am grateful to Jolyn Hersch and Stephen Laurent for conducting two of the experiments reported and to the hundreds of University of Sydney students who participated in the experiments and demonstrated such a diversity of written language proficiency.

References

Ackerman, P. (1987). Individual differences in skill learning. *Psychological Bulletin, 102*, 3–27.

Allington, R. (1984). Content coverage and contextual reading in reading groups. *Journal of Reading Behavior, 16*, 85–96.

Andrews, S. (1986). Morphological influences on lexical access: Lexical or nonlexical effects. *Journal of Memory and Language, 25*, 726–740.

Andrews, S. (1992). A skills approach: Optimising initial reading instruction. In A. Watson and A. Badenhop (Eds.), *The prevention of reading failure*. Sydney: Ashton Scholastic.

Andrews, S. (1996). Lexical retrieval and selection processes: Effects of transposed-letter confusability. *Journal of Memory and Language, 35*, 775–800.

Andrews, S. (1997). The role of orthographic similarity in lexical retrieval: Resolving neighborhood conflicts. *Psychonomic Bulletin and Review, 4*, 439–461.

Andrews, S. (Ed.). (2006a). *From inkmarks to ideas: Current issues in lexical processing*. Hove, UK: Psychology Press.

Andrews, S. (2006b). All about words: A lexicalist perspective on reading. In S. Andrews (Ed.), *From inkmarks to ideas: Current issues in lexical processing*. Hove, UK: Psychology Press.

Andrews, S., & Scarratt, D. R. (1998). Rule and analogy mechanisms in reading nonwords: Hough dou peapel rede gnew wirds? *Journal of Experimental Psychology: Human Perception and Performance, 24*, 1052–1086.

Andrews, S., Miller, B., & Rayner, K. (2004). Eye fixation measures of morphological segmentation of compound words: There is a mouse in the mousetrap. *European Journal of Cognitive Psychology, 16*, 285–311.

Baayen, R. H., Piepenbrock, R., & van Rijn, H. (1993). *The CELEX lexical database.* (CD-ROM). Linguistic Data Consortium. University of Pennsylvania.

Baddeley, A. (1990). *Human memory: Theory and practice*. London: Erlbaum.

Blachman, B. A. (1997). *The foundations of reading acquisition and dyslexia: Implications for early intervention*. Mahwah, NJ: Erlbaum.

Bodner, G. E., & Masson, M. E. J. (2001). Prime validity affects masked repetition priming: Evidence for an episodic resource account of priming. *Journal of Memory and Language, 45*, 616–647.

Bond, R., & Andrews, S. (2008). Repetition blindness in sentence contexts: Not just an attribution? *Memory & Cognition, 36*, 295–313.

Burt, J., & Tate, H. (2002). Does a reading lexicon provide orthographic representations for spelling? *Journal of Memory and Language, 46*, 518–543.

Byrne, B., Deleland, C., & Fielding-Barnsley, R. (2002). Longitudinal twin study of early reading development in three countries: Preliminary results. *Annals of Dyslexia, 52*, 49–73.

Carr, T. H. (1999). Trying to understand dyslexia: Mental chronometry, individual differences, cognitive neuroscience and the impact of instruction as converging sources of evidence. In R. M. Klein and P. A. McMullen (Eds.), *Converging methods for understanding reading and dyslexia*. Cambridge, MA: MIT Press.

Cassar, M., & Treiman, R. (1997). The beginnings of orthographic knowledge: Children's knowledge of double letters in words. *Journal of Educational Psychology, 89*, 631–644.

Castles, A., & Coltheart, M. (2004). Does phonological awareness help children learn to read? *Cognition, 91*, 77–111.

Castles, A., Davis, C., & Forster, K. I. (2003). Word recognition development in children: Insights from masked-priming. In S. Kinoshita and S. Lupker (Eds.), *Masked priming: State of the art*. Hove, UK: Psychology Press.

Castles, A., Holmes, V., Neath, J., & Kinoshita, S. (2003). How does orthographic knowledge influence performance on phonological awareness tasks? *Quarterly Journal of Experimental Psychology A: Human Experimental Psychology, 56*, 445–467.

Castles, A., & Nation, K. (2006). How does orthographic learning happen? In S. Andrews (Ed.), *From inkmarks to ideas: Current issues in lexical processing*. Hove, UK: Psychology Press.

Chomsky, N., & Halle, M. (1968). *The sound patterns of English*. NY: Harper Row.

Coltheart, M., Curtis, B., Atkins, P., & Haller, H. (1993). Models of reading aloud: Dual-route and parallel-distributed-processing approaches. *Psychological Review, 100*, 589–608.

Coltheart, M., Rastle, K., Perry, C., Langdon, R., & Ziegler, J. (2001). DRC: A Dual Route Cascaded model of visual word recognition and reading aloud. *Psychological Review, 108*, 204–256.

Daneman, M., & Carpenter, P. A. (1980). Individual differences in working memory and reading. *Journal of Verbal Learning and Verbal Behavior, 19*, 450–466.

Davis, C., & Bowers, J. (2006). Contrasting five different theories of letter position coding: Evidence from orthographic similarity effects. *Journal of Experimental Psychology: Human Perception and Performance, 32*(3), 535–557.

Davis, C. J. (1999). *The self-organising lexical acquisition and recognition (SOLAR) model of visual word recognition*. Doctoral dissertation, University of New South Wales.

Ehri, L. (2005). Learning to read words: Theory, findings and issues. *Scientific Studies of Reading, 9*, 167–188.

Ehri, L. C. (1992). Reconceptualizing the development of sight word reading and its relationship to decoding. In P. Gough, L. C. Ehri, and R. Treiman (Eds.), *Reading acquisition*. Hillsdale, NJ: Erlbaum.

Fodor, J. A. (1983). *Modularity of mind*. Cambridge, MA: MIT Press.

Forster, K. I., & Davis, C. (1984). Repetition priming and frequency attenuation in lexical access. *Journal of Experimental Psychology: Learning, Memory and Cognition, 10*, 680–698.

Forster, K. I., Davis, C., Schoknecht, C., & Carter, R. (1987). Masked priming with graphemically related forms: Repetition or partial activation? *Quarterly Journal of Experimental Psychology, 39*, 211–251.

Forster, K., Mohan, K., & Hector, J. (2003). The mechanics of masked priming. In S. Kinoshita and S. J. Lupkey (Eds.), *Masked priming: The state of the art* (pp. 3–38). Hove, UK: Psychology Press.

Frith, U. (1980). Unexpected spelling problems. In U. Frith (Ed.), *Cognitive processes in spelling* (pp. 495–517). London: Academic Press.

Frith, U. (1985). Beneath the surface of developmental dyslexia. In K. Patterson, J. Marshall, and M. Coltheart (Eds.), *Surface dyslexia*. Hillsdale, NJ: Erlbaum.

Gernsbacher, M. A., & Faust, M. (1991). The mechanism of suppression: A component of general comprehension skill. *Journal of Experimental Psychology: Learning, Memory, and Cognition, 17*, 245–262.

Gernsbacher, M. A., Varner, K. R., & Faust, M. (1990). Investigating differences in general comprehension skill. *Journal of Experimental Psychology: Learning, Memory and Cognition, 16*, 430–455.

Grainger, J., & Jacobs, A. M. (1996). Orthographic processing in visual word recognition: A multiple read-out model. *Psychological Review, 103*, 518–565.

Grossberg (1987). Competitive learning—From interactive activation to adaptive resonance. *Cognitive Science, 11*, 23–63.

Huey, E. B. (1908/1968). *The psychology and pedagogy of reading*. Cambridge, MA: MIT Press (reprinted 1968).

Kahneman, D., & Treisman, A. (1983). Changing views of attention and automaticity. In R. Parasuraman and R. Davies (Eds.), *Varieties of attention*. New York: Academic Press.

Kello, C. T. (2003). The emergence of a double dissociation in the modulation of a single control parameter in a single dynamic system. *Cortex, 39*, 132–134.

Kello, C. T. (2006). Considering the junction model of lexical processing. In S. Andrews (Ed.), *From inkmarks to ideas: Current issues in lexical processing*. Hove, UK: Psychology Press.

Kello, C. T., & Plaut, D. C. (2003). Strategic control over rate of processing in word reading: A computational investigation. *Journal of Memory and Language, 48*, 207–232.

Kinoshita, S. & Lupker, S. (Eds.) (2003). *Masked priming: The state of the art*. New York: Psychology Press.

Libben, G. (2006). Reading complex morphological structures. In S. Andrews (Ed.), *From inkmarks to ideas: Current issues in lexical processing*. Hove, UK: Psychology Press.

Logan, G. (1992). Attention and preattention in theories of automaticity. *American Journal of Psychology, 105*, 317–339.

McClelland, J. L., & Rumelhart, D. E. (1981). An interactive activation model of context effects in letter perception: Part 1. An account of basic findings. *Psychological Review, 88*, 375–407.

McLeod, C. M. (1991). Half a century of research on the Stroop effect: An integrative review. *Psychological Bulletin, 109*, 163–203.

Neely, J. H. (1977). Semantic priming and retrieval from lexical memory: Roles of inhibitionless spreading activation and limited capacity attention. *Journal of Experimental Psychology: General, 106*, 226–254.

Pacton, S., Perruchet, P., Fayol, M., & Cleeremans, A. (2001). Implicit learning in real world context: The case of orthographic regularities. *Journal of Experimental Psychology: General, 130*, 401–426.

Page, M. P. (2000). Connectionist modeling in psychology: A localist manifesto. *Behavioral and Brain Sciences, 23*, 443–512.

Paul, K. Y., & Andrews, S. (2007). Using transposed-letter confusability effects to assess lexical precision. Paper presented at European Conference on Cognitive Psychology, Marseille.

Perea, M., & Lupker, S. (2003a). Transposed-letter confusability effects in masked form priming. In S. Kinoshita and S. J. Lupkey (Eds.), *Masked priming: The state of the art* (pp. 97–120). Hove, UK: Psychology Press.

Perea, M., & Lupker, S. (2003b). Does *jugde* activate COURT? Transposed-letter similarity effects in masked associative priming. *Memory & Cognition, 31*(6), 829–841.

Perfetti, C., & Hart, L. (2001). The lexical basis of comprehension skill. In D. Gorfein (Ed.), *On the consequences of meaning selection: Perspectives on resolving lexical ambiquity* (pp. 67–86). Washington, DC: American Psychological Association.

Perfetti, C. A. (1992). The representation problem in reading acquisition. In P. B. Gough, L. C. Ehri, and R. Treiman (Eds.), *Reading acquisition* (pp. 145–174). Hillsdale, NJ, England: Erlbaum.

Pinker, S. (1997). Preface. In D. McGuiness (Ed.), *Why our children can't read*. New York: Simon & Schuster.

Plaut, D. C. (1997). Structure and function in the lexical system: Insights from distributed models of word reading and lexical decision. *Language and Cognitive Processes, 12*, 767–808.

Plaut, D. C., McClelland, J. L., Seidenberg, M. S., & Patterson, K. (1996). Understanding normal and impaired word reading: Computational principles in quasi-regular domains. *Psychological Review, 103*, 56–115.
Potter, M. C. (1999). Understanding sentences and scenes: The role of conceptual short-term memory. In V. Coltheart (Ed.), *Fleeting memories: Cognition of brief visual stimuli* (pp. 13–46). Cambridge, MA: MIT Press.
Potter, M. C., & Lombardi, L. (1990). Regeneration in the short-term recall of sentences. *Journal of Memory and Language, 29*, 633–654.
Potter, M. C., Moryadas, A., Abrams, I., & Noel, A. (1993). Word perception and misperception in context. *Journal of Experimental Psychology: Learning, Memory, and Cognition, 19*, 3–22.
Potter, M. C., Stiefbold, D., & Moryadas, A. (1998). Word selection in reading sentences: Preceding versus following contexts. *Journal of Experimental Psychology: Learning, Memory, and Cognition, 24*, 68–100.
Pugh, K. R., Mencl, W. E., Jenner, A. R., Lee, J. R., Katz, L., Frost, S. J., Shaywitz, S. E., & Shaywitz, B. A. (2001). Neuroimaging studies of reading development and reading disability. *Learning Disabilities Research & Practice, 16*, 240–249.
Rack, J., Snowling, M., & Olson, R. (1992). The nonword reading deficit in developmental dyslexia: A review. *Reading Research Quarterly, 27*, 29–53.
Rastle, K., & Coltheart, M. (2006). Is there serial processing in the reading system; and are there local representations. In S. Andrews (Ed.), *From inkmarks to ideas: Current issues in lexical processing*. Hove, UK: Psychology Press.
Rayner, K. (1998). Eye movements in reading and information processing: 20 years of research. *Psychological Bulletin, 124*, 372–422.
Rayner, K., Reichle, E., & Pollatsek, A. (2006). Cognitive processes in reading: The E-Z Reader model of eye-movement control. In S. Andrews (Ed.), *From inkmarks to ideas: Current issues in lexical processing*. Hove, UK: Psychology Press.
Seidenberg, M. S., & McClelland, J. L. (1989). A distributed, developmental model of word recognition and naming. *Psychological Review, 96*, 523–568.
Seidenberg, M. S., & Plaut, D. C. (2006). Progress in understanding word reading: Data fitting versus theory building. In S. Andrews (Ed.), *From inkmarks to ideas: Current issues in lexical processing*. Hove, UK: Psychology Press.
Sereno, J. A. (1991). Graphemic associative and syntactic priming effects at brief stimulus onset asynchrony in lexical decision and naming. *Journal of Experimental Psychology: Learning, Memory, and Cognition, 17*(3), 459–477.
Share, D. L. (1995). Phonological recoding and self-teaching: *Sine qua non* of reading acquisition. *Cognition, 55*, 151–218.
Share, D. L. (2004). Orthographic learning at a glance: On the time course and developmental onset of self-teaching. *Journal of Experimental Child Psychology, 87*, 267–298.
Shiffrin, R. M., & Schneider, W. (1977). Controlled and automatic human information processing: II Perceptual learning, automatic attending and a general theory. *Psychological Review, 84*, 127–190.
Stanovich, K., & West, R. (1989). Exposure to print and orthographic processing. *Reading Research Quarterly, 24*, 402–433.
Stanovich, K. E. (1992). Speculations on the causes and consequences of individual differences in early reading acquisition. In P. B. Gough, L. C. Ehri, and R. Treiman (Eds.), *Reading acquisition* (pp. 307–342). Hillsdale, NJ, England: Erlbaum.
Stanovich, K. E., Cunninham, A. E., & West, R. F. (1998). Literacy experiences and the shaping of cognition. In S. Paris and H. Wellman (Eds.), *Global prospects for education: Development, culture and schooling*. Washington, DC: American Psychological Association.

Swinney, D. A. (1979). Lexical access during sentence comprehension: (Re)consideration of context effects. *Journal of Verbal Learning and Verbal Behavior, 18*, 645–659.

Szeszulski, P. A., & Manis, F. R. (1990). An examination of familial resemblance among subgroups of dyslexics. *Annals of Dyslexia, 40*, 180–191.

Tabossi, P., & Zardon, F. (1993). The activation of idiomatic meaning in spoken language comprehension. In C. Cacciari and P. Tabossi (Eds.), *Idioms: Processing, structure, and interpretation* (pp. 145–162). Hillsdale, NJ: Erlbaum.

Vellutino, F. R., Scanlon, D., & Tanzman, M. S. (1994). Components of reading ability: Issues and problems in operationalizing word identification, phonological coding and orthographic coding. In G. R. Lyon (Ed.), *Frames of reference for the assessment of learning disabilities.* Baltimore: Brookes.

Weber-Fox, C., Spencer, R., Cuadrado, E., & Smith, A. (2003). Development of neural processes mediating rhyme judgments: Phonological and orthographic interactions. *Developmental Psychobiology, 43*, 128–145.

Zevin, J. D., & Seidenberg, M. S. (2006). Simulating consistency effects and individual differences in nonword naming: A comparison of current models. *Journal of Memory and Language, 54*, 145–160.

INDEX

C

D

Y

CONTENTS OF RECENT VOLUMES

Volume 33

Volume 34

Volume 35

Volume 36

Volume 37

Volume 38

Volume 39

Volume 40

Volume 41

Volume 42

Volume 43

Volume 44

Volume 45

Volume 46

Volume 47

Volume 48